LAND POLICY: PROBLEMS AND ALTERNATIVES

Land Policy:
Problems and Alternatives

Edited by
SUSAN BARRETT
School for Advanced Urban Studies,
University of Bristol
and
PATSY HEALEY
Department of Town Planning,
Oxford Polytechnic

Gower

Published by
Gower Publishing Company Limited
Gower House, Croft Road, Aldershot, Hants GU11 3HR
England

and
Gower Publishing Company
Old Post Road
Brookfield
Vermont 05036
U.S.A.

British Library Cataloguing in Publication Data

Land policy : problems and alternatives.
   1. Land use——Planning
   I. Barrett, Susan, *1942-*   II. Healey, Patsy
   333.73'13   HD108.6

   ISBN 0-566-00672-3

Printed in Great Britain

Contents

Notes on contributors

Richard Barras is with CES Ltd, London.

Susan Barrett is Senior Lecturer at the School for Advanced Urban Studies, University of Bristol.

Stuart Cameron is Lecturer in the Department of Town and Country Planning, University of Newcastle.

Michael Cuddy is planning officer in the Land Authority for Wales.

Gordon Dabinett is Economic Research Officer in the Research and Intelligence Unit, Cleveland County Council.

Simon Duncan is Lecturer in Geography at the London School of Economics and University of Sussex.

Martin Elson is Reader in Planning at Oxford Polytechnic.

Stephen Fothergill is Project Leader, Industrial Location Research Project, Department of Land Economy, University of Cambridge.

Allan Gillard is Senior Lecturer in the Department of Town and Country Planning, University of Newcastle.

Tony Gore is Research Associate in the Department of Planning, University of Wales Institute of Science and Technology.

Patsy Healey is Associate Head, Department of Town Planning, Oxford Polytechnic.

Michael Hollingsworth is Planner/Development Officer in the Land Authority for Wales.

Alan Hooper is Lecturer in the Department of Land Management, University of Reading.

Geoffrey Keogh is Lecturer in Economics in the Department of Urban and Regional Economics, University of Reading.

Michael Kitson is Research Associate with the Industrial Location Research Project, Department of Land Economy, University of Cambridge.

Martin Loughlin is Lecturer in Law, University of Warwick.

Sarah Monk is Research Associate with the Industrial Location Research Project, Department of Land Economy, University of Cambridge.

Nigel Moor is Senior Partner in Nigel Moor Associates, London.

Janice Morphet is in the Development Directorate, London Borough of Tower Hamlets.

Barrie Needham is Lecturer at the Institute of Geography and Planning, University of Nijmegen, The Netherlands.

David Nicholson is Research Associate in the Department of Planning, University of Wales Institue of Science and Technology.

Jane Robbins is with Roger Tym and Partners, London.

Urlan Wannop is Professor in the Department of Urban and Regional Planning, University of Strathclyde.

Gwyndaf Williams is Lecturer in the Department of Town and Country Planning, University of Manchester.

Preface

The collection of papers in this book arises from a Conference on Land Policy: Problems and Alternatives held in Oxford in March 1983. The Conference was organised jointly by the editors and other colleagues from the Department of Town Planning, Oxford Polytechnic, and the School for Advanced Urban Studies, University of Bristol, and sponsored by the then Social Science Research Council.

In organising the Conference, we had two main objectives in mind:

1: to bring together researchers and practitioners in the land policy field in order to relate the largely fragmented discussion within the field, and to take stock of current research activity and its contribution to contemporary policy debates relating to land policy;

2: to re-assess the research agenda of land policy, taking account of issues and problems emerging from present research and from practice.

When the idea of the conference was first mooted, we had considerable debate about the meaning of 'land policy' and the validity of land per se as a focus for research and policy intervention. As suggested in our Introductory Review, we were also concerned about the apparent fragmentation of existing research effort between disciplines, each taking a rather different view of the issues impinging directly or indirectly on the ownership, value, use and management of land. In the call for papers we deliberately cast the net as widely as possible in order to stimulate and pursue this debate. The following broad themes were identified:

1. Current land and development problems and policy responses;

2. Analysis of land use and development processes and the role of the state;

3. Land policy alternatives.

We anticipated that most papers would relate to the UK, but we welcomed contributions from overseas. The original Conference announcement generated seventy-four offers of papers, coming from almost all the disciplines identified in our Introductory Review. These offers showed a somewhat different breakdown of concerns from our list of themes. We received a large group of papers and abstracts concerned with the promotion of economic regeneration via development and investment activity. These included alternative views of the regeneration process, the role of the state, and effectiveness of existing government initiatives, ranged in focus from inner city to remote rural locations. A second group concentrated on the regulation of development activity and the redirection of development pressure, including the critical examination of the effectiveness of existing land use planning mechanisms for local policy implementation. A third (and overlapping) group was concerned with mechanisms for intervention in the land market and development process, including comparisons of the British policy framework, with those of other mixed economies. Conspicuously absent, in view of our original list of topics, were papers addressing alternative theoretical approaches to understanding the land conversion process, and contributions specifically addressing aspects of estate management, or linking detailed land management issues with the broader context of land development processes and policies. We return to this issue in our Concluding Review.

The overall scope of the Conference was defined by the range of papers offered. The thirty-four selected for presentation represented as much this range as our own starting agenda. For this volume, we have been forced to make a further selection, a difficult process in view of the high quality of the papers delivered at the Conference. A full list of these papers is attached at the end of the volume.

In putting together this collection, we have sought both to reflect the main themes and issues of the Conference papers and discussion, and to illustrate the variety of perspectives, research questions and policy problems represented in current research and contemporary practice. The collection starts with our own overview paper for the Conference. We have then grouped the papers into two main sections:

  I   Land Policy and the Development Process:
      Facilitating, Managing and Regulating Development

  II Mechanisms and Agencies for Intervention in Land
      Development Processes.

This is followed by a third section which presents two Western European examples which serve to highlight some of the distinctive features of UK land policy. Each of these three sections is introduced by a short editorial summary of the main themes and issues addressed in the papers which follow. In our Concluding Review, we reassert the importance of focussing on the land policy field, broadly interpreted, identify the central role of an understanding of the land conversion process, and re-assess the agenda for research.

We should like to express our very considerable thanks to our colleagues Paul McNamara and John Montgomery at Oxford, and Paul Burton at SAUS, for their contribution in structuring and organising the Conference; to the now ESRC for sponsoring it, and to the Short Course Unit at Oxford (and particularly Carolin Tidbury) for mounting it for us. We should also like to thank all Conference participants, and particularly those who gave papers, for contributing to the development of our own thought, and, through the evidently stimulating interchange that went on, confirming our view of the value of bringing such a range of people together. We must also record our appreciation of the efforts of those whose papers are included in this volume in meeting our editorial requirements and deadlines, and in providing much helpful advice. Our thanks also go to Jim Scott, Julie Firth, Vicky Poole and Sue Reade for help with final editting. Finally, we must note our very considerable debt to Joan Minter, who prepared the text for publication with great skill and effort.

Susan Barrett
Patsy Healey

Table 1, Chapter 12 by kind permission of Heinemann Education Books

Introduction
Land policy: towards a research agenda

PATSY HEALEY AND SUSAN BARRETT

The aim of the conference was to inter-relate the discussion of land ownership, land values, land use planning and development policies, and to review the extent to which recent theoretical work and research findings contribute to our understanding of this area of policy, to evaluation of current policy and proposals for change. In our view, a serious criticism of the post-1947 attempts to review the land question in the UK is that the issue of state intervention in land ownership and land values has been repeatedly discussed in isolation from the more firmly established system of regulatory land use planning, and, more broadly, the role of state intervention in the ownership and allocation of land and property in relation to social and economic policy. Our intention, therefore, in calling this conference, has been to re-locate the debate about proposals for public land ownership within this wider context of the nature, purposes and organisation of state intervention in land and property, i.e. land policy.

We consider this wider debate to be of particular importance at the present time because, for the first time since the 1940s, the whole area of regulatory land use planning is itself coming under critical scrutiny among politicians, and among land use planners themselves. Meanwhile, recent governments, and many local authorities, have been developing an increasing variety of promotional initiatives; for example, selective relaxation of regulatory controls, tax reductions and financial incentives for inner city areas and special "enterprise zones" as well as assisted regions to promote industry; provision of serviced land for housing as well as industry; experiments with new forms of financing. These initiatives have been accompanied by changes in institutional arrangements, from industrial development units and employment departments in local authorities to central government's urban development corporations. In effect, if not explicitly, we are witnessing a general review of British land policy, in response to the changed economic priorities created by the

1

prolonged decline of British industry, exacerbated by the
current deep recession.

However, there is at present no systematic attempt at evaluation of British land policy. This is partly for political
reasons. Each party is having difficulty in articulating a
coherent response to current economic and social conditions,
and land policy as such is not high on any agenda at present.
Yet we would argue that one reason for the fragmentation of
discussion about the various strands of state intervention in
land and property in this country, and overseas, is the lack
of a coherent academic body of thought on the subject. Contributions to political debate have drawn selectively and
unsystematically on isolated items of research and writing
emerging from a variety of disciplines, while the professions
which have grown up around land and property issues
(surveyors, town and country planners, land and property
lawyers) have a non-academic inheritance, which emphasises the
operational rather than conceptual dimensions of political
initiatives in the land field. It is our belief that a more
comprehensive and coherently developed view of land policy,
informed by academic work from various disciplines and fields,
by operational experience and by contemporary priorities in
political debate, could lead to more creative and practical
thinking about relevant land policies for the future than has
been achieved in the UK since the 1940s.

This paper attempts to provide encouragement for such an
integration of currently fragmented contributions. In Section
2, we explain what we mean by land policy. Section 3 then
reviews the "fragments" which currently, in our view, contribute to the land policy field. In Section 4, we attempt a
summary of the main issues and questions which we consider
need to be addressed. Inevitably such an exercise in review
is open to criticism on many counts, and we welcome such
criticism. Our object is not to produce a definitive statement at this stage but to contribute ideas to constructive
debate.

1. LAND POLICY AS A FIELD OF STUDY

The "land question" in any society involves bringing together
consideration of land ownership, exchange, use, management and
development, and the role of deliberate state intervention in
pursuit of social and economic goals. We view land policy as
one among the many fields which make up the arena of public
policy and one with certain distinctive characteristics. Many
of the questions that must be asked about any public policy

2

field must in consequence be applied to land policy. Taking this perspective requires us to analyse the nature of the ways in which land is owned, exchanged, used, managed and developed; the form and purpose, character and effects of state policies in the land and development field; the way various interests seek to influence the formation of policy and the operation of programmes; and which groups benefit from policies and programmes.

We thus take a broad definition of land policy. In principle it covers both urban and rural land, and policies concerning land use and development as well as land ownership and land values. As explained in Section 1, one of our main concerns in calling this conference has been to re-integrate the discussion of land use and land values in the UK, frequently treated in recent years as separate activities. We believe that this division has arisen because of the way land policy has been institutionalised in the UK (with planning departments and planners concerned with land use matters), and the separation of the more politically contentious parts of land policy (land values) from the more generally accepted programmes (concerning the control of land use). Similarly, questions of estate management – the management of the existing stock, including the relations of landlord and tenant – have been treated as separate issues from state regulation of land use and development, which has been concerned with use and development changes only. Yet we do not see any theoretical justification for these divisions.

The above position is by no means an accepted one. A common alternative in many parts of the world is to treat urban land policy as a separate arena from rural land policy. The latter is typically associated with measures of land reform designed to redistribute access to agricultural land more equitably. In many Third World countries, the problem of urban land ownership, allocation and use have only recently received any attention, with a number of seminars and discussion papers produced during the 1970s, reflecting the problems created by the rapid urbanisation occurring in so many countries (United Nations 1973, Darin-Drabkin 1977, Dunkerley et al. 1978, Koenigsberger and Groak 1980, Cullen and Woolery 1982). Yet the interrelationship between urban and rural land and property ownership and management is evident where rural land is being converted to urban use, where agricultural land is subjected to multi-use demands by an urban population seeking recreation space, or where financial institutions are seeking long term rising yield investment outlets. An important re-search question is then to explain the differences in the way urban and rural land issues are treated in different countries.

Nor do we view land policy as merely the set of instruments and mechanisms for achieving land use planning objectives, as Lichfield (1980) does. While we see land policy as encompassing planning policy, Lichfield considers land policy to fit inside planning policies. The basis for Lichfield's distinction is that interventions in the land field do not express policy ends of their own. They are merely tools with which to further policies defined elsewhere.

There is an important and interesting debate here about the categorisation of public policy in terms of its basic functions. Lowi, for example, distinguished between distributive, re-distributive, regulatory and constituent functions (Lowi, 1978). Whilst some aspects of land policy can be regarded as 'tools' and thus essentially 'constituent' or procedural mechanisms to further policy ends defined elsewhere, we would argue that many policies in the land field have underlying ends related to the distribution of property rights between the state and the individual (or private company), and the distribution and re-distribution of benefits arising from the ownership and use of land and property (see Barrett 1982a). We would also argue (see Barrett and Fudge 1981) that policy and action are not clearly separable. The core of the argument here is that 'policy' is not something that is necessarily defined prior to 'implementation'. Rather, policies evolve and change direction over time, in relation to the changing economic and political situations out of which they arise, and in relation to the instruments created to further policy ends and how they are actually used. Consequently, it is important to examine not only formal statements of policies and the instruments created to further them, but the way the use of instruments is operationalised, and the mode of operation adopted, to use a term from Offe (1975).

Yet this raises a different intellectual problem. If it is inappropriate to separate policy instruments and how they are used from the formation of policy itself, it has to be recognised that policies about land, its ownership, use and development do not exist in their own right. Just as the value of land depends upon what people want to use it for, so land policies derive from social and economic policies and produce outcomes which can only be assessed in social and economic terms. What then is the justification for any special concern with land policy?

The separation of, for example, housing policies from industrial location policies is a matter of administrative and political history and of intellectual spheres of interest, rather than arising from a theoretical premise. Yet no analysis or prescriptions of policy can operate in complex states such as the UK without some form of subdivision. Traditionally, such subdivision in the UK and elsewhere has been based on sectors of the economy. Because land and development is an input to and a requirement for each sector, it might be more appropriate to treat land and development issues as they arise within each sector, i.e. in a fragmented way. Yet the obvious problem with this approach is that the demands and needs of each sector interact with each other through the impact of land requirements for one activity in relation to others, just as they interact in relation to finance, to labour needs; and in terms of the delivery of services to clients and consumers.

The justification for a specific concern with land policy as a distinct policy field lies in the character of land and development as a resource for <u>all</u> activities. A central concern of land policy evaluation must therefore be with the extent to which the demands and needs of economic and social policies are being met. In discussing land policy we are in effect examining the way in which a necessary resource is being made available for social and economic activities. Consequently one of the distinguishing characteristics of land policy is that evaluation of it cannot be contained within its own terms. It is not enough to say, for example, that development has been 'successfully' controlled. The social and economic consequences of such regulation must also be assessed, as Hall et al. (1973) have done for the UK. This raises complex methodological problems in evaluating the effects of land policies since lengthy causal chains are typically involved. It also means that it is of limited value to discuss land policy issues within the confines of a single discipline.

2. CONTRIBUTORS TO THE LAND POLICY FIELD

The study of land and property has never been the province of a single discipline, or been the primary concern of a particular theoretical perspective, while the professions involved in land range from town planners and planning lawyers to land surveyors and agronomists. It is perhaps only those involved in developing political programmes who have taken a comprehensive view of land in economy and society, yet in recent years in the UK there has been little sign of such integrated thinking at the political level. Land issues have become split up among disciplines, and are in fact commonly treated as a minor area of concern in each discipline.

It could be argued that land and property issues should be a central concern to geographers, but in practice this has not generally been the case. Geographers, in common with sociologists and economists, tend to focus their concern on outcomes rather than process. When process has been addressed in more recent contributions to political geography, the emphasis has been on broad political relationships rather than detailed institutional procedures and practices. This approach tends to produce naive prescriptions as it treats administrative processes as unproblematic. Policy analysts and students of public administration generally emphasise administrative processes often with insufficient attention to the context in which this occurs or the substantive outcomes of such processes. This can lead to equally naive prescriptions. Professionals, in their turn, tend to use working rules of thumb, the conceptual bases of which are rarely acknowledged. A consequence of the intellectual fragmentation of the land policy field is that these deficiencies are not more clearly appreciated.

2.1 Disciplinary contributions to land policy

If we consider the contributions of the academic disciplines first, the two most significant areas in the land policy field have traditionally been economics and geography. Land economics has examined the operations of different types of land and property markets and the nature of land rent. Public welfare economics has focussed attention on the case within neo-classical economics for public intervention in land and property markets, and examined the relative merits of different types of intervention such as regulatory, financial and direct development (Harrison 1977, Hallett 1979), and provided methodologies for the assessment of the impacts of public projects on the public interest, variously defined (see for example Lichfield et al. 1975). There has been much less work on the changing land needs of different types of economic activity and there have been few empirical studies of the actual operation of land and property markets, economists disagreeing on the extent to which land and property can be properly considered as markets. In effect, the treatment of land and property economics suffers from the general tendency in neo-classical economic thought to conceptions of prices related to idealised supply and demand situations without considering the social processes by which such prices are arrived at.

For studies of the actual operation of land and property "markets", we have to turn to the work of surveyors, which is produced for consultancy purposes and often inaccessible to researchers. Because surveyors have an instrumental concern with markets, and assume the predominance of a market mechanism to allocate land and property among users and to establish prices, they rarely consider critically the way these market allocation mechanisms are working. Their main focus of interest is on specific markets in particular types of land and property in specific localities, and their approach is primarily historical, basing assessments of current prices on past price patterns. Yet in the UK, researchers and politicians have become increasingly aware that much land and property is owned by the public sector. In some parts of the world, private land and property owners and markets are responsible for the allocation and management of only small amounts of land and property, even in urban areas. In some cases, such non-private land is allocated according to market principles (to the highest bidder). In other cases, family ties, political ties, community traditions, or queuing practices may prevail. Much more comparative research on how land is owned, used, managed, exchanged and developed in different economic and political circumstances is desirable, if only to help us in the UK understand the distinctive characteristics of our own practices.

It might be thought that geographers, with their explicit interest in spatial patterns, in relation to social and economic processes, and their traditions of detailed empirical research, would have filled the gaps left by the land economists. It is geographers who have worked extensively on the locational requirements of different types of economic activity (industry, offices, shopping developments), and more recently those concerned with social and political geography have been interested in the competition for urban space. Of considerable importance is recent work by Marxist geographers on the relationship between the investment behaviour of finance capital, the nature and operation of the property sector in developed economies, the competition for land between capital, as represented by the financial institutions and the property sector, and the role of the state in assisting capital and mediating conflicts (see Harvey 1982, Tabb and Sawers 1978, Scott 1980, Dear and Scott 1981). Of particular interest here are notions of "circuits of capital", developed by Harvey and others to analyse the relationship between land and property transactions and development and the investment behaviour of financial capital (see Harvey 1981, Boddy 1981). Here geographers are working on closely related themes to those pursued by Marxist economists and architects examining the operation of the construction industry, and on the housing sector of the property industry (see the papers of the Bartlett Summer Schools (University College, London 1979-1982) on the Production of the Built Environment).

Yet, as noted earlier, many geographers still analyse patterns of land use and development in relation to social and economic demands for particular types of space without explaining the mechanics by which such space is allocated among competing demands. An example of this is the failure to examine the relation between rural land ownership and urban land allocation, land use and land value. This requires an understanding of the various land and property allocation processes operating in an area and their inter-relationships, and the pre-existing structure of land use and ownership in areas where demands are being made to convert land into different uses. Despite some interesting pioneer work on suburban land conversion processes (Clawson 1971) and a recent developing interest in urban fringe land markets both in developed countries (e.g. Munton 1983, Brown et al. 1981) and in areas experiencing rapid urbanisation (e.g. Geisse 1982), there has been little critical examination of the relation between urban land allocation and development processes within cities and the way land is owned and urbanised around cities (but see for example Johnson and Pooley 1982, Sutcliffe 1981).

Yet, as Hall et al. (1973) argued, this inter-relation is a central one for understanding the structure of opportunities available within urban areas for investment and for the needs of firms and communities. This applies not only to understanding the very different forms which urbanisation and urban development may take in Third World cities experiencing rapid expansion in demand for urban space, but equally to the US and Europe, where activities formerly based within large conurbations are spilling out in a dispersed form into surrounding countryside in search of large sites, improved access and attractive environments. In this context, the research recently sponsored by the SSRC on the Inner City in Context (see ed. Hall 1981) should provide an important contribution to our understanding.

Investigating the changing nature of land ownership patterns and urban development processes in relation to broad economic and political processes has been given considerable impetus in recent years by researchers drawing on the seminal French Marxist work in urban sociology in the early 1970s (see for example the contributions in ed. Pickvance 1976 and ed. Harloe 1977). Although much of this work has been rightly criticised for its concentration on developing general theoretical structures for the analysis of 'urban' and 'collective consumption' spheres and for its abstract and determinist models, it has encouraged studies in a number of different countries on, for example, the role of landowners, building firms and developers in extracting monopoly rent through the process of urban development. As yet, however, there are few detailed empirical studies of the land and property field which examine and test the hypotheses being made.

In Britain, this intellectual tradition has been absorbed particularly into the fields of sociology and politics. One result has been that while the geographers and economists working within a Marxist framework tend to emphasise the ways in which urban development processes are linked to finance capital, UK sociologists and political scientists focus on the role of the state and of political lobbies and movements in the allocation and distribution of resources. This is producing important contributions on the relations and spheres of interest of different levels of government and the ways in which interest groups influence the operation of government agencies (see for example Saunders 1981 and Dunleavy 1980). Some of the work within this framework has also examined in some detail the way public agencies actually operate (see for example Flynn 1983). As so frequently where land issues are concerned, relatively little attention has been paid to the land policy area in this work. Yet the analysis of land development processes and land policy is important at the theoretical level since it is an arena in which political and economic spheres at the macro scale are closely linked at the local level, in competing demands for space, and in the way the state mediates these (see Healey 1983a). The tendency for geographers and economists to cluster around the economic, and the sociologist and political scientists around the political, is thus unfortunate.

A field of academic study which arises from a somewhat different background, but yet contributes important insights into the land policy field, is that which we may broadly call 'policy studies'. The study of public policy as a subject in its own right has in general terms arisen from both practitioners' and academics' concern about the effectiveness of government intervention. At a macro political level, questions are raised about the appropriate role and scope of government in an 'advanced' industrial society, and the extent to which governments have the material or political resources to achieve what they set out to do. At a more detailed level, concern centres on the relevance and appropriateness of specific policy initiatives to problems and issues and on the efficacy of existing mechanisms for public policy making and implementation. Gordon, Lewis and Young (1977) distinguish between "analysis of policy" - essentially concerned with understanding and evaluating the substance and impact of policy, and "analysis for policy" - focussing on prescriptions and techniques for improving the substance and process of policy making. Much of the early work (notably in the USA) tended to be in the latter arena, closely associated with management and decision making techniques and often linked to vocational training in the business school or public administration tradition - reflecting practitioners' concern for prescriptions for 'better' policy and more rational decision making processes (see for example Dror 1968, 1971).

As such, policy analysis has suffered from all the problems frequently criticised in relation to procedural planning theory. Both purport to provide prescriptions for how government should define, evaluate and implement policy in general, not necessarily related to the particular characteristics of specific policy fields, nor to the distinctive social, economic and political circumstances of specific governments. However it is important not to overlook the wide range of studies that contribute to the understanding of public policy and its impacts (analyses of policy). Economics, political science and, more latterly, the sociology of organisations, can be regarded as the parent disciplines - with a certain amount of methodological tension between them (Heclo 1972). More recent research is moving towards a synthesis of various theoretical strands involving the interaction of political, economic, environmental and organisational variables (e.g. Jenkins 1978) and recognition of the need to locate analysis of the formation and operation of public policy in a political and economic context. This kind of approach to the study of policy is associated with a shift in emphasis from comparative and quantitative studies identifying and providing explanations of relationships at a high level of generality, to the use of detailed case studies of particular policies and events.

The case study approach is better developed in the USA than Britain - particularly in relation to the evaluation of Federal social welfare policies and programmes. Less attention there (and here) is given to other types of policy including land (but see for example, Barrett, Boddy and Stewart 1978, Cox 1980, Underwood 1980 and Barrett 1981), though there is now a growing interest in examining land policy as an example of public policy and comparing it with other policy areas to highlight its distinctive characteristics in particular situations. (There are, however, some valuable studies relating to land and planning issues that pre-date the 1970s literature on social programme evaluation. See, for example, Meyerson and Banfield 1955, Selznick 1966, and, more recently, Derthick 1972). Although the theoretical emphases of the case study approach have usually been different from much of the 'political economy'

studies of urban development undertaken in recent years by
geographers, sociologists and economists, its importance is in
the detailed analysis of the operation of public programmes
and public agencies. This demonstrates that the way interests
influence the state and the way the state affects interests
can only be understood by careful dissection of state
programmes into their constituent organisations, formal
procedures and operating practices, since each provides a
distinctive arena providing different opportunities for
exerting influence and producing different effects. Within
the political economy field itself, there has so far been
little work of this nature other than that of Offe (but see
Saunders 1981 and Cawson 1982), although recent research by
Darke (1982) suggests some of the ways in which Offe's
identification of different modes of policy formation in a
capitalist state may be applied in the land policy field (see
also Reade 1978, McAuslan 1980, Healey 1983b).

Before concluding this section on disciplinary
contributions, we must comment on two contributions which are
rarely considered within the debates referred to so far. The
first concerns agricultural land ownership and rural land
policy, and the second the design of the built environment.
Agricultural land reform is a central political issue in many
Third World countries, as it was in Europe in the nineteenth
and early twentieth centuries. There has been some recent
sociological interest in the changing structure of rural land
ownership as it became evident that British agri-business was
becoming linked, not surprisingly, to multi-national finance
capital (see for example Newby 1980). There is also the work
of agricultural economists and farm management experts on the
land management aspects of the agricultural industry. To date
this has not generally been linked into the wider land policy
arena, though clearly there are important issues concerning
access for urban dwellers to the countryside, conservation of
the natural environment, as well as the more traditional
concern with urbanisation and problems of green belt
management (see for example O'Riordan 1982, Shoard 1981).

The second area, discussion of the design of the built
environment, has been substantially inhibited by the
disciplinary divide between architects and social scientists.
Having contributed to the rejection of the naive environmental
determinism of an earlier generation of architects and
planners, social scientists have largely ignored this area,
apart from the interest among geographers in environmental
perception a decade ago. Yet the question of how the built
form is produced, and its impact on the users and consumers of
the space and shapes thus provided should be as much an area

of social scientific concern as the location of activities in space. The problem, of course, is that social scientists have to learn the language of three dimensional representation to move into this area. Yet social scientists cannot continue to criticise the naive social scientific theorising of architects if they make no efforts to cross the communication divide. This criticism of course applies in reverse.

The above is merely an extreme case of the compartmentalisation of knowledge which discipline-organisation produces. From time to time the divisions thereby produced are demolished by theoretical perspectives which cut across the disciplines, redefining key areas of concern and sometimes producing new "disciplines". Systems theory and quantitative modelling of social behaviour had this effect in the 1960s, mixing geographers, mathematicians, physicists and natural scientists. The new political economy is having a similar effect in uniting economists, geographers and social scientists in a common enterprise. But whereas the arrival of systems theory if anything deflected academic interest away from land and property issues, the political economy thrust, and developments within the field of policy implementation, are drawing researchers back into the area. However, current academic interest is primarily with evaluation and explanation. Yet at some stage this work must be encouraged to feed into debates on prescriptions, both at the level of the general thrust and organisation of relevant land policy for the UK, and at the level of the detailed practices of the various professions involved in land policy.

2.2   The professions and land policy

Three areas concern us here: land and planning law, surveyors and property development, and the field of town and country planning. None of these has until recently been closely connected to the development of academic thought in relation to land issues, although many surveyors and most planners are predominantly involved in manipulating land and its development, while lawyers adjudicate between them.

Many practising surveyors possess a store of detailed knowledge of land and property transactions and of the behaviour of actors in the development process which would be invaluable not only to land use planners, but to social scientists, especially in England and Wales, where we lack information on land and property ownership and values. Such material is rarely published in any systematic, as opposed to anecdotal, form. In any case surveyors tend to consider what they do an art, which it is difficult to systematise except in

12

very general terms. Yet the practices of surveyors, in their work on land and property valuation and assessment of development potential, and the very specific way in which the profession of surveyors and of the other participants in the property development process in the UK has evolved is worth much more detailed study than it has yet received.

Town and country planners, by contrast, come from a tradition of public health officials spiced with the practical idealism of the architects and engineers of the Garden City movement. The introduction of a national system of land use planning in 1947 perpetuated the attitudes that this mixture gave rise to, although the influence of social scientists; particularly geographers, has been increasingly felt since the 1960s. Planners have written about themselves a lot and there is no need to go over well-known ground (Healey 1983c). In the context of our present concern with land policy, what is curious is how little real concern town planners in practice, and the developing academic tradition in the planning schools, have actually given to land issues. There has been little research on the processes of land use change and development in which planners have been intervening, and little evaluation of actual interventions. In effect, planners in the UK and elsewhere have adopted a schizophrenic position, claiming to be engaged in translating social and economic policies into spatial strategies, yet in practice merely manipulating, with often anachronistic tools, the details of the way land is used and developed. As in many countries, in this respect they are more manipulated than manipulating, working in situations where they may have a weak political and organisational position and where the issues they are dealing with are surrounded by conflicts. Both in the UK and elsewhere, planners' ideals of what should be done have outstretched what can be done. Yet the effect of schizophrenia, the product of an idealist tradition, has been to <u>limit</u> what planners have been able to do, through lack of knowledge and understanding of the nature and capacities of the tools they <u>do</u> have available.

Thus the current reorientation among town and country planners towards "implementation" and towards understanding their specific potential role in the process of social and economic change through physical development is very much to be welcomed. Yet to develop this understanding, planners need some assistance from academics, in researching the nature of development processes, in evaluating the impact and effects of planning intervention, in assessing alternative ways existing tools might be used, and in developing ideas for different approaches and tools.

Meanwhile, as part of a wider movement to shift legal thought out of the confines of nineteenth century perspectives, there have recently been several valuable studies evaluating through empirical study the detailed operation of various areas of planning law, and assessing the general nature of planning law in the UK (Loughlin 1980a, McAuslan 1980). While such work as yet rarely relates directly to the theorising and empirical work of other social scientists interested in the issues discussed here, nevertheless, the possibilities of future integration are exciting. Social scientists and town planners have traditionally treated the 'legal aspects' of planning as a specialist concern into which only lawyers can enter with any confidence. Lawyers researching the land use planning field are now telling us that this is not so and that we have to understand the concepts of law and the principle of its operation if we are to explain the way land policy operates in the UK.

2.3 Political debate and land policy

Finally, we must not ignore the political sphere itself as a source of ideas and directions for land policy. Currently the most obvious issue of political concern is how far "privatisation" will go in the land field under the Conservative government. Yet a much more fundamental issue lies below the surface of formal political debate and current pressure group lobbying over land issues. As the country's economic fortunes have changed, so the regulation of greenfield development and urban renewal, the predominant (though not the intended) concern of the postwar land use planning system in the 1950s and 1960s, is being supplemented by a plethora of new promotional initiatives. With much less investment finance available for investment in property, attention is increasingly focussing on the management, maintenance and piecemeal renewal of the existing built stock, on ways of making positive use of unused and derelict land; and on discovering new sources of finance for investment in the built stock as the financial institutions narrow their range of investment interests. Meanwhile, where big capital is interested in investing, both central and local government have been weakening regulative controls to smooth the path for such investment. (Many of the papers in this collection discuss the problems arising from this shift.)

While issues of land ownership and land values tend to be treated in ideological terms within political debate, the land use elements of land policy have been considered, if at all,

14

in a fragmented way. Further legislative change may well only tinker about with the planning system in the manner of the 1980 Local Government Planning and Land Act. If so, the academic and professional community will be substantially to blame for failing to provide coherent and developed ideas about alternatives for land policy. This book, and the conference from which it arises, is a contribution to remedying this deficiency. The final section of this paper attempts to construct an agenda for an improved academic contribution to land policy.

3. TOWARDS A POLICY AND RESEARCH AGENDA

Evidently there is a very considerable body of knowledge relevant to land policy to be found among the academic and professional fields discussed in Section 3. The problem is that, because it is compartmentalised, individual areas of work do not take off from or cross-fertilise each other to allow the development of discussion about land policy issues. One way to reduce these barriers is to identify a set of issues and research questions within the land policy field.

We defined this in Section 2 as concerned with land and property ownership, use, exchange, management and development, and with state intervention in these phenomena. How individual researchers, practitioners and policy-makers approach the relationships within this field will of course depend on the way the links between social and economic process, land and built form and the nature and operation of the state are conceptualised. If anything, conceptual variety should be encouraged, given the inchoate nature of the field of study at present. Yet some agreement is needed on what should be theorised about, the theoretical frameworks to which individual research contributions relate, and the terms in which policy initiatives might fruitfully be evaluated. We put forward the following agenda as a possible way of providing a focus for such agreement.

Its organising principle is to consider, first, questions about how land and property are valued, owned, used, exchanged, managed and developed, in relation to social and economic processes. In the context of such considerations, the role of the state and state land policies become empirical questions. In this way, it is possible to avoid over-simple dichotomies between a 'public' and 'private' sector. A second set of questions directly addresses explicit land policies, and is concerned with their evaluation at various levels. The primary emphasis here is with intentions, interests and outcomes. The third set focusses on the way, in organisational arrangements, formal procedures and operating practices, intentions are translated into outcomes (and transformed in the process). In effect, the second two sets provide "homing-in" devices within the framework set by the first.

A. <u>Understanding land and property ownership, management practices, land and property exchange, and development processes</u>, as they relate to social and economic demands for land and built space, and the way these are articulated (via political and/or market and/or customary processes).

We suggest that this may require attack in four directions:

(1) general attitudes to land and property and how these relate to particular cultural and economic histories;

(2) assessments of the changing land and built form demands and needs of different social and economic activities and interests;

(3) land and property ownership and management practices, exchange and development processes;

(4) evaluating the extent to which the practices and processes discussed in (3) meet the demands and needs assessed in (2); i.e. how far do the producers supply the requirements of the users and consumers of land and built form.

In our view, the whole of the first area needs much more attention, with the implications for the rest of the field drawn out. Historical and comparative work would be particularly valuable here. And as noted in the previous section, it would be valuable to see more work developing the political economy perspective as it relates to the whole set of issues. But we would also suggest that there has been little recent work on the changing land and space needs of the various social and economic activities, while geographers and planners have allowed analysis of the spatial structure of the city to fall into neglect through disillusion with perspectives which once appeared potentially so productive (i.e. urban systems theory).

Yet changing technology, resources and work patterns are having significant effects which need to be traced through to their land and space consequences. One reason for this neglect of attention among planners is that the latter have been encouraged to consider developers and public service industries as articulators of demands and needs, though such development interests have in recent years been increasingly responding to other stimuli than user demand. In this context, much more work is needed on the operation of "markets" for different types of land and property, the complex and volatile nature of development processes, the multiplicity of ways in which the state acts as an acquirer, allocator and developer of land, and the impact of the changing investment behaviour of the financial institutions. Theoretically, this should encourage work on the role of the land and property sector in the economy, the interpretation of the public and private sector in this policy field, and the significance of different forms of land ownership and rent relationships.

B. The evaluation of state programmes of intervention in the above processes, at the level of intervention strategies, as well as specific projects and programmes.

In relation to this set of questions, it is important to consider not only the individual examples of state programmes, but the overall package of measures through which state actions explicitly or indirectly affect the land and property sector. We suggest it may be helpful to consider these at two levels:

(1) the analysis of a national 'package' of land policy measures, in terms of their intentions and effects;

(2) examination of the way local authorities (or their equivalent outside the UK) combine the tools available through national intervention strategies with whatever initiatives they are able and prepared to take to produce a distinctive local expression of land policy.

Neither have received significant attention for some years in the UK, largely because we have tended to take our 'land policy strategies' for granted except in respect of land ownership and value qustions. Yet these strategies provide a basic framework establishing the power relations within which local authorities, developers and other land and property interests work in respect of land use and development change. We also need much more work on how far local authorities can shift this framework to suit their own purposes. Such research involves not only detailed studies of local landownership, land markets and development processes, but of the nature of the legal and financial tools and constraints affecting local authorities and the public agencies with a role in development and land use change (see recent work by Barrett and Whitting 1983, and Boddy 1982, at SAUS).

The third area within this set of issues is:

(3) major infrastructure projects and large development projects - their formulation, and effects.

Currently there is considerable interest in how to assess the impact of such projects (as in the discussion of Environmental Impact Statements, and the role of public inquiries). With the exception of hypermarket location, this work has concentrated on public sector projects. There has curiously been little research on the effects of such projects on land and property transactions, partly because of the methodological difficulties involved in the UK. Given the shift to a promotional emphasis in British land policy, the role of large scale public investment in levering private investment and voluntary initiative is worth much more examination.

C. Understanding the way particular policy intentions and instruments are realised in organisational terms, and the consequences of this for the outcomes actually achieved by expressed policy initiatives and ongoing state practices.

Questions of organisation and procedure have typically been left, as noted in Section 3, to the policy scientists, public administrators and lawyers. We would argue that it is essential for a coherent view of any field of policy that these questions should be closely related to the substantive matters of concern in the policy field (as outlined in A and B above). We suggest, somewhat tentatively, that the key themes in this area are the relation between formal structures and procedures, and the way these are realised in operating practices; the connection between these relationships and the demands upon the state in relation to land policy; and the extent to which such structures, procedures and practices exert an independent influence on outcomes.

This might indicate the following main areas of concern:

(1) the power relations within the public sector as expressed in the formal structure of organisations and procedures for land policy, and the modes of policy formulation and implementation which these encourage, especially central-local relations; relations with the various interests making demands on the public sector; and the relations between the various public sector agencies;

(2) examining institutional and procedural innovations at the national   level to assess how far these can change   local authority behaviour and the outcomes of land policy in   a locality;

(3) within the   formal structures and procedures,   the extent to which local variations in organisational arrangements, ·. procedures and   work practices significantly   alter   the outcomes of land policy;

(4) the   significance   of   officer   discretion   and   officer ideologies (largely planners and valuers)   in   operating practices and in affecting the outcomes of land policy.

A   considerable amount of work has been undertaken   recently on central-local   relations   and   the   causes   of   variations between local authorities   (see for example, the report of the Central-Local   panel   of Jones et al.   1979 and Rhodes   1981). Although   some   of this has been linked into the   land   policy arena (e.g.   Barrett 1981),   much more effort needs to be made to   identify the contribution of the land policy field to   the central-local   relations   discussion   and   vice   versa.   In contrast,   a great deal has been written on planners and their ideologies   (see for the UK,   Gower Davies 1972,   Dennis 1970, Underwood   1980,   Healey and Underwood   1979,   Blowers   1980). However   this   needs   to   be connected   more   closely   to   the discussion   of   the   precise political   and   economic   context within   which   particular   planners find   themselves   working. Finally,   much   more   study is needed   of   the   organisational effects   of   policy innovation to supplement Barrett   et   al's pioneering work on the Community Land Act (Barrett,   Boddy and Stewart   1978).

The   area   of   study   covered above   implies   a   substantial research   programme.   Yet   many of the   questions   raised   are difficult   to   research.   Underlying   many of   them   are   the connections between social and economic process,   and land and development   patterns   and   processes.   Empirical   work   is particularly difficult here because of the long causal   chains involved   and   the multi-causal explanations needed   for   most events.   We would suggest that much more discussion is needed among researchers on problems of method.

It   is also evident from the range of issues in this   agenda that   it cannot be tackled as a single programme.   Nor   would this be desirable,   as a diversity of approaches to the issues in   the field is to be welcomed.   What we wish to   encourage, however, is contributions within specific parts of the field which recognise its broad spread and which highlight implications of one part for another. Hence, researchers, practitioners and advisers to politicians should be encouraged to relate empirical work to theoretical discussion; theoretical discussion to prescription; and to subject proposals for intervention and the interventions themselves to empirical analysis and evaluation.

The papers collected in this book address one or more of the three sets of issues identified above. Broadly, the papers in Part I address A and B, while those in Part II centrally focus on C, though there is considerable overlap between the sections. Part III illustrates the valuable insights which can be derived from comparative studies. Some of the authors work in local authorities, others are consultants, while the academics are reporting on research undertaken at different levels and within different perspectives. As our editorial notes and final chapter try to show, there are common themes running through these papers. Yet several of the authors were quite unaware of the work of their fellow authors, for the reasons we have discussed. We hope that readers will find the discussion within and between the papers as stimulating as conference participants did.

PART I
LAND POLICY AND THE DEVELOPMENT PROCESS: FACILITATING, MANAGING AND REGULATING INVESTMENT

Introduction

PATSY HEALEY

These seven papers address in various ways the nature of contemporary land and property development processes and the role of public initiatives in supporting and shaping them.

The first two papers examine the problems of supply in a particular market - that for industrial land and premises. The second two explore the extent to which private sector investment can be attracted back into a particular type of locality, the inner areas, and how one particular local authority set out to do this. The next two papers provide an overview of the office development market and private sector housebuilding, emphasising the role of land policy in managing land supply for these activities. The final paper examines a detailed example of the negotiations which characterise the planning system's exercise of its land release powers.

Fothergill, Kitson and Monk seek to emphasise the crucial role of urban-rural variations in industrial land supply in accounting for changes in the location of industrial activity and employment. They argue that, because of changing capital-labour ratios, the demand for industrial land will increase, and suggest that there may still not be enough land available for industry in Britain's main conurbations. They therefore support positive attempts to make industrial land available in the conurbations in an effort to reverse this shift. However, other papers suggest that this is not necessarily readily achieved. Cameron, Dabinett and Gilliard use similar data to examine manufacturing floorspace and employment change in the Northern region, and then go on to discuss the role of the public sector in the supply of new industrial premises. They find the experience of the Northern region differs significantly from that of the other main urban regions. The increase in floorspace was greater and a high proportion of this increase was in new buildings rather than extensions. Yet this provision, largely they conclude the result of public sector initiatives, made little impact on employment, which declined as much as in the other conurbation regions. In

examining the various public sector programmes for increasing
the supply of new industrial premises, Cameron et al note the
different perspectives of central government and local
authorities on the way such programmes operate.

The papers by Moor, and Morphet and Robbins, address the
issue of inner city regeneration. Moor reviews the arguments
for attracting private investment into the inner city. In
contrast to Fothergill et al, he suggests that the land
dimension of the problem arises from lack of demand for land
and premises, rather than inadequate supply. He adopts a
critical stance towards the capacities of public agencies to
promote and facilitate investment, though it is evident from
his discussion that the fault lies not in public agencies per
se, but in the current powers and capabilities of local
authorities. He advocates a switch in policy measures towards
financial incentives, and special development agencies, if
private sector investment into the inner city is to be
attracted.

To an extent, Morphet and Robbins agree with Moor's
diagnosis of the limitations of local authorities in the
development promotion field. In describing the evolution of
employment-generating initiatives on the part of London local
authorities, they highlight the difficulties of developing an
economic role within organisations accustomed to a social
role. They also show how "new left" Labour councillors, in
search of issues to claim for themselves, found allies in
planning departments hemmed in by narrow definitions of the
planning role. This alliance led to the innovation of
employment policy concerns as a mainline programme in many
authorities. However, although receiving considerable
political attention, the impact on the authority's actual
resource allocation was much less. A contrast may be drawn
between this example and Tyne and Wear County Council as
described by Cameron et al, where economic issues have been a
longstanding preoccupation. Many of the points relating to
the articulating of a policy response to new problems are
echoed in the papers in Part II.

Barras' paper continues the London emphasis, with an
examination of office development cycles and the way the
regulatory powers of the planning system have related to them.
In comparison with industrial investment in the previous
examples, local authorities in London have been primarily
concerned to regulate the location of offices. Yet their task
in this has been complicated by the cyclical nature of office
development. This arises because the long lead times and
"lumpy" nature of office development processes lead to

oversupply of office space in response to periods of high demand, which in turn leads to undersupply. Barras argues that office policies should be concerned not just with location controls, but with smoothing the cycle by allowing more development to proceed in downturns and less in upturns.

Barras is suggesting that the land use planning system should approach land supply with a much stronger emphasis on the flow of sites through the development process. This point is central to Hooper's critique of the current approach to housing land supply. He argues that the residential development sector is also affected by demand cycles, related to income trends and the availability of investment finance. By examining the sequence of housing land availability studies since the 1960s, he shows the limitations of attempting to conceive of land supply for development in terms of stocks at any point in time, and stresses the importance of flows, given the time scale of development and the many factors which affect when a project is likely to be initiated, elaborated and completed. He reveals the poverty of recent government initiatives on housing land availability with their emphasis on stocks. Ultimately, such a crude conception of the housing land supply problem could disadvantage both the housebuilders and those concerned to minimise landtake for development.

Finally, Elson draws on detailed work on the operation of the planning system to show how land release for employment-generating development was actually negotiated in Hertford-shire, a county on the outskirts of the London conurbation and under considerable pressure for development. Here it was planning policy to limit employment growth (and hence pressure on housing demand) by limiting land supply. Elson demon-strates that despite the technical arguments used to relate land release for employment to specified "local needs", in practice such arguments and the policies and proposals they gave rise to were devices used in a strategy to minimise landtake. The paper illustrates how the "hurdles" created by these arguments, policies and proposals were negotiated between development interests and planning authorities, and within the various tiers of the planning system. Elson also notes how policy has now changed in response to recession, with a greater emphasis on using land to attract employment-generating activities, in response to rising local unemployment. In articulating such a response within the continuing concern to minimise landtake, both county and district have been searching for ways of expressing land supply in terms of flows rather than stocks, though central government has given them little help here.

These papers serve to illustrate and develop three important themes. They firstly highlight the interpenetration of public and private activity in development processes, and the multiplicity of forms this takes. Secondly, several papers comment on the difficulties many public agencies face in adjusting their behaviour to the changed economic circumstances produced by the recession, as well as the problems created by overlapping and fragmented institutional responsibilities. These issues are a central concern of most of the papers in Part II. Thirdly, the question of land supply is addressed in various ways in most of the papers. Despite the evidence of disinventment in so many parts of the country, many public sector programmes are still premised on the assumption that a key element in encouraging or inhibiting investment is land supply. This is obviously important to facilitate continuing investment in the production of property.

To effect the task of managing land supply adequately, several of these papers emphasise the significance of the variability of both demand and supply in relation to the needs of types of firms and investors and the locational constraints on the types of site likely to be available. But, as Barras and Hooper show, land and property investment is ultimately responsive to demand factors. Structural shifts at the level of the economy as a whole have produced major changes in the type and location of land and property demanded. Public policy initiatives which act on land and supply without taking account of the structural conditions affecting demand in different land and property markets are liable to increase the amount of unused serviced land and vacant space. The inefficiencies of current approaches in an economy in recession could well lead many interests round to the view that a more coherent approach is necessary.

1 The supply of land for industrial development

STEPHEN FOTHERGILL, MICHAEL KITSON AND SARAH MONK

This paper* concerns the supply of land for industrial development. It assesses whether the supply is adequate in relation to the requirements of manufacturing industry, especially in the event of an up-turn in the national economy. Attention is also given to the extent to which the supply varies between Britain's cities and other areas. The first part of the paper describes the main trends in the demand for industrial land and the employment densities at which industrial land and premises are occupied. The second part looks at the supply of land for extensions to existing factories and for new factories.

TRENDS IN THE DEMAND FOR INDUSTRIAL LAND

Manufacturing industry's requirements for industrial land are the product of two things: firstly, the amount of floorspace needed, and secondly the ratio of floorspace to land (or 'site density'). Trends in each of these affect the amount of land that industry needs.

* This paper is based on research funded by the Department of Industry and the Department of the Environment. The views expressed are those of the authors and do not necessarily reflect the views of either the Department of Industry or the Department of the Environment.

Statistics on the stock of industrial floorspace in England
and Wales are compiled by the Department of the Environment
from figures collected by the Inland Revenue in assessing the
rateable value of property. Figure 1 shows that despite the
fall in manufacturing employment, which has been virtually
uninterrupted since 1966, the total amount of factory
floorspace in England and Wales has risen. Between 1964 and
1981 the stock of industrial floorspace (which excludes
warehouses) rose by 34.5 million sq.metres or 16.5 per cent -
approximately one per cent a year. The stock rose every year

Figure 1

The stock of industrial floorspace in England and Wales
1964-1982

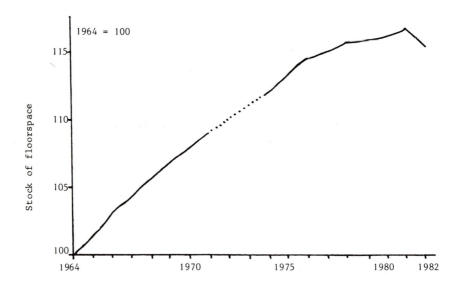

Source: Department of the Environment

during this period, although the rate of increase slowed from
the mid 1970s onwards. After 1981 the stock fell a little,
presumably as a result of the exceptional severity of the
recession at the start of the 1980s, but by 1982 it still
remained 15 per cent larger than in the mid 1960s.

Table 1 shows changes in industrial floorspace by type of
area between 1967 (the earliest year for which statistics are

available for local areas) and 1982. During these years there was a consistent and large urban-rural contrast in the net change in floorspace. In London the stock fell by 17 percent, and in the other conurbations it fell by 4 per cent. At the other end of the urban hierarchy, the stock of industrial floorspace rose by nearly 50 percent in rural areas. Thus while industry's demand for floorspace has risen overall, this rise has been concentrated in small towns and rural areas, not in Britain's cities.

The net change in industrial floorspace can be broken down into its component reductions and additions. Table 2 gives a breakdown of the gross additions to the stock of industrial floorspace in England between 1974 and 1982.

Table 1

Industrial floorspace by type of area:
England and Wales 1967-1982

million square metres

	1967	1982	% change
London	26.69	22.10	− 17.2
Conurbations	65.79	63.11	− 4.1
Free standing cities	37.19	40.76	+ 9.6
Large towns	29.67	34.18	+ 15.2
Small towns	44.32	57.55	+ 29.9
Rural areas	16.46	24.60	+ 49.5
ENGLAND AND WALES	219.82	242.30	+ 10.2

Source: Department of the Environment

Conurbations   = Manchester, Merseyside, Clydeside, Tyneside, West Yorkshire, West Midlands.
Free standing cities   = other cities with more than 250,000 people.
Large towns   = towns or cities with between 100,000 and 250,000 people.
Small towns   = local authority districts including at least one settlement with between 35,000 and 100,000 people.
Rural areas   = local authority districts in which all settlements have less than 35,000 people.

29

Table 2

Gross additions to the stock of industrial floorspace:
England 1974-1982

	million square metres	(%)
Extensions	21.4	(44.4)
New Units	17.8	(36.9)
Changes of Use	9.0	(18.7)
	48.2	(100.0)

Source: Department of the Environment

The table shows that most additions to the stock have been
through new building rather than changes of use, but what is
perhaps surprising is that factory extensions account for a
substantially greater increase in floorspace than entirely new
units. An assessment of the supply of land for industry must
therefore consider land for in situ expansion as well as land
for entirely new factories, a point generally overlooked by
most planning authorities. Indeed, in terms of its
contribution to increases in floorspace and employment, land
within existing site boundaries and immediately adjacent to
existing factory sites is more important than greenfield sites
for new industrial estates.

There is evidence that the ratio of floorspace to land has
been falling over time, despite variations between industries.
This is particularly the result of production technology
changes requiring single-storey factories as opposed to the
multi-storey buildings which were typical of the last century.
For example, if a nineteenth century four-storey building
providing 100,000 sq.ft of floorspace on a site that is
fully built-up is replaced by a single-storey modern factory
there will be substantial loss of floorspace. The site area
in this example would be 25,000 sq.ft., and it is likely that
the new factory would occupy at most only 40 percent of the
site, giving a new floorspace area of 10,000 sq.ft., which is
a 90 percent reduction.

Information on the ratio of floorspace to site area from
English Industrial Estates indicates that on their fully
developed estates the average ratio is around 30 percent.
Evidence we have collected for a wide range of factories in

30

the East Midlands also suggests that site densities have been falling, though the average ratio remains higher in cities than in small towns and rural areas. Increasing requirements for car parking, landscaping and for the circulation and unloading of heavy lorries contribute to this falling site density.

Thus the net increase in the stock of floorspace during the past two decades probably hides an even larger increase in the amount of land required because site densities are generally lower for new development.

EMPLOYMENT DENSITIES

There is no systematic evidence on trends in the ratio between land and employment, though the ratio between floorspace and land has been falling.

At the same time the number of workers employed per unit of floorspace has fallen. This is illustrated in Figure 2 which shows that between 1964 and 1982 the average number of workers per thousand sq.metres of industrial floorspace fell from 36.0 to 21.4, a fall of 40 percent or nearly three percent a year.

There is a cyclical pattern within this long-term trend. During up-turns in the economy the decline eased because of greater capacity utilisation. During recessions the decline accelerated as capacity utilisation fell. But the long-term trend is clearly downwards.

One possible interpretation of this decline in 'employment density' is that it reflects an increase in the amount of vacant and idle floorspace as British manufacturing moves further into decline. However, the scale of the increase in vacant floorspace has been modest. No official statistics monitor vacant industrial floorspce but King and Co., a firm of estate agents, produce regular estimates of the amount of vacant floorspace. Their figures are subject to certain minor exclusions - notably run-down older property and premises of less than 5,000 sq.ft - but King and Co. believe that the figures give a reasonably accurate guide to the amount of unoccupied floorspace on the market, and the accuracy of the King and Co. estimates was confirmed by a comparison we made between their figures for Leicestershire and records of vacant industrial premises compiled by the county council.

Figure 2

Employees per 1000 sq.metres of industrial
floorspace: England and Wales 1964-1982

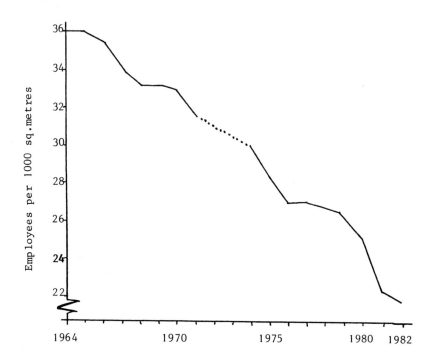

Sources: Department of Employment
           Department of the Environment

    The King and Co. data shows that in April 1982   9.54 million
sq. metres of industrial floorspace were vacant and on the
market   in England and Wales (King and Co. 1982).   This was
equivalent to approximately 4.1 per cent of the total stock of
floorspace in premises of more than 5,000 sq.ft.   This vacancy
rate is surprisingly small,   and before the recession at the
start   of the 1980s it was even lower - 1.7 per cent in April
1976, for example, and as low as 1.2 per cent in August 1979.
Therefore without denying that the amount of vacant industrial
floorspace rises during a recession,   it can safely be stated
that   the trend decline in employment density (in Figure 2
earlier) is not simply the result of an increase in the amount
of vacant floorspace.

    Our   view   is   that   the decline in employment   density   on

32

factory floorspace is probably the result of capital investment. As production techniques become more capital intensive, new machinery displaces labour on the shop floor and employment on any given area of floorspace falls. Certainly, since the mid 1960s the stock of capital per manufacturing worker has risen substantially, and the scale of capital investment appears to offer an explanation for the pervasiveness and magnitude of the decline in employment density.

THE SUPPLY OF LAND FOR FACTORY EXTENSIONS

The trends which have just been described are important because they indicate that the maintenance and expansion of manufacturing employment requires firstly an increase in the stock of floorspace because of the reduction in employment density, and secondly an even larger increase in the amount of industrial land because of the reduction in site densities. If the supply of land for new factories or for extensions to existing factories is inadequate, it could therefore have a damaging effect on manufacturing employment levels.

In order to find out about the availability of land for factory extensions we undertook a survey of industrial premises in the East Midlands during 1982. The survey covered all manufacturing establishments with more than 25 employees, and consisted of a postal questionnaire which had a response rate of 80 percent, supplemented by site visits to all the remaining plants. This information on premises was added to existing establishment data containing among other things figures on employment through time in each establishment, in order to investigate the relationship between employment change and the sites and premises which firms occupy (Fothergill, Kitson and Monk 1983b).

Figure 3 shows the relationship between employment change and factory extensions. Plants which did not extend their floorspace during the period 1968-1982 experienced a fall in employment, while factories which did extend their floorspace increased their employment. The graph shows this relationship very clearly. Figure 4 shows equally clearly that factories with a high proportion of their site vacant in 1968 increased their employment between 1968 and 1982 while those with fully built-up sites experienced a decline in employment. In other words, employment tends to increase only if factory floorspace is extended, and such on-site expansion can only occur if there is land available.

Figure 3

Relationship between employment change and factory extensions

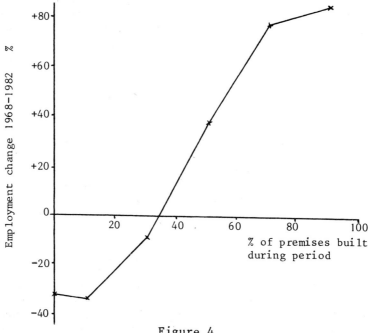

Figure 4

Relationship between employment change and site coverage

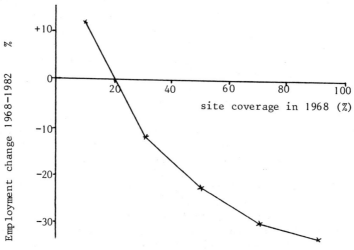

Sources: Industrial Premises Survey
           East Midlands Industrial Databank

The premises data from our survey was combined with existing data on industrial premises in the inner area of the originally collected by the Joint Unit for Research on the Urban Environment (JURUE 1980). This was adapted to compare directly with the information collected in our survey) to give a unique picture of the industrial building stock in cities, towns and rural areas. Table 3 shows that the typical picture for existing factories is one of lack of space for on-site expansion. The bulk of employment is housed in premises which have little room for expansi'on. The contrast between cities, and particularly the inner area of Birmingham, and rural areas is striking. There is a clear continuum along the urban hierarchy in the proportion of factories without room for expansion. The stock in cities is predominantly old, multi-storey, and hemmed in by other development compared with the stock in rural areas. This supports the view that one of the prime reasons for the steep decline in manufacturing employment in the cities and conurbations relative to the rural areas is the sheer lack of physical space for on-site expansion.

Table 3

The proportion of factory sites covered by buildings, by type of area

	Birmingham 1979	East Midlands 1982		
		Cities	Towns	Rural areas
% of employment in factories where buildings cover less than 50% of site	12.1	28.3	25.5	40.7
% of employment in factories where buildings cover more than 50% of site	87.9	71.7	74.5	59.3

Sources: Industrial Premises Survey
JURUE

THE SUPPLY OF LAND FOR NEW FACTORIES

No public or private agency collects comprehensive data on the availability of land for new factory building. The information in Table 4 was compiled from local authorities, most of which now keep records of land available within their areas. The data includes land available in both the short and long term, although it excludes land ear-marked for specific firms and land within the curtilage of existing factory sites. It also excludes land designated for warehousing only, though much of the land included is available for either manufacturing or warehousing (Fothergill, Kitson and Monk 1983c).

Table 4 shows the amount of land available for new factory

Table 4

Available industrial land, 1982

	hectares	hectares per thousand manufacturing employees
London	746	1.0
Conurbations	4661	2.8
Free standing cities	4213	4.3
Large towns	4418	6.3
Small towns	9732	6.9
Rural areas	6439	10.9
GREAT BRITAIN	30208	4.9

The following counties are excluded:

    Derbyshire
    Nottinghamshire
    Hereford and Worcester
    Essex
    Oxfordshire
    Berkshire
    Surrey
    Buckinghamshire (except Milton Keynes)
    Gloucestershire
    Devon

Source: Local authorities

building by type of area, expressed both in absolute terms and as the number of hectares per thousand maufacturing employees. In relation to the size of the manufacturing sector in each type of area, there is a marked and consistent urban-rural contrast in industrial land availability. Rural areas have over four times as much available land per employee as the conurbations, and nearly nine times as much as London. This shows that it is not the case that there are large tracts of land available for industry in the conurbations as a result of years of industrial decline. While there are specific areas, such as London's docklands, where substantial amounts of land are available within cities, on the whole it is Britain's small towns and rural areas, not the cities, which have by far the most land for new factory building.

The amount of industrial land available in any location is important not only because it is likely to influence the location of new factories. It also imposes a ceiling, in all but the long run, on the number of additional jobs which could be provided by new factories.

The number of jobs which might be accommodated on a given area of industrial land depends on the number of workers per unit of floorspace and on the ratio of floorspace to the total site area. Our research (Fothergill, Kitson and Monk 1983a) shows that the number of workers per unit of floorspace in new factory developments is approximately 25 percent higher than the average for the whole stock of industrial floorspace. This gives an employment density of approximately 25 workers per thousand sq.metres in 1983. Unpublished information on the ratio of floorspace to site area, obtained from English Industrial Estates (EIE), indicates that on fully developed estates one hectare of industrial land can be expected to accommodate approximately 3,000 sq.metres of floorspace. At current employment densities this floorspace would in turn accommodate 75 jobs.

This calculation allows rudimentary estimates of the employ-ment capacity of industrial land. If all the available industrial land in London (approximately 750 hectares) were to be fully developed, it would on these assumptions accommodate an extra 56,000 jobs. This number is small by comparison with the loss of 700,000 manufacturing jobs which has occurred in London since 1960. Furthermore, the potential employment capacity of available industrial land must be considered in the light of the continuing decline at approximately three percent a year in the number of workers on existing floorspace as capital displaces labour on the shop floor. Even if all the available industrial land in London were utilised, the resulting increase in employment would be entirely offset within five years by the steady fall in employment density on existing floorspace.

In practice, privately owned sites may be more intensively developed, or reach full development sooner, than the sites owned by EIE. Also, in the case of London the frequency of small sites and the need to maximise financial returns on high value land may increase the intensity of development. But even if the ratio of floorspace to total site area were as high as 50 percent the resulting gain in employment from developing all the available industrial land in London would still be entirely offset in only eight years by the falling employment density on London's existing factory floorspace.

The reason for such a relative shortage of industrial land in London and the conurbations is not entirely clear. We have argued elsewhere (Fothergill, Kitson and Monk 1983a) that the relative shortage of industrial land in cities is the result of constraints on supply, but it could be that less land is forthcoming because of a lack of demand. One indicator of this is the price of industrial land, because if lack of demand was the causal influence this might be reflected in lower prices. Data provided by District Valuation Offices to the Inland Revenue indicates that the price of land in conurbations and cities is generally significantly higher than the price of industrial land in other areas in the same regions, although there are large regional differences in price. In some cities, particularly London, the inflated price of industrial land may reflect hopes or expectations that a change to a more profitable land use such as offices will be allowed, but given the existence of planning controls it would be surprising if there were widespread expectations about change of use. Furthermore, it should be noted that the relatively high price of industrial land in the conurbations has been sustained despite the steep decline of manufacturing employment experienced there during the last two decades.

Although precise data is not available, Table 5 estimates the rate of take-up of available industrial land 1974-1982 on the assumption that the distribution of available land was approximately the same in 1974 as it was in 1982, the year for which we have figures. The table shows a consistent pattern, with a rate of take-up in London and the conurbations three times that in the towns and rural areas. This is further evidence that industrial development in the conurbations is buoyant in relation to the supply of industrial land.

CONCLUSIONS

This paper has summarised a number of aspects of the supply of
land for industrial development.   In particular, it hs shown
that   despite   the fall in its   employment   manufacturing   has
increased   its   demand for factory floorspace,   and   thus   its
demand for land.   Also, since the number of workers on   any
given area of factory floorspace is falling more industrial
land and floorspace is required in any given town or city
merely to maintain its existing level of employment in
manufacturing.   However, the evidence presented here indicates
that   in Britain's major urban areas their   is   only limited
space for the physical expansion of industry, and that   the
potential for maintaining or expanding their   industrial
employment base is therefore restricted.

The   implications of these findings for any future   national
economic   recovery   are   potentially serious.   In   the   first

Table 5

The rate of take-up of available industrial land:
England 1974-1982

	% share of total*		Rate of take-up B / A
	Available land 1982 A	New Units 1974-1982 B	
London	3.7	7.0	1.9
Conurbations	14.1	28.2	2.0
Free standing cities	18.5	10.7	0.6
Large towns	16.4	13.3	0.8
Small towns	29.7	26.5	0.9
Rural areas	17.6	14.4	0.8
ENGLAND	100.0	100.0	1.0

* counties for which land figures are not available are
  excluded from both columns.

Sources: Department of the Environment
           Local Authorities

instance, as the economy expands, spare capacity would be utilised and vacant premises would become occupied. But the relatively low vacancy rate, even in the depths of a recession, means that such slack would quickly be taken up. Further expansion would require more floorspace. Floorspace can be increased through factory extensions, new units and changes of use. But there is not enough land for on-site expansion in cities; there is not enough land for new units to provide sustained employment growth in cities; and changes of use are likely to become even less important during an upswing because other sectors would also be expanding and competing for buildings. In addition, there are likely to be bottlenecks in the development process and in the building industry itself once spare capacity had been used up.

These factors imply that an up-turn in the national economy would leave the conurbations, and the inner cities in particular, largely unaffected, as increases in industrial production and employment are pushed into small towns and rural areas where there are fewer obstacles to investment in new factory floorspace. This is undesirable not only because the burden of national economic adjustment would be heavily loaded onto inner city residents, but also because so long as obstacles to expansion remain, many firms in the conurbations are unlikely to realise their full potential for growth.

If public policy seeks to divert a larger share of any growth in industrial activity into the conurbations the central problem of land supply must be tackled. Measures to increase the supply of land for on-site expansion would be particularly necessary since, as we have noted, in factories where there is little or no room for expansion, employment tends to fall as production becomes more capital intensive and the number of workers on any given area of floorspace declines. Positive intervention to improve the supply of industrial land might include re-designating land currently reserved for other uses, and subsidising the costs of clearance, demolition and reclamation. Land prices are higher in cities; subsidised rents on publicly owned land, or sales of such land at subsidised prices, might help to redress the balance.

2 The supply of new industrial premises by public and private agencies in Tyne and Wear

STUART CAMERON, GORDON DABINETT AND ALLAN GILLARD

The local economic development policies which have expanded in
recent years have followed established Regional Policy in
giving a major role to the provision of industrial premises.
The deficiencies of the stock of industrial buildings and
sites in inner urban areas has been implicated as a major
cause of the poor economic performance of these areas.
Nevertheless, the role of the public sector in the provision
of industrial premises is now a more controversial one. The
question mark arises partly in terms of the effectiveness of
this policy instrument in stimulating a local economy and
creating jobs.

Increasingly, though, the point at issue is whether public
sector provision is desirable and necessary, or whether the
private sector can be relied upon, or encouraged, to meet the
need. The present Government's preference for private rather
than public sector action obviously highlights this issue.

Our interest in the process of supply of new industrial
premises arose out of an interest in the construction of
premises as an element of local public policy. It became

* The funding of the Department of the Environment and of the
  SSRC for the research referred to is gratefully acknowledged
  but the views expressed are those of the authors alone.

clear that, in order to examine the second of the issues mentioned above; whether public sector action is necessary; it is essential to look at the industrial development process as a whole, and at the actions and interactions of public and private agencies within that development process.

Our first purpose here is to describe the progression of our research from the evaluation of local authority economic policies, including those involving the supply of industrial premises (which examined the first issue, that of effectiveness), to a concern with the overall pattern of supply of industrial premises. Our second is to report some of the preliminary findings and to describe some of the methodological issues of research on the industrial development process.

The research has concentrated on the County of Tyne and Wear, centred on the cities of Newcastle and Sunderland. It will become clear that Tyne and Wear does not provide a 'typical' case of the industrial development process, if there is such a thing. It is an area which is notable for the long history and large scale of public sector intervention in the supply of industrial premises by national and local agencies, which perhaps make it of particular interest in relation to the issue of the role of the public vis-a-vis the private sectors.

LOCAL AUTHORITY AID TO INDUSTRY IN TYNE AND WEAR

The origins of our work on the supply of industrial premises were in a research project commissioned by the Department of the Environment to evaluate recently developed local authority policies to assist local industry in Tyne and Wear (Cameron et al, 1982). The primary reason for this study was that Tyne and Wear County Council had sponsored a Local Act, the Tyne and Wear Act 1976, to extend the powers of local authorities to assist local industry. These powers made available in Tyne and Wear in 1976, were similar to those incorporated in the Inner Urban Areas Act 1978 and Tyne and Wear, and therefore, provided an opportunity for an early assessment of their effects. The new powers in the Tyne and Wear Act covered two areas: financial assistance in the form of loans and grants and the declaration of Industrial Improvement Areas. These were not necessarily directly connected with the supply of new premises, indeed a part of the purpose was to extend the range of local authority action into new areas, such as loans and grants for plant and machinery. In initial discussions with local authorities it became clear that the powers made available in the Tyne and Wear Act should be seen as a part of a package of new initiatives to aid local industry, developed after 1974, and should not be treated in isolation. In particular, the programmes of advance factory building were another central element in the new economic initiatives and so the provision of advance factories was also evaluated in the research. In fact, the evaluation concentrated mainly on financial assistance and advance factories because the programmes of Industrial Improvement Areas were not, in most cases, sufficiently advanced to make an evaluation possible.

In the event, the study revealed that during our study period of 1974 to the end of 1979 the provision of new factory premises was overwhelmingly the most important element in local authority economic development policy in Tyne and Wear. The direct provision of new advance factories by local authorities was the largest single element of the new economic development policies we examined. In the study period, 187 advance factory units were constructed, while 149 firms were assisted by loans and grants; spending on advance factories amounted to £6.4m while spending on loans and grants was £3.9m. In addition to direct provision of advance factories by local authorities, most of the financial assistance actually provided by local authorities related in one way or another to the provision of new premises. The powers made available under the Tyne and Wear Act allowed for a range of financial assistance measures which included assistance with extending and improving existing premises and also for the purchase of plant and machinery. Despite this, local authority assistance was concerned in most cases with firms moving into new premises, either as new firms or as established firms moving from other premises. Of the 156 firms interviewed in our study, only 20 had not moved; of these 16 had used local authority assistance to expand existing premises and 4 had purchased plant or machinery. The largest single element in local authority loans was mortgage loans for the purchase or construction of premises. The largest element in local authority grants was rent relief grants given to tenants of local authority advance factories. Thus the intervention of the local authority by means of these new economic development initiatives was mostly relevant to the particular circumstances of firms seeking premises, either to establish a new firm or branch or relocate an existing one.

The main purpose of the study for the DoE was to evaluate these economic development policies; it was concerned with the question of effectiveness. It is not our intention here to look in detail at this evaluation, but the results can be briefly summarised. The evaluation was primarily in terms of the employment created by these policies, but the final conclusion was that the impact of these policies on employment was quite limited. This was not because the policies were inefficient in job creation – the calculations of cost per job revealed a quite reasonable picture – but rather that the programmes were small in scale and applied mostly to very small firms. The conclusions of the Report (Cameron et al, 1982) suggested that the most important impact was probably on the development of small firms in the circumstances when they required new or improved premises, and more generally in providing a stock of good quality small industrial units in the inner urban areas when it appeared that this was not being done either by the private sector or other public sector agencies.

THE PATTERN OF SUPPLY OF NEW INDUSTRIAL PREMISES

The research for the DoE revealed the central importance of new industrial premises in the local authority economic development policies evaluated, but not the relationship between local authority provision and other public and private sector agencies in the production of new industrial premises. As the main public sector agency, English Industrial Estates began to change its role and as the involvement of the private sector has become more central to Government policy, the question of the relationship of local authority activities to those of other agencies in this field has become more important. It was decided, therefore, to examine the overall pattern of the supply of new premises in Tyne and Wear and a new research project was started, in January 1982, supported by a grant from SSRC, on 'The Supply of New Industrial Premises: A Planning Framework'. The main aims of this project have been:

- to examine how agencies operate in difficult types of industrial localities in a sub-region,

- to examine the reasons for the pattern of investment of agencies,

- to examine the interactions of agencies, their plans and programmes and the planning framework within which they operate.

Thus the policy issue of the necessity for public sector intervention is being addressed as part of an examination of the actions of all the agencies involved in the supply of industrial premises.

The development of a methodology for the study revealed the lack of a single comprehensive data source on new industrial premises within our study period of 1974 to 1981. The most obvious source of data was planning applications and building control records held by local authorities but it did not prove possible to use these sources to produce a comprehensive picture of new premises supply. The strategy eventually developed involved three distinct types of information.

1.   The Industrial and Commercial Floorspace Statistics (IFS) produced by the DoE from Inland Revenue data were used to provide broad aggregate data on new industrial premises. The main purpose for which IFS was used was in an inter-regional comparison; comparing the Northern Region with the other Regions of England. The data for Tyne and Wear was then set against this regional context.

2.   Data on the building programmes of public agencies was collected from the three main types of public agencies involved in building industrial premises: English Industrial Estates, New Town Development Corporations and local authorities. A comprehensive picture of their programmes in the Region, and a more detailed picture of public sector provision in Tyne and Wear, was built up.

3.   Comparing the total picture given by IFS with the data on public sector provision gave a broad impression of the scale and nature of private sector provision in the North Region and in Tyne and Wear. It was decided, though, that it was not practical to attempt to obtain a fully comprehensive picture of private sector supply in Tyne and Wear. Instead, a number of case studies of industrial locations, chosen to represent a range of types of locality and of mixes of developers, have been identified. A detailed analysis of development in these areas is being carried out, and private sector developers identified and interviewed to examine the reasons for their investment choice regarding location and development choice.

INDUSTRIAL FLOORSPACE TRENDS IN THE NORTHERN REGION

The first stage of the research set a context for the detailed analysis of Tyne and Wear with an analysis at the regional level using the Industrial Floorspace Statistics and data from public agencies (Dabinett, 1982).

The Industrial Floorspace Statistics do have a number of limitations; for example, they do not include information on the type of developer (a fuller discussion of the limitations

of IFS is included in Dabinett 1982). Nevertheless, despite
these limitations, the analysis of IFS revealed certain unique
features of industrial floorspace trends in the Northern
Region. The Northern Region experienced a substantial
increase in floorspace in the period 1974-1978, as can be seen
in Table 1. It was one of a group of four regions with

Table 1

Floorspace and Employment Change in the English
Regions 1974-1980

Standard Region	% Change in Floorspace	% Contribution of New Build	% Change in Manufacturing Employment
South-East	+ 1.1	44	- 12.9
North-West	+ 0.2	38	- 15.4
West Midlands	+ 3.2	49	- 15.3
Yorks & Humberside	+ 1.3	41	- 14.0
East Midlands	+ 9.3	37	- 8.9
South-West	+ 9.5	41	- 7.1
NORTH	+ 9.5	62	- 14.9
East Anglia	+ 12.3	29	- 4.9
England	+ 3.4		- 12.9

Source: DoE Commercial and Industrial Floorspace Statistics
England (1980 and 1981) HMSO.

substantial floorspace increases, the others being East
Midlands, East Anglia and South West. In contrast the South-
East and the other major industrial regions, West Midlands,
North West and Yorkshire and Humberside had a much smaller
increase in floorspace. Clearly, though, the other 'growth'
regions are very dissimilar from the North, representing the
areas outside the conurbations and traditional industrial
areas which have been the recipients of the dispersal of
industry. The growth of industrial floorspace in the North
had certain distinct features. Firstly, the element of new

building was much more important in the North than elsewhere. The Region had the second lowest percentage increase in floorspace through extensions, but by far the highest percentage increase through new building. The average size of industrial hereditaments in the Northern Region in 1980 was large, more than twice the average size for the South-East and substantially larger than any other Region, reflecting the continued dominance in the local economy of large firms with large plants. This trend was continued in the provision of new floorspace between 1974 and 1980, units over 10,000 sq.metres representing a large part of total new building in the North. There was, however, also a dramatic increase in very small units of under 500 sq.metres. This was quite small in terms of total floorspace, and was not unique to the Northern Region, but did represent a break from the traditional pattern of supply. In all Regions of England, manufacturing employment declined between 1974 and 1980 while manufacturing floorspace increased. This difference was most marked in the Northern Region, where there was a 9.5% increase in industrial floorspace but a -15% decrease in employment, compared to +3% and -13% in England as a whole.

PUBLIC SECTOR PROVISION IN THE NORTHERN REGION

A comprehensive picture of public sector provision of new industrial floorspace was built up from public agency records. The difference in definition between this data and that provided by IFS does not permit an exact comparison, but it can be estimated that between 1974 and 1980 the public sector accounted for about 30 percent of all new floorspace. We do not have comparable data for other Regions but this appears to be a very substantial public sector contribution.

The public sector providers in the North Region were mainly English Industrial Estates, the New Towns (Washington, Peterlee and Newton Aycliffe) and the local authorities, with minor contributions from, for example, British Steel (Industries). English Industrial Estates was the most important. The North-East has received a large proportion of EIE building activity (about 50 percent of all factories built between 1960 and 1980) and EIE account for more than half of all public sector provision in the Region, and about 16 percent of all new building. Although local authorities account for only about 20 percent of public sector provision in all, their involvement in factory building did increase substantially in this period. The local authorities concen-trated on very small units with an average floorspace of only 205 sq.metres. English Industrial Estates also moved towards

the building of more small units; by 1980 their average size
of unit had reduced to 433 sq.metres. It seems that the growth
in small industrial units under 500 sq.metres noted above was
particularly associated with public sector building.

PRIVATE SECTOR IN THE NORTHERN REGION

The central feature of private sector new industrial premises
in the Northern Region was the dominance of very large units
of more than 10,000 sq.metres. This size of unit accounted
for 53 percent of all new floorspace in the study period,
compared with 30 percent for the country as a whole. It
represented about 75 percent of all private sector provision
in the Northern Region. Obviously, factory units of this kind
are not built speculatively but are likely to be designed for
specific user's requirements. It is not possible from the
statistics to identify specific developments, but local
knowledge suggests that developments of this kind are
sometimes part of the modernisation and rationalisation
process of major established industries. These processes may
also involve labour force reductions, and it could be hypo-
thesised that the dominance of units of this kind is
associated with the particularly strong contrast in the
Northern Region between floorspace growth and employment
decline.

The remainder of the private sector, producing units of less
than 10,000 sq.metres, is a very mixed category. It will
include speculative building by investor/developers and
builder/developers (Boddy and Barrett, 1979) as well as own-
account building for owner-occupation. The key feature of
this category in the Northern Region is its small size,
seemingly accounting for less than 20 percent of all new
floorspace, while in other Regions it would seem to be typical
for this category to account for more than half of all new
building.

The supply of industrial floorspace in the Northern Region
revealed in IFS presents a unique and interesting picture. In
common with the favoured outer areas of the South of England,
the North experienced a relatively large growth in floorspace,
but with many features peculiar to itself. New build, rather
than extensions to existing plant, accounts for a large part
of the growth. In the private sector very large units
dominate, while the public sector is also very large. In
contrast, the provision of smaller units by the private
sector is, comparatively, very small. Finally, the favourable

position with regard to floorspace growth is not reflected in employment.

INDUSTRIAL FLOORSPACE CHANGE IN TYNE AND WEAR

Having established a context at the regional scale, the research focussed on the main area of study, Tyne and Wear Metropolitan County. As well as the data sources used for the regional analysis, IFS and public agency records, a third data source was used for the County. This was the Significant Planning Applications File (SPAF) of the Tyne and Wear Joint Information System. This computerised record of planning applications and building completions data from local authorities in the County provides information on major new industrial developments. Unfortunately, in practice only development from 1980 could be identified with confidence from this source, so its usefulness was limited. As mentioned earlier, it was not possible to construct a comprehensive record of new industrial premises supply in Tyne and Wear in our study period of 1974 to 1981, but from these data sources it was possible to build up a picture of new industrial premises in Tyne and Wear.

The picture is similar to that of the Northern Region as a whole. Between 1974 and 1981 the amount of industrial floorspace in Tyne and Wear increased by 0.8%, considerably less than the Region, but in most other conurbations floorspace decreased. A major factor in this growth, as with that in the Region, was the provision of new premises, rather than the floorspace provided by extensions. In Tyne and Wear, even more than in the Northern Region, the public sector played an exceptionally important part in the provision of new floorspace. Certainly over half and perhaps as much as 70% of all new floorspace was provided by public agencies, mostly in advance of demand. In contrast there appears to have been only a handful of private speculative schemes in the County. There is, though, a growing trend for private finance to become involved in public speculative schemes through partnership arrangements. The types of schemes appear to be spatially differentiated with large developments on industrial estates on the periphery of the urban area and smaller, usually local authority schemes in the inner urban and riverside areas.

THE PUBLIC SECTOR IN TYNE AND WEAR

Public sector provision of new industrial premises is

49

particularly important in Tyne and Wear, accounting for substantially more than half of all new floorspace. Three
agencies have been responsible for this development; English
Industrial Estates, Washington New Town Development Corporation and the local authorities.

English Industrial Estates: Historically the English
Industrial Estates Corporation provided most public sector
advance factory units in Tyne and Wear; in the period 1974 to
1981 they accounted for 39 percent of public sector building.
Before June 1980 English Industrial Estates Corporation (as it
was then known) was an executive arm of the Department of
Industry, who determined the size and location of the factory
building programmes as an element of Regional Policy. The
allocation of building between Assisted Regions was determined
by the Department of Industry; the location of development
within a Region was decided by regional officials of
interested government departments. The main criteria for the
location of factory building was the level of male unemployment and the purpose of factory building was to bring
employment to high unemployment areas. The announcement of
programmes was very uneven, reflecting regional priorities and
government spending; these programmes sometimes related to
specific problems e.g. stimulating the construction industry,
responding to steel, coal and shipyard redundancies and, more
recently, relating to inner city policies.

The change in government in 1979 brought a complete change
in the basis of operation of what then became English Industrial Estates along with a major reassessment of Department of
Industry policy. The areas of the country covered by regional
policy were to be drastically reduced. Advance factory
building would continue as an instrument of regional policy,
but EIE was to operate more independently of the Department of
Industry, making its own policy decisions on new development
and including a greater element of private sector financing,
particularly from the financial institutions. No EIE factory
building programme was announced in 1979. In 1980 the new
pattern emerged. In the March Budget of 1980 the government
introduced an Industrial Building Allowance to stimulate the
construction of small manufacturing units, and made more than
£5m available to build 1,000 new nursery units in the Assisted
Areas with co-operation between EIE and the private sector.
In June 1980 new guidelines were issued to EIE and the 1981
Industry Act empowered EIE to undertake development using
private sector funds. Under the guidelines, EIE was required
to further central government, regional and industrial
policies, but also to conform with the best financial and
commercial standards. The guidelines included a significant

transfer of executive responsibility from the Department of Industry, with EIE itself taking on responsibility for forward planning, marketing, rental and capital valuations and selection of tenants. The Department no longer makes factory building announcements. Instead EIE produces a four-year plan with which to carry out its developments on behalf of the Department of Industry. Resources are allocated to travel-to-work areas on the basis of vacant factory stocks and need for new employment, and the plan is intended to provide the basis for 'co-operation with the private sector and local authorities with whom EIE seeks to co-ordinate its development programme'.

In Tyne and Wear provision of floorspace by EIE rose to a peak in 1979, in particular reflecting the programme of factory building as a response to shipyard rationalisations announced in 1977. Provision dropped in 1980, reflecting the lack of a programme announcement in 1979, but in 1981 a new peak of building was reached and in that year 46 percent of this was financed by private sector financial institutions, reflecting the new basis of operation of EIE.

Washington Development Corporation: Tyne and Wear is the only Metropolitan County with a New Town within its boundaries. During the study period the Development Corporation produced 39 percent of all public sector floorspace in Tyne and Wear, obviously leading to a major spatial concentration of new floorspace in this location on the periphery of the County. The Development Corporation is responsible for laying out and development of the New Town in accordance with the Master Plan. This includes providing industrial sites and premises in nine major industrial sites around the periphery of the New Town. The Development Corporation began building advance factories in 1967, ranging in size from 90 sq.metres to 4,500 sq.metres. The Master Plan was not directly affected by the policy shift in 1977 away from new towns and towards the inner cities. Since the late 1970s, though, there had been more emphasis in the Corporation's programmes on providing premises for small and local firms. The change in policy brought about by the new Government in 1979 has affected Washington as it has affected EIE, in that the Development Corporation has begun to attract private capital investment in the provision of new units and has also begun to dispose of some of its industrial assets.

Local authorities: The contribution of local authorities to the public sector provision in Tyne and Wear was only 14 percent of all public sector floorspace produced between 1974 and 1981. The local authorities in Tyne and Wear were, nonetheless, very active in the field of advance factory building and made an important contribution in concentrating on the provision of small units in inner urban areas. The County Council was the leader in this field, beginning in 1976 and all five District councils began factory building programmes between then and 1979. Newcastle City Council, however, decided as early as 1979 to concentrate on making sites available for the private sector to build factory units, and the Council have engaged in a number of partnership schemes. The emphasis on small units became more pronounced over time; for example, the County Council originally provided units of between 200 sq.metres and 1,000 sq.metres but after 1977 concentrated on workshops under 500 sq.metres.

A detailed description (Dabinett and Whisker, 1981) and assessment (Cameron et al. 1982) of local authority advance factories were included in the earlier research project undertaken for the DoE, for the period 1974 to 1980. Since 1980 there have been some important shifts in emphasis. The direct building of factory units by local authorities has become less central to this programme, having reached a peak in 1979. For example, the County Council recently decided to run down its programme of small industrial units, although this situation will be kept under review. Some of the other local authorities have now joined Newcastle City in involvement in partnership schemes. Recent factory building has been largely limited to the provision of small workshops for the start-up of new businesses, in some cases including the provision of communal services and administrative support. This is part of a wider attempt to establish new businesses, also involving various schemes of 'start-up' grants and other financial assistance, as well as advice and information services.

Private/public sector partnerships: a total of eight partnership schemes undertaken in Tyne and Wear since 1974 has been identified and these account for 8 percent of all 'public sector' floorspace provision. These include two with EIE, one with Washington New Town and five with local authorities, including three with Newcastle City Council. The EIE and Washington schemes have involved private sector funding for development carried out by the public agency, with the funding coming from financial institutions, including clearing banks. The local authority schemes have generally taken the form of a lease-and-lease back arrangement, the partnership involving a development company which builds the development, the local authority leasing the land to the developer and then leasing back the factories and undertaking responsibility for management.

Table 2

Public Sector Provision in Tyne and Wear 1974-1981
Floorspace (sq.metres)

	EIE	Washington New Town	Local Authorities	Partner ships	Total
Advance Factories	146,203	116,978	55,493	32,060	350,734
Bespoke Factories	6,696	35,921	-	-	42,617
Total	152,899	152,899	55,493	32,060	393,351
%	(39)	(39)	(14)	(8)	(100)

Source: Public agency records.

THE PRIVATE SECTOR IN TYNE AND WEAR

In Tyne and Wear, as in the Northern Region as a whole, the
provision of large industrial units over 10,000 sq.metres has
been a major element in private sector provision. It was
decided, however, not to examine developments of this kind in
detail, in that they have been provided by large companies for
their own particular requirements, not for the general stock
of industrial premises. Attention has been focussed, therefore, on the (relatively very small-scale) private sector
provision of smaller premises, as well as on those schemes
involving a public/private partnership.

This analysis of the private sector in Tyne and Wear will be
based on detailed studies of a number of industrial locations
around the County. The objective is to gain an understanding
of how new industrial premises are supplied and why; and why
there may be locational variations in this supply. The case
studies cover a range of locations from inner urban areas to
the urban fringe. Each has private sector developments, but
most are public sector industrial estates and some also
include public sector developments. The analysis of these
case study locations will involve two stages. Firstly, public
records and consultations with relevant local planning
authority officers will be used to build up a comprehensive
picture of development from 1974. Secondly, as a part of this

picture, private sector developers will be identified and a
survey of these developers will be undertaken. The objectives
of this survey will be to identify the type of developer and
the reasons for their pattern of investment and the general
pattern of their development process.

CONCLUSIONS

The research has revealed the remarkable degree of public
sector involvement in the building of industrial premises in
Tyne and Wear, and, conversely, the low level of private
sector activity. Nonetheless, it is clear that, even in Tyne
and Wear, things are changing and there is a shift of emphasis
away from direct public sector provision and towards the
involvement of the private sector.

The shift of emphasis away from direct public sector
investment and development is obviously partly a result of
central government policies. It is not clear to what extent
it also reflects a change in the willingness of the private
sector to involve itself in areas previously left to the
public sector, although there are some small-scale indications
of change, such as in partnership schemes, or where the
viability of development has been demonstrated by the success
of public sector schemes. Clearly, one important purpose of
gaining a better understanding of the industrial development
process is to identify the scope and limitations of the
private sector, and the necessity for, and the role of, public
sector activity.

The development of a position in which the public sector is
seen primarily as providing a framework for private sector
investment and development also raises the question of an
appropriate form of strategy for this role. Traditional land-
use planning viewed industrial development as a flow to be
channelled, through land-use allocations, to appropriate
locations on the basis of forecasts of employment need. The
growth of local economic development policies in the 1970s
often involved new budget-based policy plans for direct public
sector intervention. Recent changes imply a return to a
strategy based on providing a framework for private development, but an effective strategy of mobilising the private
sector will need to be based much more firmly on an understanding of the development process, and the roles of the
variety of agencies within it.

3 Inner city areas and the private sector

NIGEL MOOR

INTRODUCTION

Recognition of the problems posed by the decline of the country's older urban areas is generally dated to the setting up by the Home Office of the series of Community Development Projects, as part of their Urban Programme, in 1969. Since that date there has been a steady stream of initiatives by governments culminating in the setting up of the Urban Development Corporations for London Docklands and the Merseyside Dock Area, modelled on the New Town Development Corporation. Throughout this period, although successive governments, on the surface, have appeared to operate a generally bipartisan approach as to the need for inner area renewal, the debate as to how to achieve solutions to the problem has tended to swing between two opposing views of urban management, which reflect alternative political ideologies.

In this debate the private sector has not played a critical role, which is not altogether surprising, in that the public sector, in the shape of local government and public corporations such as the statutory undertakings and the nationalised industries, is the major landowner in the inner city areas. Nor do these areas necessarily contain a critical proportion of the country's productive capital. The seven largest inner city areas (Manchester/Salford, Newcastle/Gateshead,

Birmingham, Liverpool, Hackney/Islington, Lambeth and Docklands) contain only 8 percent of the commercial and industrial
floorspace in England and Wales.   Waste land is probably the
most characteristic common denominator of these areas;   more
than 2,000 acres in Inner London, and nearly 500 acres in a
single borough such as Tower Hamlets (London Evening Standard
1978;   Nabarro and Richards 1980).   It is this single
characteristic,   the sheer amount of waste land, together with
a series of related policy changes on the part of central
government,   that   explains the emphasis which is   increasing,
that   the   private sector should play a more positive role   in
the inner city.   These changes are principally:

i.   Traditionally,   in the provision of new housing, industry
       or   other   infrastructure,   the   inner area has   been   in
       competition with green-field sites.   Through the medium
       of the approved structure plans and the government's
       declared support for the maintenance of green belts,
       particularly in the south east, the attention of the
       private sector is being turned to the possibility of
       development in the inner areas.   There is, for example,
       little likelihood of any ministerial support at appeal
       for   industrial,   commercial or residential proposals in
       the green belt, unless exceptional national interests are
       involved,   whilst   large   areas of land lie idle in the
       cities.   Politically,   such a policy, although not
       necessarily   approved   of by the   development   and
       construction   industries,   has   a   double appeal for a
       Conservative administration.   It demonstrates to the
       generally   Labour-held   inner   area councils that the
       government is continuing a policy, largely initiated by a
       previous Labour government,   and placates the shire
       counties which increasingly hold strong anti-development
       views.

ii.   At a time of reduced public expenditure, particularly on
       capital projects,   the steady increase in the amount of
       money being invested by the government in the inner city
       areas   represents an   increasing opportunity for private
       developers.   The Urban Programme, which is specifically
       for the inner cities, has expanded from £30 million in
       1976/77, to £270 million in 1982/83, and a provisional
       sum of £348 million for 1983/84.   Even allowing for
       inflation,   this is a significant increase and although
       the   programme is meant to supplement the existing
       programmes of central and local government, which are in
       decline through spending cuts, it can no longer be
       ignored.

iii. Through the innovations contained in the Local Government, Planning and Land Act 1980, the government has staked a great deal politically on making progress in the inner areas. Principally these include the statutory land registers through which the Secretary of State hopes to persuade public land owners to release land for development, the enterprise zones which are discussed later in this paper and the Urban Development Corporations. As the Chairman of the London Docklands Development Corporation, the Secretary of State chose a property man, who had built up a property company from nothing to a diversified group with a market capitalisation of nearly £250 million.

ROLE OF THE PRIVATE INVESTOR

The aim of Government policy, according to a statement made by the Secretary of State in 1979, was 'to make our inner cities places where people want to live and work, and where the private investor is prepared to put his money'. The role of Government was to create opportunities which others can take up, for example by reclaiming land to encourage private development. This approach contrasts strongly with that adopted by the previous administration, in its 'Policy for the Inner Cities' suggests that 'The aim must be to encourage changes in the attitudes of industry and financial institutions so that they play their full part' (DoE 1977b, para 40).

During the 1980s the urban management of our cities and towns will prove to be an ideological battleground between those advocating a private sector, market-orientated approach to regeneration and those pledged to return to a high level of public intervention and expenditure. Even with strong policy support, can the private sector make an effective contribution to the solution of inner city problems? It is faced with considerable obstacles in attempting to define possible development opportunities in the inner areas if it is to maintain normal and accepted investment criteria. An 'acceptable' or 'prime' investment must, according to David Cadman:

i   provide a secure stream of income;

ii   provide an element of rental growth that gives a satisfactory hedge against inflation;

iii   be a freehold interest, or at least a very long leasehold interest (125 years or more);

iv   not involve onerous management problems;

v   be of a suitable size - the larger funds do not like to invest in very small sums, which to some means less than £1 million and others less than £250,000;   and

vi   be in a satisfactory environment. Apart from considering the building or buildings, the fund will have regard to whether the surrounding area will enhance or detract from the value of the investment now and in the future (Cadman 1979).

These views are confirmed by the most authoritative statement to date on the criteria of the institutions - evidence given to the Wilson Committee in November 1977 by the insurance companies and the pension funds:

"The primary objective of pension funds is to maximise the rate of return by investments which involve an acceptable level of risk, having regard to the nature of the liabilities. Moreover, pension funds are trustee funds and trustees are bound by legal restraints ... They cannot take too wide a view", (House of Commons 1978).

Given therefore the inevitably opportunist approach of the private sector to investment, is there a danger that an exaggerated emphasis on the inner areas of cities in public policy will be counter-productive as far as attracting new investment? Area management has had a strong following in local government during the seventies, as part of a 'total' approach to the organisation of public services and was given considerable impetus by the series of town studies published by the Department of the Environment under the general title of "Making Towns Better" in 1973. However, it has no comparison in the private sector. What then are the reasons for pursuing this focus on inner areas? The Royal Town Planning Institute has suggested five in its report on land values and planning in the inner areas:

i   Inner city areas represent particular concentrations of problems and may therefore be specially urgent or amenable to exceptional treatment;

ii   In certain areas, the scale of the problem can build up to a pattern of accumulated disadvantage, where the extent of the lack of opportunities exerts its own effect on residents;

iii   The resources of inner areas are, at present, much under-utilised. Unemployment and lack of use for skills exert their own cost on the economy;

iv   There is evident and widespread waste resulting from empty or under-used buildings, and vacant land;

v   The characteristics of the land market are distinctive, especially the role of land acquisition costs in constraining development (RTPI, 1978b).

The RTPI concluded that the private investment that had taken place in the inner areas had been limited and highly localised. Office and warehouse building on the fringe of central business districts has often been disruptive of local communities. New industrial developments would nearly always generate fewer jobs per acre than the old industries they replaced. New employment in office development was often inappropriate to the needs of inner area school leavers and the unemployed. It is a dismal catalogue and the sceptical reader might be tempted to ponder on what other, more exciting job opportunities, the Institute had in mind. The report was published in the Spring of 1978 at the apotheosis of the publicly financed approach to the solution of inner area problems and concluded that "a major redirection of public investment is called for, on a scale which society has hardly dared to contemplate". Since then there has been a shift in public spending, that has been described earlier, although nothing on the scale that the authors of this report no doubt had in mind. What has also happened, is the growing realisation that the public sector, unaided, cannot meet all the financial requirements of inner area improvement. It has become a 'Catch 22' situation in that in order to attract investors, there has to be public spending on roads, public transport facilities, schools, open spaces, etc., whilst the public sector, through increased curbs on expenditure, has less room to manoeuvre. To fully understand how this confused and inhibiting state of affairs has arisen, it is helpful to review briefly the manner in which inner city area policy has evolved during the past decade.

INNER AREA POLICIES

The Community Development Project was set up by a Labour Home Secretary in 1969, as a 'neighbourhood-based experiment aimed at finding new ways of meeting the needs of people living in areas of high social deprivation'. The CDPs were set up in twelve areas, where, with the exception of Oldham and Cleator

59

Moor in Cumberland, conditions were representative of inner city areas. The intention was that working with the local authorities concerned, the project teams would identify needs, promote greater co-ordination and accessibility of services at the field level, to foster community involvement and to build a communication bridge between the people and local services. Research was to be located in local universities or polytechnics to provide data, advice and evaluation. The reports of those teams however did not remain at this small-scale focus. Using empirical case-studies, they added up to a mighty critique of a series of inter-linked government policies for urban renewal, economic growth and environmental improvement (National Community Development Project, 1974). The original financial sponsor, the Home Office, was less than enthusiastic, and in some instances, the project teams had lost the support of the local authorities. However, during the life-time of the projects the focus of interest on inner-area problems was passing to the Department of the Environment. Under a Conservative administration, the 'Urban Guidelines' studies were published in 1973 and inner area studies of Birmingham, Lambeth and Liverpool began. The consultants appointed reported to a Labour Secretary of State in 1977. Although less openly critical of the private enterprise system than the Community Development Projects, their reports identified economic forces as the main determinant of the social deprivation found in these ideas, in contrast to the theory that such problems had their origins in the characteristics of local populations, originally promoted by the Home Office. The consultants recommended positive discrimination by government in favour of the inner areas on a 'total' area basis (DoE, 1977a).

The Government's response to these reports and its proposals were contained in the White Paper 'Policy for the Inner Cities' (DoE, 1977b). Inner city aid was to be increased from under £30 million to £125 million in 1979-80 and a fourfold approach was proposed:

i   Strengthening the economies of the inner areas
     and the prospects of their residents;

ii   Improving the physical fabric of the inner areas
     and making their environments more attractive;

iii Alleviating social problems;

iv   Securing a new balance between the inner areas
     and the rest of the city region in terms of
     population and jobs.

Local authorities were to enter into 'partnership arrangements' with Central Government, committing themselves to specific area improvements. The legislative basis for the proposals was contained in the Inner Urban Areas Act which obtained the Royal Assent in 1978. Criticism came on two main counts. The resources to be allocated were trivial against the background of the serious problems affecting inner city areas and the administrative machinery too cumbersome and diffuse. The Town and Country Planning Association was a particularly vocal critic and stated that "undoubtedly the most effective public machine for development so far devised in this country is the New Town Development Corporation, and many of the management methods of development corporations have applications to inner city problems". The TCPA were in fact to have their plea answered by means (Town and Country Planning, 1979) of another dramatic shift in the direction of inner area policy. Following their election in 1979 the new Conservative Government announced that the inner area partnership approach between central government and the local authorities would continue, but Urban Development Corporations were to be set up for the London Docklands and the Merseyside Dock area. The other new initiative, the setting up of 'enterprise zones' in a number of inner areas, which had been anticipated in a speech by Sir Geoffrey Howe to the Bow Group in June 1978, was confirmed in the 1980 Budget. Although maintaining the partnership approach initiated by the previous Labour administration, the effect of these innovations is to reduce considerably the scope for local government in inner area renewal.

WASTE LAND

It is the sheer lack of demand that typifies the inner area problem. Anyone who undertakes a train journey from Birmingham New Street to Manchester Piccadilly cannot but be struck by the enormous tracts of waste urban land, abandoned, unproductive, unsightly and neglected, visible through the carriage window. The 'de-industrialisation of Britain' is dramatically apparent (Moss, 1980).

When considering wasteland in inner city areas, it is important to distinguish between on the one hand derelict land, and on the other, unused land which remains unused because of a lack of demand or other factors not directly concerned with the condition of the land itself (Nabarro and Richards, 1980). Derelict land clearance has been eligible for government grants for a considerable period, and the emphasis is now changing to give more priority to derelict

land in urban areas. However, the greatest criticism has
focused on unused land, and various attempts have been made in
the past to try and overcome the difficulties associated with
this problem (Bruton and Gore, 1981). The usual prescription
advanced in these cases is increased public spending but given
the scandalously bad land management record of the public
authorities (in East London of the 175 acres zoned for open
space in 1951, only 50 had even been grassed over by 1975 and
most of these had no facilities) this must be open to
question. Whatever the criticisms that might be levied on the
private sector, the weight of financial pressures ensures that
management attempts to find some beneficial use for its land
holdings.

There therefore does appear to be some general agreement
that the culprits in the main have been nationalised
industries, statutory undertakings and local government –
there being in many inner city areas virtually no private
market in land. Despite various exhortations by the previous
government, there was little evidence that these bodies were
actively taking steps to bring such land into development.
The Local Government Planning and Land Act 1980 (Part X)
therefore goes further than anything before in providing for a
Register of Land held by public bodies and certain powers for
the Secretary of State to direct a sale of any land entered on
the Register. This part of the Act came into operation in
stages. A copy of the Register has to be made available for
public inspection, and the implied intention is that the
private sector, by means of the Register will search out these
sites and make a bid for the land. The presumption here is
that the constraint inhibiting development has been the actual
ownership of the land, and although not denying some of the
force of that argument, there is the suspicion that the
greatest constraint has been the lack of effective demand.
Without this, there is little prospect of the Register facilitating development.

The question of effective demand for land in the inner city
areas has become one of the major areas of concern and it is
appropriate here in that context to examine the concept of
'enterprise zones'. The planning aspects of these zones are
defined in the Local Government Planning and Land Act 1980
(Part XVIII and Schedule 32) and the financial provisions in
the Finance Act 1980.

ENTERPRISE ZONES

Since the introduction of the 1947 Town and Country Planning

Act, the majority of innovations in the system of town and country planning have come from Labour Governments. The 1980 Act is perhaps the first attempt by a Conservative Government to introduce into the system more 'market-orientated' concepts. Generally in the past during periods of Conservative Government, the administration has tended to modify and amend legislation previously passed by a Labour Government. 'Enterprise Zones' are perhaps the most significant of these innovations and it is inevitable that the genesis for the concept is political rather than administrative or technical. Sir Geoffrey Howe, in a speech to the Bow Group in June 1978, set out some of the background (Bow Group, 1978). Crediting Professor Peter Hall with the idea, launched at the RTPI Conference in Chester 1977, of opening small selected areas of inner cities to all kinds of initiatives, with minimal control, the Conservative front-bencher distinguished between three different concepts. These were:

i   The Freeport: Basically a 'free-trade zone' near an airport or seaport. Customs and Excise duties and tariffs are not payable on goods and raw materials imported into the zone. They may be exported from the zone similarly free of duty; generally after having been reprocessed. Freeport facilities already exist in several continental ports. Shannon is an example.

ii The 'Crown Colony': A largely independent community - tariff free - and exempt from most legislation.

iii The Enterprise Zone: The idea would be to set up test market areas or laboratories in which to enable fresh policies to flourish and to enable their potential for doing so elsewhere to be evaluated. The key elements would include no detailed form of planning control, publicly-owned land would be put onto the open market, rent control would be removed, there would be exemption from DLT and rates, and these conditions would be guaranteed for a substantial number of years.

The concept attracted considerable opposition. The RTPI argued that the zones would degenerate into second-rate environments and suggested instead the use of Special Development Orders or local plans tailored to the needs of small industry to satisfy economic needs without sacrificing the environment. In the event the Government was denuded with bids from local authorities wishing to benefit from the financial inducements set out in the 1980 Finance Act. Zones,

generally of the average size of 500 acres, originally put
forward as a criterion, were designated in Salford/Trafford in
Manchester, Dudley in the West Midlands, the lower Swansea
Valley, Corby, Clydebank, Belfast, Speke in Liverpool,
Gateshead on Tyneside and the Isle of Dogs in London's
Docklands. Smaller zones were also specified in Hartlepool
and Wakefield. The councils had to agree boundaries of the
zone, and accept the planning proposals and policies set out
in the 1980 Act. The Department of the Environment had to be
satisfied with the administrative arrangements. Subsequently,
eleven further zones were designated; seven of them in England
and the existing zones at Speke in Liverpool and Wakefield in
West Yorkshire were extended.

Comparing the concept that has eventually materialised with
that originally set out in the speech to the Bow Group, it is
evident that the financial measures are broadly as set out
there. These include exemption from general rates on
industrial and commercial property, 100 percent capital
allowances for commercial and industrial buildings and
exemption from Development Land Tax for ten years.

The planning procedures have generally been misunderstood
and hardly constitute the 'planning free zone' originally
canvassed and which drew a considerable amount of criticism.

Enterprise Zones are obviously an experiment and the
Department of the Environment have appointed urban and land
economists to monitor the experiment; particularly which of
the incentives has generated activity. Among the aspects
which should be considered are:

   i)   Will the result be in a shift in existing investment
         capacity to the Zones, rather than the development
         of new investment in productive activities?

   ii)   Do the proposals represent rather than a 'planning
         free zone', a definitive land-use zoning plan with
         fiscal incentives added, and therefore the oppor-
         tunity to overcome the traditional dichotomy between
         economic policy and physical land-use planning?
         Does such an innovatory policy have lessons for
         other areas within the inner cities and elsewhere?

   iii) Enterprise Zone authorities will have to consider
         very carefully the implications of the various
         fiscal incentives on the local land market. Within
         the assisted areas for example, the value of the
         incentives for new industrial building differs very

little from what it has been in the recent
past. Whatever the intentions of the policy, it is
unlikely to lead to the regeneration of industry in
those areas. On the other hand, relative to the
surrounding area, the encouragement to new
commercial development in the Zones is high. Therefore if the Zone is in an area where the only
significant incentives are for commercial development, they will have little effect if the whole area
is zoned for industrial development.

It is significant that during the course of the second round
of Zones, more than fifty English authorities submitted bids.
The Enterprise Zones have perhaps attracted the most attention
of the current initiatives but what impact are the other
innovations making on the inner urban problem?

Enterprise Zones are most explicit expressions of the
Government's attempts to stimulate demand in the inner city
areas, but they are part of a series of initiatives whose
overall aim is to increase the aggregate level of ecnomic
demand in the areas and, in the process, attract private
sector investment hitherto conspicuously absent. These
initiatives can broadly be classified as follows:

(a) Efforts to increase the awareness of inner area
    problems among the financial and business community;

(b) Specific financial inducements to stimulate and
    attract new enterprises to the inner areas, in addi-
    tion to those inherent in the Enterprise Zones;

(c) Measures, both financial and administrative, to
    improve the physical environment of the inner areas.

Using this classification, the initiatives can be grouped as
follows:

(a) Awareness:

    - Business in the Community
      Following a conference of UK and US businessmen
      sponsored by the DoE in April 1980, a group of
      leading companies formed BIC, which aims to
      encourage and assist in the extension of the
      involvement of indus-trial and commercial concerns
      with local economic and social development. BIC is

working closely with the DoE's Regional Offices to encourage the formation of local enterprise agencies. These draw their membership from a wide circle of local companies and other interests and some include local authorities and trades unions in their membership.

- Financial Institutions Group
The FIG consisted of twenty-six managers seconded for a year to October 1982 from major banks, building societies, insurance companies and pension funds to work with central government in developing new approaches and ideas for securing urban regeneration.

(b) New Enterprises:

- Urban Development Grants
The grant is designed to lever significant private sector involvement into the inner cities, providing the minimum public sector contribution necessary to enable development projects which might not otherwise go ahead to do so. A total of £70 million is available but only for projects which secure the commitment of significant private sector funds. The grants are in addition to the regional development grants available from the Department of Industry.

- Urban Development Corporations
In London Docklands and Merseyside these have been given special powers to enable them to secure the regeneration of their areas, by programmes of land acquisition, reclamation and sale to the private sector, infrastructure provisions and encouraging the development of new and existing industry and commerce.

(c) Physical Environment:

- Derelict Land Clearance Grants
The Derelict Land Act 1982 has extended existing government powers to promote the reclamation of derelict land. The Secretary of State can now pay grants of up to 80 percent of the net loss incurred in reclamation by the private sector, statutory undertakers and nationalised industries for those areas where a 100 percent grant is payable to local authorities.

- Housing Improvement Grants
  Until the end of the financial year 1983 the grant
  limit towards the cost of repairs and renovations
  has been increased to 90 percent in an effort to
  rekindle the housing improvement movement, which,
  after peaking in 1974, has since been flagging.

- Evaluation
  Any attempt to evaluate the success of the various
  initiatives will be inevitably somewhat impression-
  istic and less than comprehensive, but initial
  comment would be as follows. The Enterprise Zones
  have attracted a considerable amount of interest
  among inner area local authorities, but the
  financial institutions have shown little interest.
  By definition the zones are in areas needing more
  than their share of assistance, and therefore far
  removed from the institutional ideal of a private
  investment. Rents, although bolstered by freedom
  from rates, are not giving a good enough return to
  outweigh other investment opportunities and,
  finally, the prospects for what is essentially an
  artifically-created market may well look bleak at
  the end of the concessionary period. It is probably
  too early to judge but some sceptics now describe
  the Enterprise Zones as Conservative regional policy
  in a politically acceptable guise.

Land Registers too appear to have had an uncertain welcome.
The House Builders Federation (HBF) Report on Initial Land
Register Inspections (HBF 1984) reveals that only 11 percent
of the land is available and suitable for housing development,
with the conclusion "that those who have suggested that 96,000
acres of vacant land is awaiting development have quite
clearly been misled". The Federation estimates that less than
11,000 acres of the total amount of registered land in England
is suitable for housing.

Nevertheless, despite the pessimistic predictions of the
HBF, private housebuilding in the inner cities is on the
increase. Tom Barron, Secretary of the Volume Housebuilder's
Group, suggests that during 1982 some 6,000 private houses
were built in the inner cities and by 1985 this could increase
to between 20,000 and 25,000. It is my own view that private
residential developers can play a leading role in the inner
areas. Until now, many people have been forced out of these
areas because of lack of choice in the type and tenure of
housing. In many inner London Boroughs, there has been
practically no new private housing built for more than a

decade. Now, 2,000 houses a year are planned in London's Docklands whilst, for example, the Abbey Housing Association planned 1,000 houses in inner areas on a non-subsidised cost sale and assured tenancy basis in 1983 and perhaps 5,000 by the end of the decade.

Progress reports recently released from the London Docklands and Merseyside Development Corporations present a snapshot of the development scene in each area and allow an assessment of progress to date. LDDC building on the preparatory work done by the Docklands Joint Committee, is moving into top gear very quickly, whereas the Merseyside Corporation still appears to be absorbed by the need to agree upon strategy and plans. (But there is progress, for example, in co-operation with BAT Industries, the Corporation is converting a transit shed in the South West Brunswick Dock into sixty small industrial units).

The idea of Urban Development Grants as a way of combining public and private sector interests and encouraging investors away from traditional investment areas originated with the Financial Institutions Group. At the time of writing nearly 100 schemes have been approved by the Department of the Environment, which should result in some £51 million of private investment attracted into the inner areas primed by some £12 million of public expenditure.

It is impossible at this stage to assess whether this initiative represents a real change in the attitudes of investors and financial institutions towards the inner city. In many schemes, the risk is reduced by the local authority acting as a guarantor or the leader of last resort. The private sector appears to prefer a partnership approach rather than 'laisser-faire' capitalism. Exhortations to date have been met on their part by considerable scepticism. More positive have been the responses of some individual major public companies, the leading private housebuilders and superstore operators for example. Barratts are involved in the trust set up to renew the Cantril Farm Estate at the Liverpool satellite of Kirkby. With financial support from Barclays Bank and the Abbey National Building Society, and the involvement of the Knowlsey Borough Council, the Trust will operate like a development corporation in that it will buy out all council property in the Estate. Ultimately it is envisaged that there will be a choice of tenure for the residents. Refurbishment and new house building are envisaged.

The most articulate case for the provision of new retail developments in the inner cities has been presented by Tesco

Supermarkets (Estates Times, 1977). They suggest three significant contributions that would be made to the regeneration of inner city areas:

i) By reclaiming some of the vacant land which, well-planned and landscaped, could be significantly improved by such developments;

ii) By generating rateable income and creating certain employment gains, as well as by stimulating investment confidence;

iii) By strengthening the service base of the community and consequently providing a more attractive environment in which to live.

Support for this view has come from a report carried out by the Unit for Retail Planning Information on behalf of the National Economic Development Council (Estates Times, 1981). Based on studies of inner area shopping centres in London and Liverpool, the report concludes that inner city areas need supermarkets and superstores to provide badly needed jobs for the young and unskilled.

Some of the work undertaken by the Financial Institutions Group has been taken over by Inner City Enterprises Limited. Set up by the DoE, but not financially dependent on it, ICE is intended as a private sector service company which will seek out and promote investment opportunities in inner city areas and try to persuade the institutions to look at areas that are not their traditional areas, but are in greater need. Nevertheless, the basic problem for the institutions when considering these areas, the prospect of poor rental growth, will prove difficult to overcome.

One major conclusion emerges from this review, which is that unless there are institutional and administrative changes such as the Development Corporations adopted for the Docklands in London and Liverpool, the private sector, with perhaps an innate distrust of the local administrations active in the inner cities (which the GLC and Southwark Council's decision to pull out of the Lysander scheme proposed for Surrey Docks will do nothing to dispel) will be reluctant to become involved. The Development Corporation, criticised for its lack of accountability, is not the only model for such institutional change.

The GEAR * programme initiated in 1976 in the East End of

---

* Glasgow Eastern Area Renewal

Glasgow to renew what was described at the time as the most socially deprived city area in Europe, is a partnership between the Government, the Scottish Development Agency, the Scottish Special Housing Association, Strathclyde Regional Council, Glasgow District Council and other interested agencies, such as the Manpower Services Commission. The co-ordinating (and controlling role) is provided by the SDA. The 'quango' character of the programme may perhaps have a bitter taste for the present government, but there is no doubting its effectiveness.

In March 1983, after leaving the Department of the Environment, Michael Heseltine concluded that "we have moved through a period of exploration of many of the inner city problems where they are the responsibility of the Department of the Environment. I think we now have answers where formerly there were questions. We now need the energy and time to apply them". Unfortunately the Environment Committee set up to examine the problems of management of urban renewal did not agree with him. Reporting in May of that year, it acknowledged that the Secretary of State's presence in Merseyside had a significant impact in the generation or acceleration of new development, and the Committee was impressed with his commitment to involve the private sector in the task of regeneration, but there was concern that the mixture of agencies involved was proving counter-productive. "Merseyside's patchwork of government exacerbates the conflict of policies and thereby inhibits an overall view and co-ordinated planning" (House of Commons, 1983).

This conclusion recalls the judgement of an article in the Sunday Times in 1981 at the time of the Brixton riots:

> "But if the political will were stronger, what would be the best way of putting urban aid into effect? During our inquiries in Westminster and Whitehall last week we detected signs that some people are now beginning to doubt whether any funds can be properly directed under Britain's current local government structure.

> "To try to circumvent this kind of obstacle, one radical idea being discussed is whether the new types of city development cor-porations, funded by central government, banks and insurance companies, should be imposed on local councils. The task of these corporations

would be to haul the inner areas up to
national average stand-ards of employment,
housing and so on... The difficulties of
'Taking an area into care' for perhaps 10-
15 years are obvious but some experts now
believe only such drastic action can
work" (Sunday Times,1981).

The experiment at the Cantril Farm Estate, Knowlsey, is
perhaps the first step in this particular direction. What is
now clear, at what will be a mid-point, when looking back in
the future, over nearly a decade of inner-city policies admin-
istered by a Conservative government, is that the private
sector on its own cannot rescue the inner cities.

Not only must the overall level of economic demand be
stimulated in these areas, but the risk of uncertainty,
occasioned by the prospect of poor growth in rental levels,
must be taken account of.

4 The use of land for employment: a study of policy making and implementation in Inner London 1975-1982

JANICE MORPHET AND JANE ROBBINS

INTRODUCTION

At the present there seems to be a paradox in the relationship between the formulation and intent of land use policies geared towards the attraction of employment in Inner London boroughs and the extent to which these are being successfully implemented. This seems to be not for reasons of market interest, but the weight of organisational impetus behind established local authority land uses. The purpose of this paper is to examine the extent to which this paradox is confirmed by the examination of recent changes in land use allocation by the Inner London Boroughs, and also to investigate the relationship between employment policy, its development and the command it has over these borough resources. The extent to which this relatively new policy field has been able to establish itself as a major influence on key authority decisions will also be considered.

Before turning to these two major elements in the paper, it is important to consider the context within which this debate takes place, and the assumptive background of this chapter.

Land use policies were not favourable to employment-generating uses in Inner London before 1975. Evidence for this can be provided from a variety of sources describing individual or collective policies (Greater London Development

Plan, (GLC), 1978, Inner London Consultative Employment Group, 1976). Further Inner London authorities did not respond to marked changes in their economic structure or the status of their population. Traditional local authority policy and activity have been directed towards service delivery following the identification of client groups (the elderly, the housebound) or client areas (areas of poor access, shopping centres, expansion areas). The reorganis- ation of London local government in 1964 had more relation to the political pressure for boundary reform (Young and Garside 1982) than a substantially altered view of appropriate activity, although the review on which the reform was based, the Herbert Commission (MHLG 1960), had included in its terms of reference consideration of both structure and function. When local government reform was considered for the remainder of England and Wales, the expectations of local authority responsibility had extended considerably. Gray (1982) argues that these changes stemmed from the adoption of corporate planning ideology following criticisms of local authority management throughout the 1960s (MHLG, 1966; Department of Education and Science, 1967; MHLG, 1967; DHSS, 1968). Gray states these criticisms to be "the excessive departmentalism of local authorities, the lack of recognition of interconnections between services and the lack of attention being paid to the environments within which local authorities operated". The response to these criticisms contained in Bains (DoE 1972), Scottish Office (1973) and DoE (1973b) revolved around the need to create "all embracing comprehensive frameworks for the establishment of policy" (Gray, 1983) which were founded on the assertion that "... government is not limited to the provision of services. It is concerned with the overall economic, cultural and physical well-being of the community" (DoE, 1972).

The reform of local government in London did not proceed on these lines as Robson (1961) predicted, "the proposals of the Royal Commission do not embody any new principle of local government. They are essentially an extension and adaptation of the present system to modern conditions. The Greater London Council projected on a larger scale". In this paper we are therefore assuming that the organisational climate of London local authorities at both levels prevented recognition and appropriate action on the changing employment situations of their areas through the ordinary operation of their functions.

In considering those particularly involved in the development and implementation of policy, planners had a specific contribution to make. This is due primarily to their

73

specific education which in the period 1965-1975 emphasised the social aspects of the administration of their tasks (Cockburn, 1970). The 1968 Town and Country Planning Act also emphasised the economic, social and physical factors to be considered in plan preparation and implementation. Planners were also encouraged to extend their appropriate sphere of influence (Reade, 1982). Elsewhere in local authorities, prevailing views of corporate approaches permeated wider stages of action unconfined by existing patterns of activity. The characteristics of those actively involved in local politics within London were also changing.

The sweeping victories achieved by the Tories in many Inner London boroughs in 1968 where Labour Councils had been in control since the 1930s, encouraged Labour Councillors elected subsequently to reassess and to re-examine their role and that of their authority. Changes in the socio-economic structure and housing tenure, characterised by Islington's gentrification, but occurring simultaneously elsewhere, (GLC, 1982) brought a changing Labour Party membership. In 1974 a number of young professional Labour councillors were elected to borough councils. In some boroughs, such as Wandsworth, these changes were apparent from the early 1970s (Lawless, 1981). These new councillors did not feel constrained to define local authority activity in the same way as those traditionally in control. Indeed, their position on the left of the party indicated their acceptance of a greater interventionist, local role in any activity within their boundary. As new members in authorities where control remained with traditional or 'old guard' members, they were free to pick up and promote relevant issues outside the existing distribution of power. Many paradoxes of the Labour left's involvement in economic policy stem from this initial opportunity it provided for access to power.

Whilst these changes were taking place, the existence and extent of economic decline and unemployment within London could no longer remain hidden. These changes were first brought to attention through the publication of "London: the future and you" in 1974 by a GLC Labour administration which had regained power in the previous year. It was based on the results of the 1971 Census, which showed high levels of unemployment within Inner London. Initially there was little understanding of the extent and cause of the problem. The work by Bramley for the Lambeth Inner Area Study (Bramley, 1976) for the Canning Town CDP (O'Malley, 1975) started to highlight these problems. Their truth has been subsequently demonstrated despite attempts by the Department of Employment (through the calculation of unemployment rates) and the Assisted Areas (through their opposition to the granting of special powers - see Davies 1981, and opposition to other SE investment such as Stansted) to cover them in a cloak of South Eastern affluence.

Before examining the nature and effects of policy-making, the authors would like to state their position on two fundamental issues which are not pursued here, but are the subject of considerable debate in this field. The first is that local authorities can, through their actions, effectively maintain and promote economic development. Most of the criticism of this view is based on structural analysis, where economic decline is based on the reformation of capital. These studies exist at various levels, from those produced by the CDPs (CDP Inter Project Team, 1977; Higgins, 1978; Mayo, 1979), to those produced based on specific firm histories (Gripaios, 1976, 1977; Dennis, 1976). Although we do not wish to pursue this debate here, we would like to state that we endorse the view contained in the establishment of Inner Area Studies (Batley and Edwards, 1978) and in the RTPI's Employment Working Party Report (1979a), that there are considerable areas of discretion and manoeuvre left aside, apart or remaining from structural change. We see local authorities operating within this sphere.

Secondly, it is by no means certain that a distribution of land uses which favours economic development or employment uses will in itself maintain or create jobs (Fothergill et al. 1983a, b). We would however be of the view that land use policies which promote uses other than those primarily associated with employment would be unlikely to create or maintain jobs. Some evidence is now becoming available (R. Tym and Partners, 1980; McIntosh and Keddie, 1979) which suggests that the avail-ability of land and buildings, and security of their future employment use enables firms to establish, maintain and extend economic production. Whilst this may give rise to some job opportunities, the same land use policies will make it easier for major capital interests to regroup wherever they choose, with such processes incorporating major rationalisation and job loss. Secondly the adoption of promotional or sympathetic land use policies cannot in any way counter the loss of jobs arising from closure or relocation.

Finally, both authors have worked within Inner London for fifteen and ten years respectively, have chaired the Officers' Group of the Inner London Consultative Employment Group, and continue to be actors in the situations described here.

EMPLOYMENT POLICY FORMULATION IN INNER LONDON

Organisations adapt to changing circumstances in a variety of ways, some of which are more successful than others. In some circumstances the importance of an event or crisis evokes an immediate or strong response. However in most organisations change is generally incorporated slowly, following a response lag. In Inner London economic fortune did not occur overnight. Moreover, once the pace of decline had been noted, it was still impossible to shift entrenched national attitudes towards London's perceived prosperity.

In local authorities, officers expressed considerable anti-pathy to the embrace of economic problems even when their scale became widely known. During the latter part of the 1960s and early 1970s it became startlingly apparent that the economies of the older inner urban areas were collapsing (see CDP papers, 1974 and 1977 and the Inner Area Studies). In Inner London the consequences of the deterioration were drama-tically illustrated by the first major closure in the area, of AEI in Woolwich (Daniels, 1972), where over 6,000 people lost their jobs. This was swiftly followed by other large and small scale closures and by rapid rises in unemployment (ILCEG, 1980). Local politicians began to express concern, but there were no Departments of Employment at a local level as there were for Housing or for Leisure and Recreation. The major constraints on policy development were the lack of manpower and finance within the local authority. When ILCEG (a group consisting of the Inner London Boroughs, the GLC, London Chamber of Commerce, Greater London Trades Council etc.) was set up in 1975, only one member borough, Wandsworth, had an Industrial Liaison Officer (ILCEG, 1980). This lack of policy proved a considerable constraint (LCSS, 1977).

The issues were inevitably picked up by Planning Departments. However, the people who pursued them were faced not only with a lack of knowledge both of the powers and resources available to local authorities, but also with a lack of understanding of the events precipitating the crisis in their local economies. Through groups such as ILCEG, officers of the authorities were able to share knowledge and experience. This is reflected through examination of the changing nature of reports being presented over a seven year period since ILCEG's inception. The early years were characterised by information reports, which gradually developed as officers gained experience of policy and implementation, which could be shared. A more innovative phase emerged where the lobbying role of the Group was developed and it was able to influence other actors in the employment field (ILCEG Annual Reports, 1977-1982).

Today policies have been developed which are very wide ranging and are often at the forefront of concern for both Planning Departments and Councils as a whole. Local politicians also promote employment policy as a major tool of regeneration (GLC, 1982a). However, despite this growth in policy the exercise has been largely cosmetic in relation to the scale of the problem. More people have been employed by local authorities to work on employment, but in comparison to the scale of local authority employment as a whole, the number remains small.

At Kensington and Chelsea for example, approximately ten people are employed to develop policy for the Council on employment and to implement that policy compared to a total of 2085 employed by the Council as a whole. Table 1 illustrates the loss of industrial land over a period, with almost one third being lost between 1967 and 1981. Unemployment in Inner London (the ILEA area) continues to rise; the rate in December 1982 was 17.2% whilst between October 1980 and October 1982 it rose by 89%. Finally, the budget allocated to employment development is generally small in comparison with other more traditional areas of local authority concern.

As stated above, it is obvious that the problems are far greater than the resources to solve them at local or at national level. However there seems to be a considerable divergence between the rhetoric on the one hand and action on the other. The actions being undertaken are of a lesser scale than the development of knowledge and policy would suggest to be necessary. Further actions that are being undertaken are marginal in comparison to the scale of the problem (Lawless, 1981). Economic development remains relatively unimportant in the local authority programme in terms of resources including staff.

Turning to those in power in Labour and Tory authorities, traditional Labour elected members were strongly based in the Labour movement, possessing a strong antipathy to problems related to capital. However, economic recession and the humanism of Heath's brand of conservatism, with its recognition of the "unacceptable face of capitalism" did much to shuffle the political agendas of the two main parties. The stage was set for a shift in institutionalised conflict between the interests of labour and capital, to their coalition against the effects of world recession. In those authorities controlled by Tories, the certainty of succession had bred a benevolent paternalist representation happy to embrace an "industrial hand-maiden" view of public intervention i.e. a pragmatic rather than an ideological activity (George & Wilding, 1976).

Table 1

Land in Industrial Use in Inner London, 1967, 1974 and 1981

Authority	1967 '000 sq.feet	1967 '000 m²	1974 '000 m²	% change 1967-74	1981 '000 m²	% change 1974-81	% change 1967-81
City	1334.7	124.0	162.2	+ 31	162.3	–	+ 31
Camden	4014.1	372.9	278.8	– 25	234.9	– 16	– 37
Hackney	12979.5	1205.7	1217.7	+ 1	1192.3	– 2	– 1
Hammersmith	7173.6	666.4	638.2	– 4	591.7	– 7	– 11
Islington	9262.4	860.5	650.8	– 24	543.5	– 17	– 37
Kensington & Chelsea	1376.6	127.9	65.4	– 49	50.1	– 23	– 61
Lambeth	6296.7	584.9	516.6	– 12	394.4	– 24	– 33
Lewisham	4620.1	429.2	391.7	– 9	405.8	+ 4	– 6
Southwark	15816.2	1469.3	1110.8	– 24	977.8	– 12	– 34
Tower Hamlets	19432.0	1805.2	1226.7	– 26	1274.2	– 5	– 29
Wandsworth	7932.3	736.9	367.3	– 50	334.8	– 9	– 55
Westminster	1185.5	110.1	39.9	– 64	35.2	– 12	– 68
Greenwich	11933.8	1108.7	799.3	– 28	683.7	– 15	– 38
Total – Inner London	103357.5	9601.9	7575.4	– 21	6880.9	– 9	– 28

Source: DoE Floorspace Statistics Series II, nos 2, 4, 10.

Employment was seen as a political backwater at the
beginning of the period. It was obviously not as powerful as
areas like housing. However, new younger politicians developed
an approach within this context. In Wandsworth the Policy
Review Committee produced their own paper 'Prosperity or
Slump? The Future of Wandsworth's Economy' which outlined the
crisis of employment in that borough and the new directions
which actions by the authority could take (Wandsworth, 1976).
This process continues to occur in certain left wing Labour
authorities such as the GLC (GLC, 1982). Members in Tory
authorities have been much more willing to leave the
initiative to officers.

In order to produce innovative policies, Committees rested
heavily on the work of officers, but remained in control.
These processes are described by Davies (1981) in the context
of the petition to gain additional employment powers through
the 1977 GLC General Powers Bill. This involved several of
the ILCEG boroughs and was co-ordinated by the Group. As work
on the Bill was innovatory, officers and members worked
closely together producing evidence, argument and ideas to put
the case for changes in the powers. This working relationship
has continued in many cases. Members and officers work
together to present information to MPs and Ministers on a more
equal basis than that normally found within local authorities.

Thus a specific coalition between planners and politicians
was created as each needed the other. The politician needed
the planner to provide and develop the information base and
the planner needed the politician to put forward the policies
that had been developed. They were able to proceed in a much
more informal way than was normal for local authorities
because neither the officer hierarchy nor the senior
politicians considered employment planning to be a central
local authority concern. This is demonstrated by the lack of
Employment Committees or even Sub-Committees, in Inner London
at the start of the period.

Within a short space of time, the majority of boroughs
adopted an employment policy. In its paper 'Employment and
Industry in Greater London - a background document', the
London Council of Social Service (1977) stated that "many of
the London Boroughs have been at work on producing documents
for their Borough Development Plans for many years. It is
significant however that in the last two years many boroughs
have produced papers on employment and industry for the first
time". Since that time, several Inner London Boroughs have
had their Borough Plans containing land use policies on
employment adopted, starting with Camden (1979) and followed

by boroughs such as Westminster, Kensington and Chelsea, and Hammersmith and Fulham. In other Inner London boroughs, work is well advanced on producing strategies for employment and economic activity, e.g. Lewisham, Tower Hamlets, Hackney. This impetus to produce land use policy documents for employment stemmed largely from the coalition between members and officers of the planning departments described above. It can be seen currently at work, although not now necessarily through Planning Departments, in recently elected left-wing Labour Councils such as the GLC and West Midlands. These Councils are seeking to reverse the conventional form of local authority intervention in the economy, which assists private sector enterprises, and instead to create "alternative institutions and alternative sources of power in the ecnomy" (Ward, 1980). Such authorities are much more concerned with reallocating power to the local community. Further, they seek to demonstrate, by the implementation of their local strategies, that alternatives to the capitalist mode of production can work through greater democratic control. In addition a planned use of resources can be used to create jobs throughout the community. They are therefore seeking to change what has become the status quo in relation to employment planning and are therefore actively working with innovative officers to produce such change.

This relationship between planning officers and politicians is now changing. Increasing interest is being shown in employment issues by politicians and therefore by high ranking officers of local authorities. Employment planning and development has become a central local authority activity in many councils with an employment office reporting directly to a Chief Executive. There are several examples in Inner London including Camden, Islington and Kensington and Chelsea where this has happened. There appears to have been a decline in innovation associated with these moves. Now that employment planning has become a legitimate activity it is largely being taken over by the mainstream of local government at both levels. Thus the relationship and innovation associated with it has declined.

THE ACHIEVEMENT OF POLICY IMPLEMENTATION

Although the coalition of specific political and officer interests issuccessful in raising the employment issue high on to the political agenda, a real measure of its success must be the extent to which it has been implemented by the boroughs. Much of the literature on local authorities typifies them as Weberian 'ideal-type' bureaucracies which operate through the exercise of structural control particularly in the forms of standardisation, formalisation, centralisation and profes- sionalisation. In this case, if an issue has been accepted or adopted as one of day to day concern throughout the authority, it would be anticipated that it would permeate all decision making to its advantage. This would be in a marked comparison to the effect on policy implementation prior to acceptance. This section examines the extent to which this transmission has been achieved through the operation of the planning process, both in terms of policy planning and planning applications.

The policy framework adopted for land use decisions for employment use prior to the mid 1970s has been well documented (e.g. Lawless, 1981; Smith, 1973, 1977). Any turn-round in policy would therefore need to be executed in a number of spheres, namely land use allocation, planning decisions in favour of extending sites for new development for existing firms, industrial development, and finally the most telling, the extent to which employment uses are promoted on key or major sites.

There are problems in assessing the extent to which policies have been implemented. Firstly, recorded information only appears in published documents or committee reports, thus making the terms of debate or alternative strategies for sites discarded during the decision making process difficult to document effectively. In published plans, the mechanism for defining sites in any use will tend to be residual i.e. those sites which can be unequivocally determined for a particular use. This serves to focus technical and political debate on a defined number of key sites. There is also a further problem with the provision of change information in plans. The adop- tion of land use policies directed towards the maintenance and stimulation of employment use has been most clearly expressed in the Borough (District) Plans of the Inner London Boroughs. However, the preparation of these plans through the 1970s has meant that they themselves are of course subject to changes in perception and value weighting. This can be traced by example through the various stages of plan preparation by one of these boroughs, Islington. The draft employment topic paper (1975) was accepted as being extremely thorough and competent in its understanding of the problems of Islington's local economy and labour force. The draft plan published in 1978 contained a range of policies aimed at reducing unemployment. These policies were supported by the allocation of eight industrial development area sites (no size given) and the identification of ten potential Industrial Improvement Areas. Once the Plan had reached Deposit draft in 1980 the policies were considerably more direct in their style whilst they were supported by 10 Industrial Priority Areas, 16 Industrial and Commercial Development sites, 10 office sites (compared with one in the 1978 version) and 12 mixed use development sites. Without monitoring this process in great detail it is difficult to assess whether these increases in site allocation were due to growing awareness of the scale of the problem, or a changing pattern of value judgements concerning land use.

Apart from these problems of assessing fast change, there are others, including the non-existence of 'control' areas. More importantly it is difficult to define a 'significant' level of land use change. If a significant change is defined as a percentage increase in land allocated to employment use, this will provide a partially false picture given the low level of employment development initially. An alternative measure may be the proportion of planning applications for industrial use compared with other uses. These are shown on Table 4 although again it is difficult to assess the 'verbal steering' and the 'informal advice' offered to firms by local authorities, the GLC and the Department of Industry.

The most telling barometer of policy direction can often be the key or windfall sites which become available e.g. railway or other public utility land (see Elson's paper in this volume). In the 1960s these would automatically be developed for housing, whereas in the 1970s their fate became less certain. The availability of these sites often provided an opportunity for authorities to indicate their promotion of employment opportunities through their allocation for industrial development (e.g. York Way in Camden, Devons Road in Tower Hamlets, and in particular Nine Elms in Wandsworth). However, some examination is required of the extent to which these changes in key site allocations represent real change in authority policy.

There are three issues around which this debate revolves:

1. The extent to which the continuing change in land use allocation, moving away from employment in the last forty years, would imply a dramatic change in allocation of land uses in the last ten years, in order to achieve some kind of economic stability or reversal;

2. the changing pattern of funding for housing and the development quality of windfall sites (including their location) together promote industrial and use decisions; and

82

3. key industrial sites, although in short
    supply, are still vulnerable to diversion
    to other potentially more attractive uses.

The most generally accepted key event in the movement of industrial uses away from inner cities was the publication of the Barlow Commission report in 1940 (Royal Commission, 1940), although this report rested on the levels of high unemployment and regional disparities demonstrated during the 1930s. However, it is also clear (Martin, 1966) that industrial decentralisation had been taking place over a much longer period, with the development of industrial inner areas itself a product of an earlier decentralisation move. Barlow therefore added an impetus to an existing trend, although it is interesting to note that the main report, and in Abercrombie's memorandum of dissent, real fears were expressed at the strength of industry enabling it to retain its locational position despite the policy proposals contained in the report. At the same time Barlow's report also promoted a balance of land uses rather than a complete relocation for industry. The promotion of decentralisation in an arbitrary way was also not supported by Abercrombie in the 'County of London Plan' (Forshaw and Abercrombie, 1944). The areas of reconstruction embodied the central aims of reducing congestion and journeys to work, but encapsulated the need to provide jobs in the locality. The proposals were therefore designed to create a balance of uses rather than effect new inner city suburbs.

The extent of change which occurred in the distribution of and uses far over-stepped this notion of balance for a number of reasons. The moves to improve the environment and its health established a powerful lobby (Smith, 1973), which culminated in the establishment of clean air zones. Secondly, the extent of physical decay in the housing stock with its association with private renting became foremost on the public agenda, particularly through the establishment of the Milner-Holland report and Rachmanism. The political response came through Macmillan's drive to complete one million homes per year, a popular move from a rising politician. Further polit-ical objectives were supported by resource allocation and accompanying policy decisions for compulsory purchase etc. The effectiveness of this programme is demonstrated in Dennis (1970, 1972) and Gower Davies (1972) as stated above. Next, the degree of resource priority afforded to new and expanding towns could not have been anticipated in the 1940s. The methods of resourcing housing within existing urban areas, and the full range of land uses in the NETS programme were in stark comparison with the funding procedures and priorities for areas of reconstruction or comprehensive development areas remaining in London. Resources for the implementation of the initial Development Plans were never explicitly allocated.

The examination of changes in land use in the post war period will underline some of these points more clearly. The changes in land use demonstrated in Table 2 for industrial use show an absolute decline of 42% between 1947 and 1971, with individual borough losses ranging from 67% in Westminster to 36% in Islington (Lambeth figures are lower at a 27% loss, but the boundary changes in 1964 were more significant than elsewhere). However when the land use information for residential use is examined, the changes are far less dramatic in terms of loss, with some boroughs exhibiting considerable increases e.g. Hackney with an increase of over 50% as shown in Table 3. Inner London is shown to have an overall loss of 9%. The decision not to undertake a 1976 or 1981 Land Use Survey means that it is impossible to compare what has happened in the last ten years since the adoption of policies in favour of employment use. However some data is available from the DoE based on rating statistics. These are shown in Table 1 and demonstrate a continuing decline in floorspace in industrial use. The reduction of floorspace and land use should also be seen against the falling employment densities on industrial sites as capital is substituted for labour. The substitution of site areas on a one for one basis could not therefore in itself create the same number of jobs even if the economic climate were favourable to the creation of more job opportunities. However there has been no overall change in the pattern of decline since 1974, when more favourable policies were emerging. An additional barometer of change is the level of planning applications received and their net effect on land use. Information is only available for a short period, 1972-1976, as shown in Table 4, but it is clear that the same kind of annual pattern emerges as demonstrated before i.e. continuing net loss of industrial floorspace. Similarly with completions of planning permissions and permissions outstanding (Tables 5 and 6).

Whilst land in employment use continues to decline in net terms, considerable fears have been expressed by the property industry and the GLC at the amount of floorspace or land available for industrial use. The changes in local authority policy direction, with emphasis on implementation, has meant that each authority has promoted the development of its own industrial premises on at least one site. However, much of this floorspace remains vacant. Apart from the recession there may be a variety of reasons for this, not least the continuing low expectation of firms in being able to relocate

Table 2

Land Use - Industry, Inner London 1947, 1957, 1966, 1971

Borough	(i) 1947	(ii) 1957	(iii) 1966	(iv) 1971	Absolute Change 1947-71 (Hectares)	% Change 1947-71
City	8.1	6.9	6	5	- 3.1	- 38
Camden	54.2	53.8	30	27	- 27.2	- 50
Hackney	116.6	106.0	74	64	- 52.6	- 45
Hammersmith & Fulham	108.1	102.4	70	65	- 43.1	- 40
Islington	102.0	99.6	65	65	- 37.0	- 36
Kensington & Chelsea	27.1	22.7	14	10	- 17.1	- 63
Lambeth	60.3	57.9	49	44	- 16.3	- 27
Lewisham	72.4	76.5	59	43	- 29.4	- 41
Southwark	140.8	138.4	98	76	- 64.8	- 46
Tower Hamlets	172.0	183.0	146	109	- 63.0	- 37
Wandsworth	129.5	117.8	72	59	- 70.5	- 54
Westminster	47.8	42.5	18	15	- 32.8	- 67
Greenwich	168.8	179.7	144	120	- 48.8	- 30
Inner London/ICC Area	1207.7	1187.2	845	702	-505.7	- 42

Sources: (i) and (ii) Administrative County of London Development Plan First Review 1960
(iii) and (iv) 1977 GLC Annual Abstract of Statistics.

Note: Figures for 1947 and 1957 are based on crude amalgamations of MBs as follows:
City, same; Camden, Hampstead, Holburn, St. Pancras; Hackney, Hackney, Stoke Newington,
Shoreditch; Hammersmith and Fulham, Hammersmith, Fulham; Islington, Islington, Finsbury;
Kensington & Chelsea, Kensington, Chelsea; Lambeth, Lambeth; Lewisham, Deptford, Lewisham;
Southwark, Camberwell, Bermondsey, Southwark; Tower Hamlets, Bethnal Green, Poplar, Stepney;
Wandsworth, Battersea, Wandsworth; Westminster, St. Marylebone, Paddington, Westminster;
Greenwich, Greenwich, Woolwich.

Table 3

Land Use – Residential, Inner London, 1947, 1957, 1966, 1971

Hectares

Borough	1947	1957	1966	1971	Absolute Change 1947–71	% Change 1947–71
City	11.3	12.9	3	7	- 4.3	- 38.0
Camden	798.5	842.6	778	759	-39.5	- 4.9
Hackney	490.1	813.0	768	751	+260.9	+ 53.2
Hammersmith	567.0	598.1	575	570	+ 3.0	+ 1.0
Islington	628.5	679.1	633	581	- 47.5	- 7.6
Kensington & Chelsea	482.4	510.3	495	477	- 5.4	- 1.1
Lambeth	1604.2	1706.6	1697	1690	+ 85.8	+ 74.1
Lewisham	998.8	1078.0	1061	1032	+ 33.2	+ 1.0
Southwark	438.3	484.8	479	463	+ 24.7	+ 3.3
Tower Hamlets	1880.6	1959.6	1403	1386	-494.6	+ 5.6
Wandsworth	508.7	547.2	523	528	+ 19.3	- 26.3
Westminster						+ 23.1
Greenwich	1372.0	1542.7	1612	1592	+220.0	+ 16.0
Inner London	10525.9	11557.2	11359	9542	-983.0	- 9.0

Source: As Table 2

Note: Same borough groupings for 1947 and 1957 data as in Table 2.

Table 4

Effect on land use of planning permissions given 1972–1976 – residential and industrial uses

Net Hectares

	1972		1973		1974		1975		1976	
	R	I	R	I	R	I	R	I	R	I
City	0.1	-0.6	0.1	-0.6	–	-0.2	-0.1	-0.2	0.2	-0.8
Camden	1.7	-0.3	2.8	-1.0	2.7	-1.3	2.5	-0.4	2.2	-1.2
Hackney	2.0	-1.5	2.2	-0.8	-0.2	-0.3	3.9	-0.5	3.7	-1.1
Hammersmith	2.9	-2.5	5.7	-2.7	3.5	-3.9	1.1	-1.1	5.1	-2.3
Islington	8.9	-2.4	2.0	-3.5	3.1	0.1	1.2	0.1	1.1	0.6
Kensington & Chelsea	9.5	-0.5	3.8	-0.1	1.2	-0.1	2.0	-0.1	-0.4	-0.1
Lambeth	-2.1	-0.4	0.9	-0.7	–	-0.3	0.2	-0.3	2.0	-1.0
Lewisham	2.9	-0.3	4.7	-0.5	-1.1	0.3	-0.3	-0.2	0.2	-0.5
Southwark	0.5	-2.9	1.1	-1.8	0.6	-1.2	4.9	-1.6	-1.0	-1.3
Tower Hamlets	16.6	-5.1	3.3	0.9	1.4	-0.7	5.1	-0.9	8.4	-1.7
Wandsworth	2.6	-0.7	0.4	1.3	-0.1	0.2	4.1	1.0	9.1	1.4
Westminster	0.9	-0.1	3.4	0.1	1.9	-0.3	0.6	-0.3	1.6	-0.1
Greenwich	3.2	-1.8	13.4	1.6	3.0	3.0	3.0	0.6	6.0	-0.8
Total – Inner London	49.7	-19.1	43.8	-15.6	17.0	-4.7	28.2	-3.9	38.2	-8.9

Source: GLC Decisions Analysis

Table 5

Completions of planning permissions, for industrial use in Inner London 1974–1977

Net '00 square metres

	1974	1975	1976	1977
City	– 77	– 76	– 101	– 44
Camden	– 82	–136	– 59	– 46
Hackney	–182	–173	– 53	–134
Hammersmith	–104	– 16	– 53	– 14
Islington	–206	– 95	– 3	– 47
Kensington & Chelsea	– 8	– 50	– 126	– 52
Lambeth	– 52	–	14	–182
Lewisham	19	44	– 17	– 25
Southwark	– 13	–291	– 358	–504
Tower Hamlets	111	–254	65	–184
Wandsworth	– 64	– 50	44	–119
Westminster	– 55	– 98	– 80	– 25
Greenwich	20	31	20	31
Total – Inner London	–693	–1164	– 707	–1345

Source: GLC Decisions Analysis

Table 6

Analysis of residential and industrial planning permissions outstanding
Inner London 1973, 1975, 1976

	1973		1975		1976	
	R	I	R	I	R	I
City	22	– 446	16	– 453	78	– 573
Camden	4976	– 626	4773	– 362	5202	– 445
Hackney	5995	– 410	4228	– 70	4917	– 372
Hammersmith	2835	– 191	2699	–1163	3135	–1217
Islington	8616	–1073	9200	– 728	8468	– 548
Kensington & Chelsea	4127	– 272	4557	– 246	3353	– 126
Lambeth	7192	– 301	5485	– 287	5675	– 398
Lewisham	5546	– 118	4404	– 247	3429	– 220
Southwark	1993	– 836	7394	–1266	7215	–1079
Tower Hamlets	7439	–1001	5963	–1095	3858	–1416
Wandsworth	4927	– 252	4340	– 118	5162	– 204
Westminster	4153	– 295	4195	328	4473	– 378
Greenwich	6403	– 14	6747	7	6631	50
Total – Inner London	64225	–5835	64001	–5700	61596	–6926

Source: GLC Decisions Analysis

Note: Residential = Gross number of dwellings (total of all types of developer
Industry   = Net '00 square metres

89

or redevelop within Inner London. Secondly, many of the premises are of the same type and size, whereas the market depends on a filter mechanism with new opportunities for firms at all levels of the market starting with open yards or railway arches. Thirdly, much of this development may be on sites which were already vacant and could be assessed as being inherently unattractive prior to development for definable reasons e.g. Lea Valley, Scrubs Lane, Nine Elms, and this leads to the second main issue in industrial land allocation.

Since the establishment of the HIP process, housing development has increasingly come within tight Central Government control, although some inner boroughs maintain sizeable programmes. The most significant change has been the collapse of the GLC's role as a housing authority although it has not been divested of many of its housing sites. The general concern relating to vacant land and dereliction has also meant that there is considerable pressure to ensure that sites are put into some immediate use where this is possible. However, it is also true that many of the vacant sites within Inner Boroughs are owned by the GLC, whether on their housing or other accounts. Other major sites have often been in the ownership of statutory undertakers or public bodies which they have been forced to release as part of the current Government's approach to vacant land. Many of these sites are unattractive to any kind of development for a variety of reasons. They are often difficult to reach, such as those on the Isle of Dogs, Greenwich Peninsula or Lots Road in Fulham. There are often problems of past use, potential contamination or instability. Even in former residential areas there are problems of basements and services. In former industrial areas within LCC/GLC CDAs, the site assembly programme has been left incomplete leaving a resultant patchwork of undevelopable land. An examination of any Borough Plan Schedule for industrial sites will almost always include problem sites, for example the Hammersmith and Fulham Plan (1979) lists three major sites released from British Rail each requiring access before development, and another in private ownership is landlocked. Many of these sites are therefore not available for current development but have other issues to be determined before development can take place, whether it is land release, site assembly, relocation or access. In many ways this allocation of land which is not immediately available for use may seem reasonable practise given the requirements of a Plan for ten year programme and land supply. However, it is tempting to question the attractiveness of these sites for any development. Thus they may represent commitment to action without any expectation of implementation. In contrast, in the pursuance of housing uses, these problems rarely seem apparent as powers and resources are available to overcome them. As Hooper's paper in this volume demonstrates, this may be at the DoE's request. In addition, the local authority machine requires projects for its existence. The HIP process thus ensures programming continuity. Employment associated activities whether development or facilitating works have to take their chance in Block 5 of the Capital Programme or from general bids made of the DoE (Urban Programme, Urban Development Grant, Derelict Land Grant) or the GLC (Greater London Enterprise Board).

Therefore we would argue that many of the best or most attractive sites do not find themselves within the employment programme. Even those sites which are included are often attractive to other uses, thus bringing us to the third issue. There are many examples of good industrial sites within Inner London, available for development which are being rapidly used for other uses, such as the Morgans site in Wandsworth, Hays Wharf Southward (now Wates housing), Sainsbury's Superstore at Nine Elms (Lambeth), Granby Street prestige GLC/DoE Housing (within a CDA industrial area, Tower Hamlets). In addition, the opportunity resources which are presenting themselves through, for example, the award of Urban Development Grants supports a variety of uses. In the UDG grants which have been announced in early 1983, approximately half of the schemes were for industrial uses, but 10% were for schemes changing industrial accommodation into residential.

The current commitment to development coupled with the scarcity of private sector resources serve to ensure support for major schemes regardless of use. In addition Government policy is supplemented by the use of specific measures such as Special Development Orders, land vesting and competitions, whilst this whole approach to development is underlined through the determination of appeal decisions. Thus any development which is achievable, particularly within Inner Areas, is to be warmly welcomed regardless of its use, and the longer term options which it may serve to severely curtail.

CONCLUSIONS

The policy response to employment issues has continued to grow and has resulted in greater emphasis being placed on the allocation of land for employment purposes although against a background of continuing decline in the amount of land being used for industry in Inner London and falls in employment density on the remaining sites. Nevertheless the policies adopted for promotion of employment and economic activity

remain insufficiently resourced and do not command wide enough
support within the authorities to be successful. We would
maintain that traditional local government programmes still
command more general support and are able to have a first
charge on resources.

The success to date has been achieved by the moves of a
specific group of officers, i.e. planners, and their relationship to a specific group of Members, i.e. the newly elected
Labour Members on the left, followed by concerned Tory
Members. This position is changing in some authorities;
employment development is more supported through the provision
of budgets, staffing, Committee status and prestige. This has
had a positive effect in raising credibility. However the
kind of sites and projects available may be of such complexity
that they may ultimately have adverse effects if they fail to
deliver.

Meanwhile the recession deepens and the challenge facing
Inner London authorities grows. Increasing resources also
reduce the extent of policy innovation as they are earmarked
to fund ongoing initiatives. Further, most authorities still
employ Chief Officers with a traditional approach, many of
whom hold a position of considerable scepticism. Main local
authority programmes continue subject only to Central
Government restrictions. There is evidence of an increasingly
eager private housebuilding interest ready to make a
considerable effort to gain any developable site in reasonable
condition, regardless of zoning or proposals.

The last ten years therefore have witnessed a remarkable
change in attitude and policy response by Inner London authorities to employment problems but the conclusion must be that
the intervention by authorities in the employment field
remains essentially marginal with little prospect of change.

5 Development of profit and development control: the case of office development in London

RICHARD BARRAS

THE PROBLEMS OF PLANNING

Taking a very simplified view, it can be argued that two main problems beset the British planning system. Firstly, there is the lack of positive powers and resources available to planners, to complement the essentially negative powers of development control. Secondly, there is the danger of confusion of objectives, as the development control system is used to implement a wide range of different policies. These problems are highlighted most sharply by the recent history of the planning of office development in London, which shows just how difficult it is to intervene effectively in what is perhaps the most active, volatile and profitable property market in the UK.

At least three types of explicit policy objectives have been pursued with respect to office development in London. In ascending order of generality they are:

- to control the scale, standards of design and layout of individual buildings, according to physical planning objectives;

- to control the location of office development, in accordance with the objectives of land use or spatial planning;

- to control the overall level of office development activity, with respect to the objectives of economic development policy.

In addition, there has sometimes been a fourth, implicit objective, which is to contain what is seen as an excessive level of development profit, in accordance with the broader social and distributional goals of planning.

Not only do these objectives overlap, but they are all pursued through the medium of one policy instrument, the development control system, with all its well known limitations. There is therefore considerable scope for confused and ineffectual planning. In contrast, private developers and investors enjoy the freedom to act quickly and positively in the market, through their access to plentiful financial resources. Their main problem is the risk associated with uncertainty about future market conditions, but on the other hand they suffer no danger of confused objectives. For developers the goal is to maximise profits; for investors it is to maximise their rate of return over time subject to an acceptable degree of risk.

The following sections of the paper focus upon three particular aspects of the problems confronting planning in a property market such as the London office market, which is subject to massive inflows of development and investment capital (for a more detailed discussion, see Barras, 1981). Firstly, there is the difficulty of trying to regulate the overall level of development supply in the face of uncertainty about future levels of demand. Secondly, there is the risk that the intervention of development control will reinforce rather than counter the pronounced cycle of alternating booms and slumps in office market conditions. Thirdly, there is the problem of trying to control the location and scale of development in a metropolitan market subject to strong pressures for the intensification, outward expansion and decentralisation of development. The final section of the paper draws out the lessons for the planning of office development in London during the next decade.

Central to the whole discussion is the crucial underlying relationship between development profit and development control, which can be expressed in the following terms - the more restrictive is development control, the higher is the rate of development profit, even though the total volume of profit may be reduced. In other words, if a restrictive policy of development control is applied, the effect will be to boost the capital values of those development schemes which

are allowed to proceed, though there will be a smaller number
of new development and investment opportunities created.

REGULATING THE LEVEL OF DEVELOPMENT

A central concern of economic development policy in London in
the post-war period has been to control its growth as a
national and international office centre. The extent of
London's dominance as a national office centre can be measured
by the fact that 30% of national office employment and nearly
40% of national commercial office floorspace are located in
the capital. More dramatic is the extent to which building
capital is concentrated in London, with nearly 80% of national
office rateable values, of which nearly 60% is located in the
Cities of London and Westminster alone.

Three aspects of London's economic structure account for the
growing dominance of office activity. Firstly, in all sectors
there is the concentration of office based headquarters
functions in the capital, which has been encouraged by the
growth of large multi-plant firms through diversification and
take-overs within the national economy. Secondly, the London
economy is biased towards those service sectors with the
highest proportion of office-based employment, and in
particular financial and professional services in the City and
public administration in Westminster. Thirdly, there has been
a major post-war inflow of overseas multinational companies,
especially international banks, attracted by London's role as
an international financial centre and by much lower labour
costs than those in other European centres.

During the post-war boom, the growth of London as an office
centre was proceeding at such a pace that it became a matter
of concern at national as well as metropolitan level.
Consequently, regional policy was directed towards encouraging
the decentralisation of office activity from London, using
policy instruments such as Office Development Permits and the
Location of Offices Bureau. The twin aim was to reduce the
danger of excessive demands for labour, housing and transport
facilities within the London economy, and at the same time
divert office development to the relatively depressed, older
industrial regions. In fact, the high costs of office space
in Central London were already forcing a strong outmovement of
office firms (Dunning and Morgan, 1971). However, the vast
majority of this office relocation involved movements to
smaller towns within the South East region, offering much
lower location costs, good communications and rapid access to
London, an indigenous white collar labour force, and an

attractive working environment. Thus though decentralisation policy certainly assisted an underlying trend, it failed to stimulate the economies of the older industrial regions, as had been intended (Rhodes and Kan, 1971).

Over the past fifteen years, the sustained outflow of office firms, combined with the increasing impact of new technology on clerical employment has meant that office employment in Greater London has remained virtually static, and in Central London it has been declining (Weatheritt and John, 1979). Furthermore, the downward trend has been reinforced by the current recession. In contrast, there has continued to be strong growth in the office building stock, with the area of occupied commercial office floorspace in London growing by over 60% between 1967 and 1982. These divergent trends imply that there has been a major increase in the amount of occupied floorspace per office worker during the past fifteen years, which has helped to maintain the user demand for new office space. Three factors can be suggested in explanation. Firstly, new office technology creates its own space requirements while reducing employment levels. Secondly, for all grades of office worker, successive waves of new office development have meant increased accommodation and space standards. Thirdly, new technology has had most impact on the more routine clerical jobs, so that an increasing proportion of total office employment is in the higher professional and administrative grades who demand relatively higher space standards.

There has also been a strong growth in investment demand for new office property in London from the financial institutions. This has been sustained by the growth of pension and life funds and by the favourable returns derived from property investment in the last twenty years, compared with investment in gilts and equities. In general the growth in investment demand has exceeded the growth in user demand, with two results. One is that real investment yields have declined, bringing them more into line with the return on other assets; the other is a pressure for accelerated economic obsolescence and redevelopment of the existing, secondary office stock. Such redevelopment helps to maintain a continued supply of new prime properties which provides users with improved facilities, yet does not excessively expand the total available supply.

When attempting to regulate the total supply of new offices in London, planners must therefore take into account two important factors, which if ignored will lead them to underestimate future demand for new office space. One is the increasing amount of floorspace being occupied by each office worker, which as already noted reflects increased capital intensity in the service sector. This trend is likely to accelerate during the next decade, as the pace of office automation increases. The other factor which must be accommodated is the pressure to redevelop the older vintages of office stock, a pressure which is soon likely to extend to the first post-war wave of office building. Excessively restrictive conservation policies in response to these redevelopment pressures may exacerbate the imbalance between user and investment demand, and constrain the rate at which technical innovation is introduced into the office sector via new building.

Furthermore, restrictive development control policies may become self-defeating if they significantly boost land values and development profit, which in turn reinforces supply side pressures for new development. The rate of development profit is determined by the capital value of a completed building, derived from its rent and yield, less construction costs, interest charges and site costs. The high level of office rents in London mean that the rate of development profit may typically be in a range as high as 30-50% of the total discounted capital value of a new building in the Central Area, even allowing for high land values. The most critical components of the profitability equation are capital values and construction costs, and the long term trend in the post war period has been for a faster rate of growth in capital values, which has created a tendency for the rate of development profit to increase. This real growth in capital values in turn derives from declining yields and a real growth in rents, the latter being attributable to the combination of growing user demand and a limited supply of new development sites, reinforced by the application of development control policy.

INTERVENING IN THE DEVELOPMENT CYCLE

The intervention of the planning system in order to regulate the level of office development in London must also take account of the strong cycle of development activity, which leads to alternating periods of relative over and under supply rather than a steady market equilibrium. It is the delay of three to four years between the start and completion of a development scheme which creates the inherent cyclical trend. Increasing demand leads to shortages of space and rising rents. The resultant increase in capital values encourages developers to initiate schemes without full appreciation of

97

the total volume of development being started. Only when the first wave of developments comes onto the market, stabilising rents and values, does the level of new starts begin to slacken off, by which time a potential over-supply has been created. Speculative development then drops to a low level until this new supply is absorbed and the cycle can begin again.

Variations on the demand side may either reinforce or dampen down the successive phases of under and over supply created by the development cycle. The first post-war development boom in London, during the late 1950s and early 1960s, coincided with a period of sustained economic growth, so that the newly developed office space in central London was rapidly taken up, and market conditions remained stable. However, as economic growth slackened, the business cycle became more pronounced again, influencing the demand for new office space. Since the late 1960s, this demand cycle and the development cycle have tended to run out of phase, since successive business cycle upturns have helped to trigger off a new wave of development starts which are only completed in time for the subsequent economic downturn.

This is the basic explanation for the instability created in the London office market during the second major post-war development boom of the early 1970s. In central London, available prime space from the previous boom had declined to a very low level by 1970, generating a high level of new development starts. At the same time, the start of the "Barber boom" in the national economy in 1971 further exacerbated the shortage of available space, accelerating the rise in rents and encouraging a further wave of new development. These schemes began to reach completion in 1973, just as the Barber boom was ending. The result was a collapse of rents and a rapid switch from severe under-supply to even more severe over-supply, coinciding with the mid 1970s recession.

The modest economic recovery of the late 1970s increased the take-up rate in the London office market once again, so that from 1977 available space started to decline and rents to rise. Consequently, a new wave of development started in the City in 1977 and has subsequently spread to the rest of London. By the end of 1979, available space in central London was again limited, rental growth had peaked, a third post war development boom was in full swing, and a new phase of over supply could safely be predicted for the early 1980s (Barras, 1979a). What could not be predicted was the severity of the recession after 1979/1980 which, combined with a larger volume of new development than in the early 1970s, has led to a current over supply which is probably more severe than that in 1975/1976 (see Jones, Lang, Wootton, 1982; Ellis, 1983, for reviews of current conditions in the Central London office markets).

The processes which create the development cycle are reflected in a pronounced cycle in the rate of development profit (Barras, 1979b, for details of the calculations). Profitability is highest right at the beginning of the development cycle, when conditions in fact appear most unfavourable. Thus buildings started in 1958, 1966-1968 and 1976-1977 were completed in time for letting at each subsequent peak of the cycle, when values were highest. Conversely, the developments started during each boom (e.g. 1962, 1972/1973 and 1979), when development conditions were apparently most favourable, were only completed in time for the subsequent slump - which explains why each cycle tends to produce an over supply of office space.

The crucial question as far as the planning system is concerned is whether or not development control policy should be used to counter the instability created by the booms and slumps of the development cycle. The arguments in favour of such an objective are that it would reduce the volatility and uncertainty of market conditions, to the benefit of developers, investors and occupiers, and minimise the negative externality effects created by the cleared sites and vacant buildings which are left at the end of each boom. However, if this is to be an objective of planning policy, then develop- ment control must be exercised in a manner opposite to that so far pursued in the post war period, when it has tended to reinforce rather than smooth out the cycle.

What has happened is that controls have been relaxed during each development upturn and re-imposed more severely during the subsequent slump, whereas a truly counter-cyclical policy would attempt to control each upturn, when profitability is highest, and relax controls in a downturn. Thus the mid 1960s "Brown Ban" on office building in London and the mid 1970s reinforcement of ODP policy, both by incoming Labour govern- ments, were a reaction to the onset of oversupply. Correspon- dingly, the relaxation of ODP controls after 1970 and their abolition in 1979, both by incoming Conservative governments, added impetus to development booms which were in any case underway.

This sequence of changes in development control policy has combined not only to sustain the cycle, but also to boost the average level of development profit by moderating the effect of each slump. Thus Marriott (1969) points to the beneficial effects of the introduction of ODPs upon office rents and values during the mid 1960s period of over supply, while the DoE's own Office Location Review (1976) considered that "The overall effect of the (ODP) control may be to maintain cyclical instability but at a higher average level of rent". If the GLC imposes a new phase of restrictive development control in response to current over supply, it will be in danger of continuing the policy sequence which has reinforced, rather than countered, the post war cycle in the London office market.

CONTROLLING THE LOCATION AND SCALE OF DEVELOPMENT

The growth of user demand for new office space, reinforced by the pressures of investment demand, has been accommodated within London in three ways. Firstly, the intensity of building in the traditional central office area has been increased through redevelopment. Secondly, the functional boundaries of the Central Area have been extended by office development on its fringes. Thirdly, new office centres have been developed in the suburbs. Each of these trends have posed a different set of problems with regard to the formulation of planning policy.

The intensification of the building stock through redevelopment, particularly in the Central Area, is a process which is closely related to the rapid concentration of capital which has taken place within the development sector. This has seen the emergence of large conglomerates which can undertake the planning, funding and construction of new schemes. In particular, the sector has become dominated by the financial institutions (Cadman, 1983). They started by providing fixed interest development finance for property companies, then moved to sharing the equity of development schemes, and now either engage directly in development through subsidiary companies or provide forward funding for schemes which they purchase on completion. The property companies, which in the 1950s and 1960s used to control the sector, have been relegated to the role of development agents for the financial institutions, and the main challenge to the institutions is now coming from the large construction companies with a sufficient capital base to fund their own development subsidiaries. The institutions and construction companies are thus able to retain an increasing share of the development profit which they previously helped to realise, but shared with independent property companies.

The intensification process results from increasing competition to develop prime sites, particularly those in the Central Area where rents and profitability are highest, combined with escalating building costs which necessitate ever larger volumes of capital investment. The process is manifested both in terms of higher redevelopment densities and the assembly of larger individual development sites. As a result there were, for example, six office schemes of over 300,000 square feet under construction in the City of London in the current development boom, costing at least £50 million each, compared with only five such schemes completed in the previous twenty years. Developments of this scale inevitably put pressure on the planning system, in terms of design criteria such as building height, maximum plot ratios, and the listing of older buildings which may be part of a large site which is being assembled for redevelopment.

The difficulties of finding and assembling suitable sites for large scale redevelopment schemes are imposing an increasingly severe constraint on the intensification process within the traditional office area of Central London (Stevenson, 1981, on the shortage of large redevelopment sites in Westminster). Consequently, there has been growing development pressure to extend the boundaries of the central office area, by undertaking schemes in inner city areas previously in other industrial, commercial or even residential uses. Such schemes have been constructed, or are planned, for the northern and eastern fringes of the City, in Tower Hamlets, Hackney and Islington; in the southern part of Camden; to the south of Victoria in Pimlico; and, most controversially, on the South Bank, in Lambeth and Southwark.

This development of the "extensive margin" of the central office area is currently generating an intense debate, within both local government and the development industry. Firstly, since these areas have not previously been in office use, there is considerable uncertainty about the potential level of user demand. This uncertainty affects both planners, in terms of their development control decisions, and investors and developers, for whom the rents achievable on such schemes remain very much an unknown quantity. The difficulties of letting space in one or two ambitious schemes recently completed on the City fringes clearly illustrate this problem, though it must be remembered that if they are successfully let these pioneering schemes will probably yield a considerably above average rate of development profit. Secondly, office developments in these areas tend to conflict with existing Borough or GLC plans, which propose a continuation of smaller scale residential and industrial uses, consistent with the

traditional land use patterns and economic structure of Inner
London. Consequently, many of these schemes, particularly on
the South Bank, are being vigorously opposed by the local
authorities concerned.

   The problems posed by the extension of the central office
area are magnified because several very large vacant sites are
becoming available in inner city areas, due to the ending of
traditional uses such as warehousing and dock facilities, and
these present opportunities for office development projects on
a scale never before achieved in London. In particular, South
Bank sites such as Vauxhall Cross, Coin Street, Kings Reach,
Hays Wharf and Surrey Docks could, if present proposals proceed, add several million square feet of new office space to
the London stock, with two or three individual schemes eventually providing up to one million square feet apiece.   Not
only are such schemes larger than any built in the City of
London, but they also produce a large net increase in the
total stock since they are not replacing older office
buildings, whereas in the City, redevelopment schemes may only
produce a 50% net increase because of demolitions. The extension of large scale development beyond the traditional office
centre will thus have a dramatic impact upon the total future
supply of office space in London.

   The final locational aspect of office development in London
is the emergence of several major suburban office centres
during the post war period. This trend should be recognised as
part of the wider decentralisation process in response to high
Central Area location costs which has already been referred
to. The result has been a strong demand for suburban offices,
which has been reflected in a faster rate of rental growth
than that achieved in the Central Area over the period 1965-
1982 (Investors Chronicle/Hiller Parker, 1982). Though large
office schemes in suburban centres can create potential
conflicts with other land uses, as well as traffic congestion
and parking problems, there has in general been less planning
opposition than that being generated in response to proposals
to develop sites on the fringes of the central office area.
In fact, in some areas such as Hammersmith, there has been a
positive welcome for office development as a source of jobs,
rating income and "planning gains" (McKee and Martinos, 1981).

   The growth of suburban office centres has not, however, been
uniformly spread, since the strength of user demand, and thus
the level of rents and development profitability, seems to
depend critically upon the accessibility of a centre in terms
of the metropolitan road and rail networks. Thus the rapid
development of Croydon as an office centre in the 1960s was

based upon fast rail links to Victoria and to the white collar commuter belt to the south of London. During the 1970s, the focus of suburban office development moved to the western corridor linking Central London to Heathrow via the M4, with the subsequent growth of centres such as Hammersmith, Ealing and Hounslow. As far as the 1980s are concerned, the dominant factor will be the completion of the M25 around London, which will certainly encourage further decentralisation of offices to the Outer Metropolitan Area.

OFFICE POLICY FOR THE NEXT DECADE

The formulation of office policy for London during the next decade should take into account the following features of the current situation:

(i)   There are clear signs that the current recession is forcing many large organisations either to rationalise their use of office space in Central London, or to decentralise to cheaper accommodation outside London.

(ii)   There is currently a major oversupply of office space on the London market as a result of the third post-war development boom, though there is continued evidence of demand for new prime property from the financial and professional service sectors.

(iii)   Much of the currently vacant office space is in secondary buildings which are becoming obsolescent, and since these are forming a growing proportion of institutional investment portfolios, there will be increasing pressure for their redevelopment.

(iv)   There are a large number of schemes in the pipeline ready for the next development boom in the second half of the 1980s, and many of these are massive projects on controversial South Bank sites which, if developed, will create a large increase in the total office stock in London.

(v)   The increasing impact of information technology and office automation during the next decade is likely to be manifested not so much in a reduced aggregate level of demand for office space, but rather in a changed pattern of demand, with a trend to smaller, more dispersed and technically more sophisticated office units serving both large and small organisations.

(vi)   The completion of the M25 orbital motorway in 1986
       could have a dramatic and damaging effect upon the
       economy of London, accelerating the decentralisation
       of commercial and industrial activity which has been
       in progress throughout the post-war period.

With these factors in mind, it is vital that planning policy
is directed towards controlling and shaping the **next** wave of
office development in London, rather than merely reacting to
the over-supply created by the last wave. In formulating
office policy for the next cycle of development, three major
objectives would seem to be desirable:

- to reduce the sequence of boom and slump conditions
  which have so far affected the London office market in
  the post-war period;

_ to promote a positive office location strategy which
  meets the future pattern of user demand in terms of
  accessibility, size of units, layout and technical
  facilities;

- to allow a level of development sufficient to accommodate both existing and new office firms in London at
  rents low enough to compete effectively with rents in
  the growing office centres in the remainder of the
  South East.

This last objective is perhaps the most crucial to pursue,
for otherwise the next decade could witness a major loss of
office employment in London, similar to that which has already
occurred in the manufacturing sector, and this could have
severe long-term effects upon the viability of the metropolitan economy as a whole.

Any planning policy which is interpreted as broadly favourable to the continued growth of offices in London may be
attacked as also favouring the very high rates of profit
obtained from office development. However, as pointed out at
the beginning of this paper, the paradox of the British planning system is that the highest rates of profit tend to be
achieved when restrictive development control policies are
applied. Nevertheless, this still leaves the problem of how
the community at large can obtain a share of the high rental
income and capital values created by the issue of development
permissions - a problem which has remained unsolved ever since
the 1947 Planning Act, and which appears in its most acute
form with regard to office development in London. Perhaps all
that can be said in this context is that local authorities

should be seeking to intervene more **positively** in the development process, using the powers of development control to create development schemes which can attract both private and public investment capital under various types of equity sharing arrangements. There may be a case for establishing a Development Agency for London, which can combine the functions of planning, property development and investment, matching public sector capital to that of the financial institutions, in order to ensure a continuing supply of office space which both meets user demand and conforms to the goals of strategic planning policy.

6 Land availability studies and private housebuilding

ALAN HOOPER

INTRODUCTION

Concern over the amount of land available for private housebuilding has been expressed by different agencies intermittently ever since the passing of the 1947 Town and Country Planning Act. Until recently, this concern attracted little sympathy from within the planning profession, being attributed either to the cyclical (and therefore transient) character of the housebuilding industry under 'boom' conditions, or to special pleading on the part of a particular interest group (those housebuilders seeking to take a trading profit in land as well as housebuilding). From the late 1960s until the present, a series of investigations into land availability for private housebuilding has accompanied the growing political prominence of the issue. These investigations have gradually revealed the complexity surrounding an issue which, all too often, has been presented in the simplistic terms of land <u>stocks</u>, and have pointed the way towards the establishment of a comprehensive procedure or method for assessing the availability of land for private residential development.

At the same time, successive governments, with different political complexions, have from 1970 sought to encourage the release of land for private housebuilding through the release of circulars by the Department of the Environment. Though these have tended to create a policy ambiguity at both the national and local level (in terms of containing urban growth, largely through the instrument of green belts), they have served to extend the information base essential to any successful monitoring of land availability. The Local Government Planning and Land Act 1980, by bestowing upon the Secretary of State for the Department of the Environment powers to direct a local authority to make an assessment of development land (S 116), has transformed what had hitherto been a discretionary into a mandatory activity on the part of local authorities. More than this, Circular 9/80 (DoE 1980a) (which though preceding the 1980 Local Government, Planning and Land Act, sets out the recommended procedures for assessing land availability for private housebuilding) advocated a specific methodology to be adopted in future studies, based on only one of the preceding investigations or research reports, namely The Study of the Availability of Private House-Building land in Greater Manchester (DoE 1979). This study initiated a succession of joint studies, as recommended by Circular 9/80 (DoE 1980a), between local authorities and builders' representatives, encompassing both the Metropolitan and non-Metropolitan Counties in England. Twenty-four such studies had been initiated to 1981, with fourteen completed (Dobson 1981).

It is an urgent necessity to investigate the interrelationship between Structure Plan allocations of land for private housebuilding, and the joint-study assessments of land availability. This interrelationship is of pressing practical relevance for the planning profession, the housebuilding industry, the Planning Inspectorate and the judiciary. As is so often the case, this pragmatic topicality disguises an issue of more enduring complexity concerning the changing interrelationship between the structure and method of operation of the land-use planning system on the one hand, and the house-building industry on the other. An investigation of one component of one policy field (the methodology of land availability studies) can thus serve as a starting point from which to assess the progress of the implicit review of British land policy noted in the Conference introductory review paper.

LAND SUPPLY FOR PRIVATE HOUSING - THE PIPELINE MODEL

Under the regulatory or responsive style of land-use planning established since 1947, the planning system emphasised one specific component of the process of supplying land for development - that of land allocation. House-builders, on the other hand, are oriented towards land availability, and availability need bear no direct and simple relationship to allocation. Inevitably, therefore, there will be differences in perspectives, objectives and interests among the agencies involved in the land conversion process for private housebuilding (DoE, 1975, Barrett, 1982b). In the absence of a close relationship between allocation and availability, the system of control of development always promised to be the most likely battlefield over which conflicts would be fought out. It is part of the argument presented in this paper that the site of this conflict serves to disguise a more fundamental opposition between the system of development and the system of land-use planning as they pertain to private residential development.

In order to clarify the nature of the land conversion process in any field of development, a model of the overall process is required which can generate a useful operational methodology for studying empirical outcomes. Until recently, such a model was missing in the field of residential land conversion, but research over the last decade has gone some way to remedy this deficiency. After initial commentaries and research reports concerned with an essentially static perspective of estimating stocks of land for private housebuilding (Annual Reports of the Land Commission, 1968, 1969; Hall, et al, 1973; Shankland Cox Partnership, 1972, 1973), the 1975 'Housing Land Availability in the South East' report marked an important methodological advance by developing a method of assessment oriented towards flows of land through a development 'pipeline'. Essentially, the method involved the separation of the process of supply of residential land into four phases (allocated; outstanding permissions not started; under construction; completion) and tracing the movement of stocks of land through these phases over time (a 2-year period).

A second study by the Joint Unit for Research on the Urban Environment of the University of Aston in Birmingham for the DoE examined similar processes in what was then the other main area of 'pressure', the West Midlands. Again the researchers stressed the significance of a research method relating allocation to availability, and oriented towards a dynamic flow perspective rather than a static snapshot approach (JURUE, 1976). The residential land conversion process was depicted along the lines of the pipeline model established in the 1975 DoE study, but with the phases disaggregated to include more detail in relation to the interface between developers and the planning system (JURUE, 1977). In order to relate land stocks to flows through the pipeline, data was gathered concerning:

i) the stock of land available in various categories at the beginning and end of the relevant period;

ii) the identification and measurement of land flows into the system - as defined primarily by planning permissions;

iii) the identification and measurement of land flows out of the system - as measured by housing starts and completions or lapsed permissions (JURUE, 1977b).

The empirical research carried out by the JURUE researchers related largely to (ii) and (iii), focusing upon three main dimensions:

		Dimensions
i)	the volume of land flows	aggregate
ii)	the rate of land flows	temporal
iii)	the spatial distributions of land flows	spatial

(JURUE 1977)

The focus upon the impact of planning control in the <u>process</u> of land conversion was continued in the study by the DoE in 1978, 'Land Availability: A Study of Land with Residential Planning Permission'. This concentrated upon only one stage in the overall land supply process (that between planning permission being granted and construction being undertaken) over a 2-year period, but extended its sample coverage to England as a whole, rather than being confined to the 'pressured' areas as had the two earlier studies. The study retained a 'process' perspective by charting the rate of implementation of sites with outstanding permission.

It can be seen that whilst all studies adopted a dynamic, process, 'pipeline' model of land conversion, over time attention became diverted from the structural attributes of the model to the rate of progress of allocated land towards permission (i.e. to those delay characteristics which fell within the ambit of the development control process). Indeed, the 1975 DoE study had warned that such myopia would detract from a "more general view of land supply as a <u>process</u> which examines the aggregate effect that the mechanics of the process have on the overall stocks and flows of land" (DoE, 1975). By emphasising the crucial <u>structural</u> characteristics of the land conversion pipeline the <u>DoE model</u> was able to point to the drip-feed characteristic of this process, i.e. that the rate of movement through the supply pipeline was dependent upon (a) the level of demand for private housebuilding and (b) the allocation of new land.

One of the most interesting empirical conclusions of the studies was that whenever a shortage of land for private residential development had been experienced in the 'pressured' regions (for whatever characteristic or set of delay factors), the response of the land-use planning system had been to release unallocated or 'white' land - over 50% of permissions in the case of the South East study, and two-fifths of all land released in the case of the West Midlands study (DoE 1975; DoE 1977). Both studies point to an apparent mismatch between plan-making and the implementation aspects of development control that this implies (DoE 1975, DoE 1977a - see also Cuddy and Hollingsworth). In the future, the role of such incremental releases of land (in addition to formal allocations in statutory development plans) is likely to be crucial in managing the relationship between land stocks and flows through the land conversion pipeline.

The review entitled 'The Land Market and Development Process' published by SAUS (Barrett 1978) commented on the heuristic advantages of the 'pipeline' model, with its descriptive emphasis upon an holistic perspective on the events involved in the physical land conversion/development process. Taking the existing development context as given, the SAUS researchers argued that the model facilitated snapshot assessments, but that any more dynamic orientation was precluded by the structural characteristics of the model, which artificially fossilised existing development agencies and relationships (Barrett 1978). Their suggestion for the substitution of a development or finance conversion perspective is a specific attempt to more closely replicate the structural logic of the private development process (Barrett 1978) and subsequent research attempted to map the interface between this process and public agencies involved in facilitating land supply (Barrett and Whitting, 1980, Barrett, 1982b).

It thus becomes crucial to a proper understanding of land/development/finance conversion models that they be located in a development context establishing the precise mix of public/private agencies providing the central dynamic to the implementation process. Once this context is established, it becomes possible to relate to the processes in land supply identified by Barrett (1982b), namely land allocation and land availability. It is in this sense that land conversion models are often thought to be 'neutral' (DoE, 1975) - they are neutral insofar as they fail to specify the development context which determines the logic of their operation.

To summarise, the sequence of research reports in the late 1970s emphasised:

(i) the need for a conceptual model within which to locate the process of land conversion for private residential development, in order to generate an explanatory understanding of the causal factors determining the relationship between the demand for, and the supply of, land;

(ii) the need for such a model to be process and dynamic in orientation, i.e. to explicitly integrate a temporal perspective in which the snapshot pictures of land availability could be contextuated;

(iii) the need for this model to include all relevant agencies in the development process, both public and private, and to avoid a narrow concern exclusively with the statutory planning process in general, and the development control system in particular;

(iv) this model to include not only traditional physical and land-use related factors affecting development feasibility, but also economic factors and their interaction with physical factors over time.

LAND AVAILABILITY FOR PRIVATE HOUSEBUILDING

It is in the above context that the Study of the Availability of Private House-Building Land in Greater Manchester (DoE 1979) should be judged (Hooper, 1979). Only a perfunctory reference is made to earlier studies, and that from a perspective of the adequacy of stocks of land the Department of the Environment suggesting that, on the basis of the evidence available from earlier studies, there was no net national shortage of housebuilding land, but rather "a variety of local problems" (DoE 1979). DoE Circular 44/78 had urged co-operation between local authorities and builders to produce realistic local appraisals of the availability of house-building land, and the Greater Manchester study represented the first of many joint efforts between housebuilders and local authorities. The emphasis throughout these studies has been upon the production of realistic assessments, and most of the differences in interpretation of the results between housebuilders' representatives and local planning authorities (and agencies representing them) have concerned the interpretation of the term 'realistic'.

What is striking about the aims of the study (to establish a common perception amongst the participants about the availability of land and to identify specific problems; to identify generally applicable lessons about land supply and planning policies, and to provide a better understanding of the structure of the housebuilding industry and how it operates; to devise a simple method of appraisal; to create a framework for regular and effective liaison between local authorities and builders) is that the methodology adopted is almost exclusively oriented to only the two last objectives, and is designed to focus overwhelmingly upon the adequacy of stocks of land for private housebuilding. The first two objectives would be much better served by developing the research which had taken place throughout the previous decade, and reviewed briefly above. Yet the report saw itself as being "the first study of its type" (DoE 1979), which could only be true in the sense of the involvement of housebuilders and local authorities in the estimates of availability.

The earlier studies, whether of the pipeline or land conversion type, had sought to develop a relatively neutral methodology, which would serve to 'locate' various agencies and factors in the process of land supply. Recognising the different interests of the actors involved, such an approach facilitated the interpretation of the results by establishing a method which explicitly covered all the agencies in the supply process (landowners; planners; developer/builders)and all the sequences in land conversion. The Greater Manchester study is characterised, on the other hand, by the development of a method which emphasises the assessments of stocks rather than flows through a pipeline, introduces economic factors but in a partial and uncritical way, adopts a definition of availability which permits additions to (and deductions from) stocks in an unstructured manner, and is based on a surprising agreement between local authorities and builders concerning the dwelling capacity of the land stock.

DoE Circular 9/80 "makes it clear that land identified as suitable for housing must be free, or easily freed, from planning, physical and ownership constraints, be capable of being economically developed, be in areas where housebuyers are prepared to live and be suitable for the wide range of housing now demanded. For the commercial judgements to be made, consultation with the housebuilding industry is essential" (DoE Press Notice 153 of 1980). This is to be

112

achieved by requesting local authorities to ensure that there is a five years' supply of private housebuilding land at all times, based on (paragraph 7) the 'simple method' set out in the Appendix to Annex II of the Greater Manchester Study. The Appendix to the Circular recognises that such land availability studies will be snapshots, with attempts made to estimate completions "firstly over the study period by year, and then over the following five or so years in toto. If the authority cannot produce this sort of annual assessment within a reasonable period, their view of total production during the first five year period would be a reasonable second best". Clearly, it will be necessary to closely monitor and revise all the parameters of such studies year by year if an accurate picture of land availability is to be obtained, even on the limited basis of the methodology adopted in the Greater Manchester study.

Whereas all circulars relating to land availability had hitherto been advisory, Circular 9/80 (DoE 1980a) was given a unique status by s116 of the 1980 Local Government Planning and Land Act 1980, in that the Secretary of State has powers to underline direct a local authority to make an assessment of development land, and this assessment is to be made, following Circular 9/80, using guidelines based on the prior study carried out in Greater Manchester in 1979.

The weaknesses of the methodology involved, noted above, have been outlined in detail elsewhere (Hooper 1979; 1980), but can be summarised as follows:

(a) the method emphasises stocks rather than flows, producing a snapshot at one point in time.

     All previous research reports had attempted to disaggregate the movement of stocks through the land conversion pipeline, and to determine the rate at which land moved forward to completion in terms of (a) new additions to stock (b) the rate of implementation of permissions (c) the efficiency of operation of the component parts of the developing pipeline. The Greater Manchester study is concerned with the constraints that apply to a particular stock of sites at a particular point in time. As Barrett notes, time scale is a crucial "determinant of the relative importance of different feasibility factors. This poses a question on the role and value of joint studies on housing land availability: can they do more than make this point in relation to sets of specific sites" (1982).

(b)   For the first time, the Greater Manchester study
      introduced economic as well as physical factors into
      the estimation of land availability. Yet problems
      occur in the treatment of both types of factor, and
      it is arguable that too great an emphasis is given to
      economic factors in terms of the robustness of the
      information on which such factors are estimated.

      In the first place, the common perception of land
      actually available for private housebuilding arrived
      at involved a reduction in original estimates from
      3,100 acres to 2,300 acres. This process involved
      the exclusion of land considered to be unavailable
      for a variety of reasons, chief of which (33%) were
      marketing constraints. Because unserviced unpermis-
      sioned land comprised only 10% of the annual average
      development (though it comprised 40% of builders
      stocks), the report considered "it may be more
      sensible to discount it in assessing how much land
      builders own which is available for development". It
      is not clear from the report whether this is a
      planning or an infrastructure/services constraint.
      But it seems odd to exclude such land, when the
      original definition of availability is not confined
      to land with planning permission.

      The reason for the high proportion of deductions from
      stocks for marketing constraints is related to
      perhaps the most contentious aspect of the
      methodology, the market-banding principle. The
      report introduces the notion that effective demand
      for private housing can be disaggregated in terms of
      lower, middle and upper market categories, defined in
      terms of dwelling size, type, density and price.
      This is relatively straightforward, but the House
      Builders' Federation then link this classification to
      categories of land, though in a rather unstructured
      manner in relation to geographical location,
      environmental assessment, accessibility etc. The
      report therefore argues (on the basis of little real
      evidence) that "the land needs of each market band
      are fairly distinct (although there is some scope for
      flexibility depending upon the general quality of the
      site and its location)" (DoE 1979). It is claimed to
      be realistic to disaggregate both available land and
      anticipated need or demand by type in this manner, in
      order to avoid real shortages. Yet the borderline
      between each band is admitted to be fuzzy, though it
      is claimed that "broadly speaking they are not

interchangable" (DoE 1979). No attention is paid to the changing basis of finance for home purchase (which, over time, can radically alter the structure and form of market bands), to the interrelation between local housing markets which are recognised, in Vol.2, Annex XVIII, not to "operate in isolation but are closely interrelated", or to factors such as the design and layout of developments, which can markedly determine where a completed development is located in terms of 'land' or 'market' bands. The limited empirical search available gives grounds for questioning the suitability of housebuilders as the appropriate agents for making these general environmental assumptions (Nicholls et al 1981).

As the report notes, in practice "sites will compete with one another to satisfy demand, forming a queue, with the most attractive (from the builders' viewpoint) being developed first, and others later" (DoE 1979). To build market banding into the methodology is to institutionalise this phenomena, leading to a wasteful utilisation of serviced land in designated plan areas lacking any apparent effective demand within some notional banding category. Inevitably, in practice, the effect will be to locate lower cost housing in the least desirable locations, and high cost housing in the most favoured locations. Whilst this is a natural market tendency, its formalisation in statutory land-use planning would mark a substantial departure in post-war planning practice.

A second marketing factor relates to the dwelling capacity of sites in relation to the local housing demand on an annual basis. Thus large sites have to be phased in release in relation to demand, reducing their annual capacity as a contribution to real availability of private housing. Such downward revisions are clearly related to the level of effective demand, and can change dramatically over the typical three-year housbuilding cycle. Unless the programme of land availability is closely monitored on an annual rolling basis, any five-year estimate can readily be exceeded by bringing such developments on stream at a more rapid rate. This is a very difficult process to control in planning terms, given the current instruments available. A major determinant of the rate of implementation of permissions will be competitions between builders, and in its own methodological criticisms the Greater Manchester study points out that a mere aggregation of individual builder's estimates of production will overestimate the total required in any one period due to this failure to make allowance for competition between sites (DoE 1979).

By invoking these marketing factors in an uncritical manner, the tendency is to push up the projected land requirements of the housebuilding industry, and to depress the stocks of land available for private residential development. Nor is it accurate to assert that the study "... is not a static, once-and-for-all picture, but is intended to form the basis of a continuous monitoring system and to provide an increasingly accurate assessment of rates of use of building land and of future requirements on an annual basis" (Humber, 1980). Such a monitoring exercise would require annual reviews and would involve breaking the land conversion process down into its constituent parts. If this is not done, and if the ambiguous definitions used in the study are utilized, deductions and additions to the snapshot pictures can be made in a random and ad-hoc manner. It has been claimed that "... the system established and validated by this study, and already put into effect in other surveys, is a genuine monitoring system that allows and encourages self-correction over time" (Humber, 1980). Without the more rigorous methodological framework outlined in the earlier research reports, such a view is unrealistic.

(c)   The physical definition of availability adopted in the study was obscure - it included not only sites with outstanding residential planning permission, but also "sites expected to sustain new private house completions during the study period" (DoE 1979). The planning status of such sites was not indicated, and may have included 'white land'. Since such estimates were arrived at on a District-by-District basis, the accumulative effect in strategic terms could be considerable, but is disguised by excluding other sites with permission, but with development constraints (including such non-physical factors as unwilling vendors, factors which can change significantly over time).

(d)   As noted elsewhere (Hooper, 1979) the method adopted in the study involved a joint estimate of dwelling

116

capacity on the sites comprising the agreed stock. Authorities and builders agreed on every site, which is surprising given the findings of the 1978 DoE study that a significant delay in the development process is caused by applicants seeking to increase the density of approved development, involving a net change in dwelling capacity for the sample studied of 25%. The study had clearly anticipated disagreement by retaining the services of an independent surveyor, but in the event his services were not required. If this apparent agreement subsequently disappears, and densities are increased, a significant over-provision could be provided.

The whole issue of capacity of existing land stocks has received scant attention, notably the very rough-and-ready estimates made by most local planning authorities of existing built-up areas to absorb (through infill, plot sub-division and redevelopment) some of the demand for new housing.

As noted in a previous commentary (Hooper, 1980) "Far too much reliance has been placed on the findings and method-ology of the Manchester Study". It is unfortunate, if unsurprising, to find that the subsequent joint land-availability studies have in general adopted the methodology of the Greater Manchester study.

In view of the considerable attention given to the issue of land availability over the last decade, it is striking that the majority of the empirical research has been unanimous in its overall conclusion - that from the perspective of land stocks (i.e. from the perspective of all land availability circulars), there is no overall shortage of land for private residential development. This has been the consistent result of the research reviewed above, whether at the national, regional or metropolitan level, and whether concerned with the pipeline as a whole, or with that which falls within the purview of the statutory planning process. This is not to say that shortfalls have not been identified, nor that land availability is a non-problematic area. However, in the bald terms of land stocks (defined usually in terms of a 5-year period), it has proved singularly difficult to identify a problem of any magnitude. This has been true not only for metropolitan counties (the Greater Manchester study being 80% accurate on the basis of a generous methodology (Hooper, 1980), and the Tyne and Wear Study showing a discrepancy between allocation and availability of only 1.5 per cent (Wenban-Smith, 1980), but also for the non-Metropolitan counties. An examination of the joint land availability surveys published to date shows that the majority have sufficient available land to meet the requirements set out in the respective Structure Plans within the context of Circular 9/80.

This overall perspective is confirmed by two further reports. In 'Housing/Land in South-East England' (November 1981), produced by the Standing Conference on London and South-East Regional Planning and The House-Builders Federation, the results of ten of the eleven joint land availability surveys in the South-East are analysed. The overall conclusion reached is that, following the methodology adopted in the Greater Manchester Study, sufficient land is available for the South-East counties as a whole (outside Greater London) for the next five years to meet Structure Plan provisions. Subsequently, the Association of Metropolitan Authorities produced 'Land for Private House-Building' in June, 1982, based on a regional survey of metropolitan county authorities. Its conclusion is unequivocal: there is no evidence that land availability is a major constraint on the private sector housing programme at present. The AMA notes that the majority of private sector development in any event occurs in the shire counties.

It would be quite erroneous, however, to conclude on the basis of this research that land availability for private housebuilding is unproblematic. Such a conclusion only follows from the objectives and methodology adopted in the joint land surveys. At the heart of this method is a central preoccupation with the assessments of stocks at one point in time (Hooper, 1982), and then projecting forward completion rates for a five-year period. As discussed above in relation to the original Greater Manchester Study, this overwhelming concern with stocks of land leads to a relative neglect of the process of movement of flows through the development pipeline. None of the joint studies has attempted to replicate, or extend, the models of the development process outlined at the beginning of this paper, despite the central importance of doing so emphasised by the researchers concerned (JURUE, 1977, Barrett, 1978). In the absence of such models, it is not surprising that the data-base differs between local authorities. Whilst the majority refer only to allocated land or land with permission for residential development, some exclude land not currently with permission (e.g. Surrey); others include land which does not have permission nor is formally allocated in development plans, but to which development is committed in principle (e.g. Berkshire, Bedfordshire). One includes land shown on "any plan used for development control purposes" (Cumbria). Whilst some authorities include land in draft local plans (e.g. Oxfordshire), others exclude it (e.g.

Hampshire). Few follow the example of West Sussex and explicitly adopt a pipeline perspective, though even here the level of disaggregation does not match the complexity of the land conversion pipeline indicated by researchers concerned with the land supply process.

It becomes very difficult, therefore, to assess the role and planning status of new additions to stock. The 1975 DoE study and the 1977 JURUE study had been concerned by the large-scale release of land on sites not previously allocated for residential purposes. Whilst such release has traditionally provided the flexibility absent from much statutory land-use planning, research has confirmed that in flow terms it is precisely this category of land that is commonly associated with delay characteristics (JURUE, 1977).

Likewise, it is difficult to assess the rate of implementation of permissions (especially in the completed-occupied category, several reports indicating the problems associated with this stage), and therefore the relative efficiency of operation of the component parts of the development pipeline. Whilst some authorities propose an annual review, others propose biennial reviews, or longer. In the absence of an annual review, disaggregated to include all the components of the land conversion process, the picture which emerges is one of comparative statics, with snapshot comparisons of the land availability situation at different points in time, and no guarantee of any reliable parameters.

The general optimistic perspectives on stocks should be considered in the context of the conservative methodology inherent in the Greater Manchester Study approach, widely adopted in the joint surveys. Thus, many of the latter excluded land which, though allocated or with planning permission, were jointly considered to be unavailable for immediate development. Following the advice of Circular 9/80, (Doe, 1980a) local authorities have generally excluded land with "planning, physical and ownership" constraints, so that the tripartite meetings to discuss availability generally resulted in a reduced estimate of land availability. It is of particular note that, once excluded, such categories appear to have attracted little attention in terms of their contribution to land development. Optimistically, one would expect the process of review to investigate the problems further, but the methodology adopted generally provides no firm guarantees that this will be done in a structured manner, particularly in relationship to ownership factors. Only the Dorset study explicitly notes that such excluded land, whilst likely to remain undeveloped in the prevailing economic circumstances, should not automatically "... be discounted from the overall short-term land supply, if this were to lead to a claim of shortfall in supply and pressure for additional land to be made available elsewhere" (South East Dorset District Council/HBF, 1982). The House Builders' Federation indicated in the study that such a view ignores the central thrust of Circular 9/80 (DoE 1980a).

Greater difficulty was experienced in relation to potential deductions from the available stock for economic reasons. In terms of projected production rates, the general approach followed is to accept the house-builders' estimates. Yet even in the original Greater Manchester Study, builders' estimates of demand had been called into question (e.g. Vol.2, Annex X, p.56), and several of the joint studies expressed reservations in this regard. The Kent study noted that "Judgements regarding likely production rates that stem from marketing factors inevitably reflect the state of the market at the time the exercise was conducted and this requires annual re-appraisal to reflect changes in market outlook". Nevertheless, again influenced by Circular 9/80 (paragraph 5) most authorities have reduced their estimates of availability to take account of marketing factors. Authorities are therefore now considering not only amount of land and type of land, but amount of demand and type of demand - the Kent study explicitly commenting upon "the nature of the demand" (Kent Planning Officers Group/HBF, 1981) in making provision for new land allocations. But Kent simultaneously note that production rates on large sites can be increased by encouraging a greater mix of developers, rather than one large developer - competition between producers will therefore affect the rate of development, and not merely the supply of land in itself. Several of the reports note the methodological weakness of merely aggregating individual site capacity estimates by individual builders (e.g. Berkshire).

In relation to the market-banding principle adopted in the Greater Manchester Study (Hooper, 1979), the joint studies are more ambiguous in their conclusions and coverage. Whilst some (e.g. Buckinghamshire) found a marked difference in avail-ability by market-band throughout the county, a majority found that the largest category was (as might be expected) the 'middle' range. However, the basis for establishing the categories varied greatly between local authorities, relating to price, location, density, etc. The Buckinghamshire study noted that "It cannot be overemphasised that the price ranges and the various prices allocated to those ranges according to the District concerned are only intended as a very approximate guide" (4). Noting the very approximate guidelines outlined

in the Greater Manchester Study in this respect, it is perhaps
not surprising that difficulty has been experienced in
assessing market-banding availability. Given the apparent
ease with which sites can be reclassified under conditions of
different demand, especially between 'low' and 'middle' bands
(e.g. the Cumbria study), the reliance on subjective
assessment of such factors by housebuilders, and the practical
difficulties involved (e.g. in the Lancashire study), it is
not surprising that this aspect remains one of the weakest
aspects of the whole methodology.

The question of the capacity of available land stocks is
also brought to the fore by the joint studies. As noted with
the Greater Manchester Study (Hooper, 1979), it is surprising
to find unanimous agreement on site capacities arising from
the tripartite meetings, when earlier research (DoE, 1978) had
revealed a potential increase in dwelling capacity from
outline to detailed planning permission of as much as 25%, the
report noting that, "The dwelling capacity estimate for the
outline component of the total stock of outstanding permission
is therefore the most likely component to be inaccurate" (DoE,
1978). In this respect, the commentary on the Kent study
indicates the need to closely monitor the interrelationship
between household demand and new housing supply, for changes
in the size of household leading to smaller households will
produce reducing land requirements (Part 3, Kent Planning
Officers Group/HBF, 1981). Annex A to Circular 22/80
Development Control - Policy and Practice (DoE 1980b) indicates
(paragraph 12) that it is Government policy to encourage the
provision of dwellings for one and two person households, and
to increase the intensity of use of land in existing built-up
areas, both factors tending towards a reduced land-take.

It is noteworthy in this respect that many of the joint
surveys include an estimate of the capacity of small sites,
including infill and redevelopment sites (e.g. Kent). The
basis for such estimates varies, being generally either the
existing stock with planning permission (accepting some non-
implementation but envisaging a continuing flow) or the
average for the last five years as indicated by completions.
In any event, this aspect of land availability has received
nothing like the detailed scrutiny given to large sites, and
the inter-relationship between small and large sites and small
and large housebuilding firms remains an unexamined
phenomenon. The whole drift of recent land availability
circulars has focused attention on the large greenfield sites
peripheral to urban areas, and the consequences for
intensification and regeneration within existing urban areas
has been largely ignored. Again, this is a structural

consequence of the methodology adopted in the joint studies. The implications for this for the successful achievement of strategic planning policies has only recently been recognised. A report from the Greater Manchester Council's planning department recently indicated that, due to the reduced level of new housing construction "it is now extremely unlikely that all of the land required (by the structure plan) to be released will be developed", resulting in an increase in choice of sites for developers which, in turn, could lead to green field sites being developed at the expense of sites in the urban area. The report concludes that: "This would weaken the implementation of the central themes of the structure plan which are the redirection of development to the older parts of the conurbation, in particular the older, inner areas, in order to assist in the economic regeneration of these areas and to protect valuable open land" (Planning Bulletin 1982, p.177). It should be noted that this problem is exacerbated by the whole thrust of policy in relation to land availability since 1970, and it is particularly ironical that it should have been first encountered in Greater Manchester!

However, at the root of the whole question of land availability is the interrelationship between housing demand (both 'real', in terms of need, and 'effective' in terms of market demand) and land supply. At the national level, this would require an estimate of strategic new housebuilding requirements. Such estimates have not been published since the 1977 housing 'green paper', when the annual rate of new building in Great Britain was projected at around 300,000 dwellings a year up to 1986. The Joint Land Requirements Committee's 1982 report 'How Many Houses Should We Plan For?' notes that only 241,000 dwellings were completed in 1978, 209,000 in 1979 and approximately 200,000 in 1980 and 1981. Despite objections, the past Secretary of State refused to update the 1977 projections, yet the Joint Land Requirements Committee point out that without them "county councils have no national framework to indicate the appropriate scale of the dwelling requirements in structure plans". In order to attempt to overcome this difficulty, the Joint Land Requirements Committee projects, on a variety of assumptions, a rate of new build to achieve the conditions outlined in the 1977 green paper of 270,000 dwellings a year. Depending upon assumptions concerning economic performance, land requirements on an annual basis from 1983 are seen to lie within the range 200,000-250,000 dwellings a year for Great Britain, equivalent to 215,000 - 220,000 dwellings a year for England (1983, 1).

The Joint Land Requirements Committee suggested that English structure plans currently allocate enough land for around

180,000 - 190,000 dwellings a year, somewhat short of the 220,000 estimate of need (JLRC, 1983).

The County Planning Officers' Society, however, estimates that present structure plan policies indicate land availability of a minimum of 214,000 - 221,000 dwellings per annum, and therefore reject any suggestion that there is a shortage of land in strategic terms (JLRC, 1983). As can be seen from the joint land studies, this is indeed the conclusion based upon existing stocks and upon the policy premises of structure plan targets (based upon essentially demographic projections of real need). But important differences appear to underpin the basis of the calculations, including allowances for small sites, 'replacement' houses and proposed Structure Plan alterations, not included in the JLRC calculations (Swann and Long, 1982). These are some of the contentious issues between house builders and county planners revealed by the joint studies, and it is inevitable that they should form the basis of disagreement, since the methodology adopted systematically excludes them from the main focus of calculation.

If an examination is made not simply of the stocks of land, but of their rate of release, the situation becomes even more problematic. Virtually all of the joint studies, and espec- ially those in 'pressure' areas where containment policies are most consistently applied, indicate a steep reduction in the rate of annual dwelling completion over the first 5-year period. In some cases, this will involve "an annual produc- tion in years four and five below the expected annual rate of output taken from the Structure Plan housing policies". The estimate of the House Builders' Federation in 1981 was that in England "the Structure Plans would not allow an annual rate of build which exceeded 205,000 houses" a rate roughly approxi- mate to the 1979/1980 rate of completions "acknowledged to be the lowest totals for the last 50 years" (Dobson, 1981). Indeed, it is clear from the joint surveys that one of the reasons why stocks are not being depleted is the low annual rate of completions over the last four years. Yet, even taking this factor into account, several of the studies (e.g. Kent, Oxfordshire, Cumbria) identified potential shortages after the initial plan period (1985/1986), implying additional releases.

A further complication is that of the relationship between the rate of recent completions, and the strategic land use objectives of the Structure Plans. Several of the joint studies (Oxfordshire, Kent) indicate that planning policy is to reduce the annual rate of build in the latter part of the Plan period, in line with demographic projections. Indeed, the Oxfordshire study explicitly notes that "... the housing provisions in the Structure Plan should not be regarded as targets for growth", adding, "Some local plans have already been prepared in accordance with the principle of using a figure below the full Structure Plan housing provisions" (Oxford County Council and Oxfordshire District Councils/HBF, 1982).

This calls into question two aspects of 'land availability', firstly the derivation of projected building rates and secondly the status of 'land availability' policy in comparison with Structure Plan policy. In relation to projected building rates, most studies utilise the residual method advised by the Department of the Environment, calculating the rate on the basis of the number of dwellings remaining to be built by the end of the plan period, and assigning them to early or late phases of release (i.e. up to 1986 and to 1991). This residual method (used, for instance, in the Oxfordshire study) has been attacked by Mackie, who argues that the formula is dependent upon the relationship between the initial structure plan requirement, completions to date and the number of years left to run in the designated period. Where authorities experience below projected completion rates, the residual formula indicates further land release to meet an increasing 5-year requirement and vice versa (Planning 479, 1982). Effectively, this means that when housebuilding increases, restrictions will increase, and in non-pressure areas further land will tend to be allocated than is, in fact, required. This seems to be borne out by the joint studies published to date, and explains the pressured counties response to both maintain containment (in relation to projected demographic growth) and make ad-hoc releases in Local Plan designations. The example of Greater Manchester has indicated the reverse situation under conditions of reduced housebuilding activity. Inevitably, matching the Structure Plan provisions to land availability studies requires some assumptions to be made on completion rates, and the available evidence indicates that the current approach simply does not reflect market processes in any informed way. This is perhaps unsurprising given the difficulties associated with making allowances for such factors in Housing Investment Programmes and Strategies (Leather, 1979). It seems clear, in the absence of published information to the contrary, that the attempt to link HIPs and Structure Plans via regional offices of the DoE is bound to be a hit-and-miss affair in the absence of firm national and regional targets. Yet these targets will only have real meaning in terms of land supply if a more robust methodology is adhered to in monitoring and structuring the process of land conversion to housebuilding.

The precise status of policy in relation to land availability remains unclear. The effect of Circular 9/80 (DoE, 1980a), compounded by Circular 22/80 (DoE, 1980b), is to require a five year's supply of land for private housebuilding at all times, based upon a generous interpretation of genuine availability (along the lines indicated in the Greater Manchester Study). Crucially, "the amount and location of land required to make up that supply should now be derived from the housing policies and proposals if approved structure and local plans" (paragraph 4, Circular 9/80), and it is pointed out (paragraph 9) that "In determining planning appeals for residential development, the Secretary of State will take into account whether, in the context of the advice in this Circular, sufficient housebuilding land has been identified as available for development in the area of the district". Recent successful High Court challenges to the planning appeal decisions have confirmed (a) the legal obligation of the Secretary of State and planning inspectors to take into account the provisions of Circulars 9/80 and 22/80 (their "discretion becomes strictly limited by those policies (in circulars) just as if they were set out in a statute" (Purdue, 1982)), and (b) notwithstanding the existence of a joint housing land assessment, the approved structure and local plans must contain a provision for a 5-year supply of land. Arguments relating to proposed releases on Structure Plan review fall outside the thrust of Circulars 9/80 and 22/80.

It is in this light that Dobson's comment that "So far in none of the areas where a shortage has been identified has the local planning authority taken any action to make up the shortage by allocating additional land which can be utilised within the five year period" (1981) should be noted. As we have seen in the joint land availability studies, several counties propose such reviews nearer the critical period (1985/1986), yet in the light of Purdue's comments this may leave them exposed in any planning appeal. This makes Wenban-Smith's appeal for annual statements in relation to formal Structure Plan reviews particularly pertinent, especially in relation to the problems of peripheral restraint in the Metropolitan County areas. As he notes, whilst the Secretary of State has approved the basic containment strategy, he has nevertheless "exacerbated the problem by adding further peripheral land on approval and at appeal" (Wenban-Smith, 1983). Recent decisions by the Inspectorate in relation to Green Belt plans for Sheffield and Greater Manchester indicate that the arguments concerning land availability are increasingly likely to focus on Structure Plan policies in relation to Green Belt subject plans. The draft memorandum on structure and local plans has raised precisely that issue, in relation to the ability of local authorities to control not only the amount of land released, but its flow in terms of phasing.

It would appear that practical necessities will compel all parties concerned to return to first principles and re-examine the whole basis of the interrelationship between land allocation and land availability. It is clear that the current approach, whilst preserving a facade of co-operation between the main agents involved in the land conversion process, in fact serves to obscure the fundamental issues underlying land policy in relation to residential development.

7 Containment in Hertfordshire: changing attitudes to land release for new employment-generating development

MARTIN ELSON

INTRODUCTION

Since the 1950s local authorities in the South East outside London have operated policies of development restraint. These were designed to halt the spread of towns by reducing the rate of conversion of open land to urban uses to a minimum. Restraint has often been seen as the operation of green belt controls in isolation. This paper describes the links between restraint policies for employment and the land protection and conservation aims of one such local authority, Hertfordshire.

In response to continued demands for more land for employment uses and housing, and as a result of the new format of plans under the 1968 Planning Act, restraint has developed as a set of relationships between activity-based policies in structure plans and land-based policies in local plans. This relationship has come under strain as the local authorities have sought to adjust to rapid industrial change which has become manifest in the area since 1980.

This paper charts this process of adjustments in a situation where the usual mode of planning has been that of 'regulatory' development control and negotiation rather than promotional work. The paper therefore discusses the roles of different 'interests' - developers, development agents, land owners and local authorities in negotiating changes in planning policy.

It also includes discussion of the influence of different levels of administration - District, County and Central Government in the evolution of policy.

The detailed discussion relates to Dacorum District in Hertfordshire and is restricted to industrial and warehousing development. The need for rapid policy adjustment in the face of apparently irreversible decline, particularly in the manufacturing sector, is common throughout the country. Areas such as Hertfordshire are seen as increasingly important nationally as it is in such locations that finance for new development is readily available, and a change in attitudes to land is likely to result in the creation of new activity. Areas with good economic potential provide a valuable locale for investigation of the mechanisms of policy adjustment, the modification of the public interest orientation of planning authorities in the face of the market interest orientation of developers.

THE DEVELOPMENT OF POLICY

Restraint policies developed in response to pressures for development in the 1950s. At this time Hertfordshire was a growth County with four new towns; Hemel Hempstead, Welwyn Garden City, Hatfield and Stevenage, importing population at a faster rate than jobs could be provided. The first Development Plan in 1952 was concerned to manage this growth 'in order to maintain the attractive rural character of the County'. The idea of retaining the County environment, an area typified by medium sized towns and villages in an attractive setting, implied parsimony in the use of the County's land resources. It remains the mainspring of the land use policy stance. The first manifestation of this idea was containment, put into place by the approval of green belt policies in 1954. The close pattern of towns would thus retain their individual identities by the use of planning controls designed to avoid coalescence and preserve the countryside. The second policy was to allow the siting of a small amount of new employment-generating development, as found necessary, to provide jobs for the anticipated growth of the local population. The third preoccupation was to obtain the necessary investment in infrastructure (roads and sewerage) and other services (schools) to match growth and improve conditions for local residents.

The philosophy in respect of land release at this time is best expressed in Circular 42/55 (MHLG, 1955). Here towns in green belt zones were recommended to develop policies to deter job growth. If job growth did take place in a situation of labour shortage this would generate demands in green belt land for housing the resulting in-migrants thus defeating the environmental objectives of policy. By 1955, in response to this situation, informal employment policies, designed to restrict development to that by local firms only, had been approved for the south of the County. In the following five years they spread quickly to the remainder of the County (McNamara and Elson, 1981a).

After local government reorganisation, employment policies constituted an elaboration of these themes. Economic analysis suggested that the 'growth spiral' and its accompanying repetitive demands for more land for employment-generating development and housing would continue. Public participation suggested that the County had 'taken its share' of new growth and should concentrate on improving services to the existing population, keeping out new firms that would compete with existing firms for labour and, at the same time, protecting the environment. These attitudes had two-party political support at a time in the mid-1970s when there was strong representation of Labour and Conservative groups at County Hall. In response to these representations the 1976 Structure Plan evolved policies designed to 'balance' the need not to impair the efficiency and productivity of existing Hertfordshire firms with the strong locally-expressed environmental concerns. In creating this balance the County could instance the support of the Regional Strategy (SEJPT, 1970). However, this was not the decisive factor. Restraint was a locally-generated political imperative which planners sought to develop into a set of guidelines for the use of land and for development control.

ACTIVITY RESTRAINT

By the mid-1970s Hertfordshire had established a strong, healthy and varied industrial structure based on electronics, printing and paper, aerospace, medium and light engineering industries. During the period 1961-1971 employment in the County had grown at a faster rate than population. Accordingly the Structure Plan of 1976 aimed to work towards a balance of population, employment and housing in each District by 1991. In order to do this the population was projected assuming no changes in the balance of migration to and from the County. It was thus basically a natural increase calculation leading to a level of increase in jobs and housing to be aimed for in five year periods within the life of the Plan.

In considering the level of activity in terms of jobs that this population would require, labour supply and demand forecasts were made. The supply forecasts involved predicting the number who would be potentially economically active, deducting allowances for assumed levels of daily out-commuting, those changing jobs, and those not seeking jobs (the 'occupational pensioners'). The demand forecasts relied on a shift-share analysis by industrial sector, together with qualitative information on the likely performance of sectors in the future. Comparing supply and demand figures for future dates, the number of new jobs to be provided for within the policies in the Plan was established. The calculations indicated that the demand for labour across the County would probably exceed the labour supply by 26-29,000 by 1981 (Hertfordshire County Council, 1976).

In 1972 the County had produced a non-statutory development plan review, entitled 'Hertfordshire 1981', containing land allocations for industry and warehousing to 1981 (Hertfordshire County Council, 1972). When industrial land occupancy figures were applied to land with and without permission, but shown as committed in the Plan (194 hectares across the County), it was concluded that no new land releases were required over the 1976-1981 period. Outside areas shown for development, Metropolitan Green Belt policy applied in the south of the County, and green belt policies were to operate on an interim basis in the remainder.

The policies of the submitted structure plan stated that where a significant increase in employment was proposed permission would be refused unless the applicant could demonstrate to the local planning authorities that it was essential in the national or regional interest, or desirable in the local interest, for the activity to be located in the County. Development would be restricted to 'limited' expansion of existing Hertfordshire firms which the planning authorities were satisfied needed to remain in the County. Where it could be established that firms did not need to remain in the County they would be encouraged to relocate elsewhere in accordance with regional policies. Permissions would be subject to occupancy and named user conditions. There was some support for appropriate provision for small firms on redevelopment sites and in other cases where provision was acceptable in local planning terms. Prophetically the Plan also stated that in the event of a marked and prolonged deterioration in the overall employment situation in any District, appropriate new firms would be permitted into Hertfordshire on land committed for industrial development.

In the case of regional warehouses applicants would have to
show a need to be located in the County. All warehouses were
to be sited within the 1976-1981 land allocations in
'Hertfordshire 1981'. Only warehouses serving the local
community would be acceptable in principle, although in all
cases it would have to be established to the satisfaction of
the planning authorities that land already allocated for
industry would not need to be reserved for an existing
Hertfordshire industrial firm (Hertfordshire County Council,
1976).

These policies, restrictive in nature, suggest the erection
of a set of hurdles which applicants must argue around to
establish the principle of development (there are, in
addition, other layout, site coverage and environmental
guidelines). Applicants from outside had to provide a range
of justifications as to why they should locate in the County
or District. In practice this went some way towards reversing
the onus of proof which normally obtains in development
control. The policies were designed primarily to reduce the
amount of new land required to be released. Any significant
employment proposal which would cause housing demand to arise,
which could not then be accommodated within existing
settlements, would be refused for this reason. The policies
were designed also to exclude speculative development in that
the planning case was argued in terms of the characteristics
of the industrial or warehouse <u>activity</u> proposed. Without
knowledge of an occupier's activities no assessment could be
made. They are also designed to husband the remaining land
resources with the benefit of planning permission. Accepting
'non-essential' activities would use up committed land too
quickly, thus putting pressure on the authorities for more
land release.

The number, style and wording of these policies resulted in
a forum for the process of development control with particular
attributes. Firstly, they invited extensive negotiation over
the principle of development in addition to that over detailed
matters which prevails in non-restraint areas. The
negotiation is invited from a set of presumptions <u>against</u>
permission thus giving maximum strength to the local
authorities in the negotiating process. In order to conduct
this negotiation applicants have, without exception, used
agents. Local agents, because of their knowledge of the
nuances of restraint, have handled around eighty per cent of
the proposals for new development. For their part the local
authorities have developed a battery of monitoring information
much of which can be used to effect in such negotiations to
sustain activity-based arguments. Secondly, the policies

include wide scope for discretion by the local authorities in what they will choose to regard as locally-acceptable development. For example, the definition of what amounts to a 'significant increase' in employment has no specific numerical connotation. Significance is related to the number and composition of the workforce in the proposal in relation to that available in the District, and is therefore a one-off assessment. What constitutes an employment increase that would cause unacceptable housing demands is also an element of discretion. Also whether a proposal involves a new activity, as opposed to an increase in an existing activity, is a matter of interpretation. Analysis of the full policy text for industry and warehousing alone suggests that there are fifteen such points of discretion included (Underwood, J., 1981).

POLICIES IN ACTION

In order to demonstrate these policies in action an analysis was undertaken of one policy area, Dacorum District, in West Hertfordshire. Having a population of 11,000 in 1971 and 12,000 in 1981 the District is centred in Hemel Hempstead New Town and includes Berkhamsted and Tring. There are narrow tracts of open land between the main settlements which the planning authorities and local residents are keen to preserve. The physical setting is particularly attractive with two of the three towns lying adjacent to the Chilterns AONB. This, combined with the ease of commuting, and the presence in the area of expanding manufacturing and warehousing companies (especially in the scientific and high technology sectors in Hemel Hempstead), has led to severe pressures for land release. The main Maylands Avenue area of Hemel Hempstead (Figure 1) represents a particularly attractive location to industrialists offering the potential of large freehold greenfield sites under one mile from an existing M1 Motorway junction and within three miles of a proposed M25 junction. Most of the small amount of land allocated for development is in the ownership of the Commission for New Towns (CNT).

As already stated policies expressed a concern to husband allocated land in a situation where the County were concerned about the 'abundance of their commitments' in terms of outstanding planning permissions (DoE, 1977). This had the effect of maintaining the 'monopoly' positions of the very few owners of such land. As these were only willing to develop under certain terms, only limited types of industrial and warehousing financing arrangements could be contemplated by those seeking to develop. The most attractive greenfield sites were in the ownership of the CNT. Here the CNT were

willing to sell serviced land to firms who would pay
industrial land values. Planning policies meant that land had
to be sold to local firms with specific proposals for
development or the more attenuated process of establishing
regional or national need entered into. Firms have commonly
developed using sale and leaseback arrangements with financial
institutions. In Tring the main industrial land, allocated as
a result of a departure from the County Development Plan in
1965, was owned by a small industrial developer. His
intention was to obtain tenants for purpose built premises who
would bring the highest and most secure rates of return. The
finance for this enterprise was not dependent on institutional
involvement. The site was marketed as an entrepot for firms
from the Midlands and North seeking a base within reach of
Heathrow where goods could be repackaged prior to air freight,
or as a southern distribution point. Owing to its location
and the traffic problems of the A41, this site is much less
attractive than the CNT land. Development has, consequently,
been slow with much conflict between the local authorities and
the developer over the acceptability of proposed occupiers.
In the absence of restraint policies such a developer would
have erected premises on a speculative basis. The third
opportunity was for the development and redevelopment of
existing land in the ownership of statutory undertakers (old
railway and gas works land), and the fourth was for the
redevelopment of some of the paper mills, historically sited
along the Gade Valley, but undergoing a period of rapid
rationalisation and change.

During the period 1974-1979 the restraint policies acted as
a powerful deterrent to certain types of firm. Over ninety
per cent of applications were from within the County. The
deflection process operated by three main mechanisms. Firstly
agents, well aware of the firmness of the policy and unwilling
to compromise their relationships with the planning
authorities, would only submit applications which they
considered had a reasonable likelihood of success within the
policy. Secondly, the planners dealing with inquirers would
suggest that firms consider 'growth' areas nearby such as
Milton Keynes, Aylesbury, Northampton or Peterborough.
Thirdly, from 1975, the County operated a system of sending
lists of planning applications for industry and warehousing to
the growth areas, and to local authorities in the Development
Areas such as South Wales. The best example of deflection is
the proposal for over 250 new jobs in the British Standards
Institution in Hemel Hempstead which, following negotiations,
located in Milton Keynes.

The attitude of the planning authorities would normally be

clear before an application was formally submitted. As a result only eighteen per cent of new manufacturing floorspace was refused in the period, and the level for redevelopment and change of use was lower than this (see Table 1). The land take proposed for new development was fifty one hectares but this was reduced by half largely by refusal of warehousing applications (see Table 2). Approximately three quarters of the land approved was already located in development plans. Certainly the land-based containment aims of planning were secured during the period.

Table 1

Applications and Floorspace in Applications for Employment
Generating Development: Dacorum 1974-1979

	applica-tions	1000 sq.m.	refused 1000 sq.m.	percent refused (floorspace)
manufacturing				
new	18	43.7	8.1	18
redevelopment	66	37.9	6.3	13
change of use	14	11.1	1.3	12
warehousing				
new	20	78.7	17.3	22
redevelopment	26	56.3	12.0	21
change of use	5	3.2	3.2	12

Source: Terry and Elson 1981

Table 2

Proposed Land Take in Applications for New Employment-
Generating Development: Dacorum 1974-1979

	hectares in applications	refused (hectares)	per cent of land in refusals
manufacturing	11.86	2.35	20
warehousing	39.40	23.45	59

The second aim of restricting development by firms from outside the County was also, on the whole, effective. Six out of seven large speculative warehousing proposals were resisted as was one of three manufacturing proposals. There were no new warehousing applications from named firms from London and the rest of the South East, and three of the four manufacturing applications within the same category were refused (see Table 3). Data on conditions suggest that over ninety per cent of new industrial and warehousing approvals had Hertfordshire named user and occupier restrictions (Terry and Elson, 1981).

Table 3

Planning Decision by Proposed Occupant:
Dacorum District: 1974-1979

proposal/ occupant	number of applications	number refused	number of applications	number refused
	manufacturing		warehousing	
speculative	3	1	7	6
5+ years on site	45	7	12	3
-5 years on site	10	0	12	2
in Hertfordshire	21	3	15	6
rest of South East	4	3	-	-
not known	15	4	14	6

These data refer to primary uses. The low cut-off points are 140 sq.m. for manufacturing and 280 sq.m. for warehousing.

Source: Terry and Elson (1981)

The third major policy, that of limiting development to some expansion of existing firms that could justify a need to remain in the County, and which did not have significant employment effects, was not implemented. Local (District) elected representatives were not willing to hinder the extension of local premises or to see them removed from the area. In any case the Structure Plan was posited on the view that policies would not be so severe as to harm the efficiency and productivity of existing firms. At the Examination in

Public of the Plan in 1976, local firms and the CNT argued that this policy conflicted with the above general intention of the Plan (DoE, 1977).

From detailed case studies of individual applications it is clear that the District Council were more inclined to take each proposal 'on its merits' adhering to the more simple land-based guidelines in 'Hertfordshire 1981'. The County, on the other hand, sought to operate the policies using their activity-based criteria. The District would not use activity arguments in isolation as reasons for refusal preferring to keep to land allocation, green belt, and other more familiar and tested planning reasons.

The major points to emerge from the 1974-1979 period are the following. Employment policy only impinged on some readjustments to market conditions or changes in investment; those resulting in the change of use of a building, the erection of a new building, or changes in the external appearance of premises. It would be quite possible for large changes in manning levels for example to occur without any recourse to the planning authorities, if no physical development was required to effect the change. Many firms became skilled in the art of re-organising their utilization of space to avoid the need for permission, a process similar to that noted by Hall (Hall, 1973).

Secondly, the effects of the policy are perceived as arbitrary by industrialists and development agents. For example a firm situated less than a mile outside the boundary of Dacorum was refused permission to move into the District because it was an 'outsider' firm. Yet a firm from Royston over sixty miles away would , other factors being equal, be in accord with policy. (The firm involved subsequently obtained permission after showing it would not create new housing demands in Hertfordshire as virtually all its employees already lived within the County). Another firm, ostensibly a warehouse from another part of Hertfordshire, was in the position of having to prove that the allocated land upon which it sought permission was not required by a Hertfordshire industrialist. However, following negotiation it transpired that the firm also carried out activities which 'added value' to the products stored by assembly. It therefore could be seen also as manufacturing and was released from the need to satisfy the criterion. In order to prove a need to be in the County, some warehousing applicants hired agents to carry out property searches over large parts of the north west sector of the Metropolitan Green Belt zone to establish that no other suitable premises were available. One firm produced an analysis of forty-five alternative properties over three counties, suggesting why they were not suitable. At this point the authorities considered that sufficient effort had been made to find an alternative and granted permission. However, the criterion of need to be in the County that they had satisfied was related to local property conditions and not the definition of need in the Structure Plan.

In summary, policies benefitted employers and firms already in Hertfordshire by allowing in-situ expansion and relocation, and affording protection from labour competition by incoming firms. In doing this they aided locally-based multinational firms as well as those providing a local service. They accommodated locational readjustment within Hertfordshire (one of the largest categories of proposals approved – Table 3), but altered the intentions of industrialists if readjustment involved crossing the County administrative boundary. As employment conditions within London deteriorated in the 1970s this was fully supported by the GLC who wished to see even firmer restraint of employment in Hertfordshire. The policies to restrict new greenfield developments made the redevelopment and expensive refurbishment of industrial premises a feasible proposition and, until recently, this has been the main opportunity for new institutional investment. Redevelopment has been the main vehicle for any change in the profile of development interests active in the area.

The major exceptions to policy have been based on national interest arguments. A development involving 275 jobs in aerospace was permitted in Hemel Hempstead in 1976 based on national defence arguments. Although directly against all the arguments of matching available skills to skills demanded by incoming employers, in that it sought just the mainly graduate scientific skills so short in the County at the time (and thus likely to create maximum housing demand due to inmigration on the national job market), the County was unable to resist Central Government pressure. Thus with locally-based firms catered for, and with some large firms using national interest arguments successfully, those discriminated against by the policies were medium sized, and some large 'mobile' firms who had no premises in Hertfordshire prior to investigating possible sites there, and could adduce no particular reason to be in the County. The policy therefore sought to hold down the level of activity to that suited to local needs but was not fully successful in controlling the types of activity generated to those serving local community needs. The level of success achieved depended on, primarily, the deterrent effect of policies and their long history of application in the County. There was little challenge on appeal during the

1974-1979 period, and no significant appeal decision went
against the County's policies in our study area.

ACTIVITY POLICIES AND LAND

From the submission of the Structure Plan in 1976 to its
modification and approval in 1979, we are thus tracing a
period where the supply of new industrial land in Dacorum was
drying up. By 1977 the Commission for the New Towns were
claiming that no new sites in their ownership (that is sites
not already under negotiation) were available. In the 1971-
1977 period, permissions had been granted for the development
of a number of sites at Area A on Figure 1, the majority of
which were for firms requiring extra space, but already
located on the same industrial estate. Many of the 'high
growth' computer companies have a number (up to six or seven)
of separate sites in the town as a result. An area of land at
Three Cherry Trees Lane (Area B in Figure 1) indicated in
'Hertfordshire 1981' as 'for users with a very low employment
potential' was granted permission before 1974.

In 1976 and 1977 a number of major applications were made on
CNT land adjacent to the industrial allocations. Two are of
particular interest. The first, a proposal to site a regional
food distribution warehouse, was on land where permission had
been granted for a warehouse ancillary to an existing locally-
based manufacturer in 1974. Although not allocated in the
development it was therefore a 'soft' site. The proposal was
large involving over 10,000 square metres of warehousing and
the creation of 200-250 jobs. The applicant was clearly a
non-local firm but produced a computerised model showing Hemel
Hempstead as its optimal location. The County argued that the
existing permission was not a general commitment but was a
commitment only for local needs, that is development ancillary
to existing manufacturing industry. The applicant had not
demonstrated a need to be in Hertfordshire. The District
Development Control Committee were in favour of the
development and, advised by their officers, felt that the
arguments about a local versus non-local commitment and need
to be in the County would not be sustainable at appeal. Local
unemployment figures showed that the jobs could be filled from
within the Town (Smith, 1979).

The second case, an application by a Dacorum based computer
manufacturing company was again large (7,500 square metres of
manufacturing together with offices) and was on land with no
notation in 'Hertfordshire 1981'. Although adjacent to the
then existing land allocations this was land treated by the

local authorities as 'land over which green belt policies applied' (it was not formally approved MGB). The new premises would allow the firm to concentrate its activities, at that time on six separate sites in Hemel Hempstead, on to one site. It was therefore considered by the applicants to be a relocation in the interests of the efficiency and productivity of this existing local firm. The County was of the view that green belt policies should prevail and that the case made by the firm to remain in the Town was not strong enough. As this was a local firm seeking to improve its productivity and as the firm would lose its main resource, highly qualified staff, if forced to move out of the area, the District felt the proposal should be approved. Although County and District members could not agree a common approach to the proposal, planning permission was granted. The permission was not taken up by the first applicant but by another, this time multinational, computer manufacturing company already with premises in Hemel Hempstead.

Thus by the time the local plan was being prepared in 1978-1979 decisions on industrial and warehousing proposals were pre-empting its content. Another delaying factor was the length of time taken to approve the Structure Plan and the changes to policy introduced by the Secretary of State. Statutory planning was lagging behind decisions emerging from the interplay of development interests represented by the Commission for the New Towns, restraint interests represented by the County Council and local pressure groups in Dacorum, and the more pragmatic and facilitatory approach of District Councillors.

In his amendments to the Structure Plan, the Secretary of State deleted the policy that only 'limited' provision should be made for existing locally-based firms, replacing it with a statement that 'adequate' provision should be made. Also the restriction of permissions to committed land as of 1976 was deleted, as it was considered unduly restrictive. This gave Districts scope to switch commitments around in their areas within the totals implied by the labour supply estimates of the Plan. These proposals went some way to satisfying the CNT who had argued at the Structure Plan EIP that there was insufficient scope for in-situ expansion, relocation within the County, or for locally-arising new firms in the policies of the Plan.

By 1980 the County had submitted alterations to the Structure Plan which revised the control totals for Dacorum from land for 4,100 jobs in the 1976-1986 period to land for 5,000-5,400 jobs. Trends towards lower worker density in industrial and warehousing premises were acknowledged by a reduction of the assumed density for industry from 140 to 100 persons per hectare of allocated land (Hertfordshire County Council, 1981). The local plan calculations, published in 1981 and based on the amended Structure Plan of 1980, are shown in Table 4. Importantly they assume:

(a) that 1976-1979 permissions will be taken up;

(b) that there is land within existing industrial curti-lages which can be considered part of the land supply; and

(c) that there are some small vacant sites that will be taken up.

Based on this calculation new land for 1,500 jobs was required to be allocated in the local plan. Some 16.2 hectares over and above that in the 1972 Development Plan were shown, the majority of it in the Maylands Avenue area of Hemel Hempstead.

Table 4

Assessment of Employment Potential: Dacorum District

i. Jobs provided for by implementation of permissions (industry, warehousing, offices) October 1976–September 1979	1000
ii. Jobs provided for by shopping permissions October 1976–September 1979	300
iii. Vacant sites (excluding land within curtilages)	200
iv. Land within curtilages of existing firms	1400
v. Shopping proposals (estimated)	500
vi. Office proposals (estimated)	100
TOTAL	3500

Source: Response to CNT objections to 1981 Deposited Local Plan, (Dacorum District Council, 1980).

Much of the land already allocated had planning permission and some had buildings which were already occupied. In the Hemel Hempstead area (Area C, Figure 1) only small amounts remained. As soon as it was shown in the Draft Plan, negotiations with developers commenced such that by the time of the Local Plan Inquiry all of the allocated land was either the subject of permissions or was at advanced stages of negotiation. CNT claimed at the Local Plan Inquiry that of the 14.5 hectares identified in the Plan for industry for the 1976-1986 period some 11.3 hectares had already received planning approval by May 1981.

At the local plan inquiry there were six objections to the employment land allocations and two further objections to the general tenor of employment policies in the Plan (DoE, 1981). The CNT, as major objectors, sought to demonstrate that there was insufficient new land zoned for industry and warehousing in view of the speed of take up of allocated land and that increases in local unemployment - a significant factor from the middle of 1980 - made it imperative that more land be released. They suggested the allocation of a nine hectare site, adjacent to existing allocations, which had already been serviced by the CNT (Area D, Figure 2).

By this time local planning was being overtaken by macro-economic circumstances. For the first time in thirty years the County was experiencing a wave of large firm closures mainly in the older engineering and print and paper industries. In the 1976-1980 period, notified redundancies had run at 2,500 to 3,500 per year in the County. In Dacorum, notified redundancies increased sixfold between 1976-1979 and 1980-1981. In the year 1980-1981 there were over 10,000 in the County (although they have since reduced in 1982). Of course, internal company processes of rationalization, product innovation and new investment, now well documented by other studies, were having increased impacts on the rate of local unemployment (Massey and Meegan, 1982). Such changes, not amenable to monitoring or prediction by planners, shifted the emphasis of the 'activity balance' arguments in the County. Instead of trying to keep labour demands down to the level arising from the local population the local authorities were now faced, despite the use of more land for industry, with trying to increase labour demand to soak up unemployment. This now became the new de facto definition of local need. How has it been expressed and what are the implications for land?

POLICY ADJUSTMENTS

Concern about unemployment has been articulated through district councillors and local trades union and employers organizations. This led to negotiations between District Councils and the County with a view to the selective removal of certain constraints. The 1980 Act gave the District more power to determine planning applications and many of the criteria for justifying local need were being interpreted more liberally in the face of rising unemployment. In Dacorum unemployment rose from 3.2 per cent in May 1980 to 11.4 per cent in September 1982. In 1981 the County relaxed occupancy controls on small industrial units of under 235 square metres, reflecting what was already increasingly occurring at local level, as well as advice about small firms contained in Circular 22/80 (DoE, 1980b, Hertfordshire County Council, 1981).

Unemployment in the County rose from 10,000 in early 1979 to 30,000 in late 1981. As a result, studies were carried out to establish whether employment losses were permanent or whether they would be replaced should there be an upturn in the economy. From information on company intentions, redundancies and other sources, it was concluded that 'some 10-12,000 full-time jobs net have been lost, which are unlikely to be recreated'. As a result policies have been adjusted to allow an additional 5,000 manufacturing and 2,000 service jobs into the County.

The policy now allows outsider firms to locate in Hertfordshire on sites identified for redevelopment only, not on green field sites. In Dacorum some 2-3,000 jobs were considered to be associated with possible industrial redevelopment sites, and some offices with a regional function would be allowed into Hemel Hempstead (Hertfordshire County Council, 1982).

These policy adjustments are based on the view that around two thirds of the jobs lost are cyclical in nature and only one third is 'structural' unemployment. The location of 12,000 more jobs in the County, it is argued, would then recreate the 'balance' sought in structure plan policies. However, the full balance is only restored if the other 18,000 jobs reappear as a result of an economic upturn. There is no evidence of this latter part of the equation occurring. It is significant that in Dacorum the refinements do not imply the release of any more land. Thus the environmental aims of the Plan will be protected by a new two-tier property market; the first reserving the remaining greenfield sites for locally-based firms, the second involving only redevelopment sites for

outsiders.   This overlies the old two-tier market of land and
premises with and without local user conditions.

At the local level however, events have taken a different
turn.   In Dacorum, industrial land supply for the ten years to
1986 based on a local needs criterion, had been used up by
1982.   The number of houses built in the 1976-1981 period was
almost   double that allowed for in the   Structure   Plan.   The

local authorities proposed, in order to return to a state of
balance by the late 1980s, that excess rates of development
should be 'recouped' by reducing rates of development later in
the plan period.   The Inspector at the LPI contended that
whilst some measure of retrenchment should occur it should be
spread over a ten year period from 1981 to 1991.   This
involved Dacorum District recasting their local plan for this
new longer time period.   At the same time the Department of
the Environment objected to the definition of green belt
boundaries, coincident with the limits of land allocations, in
the local plan.   They argued that areas of land should be left
between allocated land and the green belt to allow for the
longer term needs for development in the area.   In the interim
such areas would be protected by 'special restraint policies',
although it is difficult to escape the view that these
represent the re-creation of white land as under Circular
50/57 (MHLG, 1957).

Faced with the need to allocate a further five year supply
of land for employment, and the increasing worries of local
councillors over job losses, the District in 1982 made their
most bold move away from restraint.   The revised Local Plan of
1982 allocates the nine hectare site, sought by CNT at the
Local Plan Inquiry, in Hemel Hempstead for industry from 1986-
1991 together with a small area of two hectares for a local
computer machinery company in negotiation with the authority
at the time of drawing up the Plan (Areas D and E,   Figure 2).
They have also indicated a thirty hectare site north of the
Lane as 'land reserved for long term industrial development'
(Area F,   Figure 2).   These two 'allocations' mark the largest
area of land identified in Dacorum for industrial development
since the pre-restraint days of the First Review of the County
Development Plan in 1964.   The thirty acre site is to be:

"... considered as potential industrial land,
the timing of its development being subject to
the results of monitoring the availability of
industrial land and a review of employment
structure". (Dacorum District Council, 1982).

143

It had previously been the subject of deemed permission for 600 local authority dwellings in 1976. The nine hectare site scheduled for development post-1986 now has the following qualifications attached:

"... in order to prevent premature incursions into land intended for development later in the Plan period proposals for employment-generating development on new sites other than these identified will be resisted unless it can be shown that there are no suitable alternative sites within existing industrial areas". (Dacorum District Council, 1982).

A second local plan inquiry has recently taken place and the Inspector's Report is awaited.

It would appear from this sequence of events that the criteria for land release at local level are changing in response to pressure from local and national interests. A situation akin to a rolling supply of industrial land is being created because the criterion of activity balance suggested by the County in the 1970s is so far from being realised. In 1977 it was difficult for applicants to obtain permission on the argument that there was no other suitable land available. Now if this can be demonstrated, part of the 1986-1991 land reserve will, it appears, be brought forward. Some scope for discretion is maintained by local authority power to interpret the term 'available'.

The 1982-1983 annual County assessment of policies has found that permissions for the 10-12,000 'slack' in the activity-balance equation have not been forthcoming and so the relaxation will be continued for a further year. In response to likely pressures for warehousing from the M25 the County approved, in January 1983, the identification of warehousing land in local plans, but only within redevelopment sites. A promotional campaign to explain the logic of restraint policies is also being mounted in 1983. It will stress that high technology industry will be welcome in the County on existing industrial sites and allocations as long as there is a production component to the project (Hertfordshire County Council, 1983).

The situation in 1983 thus contrasts starkly with that of 1977. At a time when some land restraints are easing, the volume of mobile activity (firms) is at a very low level. There is no shortage of investment capital willing to create speculative industrial space in the County but bowing to such

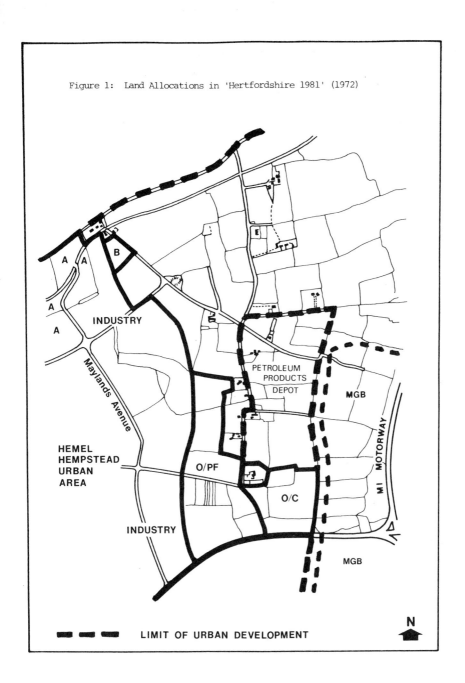

Figure 1: Land Allocations in 'Hertfordshire 1981' (1972)

A A A
B
A
A
INDUSTRY
Maylands Avenue
PETROLEUM PRODUCTS DEPOT
MGB
HEMEL HEMPSTEAD URBAN AREA
O/PF
O/C
M1 MOTORWAY
INDUSTRY
MGB

N

■ ■ ■ ■ LIMIT OF URBAN DEVELOPMENT

145

pressure would not solve the County's problems. Using Hertfordshire as a location to store the capital of the pension funds in buildings will not solve the County's unemployment problem if they are not occupied. Thus the County has sought to restrict this activity to redevelopment sites. There is more vacant industrial property in the County, some of it modern, than at any time since 1947, yet the pressures are for more greenfield development and the newly fashionable high specification industrial parks in green settings. The attitude in 1983 is that every effort will be made to accommodate genuine industrial activity, as opposed to speculative development, in the County. Deflection is no longer part of the vacabulary of local planners.

The District, on the other hand, may be accused of confusing the allocation of land with the creation of new activity which will reduce employment. At a time when the need is to create, generate and sustain economic activity allocating land per se will do little. So the argument now, as before, centres on the terms under which industrial location or relocation will be allowed to take place. The County is urging outsiders to keep to (more costly) redevelopment sites, the development industry is seeking the (more profitable) greenfield sites. If Hertfordshire refuses outsiders permission on new greenfield sites, will other Counties in the outer South East lure them away? If relaxation of land restraints occurs then the local population will have to put up with the physical extension of towns and continued impetus in the demand for more housing. This latter solution has been resisted in the past. But, in 1983, can the County both locate the new jobs it needs and pursue its environmental and containment aims in the same way?

CONCLUSIONS

What has been traced here is an experiment in activity based planning policies, devised as a technical planning solution to a locally-politically acceptable set of priorities. It was blown off course by macro-economic and intra-industry changes, the local implications of which could not be foreseen. These in turn had repercussions on local perceptions of the priorities for land use planning, which have dictated that adjustments be made. Some would argue that there has been a basic change in policy stance towards employment-generating development, although for sound tactical reasons the new, more relaxed criteria for assessing applications still operate under the banner of restraint.

The link between land and activity was easier to manage using old-style development plans as both elements were contained within one document and were 'managed' by one group of elected politicians. The two-tier system was envisaged by the County as manageable in the same way. The ten District Plans would add up to the equivalent of the old Plan. However, in post-1980 conditions policies emanate from County and District levels with the latter increasingly making initiatives independent of the flow of intelligence from the former.

In technical terms the link depends on assumptions about such matters as the take-up of planning permissions, vacant land, and the levels of occupancy of industrial space. For example, if it were assumed that only eighty per cent of past commitments were to be taken up in any five year period, then greater amounts of land would require to be released. Similarly it were assumed that the density of occupancy of industrial sites was 60-65 per hectare (as in the Greater Manchester Structure Plan) instead of the 100 in Hertfordshire then, again, further land would be required to be released. The calculation of these factors and assessments of land supposedly 'available' within existing curtilages are all variables as important as determining the acreage of land identified in plans as variations in the definition of local need or locally desirable development.

It has been clear for a number of years that the relationship between activity levels and extra increments of working space is breaking down. For example one proposal which obtained an Industrial Development Certificate for 4,500 sq.m. involved twenty jobs; another warehouse of 22,000 sq.m. involved less than ten jobs. Indeed extra space may now be associated with a reduction in numbers employed. It is instructive to note that Park Royal Estate in West London has now only 29,000 employees whereas there were 45,000 on the same site area in 1966 (Bernard Thorpe and Partners, 1981). This would imply that the more modern Maylands Avenue Estate in Hemel Hempstead would have to increase in area by over one third in under twenty years to retain the same numbers in employment (see Fothergill and Gudgin, 1982). Acceptance of such changed relationships would involve a considerable reassessment of containment policies in the County and the adoption of quite different attitudes to the loss of agricultural land.

What emerges from case studies is the crudeness or bluntness of the land use planning tool. The task involves an attempt to balance skills in the emerging labour force with the skill requirements of firms applying for planning permission. Without any reliable information on either at the local level, it has proved an unrealistic task in practice. The objective of isolating and providing for the implications of employment change in terms of <u>new land</u> seems even more probable. It is more realistic to see the planners as performing the quasi-political task of minimising the amount of land taken as a result of the pressures placed upon it. The restraint policy stance is a way of minimising these pressures in the first place.

Land is only of importance to industrialists when they cannot obtain it in the location they consider is essential to them. A number of plans in Northern England, such as those for Greater Manchester and Tyne and Wear, have set out to make land an insignificant restraint in industrialists' decisions. Any restraint policy imposes costs even if they are only psychological in having to adjust to expanding on a site 'up the road' instead of adjacent to existing premises. As such policies have Ministerial approval we must presume that the costs of restraint to industry of regional and national economic importance were seen as acceptable (although, of course, they have never been quantified). This was so in the past when mobile jobs were in greater supply. Now it is argued that it is in the national interest for Hertfordshrie to free up far more land for employment-generating development. At the same time the Department of Industry argue, the green belt can be maintained.

If central government wants to change the policy stance from a local needs to a rational needs criterion, it has a number of alternatives. It can alter Structure Plans and Local Plans, it can allow appeals or, more indirectly, it can issue Circulars. At present both the Department of Industry and Environment would like to see a loosening of restraint policies in Hertfordshire. In abandoning regional planning the Government has lost one of the levers it had to enforce the national over the local interest. Informal negotiation and officer level contacts between the two levels are perhaps the processes most in use with alterations to statutory plans representing the results of these negotiations.

This account suggests that formal plans play a restricted role in identifying new land. The <u>process</u> of plan making provides a forum where the stronger interests can assert their positions and shift the consensus. Dacorum's experience with local planning suggests that formal local planning is not a forum for reconciling interests. Where they may be basically irreconcileable we find a continuous renegotiation of the

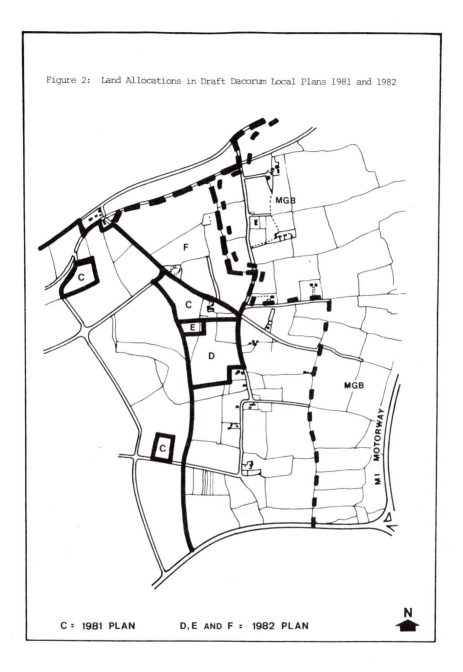

Figure 2: Land Allocations in Draft Dacorum Local Plans 1981 and 1982

C = 1981 PLAN   D, E AND F = 1982 PLAN

apparent status quo rendering the criteria for development control more and more tenuous. In 1982 the interests that gained the upper hand were the development interests, especially the CNT. They did this because District elected representatives came round to the view, for the first time in twenty years, that much more industrial land was needed. The local environmental lobby had not got any weaker but it had nevertheless lost ground. This is because the two elements of the local interest, environmental protection and the need to protect local firms from outsider competition for their labour, had diverged. The intervention of the DoE over the green belt issue was as much occasioned by a substantive concern to loosen restraint as a procedural one to gain adherence to a twenty-five year old Circular.

If the local authorities cannot mediate conflicts of interest at the local level then the case for some mediation at higher levels of administration seems clear. However, central government is not able to deliver this. The Ministry of Agriculture are stating that it is in the national interest to retain agricultural land and the Department of Industry are stating that new high technology industries will have to be allowed to grow adjacent to existing concentrations of expertise. Is it in the national interest to open up the outer South East to development? Will the twin costs of leaving infrastructure already provided in the northern regions unused, and paying for new infrastructure in the South East for new development, be a wise use of national resources? The answer is that some powerful sections of the present Government have decided it is the only course open as the depth and intractability of employment problems are appreciated.

PART II
MECHANISMS AND AGENCIES FOR INTERVENTION IN LAND DEVELOPMENT PROCESSES

Introduction

SUSAN BARRETT

The six papers grouped together under this heading in many ways build upon and elaborate the discussion emerging from Part I concerning the appropriateness of existing intervention mechanisms and agencies in the face of economic change. The papers challenge some of the conventional wisdoms concerning the nature of the development process, the interactions taking place between groups of actors involved in it, and the role of state intervention in a mixed economy. They also raise questions about conceptual constructs and methodologies appropriate to the study of land policy and the development process.

These, like the earlier papers, tend to take as their focus substantive policy issues or recent policy initiatives and relate them directly or indirectly to the political and economic changes of the past decade. Superficially at least, many of the policy shifts associated with this decade appear to have been motivated by criticisms of governmental effectiveness, including lack of efficiency, inappropriate use of powers and lack of responsiveness to changing circumstances. Underlying the managerial language of such criticisms is the more fundamental debate concerning the supremacy of the state versus the market as the mechanism for allocating scarce resources. In the arena of land policy, state intervention in furtherance of 'the public interest', impinges very directly on individual property rights and economic interests. As a result, the managerial and political dimensions of the effectiveness debate often merge and become confused in divergent definitions of the meaning and proper scope of the public interest. The papers pick up in turn issues of efficiency, interpretation and use of intervention powers and responsiveness to change. In so doing they also expose the importance of conceptual and ideological constructs in shaping the manner in which policy 'problems' and 'solutions' are defined.

The first two papers look at policy issues which have featured on the political agenda throughout the history of the contemporary planning system - land availability and public sector land holdings. Central to the current debate, and embodied in the provisions of the 1980 Local Government, Planning and Land Act, is the view that public agencies are failing or inefficient in carrying out their responsibilities for managing the use of land. On the one hand local planning authorities are seen as failing to ensure that land is available to meet development 'needs'; on the other, public agencies are characterised as poor estate managers and are criticised for excessive holding of vacant or under-used land.

Cuddy and Hollingsworth, in their paper on housing land availability studies, accept the inefficiency argument in so far as they consider that local planning authorities failed to pay enough attention to development feasibility (in both physical and market terms) when allocating land or granting planning permission in response to the government's land supply 'panic' during the early 1970s development boom. Lack of any review of subsequent take up of permissions led, in their view, to undevelopable land being counted in later assessments of land availability. This fuelled the housebuilders' pressure on central government and led to the joint House Builders Federation (HBF)/local authority land availability studies, which resulted in the 5 year land supply requirement subsequently reinforced by sanctions in the 1980 Act. However, from their review of the evolution, methodology and results of joint HBF/local authority land availability exercises, they argue that it would be wrong to see such studies as providing a mechanism for central government to implement its policies or as an objective analysis of land needs. Rather they suggest that the agreements reached between local authorities and housebuilders represent bargains struck between parties pursuing strategies and tactics in the furtherance of their own interests. They see what is going on in such studies as a process of negotiation in which neither party to the negotiation has control over its own delivery system. It is not a simple win/lose game, but a strategic negotiation for flexibility of manoeuvre in an uncertain environment. Both parties stand to gain from not committing themselves to a firm outcome 'contract' yet maintaining the negotiation process. Thus the authors argue that the main value of the studies lies in the process itself as a basis for reviewing performance, and as a means of learning more about the short/medium term flow of land through the development process.

Gore and Nicholson also emphasise the importance of understanding the dynamics of land conversion (a theme addressed earlier by Hooper) as a basis for developing a framework for the analysis of public landownership. Their paper is based on research into the extent and causes of vacant and publicly owned urban land in South Wales. Essentially they argue that studies of vacant land stocks have little value unless carried out within a conceptual framework which:

a) enables vacancy to be disaggregated according to the points in the development process at which it occurs; and

b) offers a means of linking the existence of vacancy to influences outside the development process.

They use a variation of the pipeline model developed by Barrett, Stewart and Underwood (1978) to demonstrate the clustering of their survey sites at specific stages in the development process: use, construction, beginning and end of development feasibility, and in the stock of redundant buildings. Their case study work suggests that the apparent clustering of sites at various stages may disguise differences between them in development prospects, which will be differentially influenced by the complex interaction of external factors with the motivations of those involved with the sites as landowners or developers. From this they argue the need to understand how and why different agencies hold land or engage in development activity and the nature of contingencies that combine at any one point in time to influence or constrain their actions. Drawing on the institutional approach developed by Massey (1980) they put forward a framework for the analysis of agency land ownership that includes consideration of the industrial legacy, political context, functions, powers and duties, organisational structures and relationships.

Two important conclusions emerge from this analysis. First, the paper illustrates well how the conceptual approach chosen for analysis affects the definition of the 'issue'. By moving away from the measurement of stocks towards the concept of flows of land, combined with the analysis of the role of land ownership in the context of agency operations, 'vacancy' or 'land holding' changes its meaning. Second, on the basis of this approach, the authors question the validity of the concept of land policy per se. If existing patterns of land ownership and use are the result of complex interactions, then policy measures must address these mechanisms and relationships rather than merely the patterns they produce.

The next two papers are concerned with the way in which specific parts of the existing statutory planning framework are interpreted and used in regulating development. In different ways both look at the scope and limits provided by the legislation for local planning authorities to recoup or appropriate development gain, set in the context of current debate about the degree to which development control can, or should, be regarded as a bargaining rather than regulatory process.

Keogh addresses the interrelated issues of bargaining through planning control for the public realisation of development gain, and the use of planning agreements to do it. He sets the issues and debates within the theoretical framework of welfare economics to focus attention on the planning system as a mechanism for intervening in the market to achieve the efficient use of land. On this basis, he argues that local planning authorities are entirely justified in using their powers of intervention to realise 'planning gain' on behalf of the community, and that they should perhaps have a responsibility to do so. Under the existing legislative framework development rights have been vested in the state, but rights to use and own, and trade in land rights remain with individuals. He argues that if owners and users can trade in property rights, it is theoretically consistent for the State also to trade its rights in the market place. He is thus challenging the coherence of current arguments which suggest that it is 'improper' for authorities to bargain for planning gain secured through their powers under Section 52 of the 1971 Act and elsewhere. Further he suggests that if a welfare economics view is taken of the planning system, such agreements cannot logically be limited to on-site provision of physical infrastructure (as suggested by the recent report of the Property Advisory Group (DoE 1983)); efficient use of resources may require the pooling of planning gains from a number of developments, possibly in the form of cash initially. This, however, leaves unsettled the question of the appropriate spatial level at which to extract planning gain, and the problem faced by authorities which experience little development demand and may need to offer incentives - negative planning gain - to attract development.

Loughlin takes a somewhat different perspective to address similar issues. By focussing on the question of infrastructure provision, he attempts to deal with the question of the role of local authorities in obtaining planning gains and the type of gains that may legitimately be obtained. Most forms of infrastructure may be defined as 'public' or 'merit' goods that have traditionally been provided by the state. On the one hand, increasing pressure on public finance is leading local authorities and statutory undertakers to seek to transfer infrastructure costs to, or obtain contributions from, agents of development. On the other, the public provision of infrastructure itself contributes to the 'unearned' value of a site. He argues that this latter aspect merits greater attention when looking at the issue of obtaining contributions to the costs of provision. The paper examines the mechanisms open to authorities via conditions attached to planning permissions, statutory charges and the use of planning agreements, and evaluates the legal limits of their use as interpreted by the courts.

He suggests that there has been an unduly limited definition of the limits of conditions due to emphasis on individual units of property as opposed to use of the 'planning unit'; an accepted legal concept in other areas of court rulings related to the control of development. Whilst he sees the logic in attempting to standardise the existing fragmented system of statutory charges, he suggests that there are benefits to both developers and local authorities in maintaining some flexibility and discretion. He thus argues the merits of greater use of Section 52 planning agreements, which he sees as giving both sides the discretion to negotiate contributions if considered feasible, necessary or desirable. His conclusions are thus very similar to those of Keogh - but from a rather different base.

What emerges from these papers is a view that planning in a mixed economy could and should - even with the limited 'tools' provided by existing legislation - operate more positively within the market paradigm. The use of negotiation and bargaining in the planning process may be regarded as a positive and appropriate response to coping with uneven economic opportunities (in spatial and sectoral terms), and for achieving social benefits. It could be argued that it is not necessarily the formal framework of rules which prevents planners from negotiating and using their bargaining power to further social welfare objectives, but rather the political interpretations and interest group pressures which are seeking to restrict the scope of social action.

The last two papers in this section look at the operations of specialist agencies set up by central government to achieve particular developmental objectives. Both papers address the question of the value of using such specialist agencies as instruments of intervention and consider the motivation for, and future direction of, such policy responses.

Williams considers the contrasting approaches towards problems of rural development adopted by Mid Wales Development (Development Board for Rural Wales) and by the Development Commission. His analysis and comparison of their achievements is set within an evaluative framework that considers the development model being adopted; the motivation for creating the particular form of agency; the political logic of agency creation, as well as performance criteria such as financial effectiveness, political control and local accountability. He concludes that in physical terms both have contributed to the promotion and support of rural development opportunities, but that their future effectiveness may be more questionable because of the slowing down of growth stimuli and limits placed on their scope for addressing wider rural land use issues. The question of the real impact of such agencies on the local economy is more difficult to assess and raises questions about evaluative criteria and the developmental 'model' intended. Such agencies may have a valuable 'incubator' role in the local market, but may also set up local conflicts (the territory versus function problem). Given recent economic and demographic changes overtaking the original logic for their establishment, such specialist agencies may well become 'programmes in search of a policy' - with increasing policy tension emerging between both central government and the agencies, and between agencies and local government.

Wannop picks up many of these issues in his analysis of the Scottish Development Agency's area based initiatives; in particular its role in the GEAR project in Glasgow whereby the SDA is operating alongside other existing agencies, most significantly the local authorities and the Scottish Special Housing Association. The paper addresses two main questions. First, it considers whether the managerial role assigned to SDA in the GEAR project represented a deliberate by-passing of local political autonomy on the grounds of the perceived failure of the local authorities effectively to address inner city problems, or a necessary change of impetus in response to changing circumstances. Second, it addresses the degree to which a special agency of this kind has a catalytic influence on existing agencies as assumed by the responsiveness argument.

Wannop concludes that whilst a project such as GEAR can be seen as a response to policy failure in practice, the operations of SDA in this context work mainly by agreement with existing agencies, and by avoidance of the open conflicts arising in the case of the London Docklands Urban Development Corporation. He suggests that it may be appropriate to see much of GEAR as a current version of the 1950s response to the same physical issues via Comprehensive Development Areas (CDAs). However, whilst resources are channelled into the specific areas chosen for investment, there has been no real increase in overall urban investment. Because the area focus in practice may be drawing attention away from loss of resources elsewhere, wider benefits depend upon the demonstration value of projects in encouraging more effective use of resources in other places.

Both these papers point to the complexity of alternative agency evaluation, and to the multiplicity of objectives involved in their establishment and operations. The papers also add a further dimension to the debate about the nature of land policy and mechanisms for state involvement in the land market and development process which will be returned to in the concluding chapter.

8 The review process in land availability studies: bargaining positions for builders and planners

MICHAEL CUDDY AND MICHAEL HOLLINGSWORTH

INTRODUCTION

The vogue for land availability studies in the later 1970s
and early 1980s has its antecedents considerably farther back
in the history of British Town Planning. The 1947 Town and
Country Planning Act envisaged that land, once granted
permission for development, would retain it in perpetuity. It
was intended that the 100% development charge provided for in
the Act would enable land to be freely bought and sold at its
existing use value, thus lessening the temptation to hold land
granted permission for speculative reasons. As Hooper (1980)
points out:

> "The amendment of the 1947 scheme in 1953/54 and
> 1959 did far more than merely abolish the
> development charge and the basis for
> compensation for land compulsorily acquired or
> subject to planning control - it distorted the
> whole developmental context in which the 1947
> scheme was intended to operate".

The gradual realisation of the problems that old
unimplemented permissions caused when statutory plans were
reviewed led to the introduction of time-limited permissions
in the Town and Country Planning Act 1968. Such a change

seemed to presage a new era of flexible planning where the
renewal of a planning permission was treated in the same way
as totally new proposals. This was not to be.

It was, perhaps, inevitable that the discretion allowed to
planning authorities by the 1968 Act would be curtailed, not
least because the granting of permission for housing in
particular is paralleled by various commitments to spend
public money to enhance the physical and social infrastructure. An equally powerful reason for preserving the
status quo is the increment in value which a planning
permission is perceived (sometimes wrongly) to give to land.
This value can only be realised through sale or development;
but even where this development value cannot be realised
immediately, its perceived existence is usually strongly
defended in the hope of finding a market. In this way, the
assertion of property rights intrudes into planning
considerations.

Department of the Environment (DoE) Circular 17/69 presumed
this state of affairs when it laid down fairly strict criteria
for refusing renewal i.e.

a) There has been some material change of planning circumstances since the permission was granted (e.g. a change in
planning policy for the area or in relevant highway
considerations);

b) Continued failure to begin the development will contribute
unacceptably to uncertainty about the future pattern of
development;

or

c) The application is premature because the permission still
has a reasonable time to run.

It is also indicated in paragraph 16 the ease with which a
permission could be commenced through carrying out minor
"specified operations" thus avoiding the problem of renewal.
The only other alternatives open to an authority were to seek
the Secretary of State's support for a completion notice or to
revoke the permission, thus entailing compensation at the
market rate. Neither of these alternatives has often been
used by authorities. In general therefore, because of the
limited scope for excising past allocations, when planning
residential development, changes in local planning policy have
been incremental rather than radical i.e. it accepts what has
gone before.

We believe that many of the problems subsequently encountered by planning authorities and builders in the latter part of the 1970s arose because the land on which some of the permissions were granted in the early part of that decade was not scrupulously examined for infrastructure costs and marketing characteristics. Authorities were urged through Circulars DoE 102/72 and Welsh Office 234/72 (DoE, 1972) to release more land because the escalation in land values, which occurred at that time, was ascribed — wrongly some have argued — primarily to land shortages (see for example, Hallett (1977)). This rapid escalation must have persuaded both planners and land owners that the practical problems of development would be overcome simply because the potential value of the land would offset the costs inherent in overcoming them.

An examination of the relative changes between construction costs and plot values during the 1970s (see Figures 1, 2 and 3) reveals that this assumption proved incorrect, and the absolute falls in plot values in the middle part of the decade as against steadily rising construction costs gives a clue to why many permissions were not taken up in the latter part of the decade. Unfortunately, most planners were largely unaware of this change of circumstance and in the many Structure Plans which were being produced at that time, they tended to accept old commitments as a fait accompli.

The response of most county authorities in South Wales, for example, to the treatment of old planning permissions, was to accept them as commitments in their Structure Plan with relatively little examination of the problems encountered by prospective developers and why they had not been implemented.

The Land Authority for Wales (LAW), with its role of acquiring development land, started its effective operation when the majority of Structure Plans were well past their formative stage. Therefore, there was relatively little opportunity to question the supply side of the building land equation prior to the Examination in Public of these plans. It did, however, become clear within the first two years of the Authority's operation, that there existed a situation of "famine amongst plenty" in respect of housing land in parts of Wales. It was at this time that the earliest Land Availability Studies were commenced by LAW, more or less at the same time as they were being undertaken in other parts of the country, and for similar reasons.

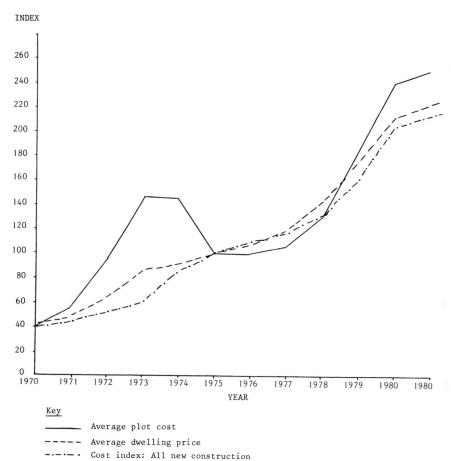

Figure 1

House Building Cost Indices (1975=100)

Key

———— Average plot cost

– – – – Average dwelling price

–·–·–· Cost index: All new construction

Source: HMSO Housing Construction Statistics 1970-1980

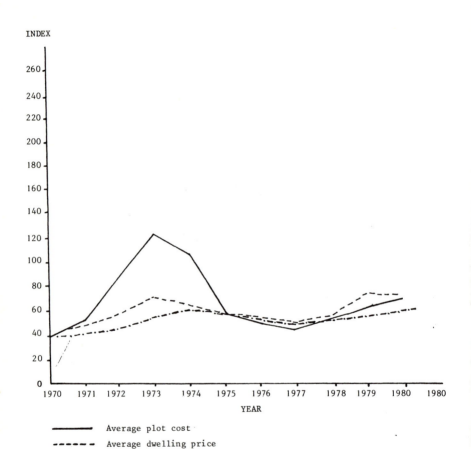

Figure 2

House Building Cost Indices (1975=100)
Modified by Inflation Rate

Average plot cost
Average dwelling price
Cost-index: All new construction

Source: HMSO Housing and Construction Statistics, Central
Statistical Office 1970-1980

164

Figure 3

Housing Land Cost/Construction Cost Index (1975=100)

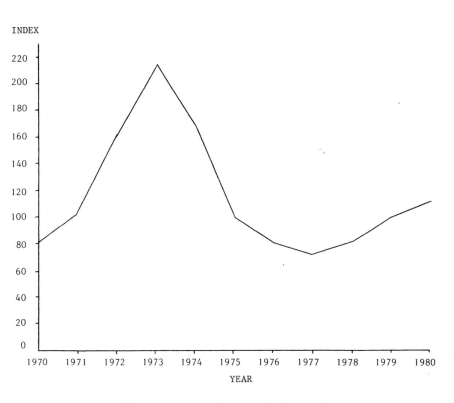

Source: HMSO Housing and Construction Statistics 1970-1980

THE EVOLUTION OF LAND AVAILABILITY STUDIES

The Guidance Given by Government

Ad hoc land availability exercises have been required since 1970. DoE Circular 10/70 which followed closely after the winding up of the Land Commission, contained all the main elements to be elaborated in subsequent circulars. In particular it noted the desirability of regular discussions with representatives of the building industry. Authorities were to be ready to participate in discussions on request, with the focus on areas of shortage where there was an urgent need for release of land to meet foreseeable needs for at least the next five years.

Subsequent circulars were variations on these themes and served in particular to narrow the area of discretion allowed to local authorities, through requiring them to perform certain tasks and through defining terms more closely. They also reflected a growing recognition of builders' requirements. The five year supply criterion remained undefined in DoE Circular 10/70, and reference was to "discussions" with builders without any specified format. Two years later in Circular 102/72 (DoE, 1972) criteria were specified and enough land was to be given planning permission to allow for problems in land coming forward. Authorities were reminded three years later to provide for periodical up-dating. Some three years after this, DoE Circular 44/78 went to some pains to describe the builder's role, his problems, and introduced for the first time the concept of marketability. The Circular's broader purpose was to revitalise the Community Land Scheme and it set relationships between local authorities and builders within this context i.e. the situation in which major untaxed development gains would no longer accrue to the landowner. The memorandum attached to the Circular is written with unusual perspicacity.

> "There should be no surprise or disappointment if the establishment of a constructive dialogue between the two sides sets off to a faltering start in places, and takes time to function properly. The house building industry cannot be expected to speak with a single voice. Perseverance and a recognition of the very different starting points of the two sides are essential. Each may have a good deal to learn from the other".

The underlying assumptions against which this Circular was

written were soon to disappear with the repeal of the Community Land Act. The Circular, however, provided the backing and the framework for the "Manchester Method", which, in essence, was no more than a systematic treatment of the items included in the Circular as initially applied in a pilot study of the Greater Manchester area.

Arrangements have been further codified in DoE Circular 9/80. In Wales the parallel Circular Welsh Office 30/80 was written to include the studies already initiated by the Land Authority. Circular 9/80, besides recommending the Manchester Method, also introduced a revised five year supply criterion which in future would be assessed against Structure and Local Plan policies. Most significantly, the Secretary of State has since been given powers in the Local Government Planning and Land Act 1980 to require these assessments.

A few broadsides were fired at the Manchester Method as it first began to gain acceptance in local authority planning circles. These were concerned to warn against abandoning a broader planning purpose, and to guard against the dangers of special pleading and undue emphasis which might follow from meeting with self-selected groups of builders, as Hooper (1980) pointed out:

> "The research (in Greater Manchester) reflects uncritically the views of a pressure-group (the House Builders' Federation)".

Shepley (1982) elaborated on this when he stated that:

> "There are dangers of their (Land Availability Studies) becoming, in effect, non-statutory subject plans, circumventing the local planning process and avoiding public scrutiny".

Land availability studies have therefore developed from loosely structured ad hoc exercises to exercises based on a preferred methodology backed up with statutory powers. At the time of writing these MK2 studies were enjoying something of a honeymoon. But as with most marriages, especially of convenience, the honeymoon cannot be expected to last forever. We chart the likely pitfalls below.

The Participants

To the surprise of some commentators, a broad understanding is developing between planners and builders around the

methodology; though **reasons for the willingness to get on with**
"the job" can more easily be ascribed to the builders side of
the marriage than to the planning side. The builders, as
represented by the House Builders Federation, having got their
act together and much of their argument across to Central
Government, were keen to follow through their advantage. They
have been participating with the Royal Town Planning Institute
in the Joint Land Requirements Committee which held out the
prospect of an agreement with planners on a national aggregate
land supply figure. This prospect, for reasons covered
elsewhere, but implicit in what is said below, has become
somewhat fudged (see for example, Hooper (1982)). Meanwhile
at the local level agreed surveys have become the rule rather
than the exception.

Although builders are not a unified group, the modus
operandi and objectives which may be present in rival firms,
however diverse, are tangible and arise out of a common
perception of the system in which they operate. The reason
for town planners' commitment to the exercise is more
difficult to discern; they presently lack a coherent self-
image as the planning literature points out (see for example,
Healey and Underwood (1979)). The only explanation we can
hazard is that the exercises provided an opportunity to be
involved in a dialogue with the "real world" at a time when it
is increasingly apparent that they had less influence on the
workings of the space economy than their plans supposed and
post 1947 legislation allows.

The factors noted above - a methodology strongly influenced
by one particular pressure group, a reluctance to look beyond
this methodology on the part of the planners who nevertheless
have a statutory obligation to do something, provide a context
in which ends may be obscure and outcomes uncertain. We
develop our view of possible consequences in the remainder of
this chapter.

LAND AVAILABILITY EXERCISES AS GAMES

Are They Games?

We suggest that despite any claims to the contrary, the land
availability survey is not an objective process, irrespective
of the particular method. If we take the method advocated in
Circular 9/80 (as this has achieved prominence), despite its
factual detail, it still contains sufficient subjective
elements internal to the process to enable us to talk in terms
of both words and numbers games. The extent to which these

are developed will depend on attitudes and perceptions of the participants and their appreciation of the exercise as a game.

It was considered initially that one might postulate Land Availability Studies following a simple quasi-mathematical gaming strategy. In this game the planners seek to justify and defend the particular policy stance they had taken. The builders, by contrast, seek to gain further releases of land in new, and more favourable, locations. The reason why builders would seek to do this is that a broader array of sites gives them greater access to marketable land, and removes the fear that in a rapid upturn of demand they may lose out in the scramble for those areas which can be built on immediately; the more difficult or less marketable sites tending to remain undeveloped.

This is a useful idea insofar as it suggests simple strategies which participants might pursue. In particular they might try to avoid, at least initially, a zero sum game in which one partner loses. However, it ignores the unpredictability of the powerful external forces acting on the participants which condition their "play" and obscure objectives. For example the Water Authorities, other statutory bodies, and the Highway Authority (the County Council) all have their priorities and these are not necessarily tailored to planning schemes.

The simple game thesis also requires that builders act in a monolithic fashion and that planners have an unambiguous conception of their role, and the goals which they are pursuing. Neither of these conditions holds. Builders are not a single body with a single purpose. There are several builders' organisations, the House Builders Federation (HBF) a grouping within the National Federation of Building Trades Employers (NFBTE), and the Federation of Master Builders (FMB) which often can be quite hostile to one another. Even the dominant one in Wales, the HBF, has a very diverse membership, ranging from the small family firm right up to the huge national "volume" companies such as Barratts and Wimpeys (whose share of the market has doubled in the last decade), and could more correctly be described as a loose confederation which promotes the industry and acts as a pressure group at the national level. Their main function at a local level is to resolve the myriad problems their members encounter with Unions, Local Government and other agencies in their building work. The truth is that builders are in direct competition with one another locally and their umbrella organisations cannot overtly negotiate with the planning authority to advantage one of their members at the expense of another.

Hooper (1982) comments on the basis of a survey conducted by the FMB:

> "That it is the small and medium sized firm which is encountering the problem of land availability - 67 per cent of such firms expressed concern over land banks, but only 38 per cent of larger firms".

Shepley (1982) goes further and asks:

> "How representative are the particular house builders who happen to be involved in local negotiations? Do they represent the whole industry? Or just the larger house builders (but interested in small urban sites)? Or even, as has sometimes been unfairly alleged, do they simply represent themselves?"

Whilst the planners' formal position is more clearly defined and constant, it too is liable to change. Central Government can give new directions through the issuance of Circulars and Policy Notes; local members can change their views or be replaced by those of a differing political sympathy; and lastly the planners themselves can review their professional position against some emerging new view of their role.

To summarise, therefore, it appears that neither of the principle protagonists is in a position to guarantee delivery in any agreement which may have been concluded between them. The local district planners cannot ensure that land identified for development can be granted planning permission, insofar as their elected members might oppose it or some unforeseen legal or technical problem could arise. The builders' organisations cannot agree to build houses in accordance with the planning authorities' policies because they do not control their individual member companies' strategy (of which building may be only a small part), nor can they predict the fluctuations in demand which result largely from nationally determined fiscal policy.

What Then is the Nature of the Game?

As Hooper (1980) has pointed out:

> "The planning system and the house building industry operate not only with a different

definition, but with a different conception, of
land availability - the former based on public
control over land use, the latter on market
orientation to the ownership of land".

Nevertheless, a dialogue has been established between them and
a consensus of sorts has emerged. In achieving this, the
authors of this paper believe that there must be a strong
element of role taking on the part of all participants. This
dialogue is set within the context of mutual recognition of
the limitations and uncertainties of each party's position
but, more importantly, a recognition of the sanctions or
penalties which will result if an agreement is not arrived at.
The builders main sanction if they fail to agree an effective
five year supply is confrontation through the appeals system
or recourse to the Secretary of State under the Local
Government Planning and Land Act 1980. Decisions on release
of new land would then be taken out of the hands of the local
planners and determined by the Secretary of State or his
Inspectorate, which is rather unpredictable. The main
sanction the planners have is that they can end the dialogue
and take a very obstructive attitude on new land release, and
possibly make allocations which the building industry might
find hard to implement. Such decisions could be challenged
through the appeal mechanism but this is time-consuming and
may result in there being an insufficient supply of suitable
land at crucial times.

The State of the Art - How the Game Runs

The framework provided by the Manchester Method (Annex 6 of
DoE Circular 9/80), as we have suggested earlier, although
detailed is no more objective than methods used by local
authorities prior to Circular 9/80. Indeed, Hooper (1980) has
made some telling criticisms of its apparent lack of interest
in relationships uncovered in earlier research and the Land
Authority for Wales has adopted a different approach in Wales.
However, there are benefits; apart from being commonly adopted
- a major achievement in itself - the Method provides a basis
for focussed discussion with a means for arriving at a
consensus which is seen as legitimate by the participants. In
this it has a similar rationale to the Delphi and other
techniques promoted by the Institute for Operational Research,
in the late 1960s early 1970s, which keep people talking and
provide a basis against which to review results at regular
intervals.

Any method also has its own internal logic which to some

extent shapes proceedings and outcomes. It is claimed that
this particular method:

    i. allows local authorities to distinguish more clearly
    the factors that determine the real availability of land
    by identifying factors operating in a particular market;

    ii. demonstrates the value of measuring the rate of
    building against policies and plans;

    iii. provides a basis to promote further land release if
    existing land will not allow policy requirements to be
    met;

    iv. provides the basis for continuous monitoring (see
    Humber (1980)).

The method need not, of course, necessarily lead to further
land release as implied above. After one round of exercises,
if the basis of the market analysis revealed that the land
bank is found wanting, it would be open to the planning
authorities to consider releasing further land with all that
this means in modifying adopted plans. There could be other
options through, for example, the re-negotiation of the basis
of the position paper or re-scheduling the rate of
construction. In any one round of discussions there is ample
scope for words and numbers games. In our experience the
attitudes adopted to such key concepts as "availability" vary
widely, despite the assistance given in the circulars, and, we
suggest, are not in the short term susceptible to any one
objective definition or test. Ultimately they rest on some
negotiated set of criteria which may be subsequently varied,
or given different weight.

The Manchester Method, as with any method dependent on
estimation and judgement, allows scope for further tactical
manoeuvre by the participants. For example, during site
analysis builders will usually press for the rate of
development to be slow, building up late in the period under
consideration, whereas planners will argue for a more rapid
rate of site completion. The aim of the builders is to create
the appearance of a shortfall in the crucial early years of
the cycle whereas the planners will endeavour to show .that
short term demand has been catered for. The system adopted by
the Land Authority for Wales attempts to accommodate both a
rate of development and a site categorisation, applying the
former to sites which may be considered immediately
developable and the latter to sites with problems or
constraints which may be solved or overcome. We have found

that the main thrust of the builders has been to maximise the problems that particular sites have and to relate these to uncertain marketability. It seems in retrospect that, in the context of the rapidly fluctuating cycle of demand for housing, too little attention has been paid to the lead-time necessary to solve those problems i.e. a builder may well initially consider it worthwhile to tackle the problems on a particular site, but if these take a considerable length of time to resolve, the uncertainty of demand with which he has to contend may well force him to the conclusion that the risk involved outweighs the potential gain.

One of the other difficulties encountered in these studies has been the treatment of land without planning permission but with some other form of approval. Circular 9/80 advocates that sites with and without planning permission should be included, but the Land Authority for Wales only admits sites with planning permission, or those recently lapsed, as potentially defining a five year land bank. In our experience "zoned" land is difficult to deal with even when included in a statutory adopted plan, insofar as boundaries can shift, densities change, or some unforseen difficulty in site conditions or infrastructure arise. If, as we later argue, the land availability exercise is part of a process, then these sites should appear with permission in due course, so little is lost if they are temporarily excluded.

Can We Learn Anything from History?

Looking at the recent history of land availability we would suggest that, as with many other aspects of policy, it has tended to be a stable door policy in that in the circumstances the particular policy was designed to confront change before it is fully implemented. This is particularly apparent when dealing with the building cycle.

Despite there being a general consensus, after the failures of 1972 and 1977, that land supply should be geared to cope with booms, demand had been suppressed by high interest rates and the deflationary policies of the Government just as the MK2 land availability exercises were beginning. The general effect of this low demand (outside the "sun belt") has been that the pressure placed on planning authorities by builders is less than in earlier, more prosperous periods. Often in our experience, the builders have not even been able to develop many of the sites with permission and no obvious constraints. Any temptation for either party to withdraw from discussions has initially been tempered, we imagine, by the knowledge that this might be politically maladroit, even though the discussions might not be producing as much as had been originally hoped for. There are signals of discontent, however, despite the Joint Land Requirements Committee. The present HBF President (Woodrow 1982) has publicly stated his dissatisfaction with the national aggregate land supply:

> "We need a more positive land release policy for the future. The industry has land for 1983 and 1984, but if the market is going to improve and if all our sales take off, our current land holdings will quickly be exhausted".

In our experience, certain planning authorities have responded to this pressure by examining the commitments and endeavouring to remove some of them in order that new allocations can be made within the overall targets for land supply. The problems of refusal to renew permission have been referred to in the introduction, although this situation may improve with planning charges since an applicant now has to judge the value of a permission against the cost of the application. The use of the completion notice has been contemplated, but these appear to be even more difficult to enforce because when they are approved by the Minister (and this is not very often) builders usually have a lengthy period of grace to complete the development. They are usually successfully resisted on the basis that market conditions are unfavourable and that it would be unreasonable to require compliance, and this is now well-established by legal precedent.

In relation to statutory plan-making, the reviews of the Structure Plans which are currently commencing in Wales, will probably pay more attention to land-supply and the problems of the private house-building industry. This is not simply in response to the pressure from the industry, but also a recognition that the successful implementation of the plan can be prejudiced by a failure to achieve house construction targets. In particular we believe there is a greater consciousness of the problems that large sites exhibit, and a greater understanding of the need to ensure a flow of land onto the market rather than merely establishing a land bank, along the lines that Hooper (1982) has described. At the local plan level, the more progressive authorities are showing themselves willing to listen to arguments about infra-structure and rates of land release, and now incorporate major sections on resources and implementation. There are also instances where planning authorities have made reference to possible contingency sites if the land supply figures can be shown to be inadequate.

174

The Impact of the Game Beyond Planning

Much of the literature on this subject has concentrated on the impact on the planning system. The conflict between builders has implications beyond this sytem, most notably in the land markets and the response of owners of land to planning decisions (or indecisions) and policies. An exercise carried out in the Land Authority for Wales on registration of land as stock in trade by the developers, under the Community Land Act 1975, revealed some 6500 hectares of potential residential land, at least 40 per cent being agricultural and without any form of planning approval; in some counties registered land with planning approval fell below 20 per cent of the total.

While it should be noted that the definition of builder and developer was applied quite widely (it included pension funds, for example) this reveals quite how the anticipation of planning permission can induce changes in the pattern of ownership. While some of this land continues in agricultural use, the hope that a more valuable use could be obtained, can result in its being used at less than its maximum potential. This situation also arises on unused or underused inner-area sites, where the anticipation of a change can lead to the land being kept idle. In our experience such situations are likely to arise more where there is an out-of-date plan or where the approved planning framework is particularly unrealistic in its approach to the release of development land, where, for example, reasons for refusal to release land are based on ill defined notions such as "prematurity" or "undesirability" rather than some firm and explicit planning principle. The activities of developers in acquiring unallocated land is an understandable precaution, and can often produce considerable returns, but the operation of this on a large scale must inevitably be counter-productive. The developer may have a large amount of working capital tied up, the land itself is very often unused or underused and the planning authority have to spend time resisting such development in appeals when they could be proceeding more rapidly with the production of up-to-date plans.

CONCLUSION

The authors of this paper consider the undertaking of land availability exercises to be a worthwhile pursuit despite many of the misgivings that have been expressed from within the planning profession. The house building industry is one of planning's most significant clients and it would seem strange indeed if the dialogue between them were to be curtailed. If it is felt that planners are taking too little notice of their other "clients", then a better response would be to establish a more effective means of communicating with them, rather than treating all with equal deafness. That being said, it has to be pointed out that there will be areas where builders and planners pursue common aims, and those where they will be in conflict. The latter arises particularly where there is a desire by the planning authority to protect some aspect of the environment, where it is the aim to maintain non-urban land uses and where there is a need to maximise public investment in social and physical infrastructure. The existence of this conflict has not prevented the dialogue taking place and there is, in the author's experience, a tacit acceptance of it by both sides in the discussions on land supply. It is our view that the final agreed assessment of land supply represents the bargain struck between the parties rather than an objective assessment of future land supply. We believe that this holds particularly where the forecasts relate to longer term predictions of construction and likely land availability i.e. beyond three years. This is because the nature of demand for housing and the supply of finance to resolve many of the sites' problems, are highly volatile and not susceptible to long term prediction. As such, these forecasts could be regarded as aspirations or bids within the planning system, rather than contractual commitments. It should be noted at this juncture that we believe that it is outside the remit of the land availability studies to influence the structure of the house building industry, although there has, as Smyth (1982) observes, been a move in:

"the industry, which has been highly fragmented,
to become increasingly concentrated".

In a free-market system the planning authorities cannot guarantee that any particular builder or group of builders will obtain ownership of allocated land.

If the bargaining between planners and the building industry is to develop beyond the present position, there needs to be a system of checks and balances so that neither one side nor the other abuses the system. As we have stated above, the predictions of future land supply can be regarded as "soft" data at best, but as time passes, the efficacy of these predictions can be tested against the performance of both parties in a review process.

This review of the performance of both the planning authorities and the builders gives an opportunity to examine the realism of the forecasts and an insight into the motives of the party making them. If it can be shown that a planning authority has consistently overstated the likely supply of developable land, or the builders (individually or collectively) constantly overestimate likely demand, then less weight should be attached to their view when the extent of land supply is questioned at appeals or local plan inquiries. It should be stressed that such a sanction should only come into force where there was a long history of overstating the case rather than a single erroneous forecast, because, as anyone involved in the industry could affirm, the conversion of land is fraught with unforeseen, and unforeseeable snags.

A consensus seems to be emerging around the importance of reviewing the land supply, and ensuring either that the total amount of land carrying forward matches that which is being used up by developers, or at least is consistent with the forecasts made in the relevant Structure and Local plans. Humber (1980) states that:

> "This study (Manchester) is a genuine advance on earlier studies in that it is intended to form the basis of a continuous monitoring system, and to provide an increasingly accurate assessment of rates of use of building land and of future requirements, on an annual basis".

Hooper (1982) states that:

> "It is a striking indictment of both parties prior to the period associated with the reor-ganisation of local Government that so little systematic knowledge has been accumulated of the detailed process of land conversion to house-building, in a context where land use planning had been institutionalised for a quarter of a century, and which had had to cope with succes-sive periods of boom and slump in house-building. One of the main factors accounting for this situation can now be seen to be the absence of an awareness by each of the respective agencies of the structure of constraints under which the participants in the land conversion process have had to operate".

If the importance of the process of land conversion is accepted, what improvements can be made to Land Availability Studies? In our dealings with builders, we consider that one of the areas of greatest concern to builders is the short- and medium-term supply of land which is capable of immediate development. The reason for this is that the demand could rise rapidly and unpredictably and no builder would wish to be inhibited by the lack of a suitable land bank in such a situation. (This is the argument underpinning a new draft circular published on 12 July 1983 by the DoE). We would therefore suggest that the robustness of the land supply over this critical three year period be tested against a range of possible demand situations, and if it would not stand up to a sudden upsurge in the market, an examination of what measures could be taken by the local authorities and other public bodies should be undertaken to see if this could be remedied. If the combined efforts of such bodies could not ensure a flow of land onto the market to cope with demand that the structure and local plan foresaw, we would suggest that measures be undertaken to re-examine the existing planning framework as a matter of urgency. A failure to do this will lead, as in the past, to a rapid upsurge in housing land prices, pressure on the Government of the day to issue circulars to "deal" with the situation and a further round of instant planning such as we saw in the early 1970s.

9 The analysis of public sector land ownership and development

TONY GORE AND DAVID NICHOLSON

INTRODUCTION

The work reported here has its origins in a research project
into the extent and causes of vacant urban land in Wales
(Bruton and Gore, 1980). This project has led to two distinct
lines of enquiry:

1. a detailed analysis, via case studies, of sites in
   South Wales identified as both publicly owned and
   vacant in 1979, and

2. the development of a framework for the analysis of
   public landownership in general.

These two approaches to the topic of public landownership are
complementary and together identify the wider issues within
which the subject must be placed. Sections 2 and 3 below
summarise the results of the case study work, while Sections
4, 5 and 6 outline the wider analytical framework and apply it
to the landholdings of the British Railways Board in South
Wales.

A MODEL OF THE PUBLIC SECTOR DEVELOPMENT PROCESS

The case study method is commonly used to investigate

processes of use cessation and redevelopment on individual
vacant sites (see, for instance, Cantell, 1977, and Department
of the Environment, 1975), but is not completely satisfactory.
An essential feature of the method is the difficulty of
deriving meaningful and legitimate generalisations, which
stems from the twin factors of locational uniqueness and an
atheoretical approach (Lebas, 1977). This problem, of
extracting the general from the particular without losing
sight of the latter, is faced by all research based on case
studies, where "it is necessary to balance the ultimate
uniqueness of each case with the need for a more general, but
still meaningful abstraction" (Department of the Environment,
Housing Research Foundation 1978). The final justification
for the use of the method must rest on the extent to which
this dilemma can be successfully resolved. What is required
to overcome this problem is a general framework against which
the mass of information generated by the case studies can be
viewed and interpreted.

This prescription has not been met by existing research on
vacant urban land, despite the common use of the case study
method. Instead, current research emphasises description
rather than explanation. The principal weakness of this
material is an over-emphasis on the form and features of
vacant land at the expense of the factors operating over time
to create, sustain, and remove it; work has halted at a
recognition and crude quantification of the state of vacancy
without perceiving the explanatory importance of aspects of
transition. As a consequence, the literature fails to provide
a coherent framework for the analysis of case study material.
These deficiencies of existing work suggest that a more
fruitful line of attack is to view vacant urban land as part
of a process. From this perspective, vacancy is situated
within the processes of urban development and redevelopment,
so that the main focus is no longer the environmental form
itself but instead the factors which are involved in its
creation and removal.

To date, the most sophisticated model of the development
process is that developed by Barrett, Stewart and Underwood
(1978). This model is a three stage categorisation of the
events involved in land development; the stress on transition
means that it is most suitable for the analysis of processes
affecting urban land. However, as noted elsewhere (Humphreys,
1980) the model only encompasses half of the relevant factors,
in that there is no attempt to identify the processes by which
new vacant plots are created, the discussion being confined to
how they move out of this condition. Since these processes
are of central interest here, the model given below, while

based on that developed by Barrett, Stewart and Underwood, incorporates a new fourth stage to deal with the creation of vacant land, as well as embodying a number of changes reflecting the specific concern with public sector development.

The framework describes the main activities of the public sector in the development process (Figure 1). The model relates not to changes in land use but to "the basic sequence of events involved as land changes from one state of development/use to another" (Barrett, Stewart and Underwood, 1978). Sites passing through the pipeline remain vacant until the construction stage of the implementation leg, i.e. until the development process is almost complete. The approach places little emphasis on the appearance or use of the land in question, but stresses instead sets of events and conditions which have to be fulfilled before development can take place. This allows activities and events in the policy and feasibility legs to be discussed, despite the fact that progress along these legs will not usually be reflected in any significant physical change in the condition of the site. This position focusses attention not on the explanation of a single phenomenon, delay in re-use, but onto a series of sets of specified events in the process, each of which may have some bearing on the flow of land through the pipeline.

The vacancy stage of the model covers events in the process which convert public sector land uses into the stock of redundant land and buildings owned by this sector. This stage employs the distinction made by Burrows (1977) between three sets of factors which, taken together, account for cessation of land use. According to Burrows, the continuation of a given use may be impossible, unsuitable or undesirable. For the public sector, reasons for the impossibility of continuing a land use range from the exhaustion of minerals to the completion of tipping. Similarly, it may be unsuitable to continue a land use as a result of problems of mineral exploitation (declining quality, increasing mining difficulties) or inappropriate activity (town gas making, rail transport). Lastly, continuation of use may be undesirable where resources for development are better invested elsewhere, on other sites or on other activities; this would include, in the case of owners such as British Rail or the British Steel Corporation, the rationalisation of plant and installations.

Land passes into the vacancy stage as a result of these processes or from other public sector activity in the implementation leg, such as slum clearance. The designation of land as 'surplus' at this point can lead to disposal to the

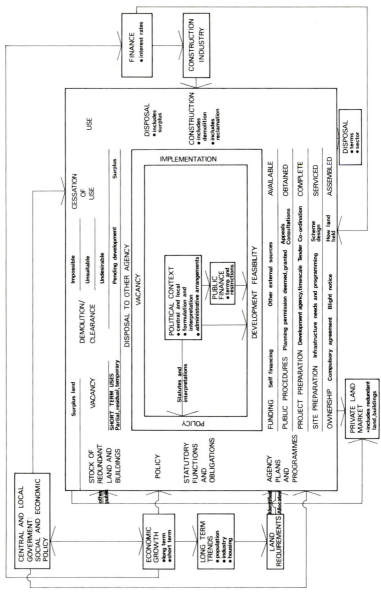

FIGURE 1 : THE PUBLIC SECTOR DEVELOPMENT PROCESS

182

land market or acquisition by a different public agency. The
most important external influence on this leg of the process
is economic growth mediated by Government social and economic
policy. For instance, the extent to which it is unsuitable to
continue a land use such as steel production in a poor
location and with obsolete plant is determined on the one
hand by changing trends in world steel production, mediated on
the other hand by Government policy towards the nationalised
industries and by social and political considerations.

The policy leg describes the stage in the process where a
number of external influences combine to translate the general
functions of an agency, often statutory, into plans and
programmes relating to land development activity or future
land use. These programmes take a number of forms, and make a
variety of statements about land supply, requirements and
allocations. Examples range from assessments of the land
requirements dictated by extension of services, or by the
fulfillment of other statutory duties such as education
provision or municipal housing, to more general statements
such as structure plans or analyses of residential and
industrial land availability.

A number of parallel streams make up the development
feasibility stage, each of which relates to a particular
influence or constraint (such as funding) and each relevant to
the passage of a piece of land through this stage to
implementation. The framework avoids assumptions about the
relative importance of, relationship between, or time sequence
within the different streams.

An important function of the public sector in the
development process is the bringing forward of land for
development by such means as site assembly and servicing. In
the model, this activity takes place within the various
streams of the feasibility stage, and when complete the site
may leave the pipeline via disposal. Alternatively, sites
pass into implementation, the stage of actual development,
incorporating construction and transfer into use and
occupation.

The model distinguishes between internal events and external
influences on development. As regards the latter, emphasis is
given to government policy and to public finance, probably the
two most important influences on the carrying out and timing
of public development.

First, the wider processes of public policy formulation
generate the context within which the public sector

development process operates. Government policy towards land is only one of a number of policy areas which impinge on the process. Both local and central housing policy, for instance, are prime determinants of the volume of local authority housebuilding and thus of involvement in the process.

Second, a major constraint on all parts of the process is the availability and terms of finance. The public sector pipeline draws on funding from three sources: the external sources of the private finance market and of public finance, and from internally generated funds. Different agencies will draw on different combinations of these sources, combinations which will have wide implications for the ability of these agencies to control both the timing and extent of their participation in the process.

APPLICATION OF THE PROCESS MODEL

General findings

Analysis of the current (1981) positions of the study sites within the process indicates that clustering occurs at certain points (Figure 2). These are at use, construction, at either end of the development feasibility leg, and in the stock of redundant land and buildings. In addition, a number of sites are lodged within particular streams such as those dealing with public procedures or ownership. These relate to problems specific to such sites which, until removed, prevent further progression along the pipeline. There seems to be a more general difficulty in initiating sites along the 'feasibility' leg as a whole, even though firm intentions for land use exist as a consequence of the various stages of the 'policy' leg. In contrast, those located at the start of the 'implementation' phase have passed successfully through each stream of the previous leg; development on all these sites is about to commence.

The wide distribution of sites within the framework confirms the suitability of the overall process viewpoint to the study of land vacancy, for without this perspective it would not be possible to differentiate between the sites which are located between the vacancy and construction stages of the model. In addition, the fact that many sites are either in use, under construction or are about to pass into implementation challenges the view of many writers that vacant urban land is a "major and enduring feature of urban areas" (Burrows, 1977). This point is reinforced by the fact that relatively few sites remain within the stock of redundant land pending initiation of the re-use process.

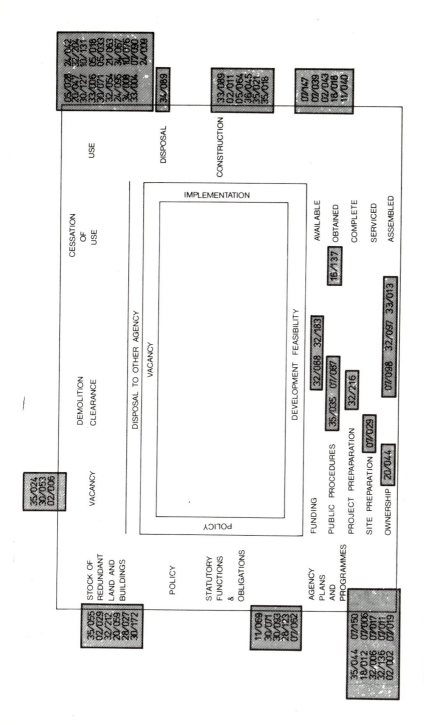

FIGURE 2: POSITION OF CASE STUDY SITES WITHIN THE PROCESS

185

Development feasibility

Further analysis however suggests that these similarities of position disguise more fundamental differences in site development prospects. While one-third have successfully reached implementation in the two year period between survey and case study work, these sites form a heterogeneous group, the single common feature being their position within the pipeline. This may relate more to an advanced position within the process when originally surveyed than to any intrinsic characteristics. Similarly, those sites located in development feasibility have little in common except this position. For instance, though several sites are currently being actively marketed, it cannot be assumed that construction will begin soon. The aim on one site is to establish a price with which to bargain with other public agencies, while another site, held by the Land Authority for Wales (LAW), is being sold in order to realise an asset rather than promote development. This points to an important feature of the development process, namely that those public agencies who participate may do so with other goals than the promotion of site re-use, though this may be a secondary objective. For example, planning permission is being sought on several sites within the 'public procedures' stream, not as a preparation for site development by the nationalised industries who hold the sites, but as a prelude to disposal. In these cases, permission is required for two reasons: first, to allow disposal to proceed, since it is unlikely, given the special planning and development problems involved, that any takers could be found without the carrot of permission; and second, to maximise the capital return received from the sale of the land. Agency strategies in the process, therefore, may be adopted for a number of goals, far removed from those of successful development or of efficient progression of sites through the pipeline. The emphasis here is on the inherent complexity of the process, as those agencies seeking site development attempt, in pursuit of this aim, to influence the operations of those with different objectives.

Further examples of this point arise when factors governing the flow of sites through the pipeline are considered. These influences operate both simultaneously and sequentially; there is no guarantee that when a particular set of difficulties is successfully eliminated, others will not arise. Furthermore, sites have successfully to negotiate each stream of the feasibility leg before construction can proceed; none of these streams are sufficient for development, but all are necessary. Particularly important is the site preparation stream, for here a wide range of constraints to development can arise,

186

though their individual influence is variable. Physical constraints, for example, tend to be site specific, and though they affect a large number of study sites, do not necessarily prevent development, as they can normally be expressed in terms of extra preparation or construction costs. In contrast, other aspects of site preparation are more problematic; in particular, the resolution of access and servicing problems on a number of study sites depends upon the actions of agencies with longer and geographically wider horizons than those involved with one individual site. Herein lies the important role of the statutory undertakers as suppliers of services and infrastructure, while the county councils as transport authorities have a major part to play in removing both local and strategic access constraints on site development.

The dimension of ownership

The relationships of the public bodies involved as owners of the case study sites to the process further underlines the complexity involved. These relationships are basically determined by agency statutory functions, though other factors - the involvement of other bodies on the same site, the availability of finance, and the influence of central government - are also relevant.

Statutory roles vary enormously, from mineral winning to electricity distribution and the provision of health care, but it is possible to draw a distinction between agencies whose remit primarily involves them in the promotion or implementation of development, and those whose participation in the process is essentially a side effect of some other objective. These two groups are not internally homogenous. Among the development agencies, for instance, LAW has a 'pure' landowning role where land is a vehicle for investment as well as the agency's prime resource. Similarly concerned with promoting development, the Welsh Development Agency (WDA) provides funds for reclamation schemes and carries out its own factory construction programmes. Differences arise over sources of finance, for while both agencies' level of activity is set by the availability of funds, LAW is required to be self-financing while the WDA may tackle more costly projects as far as resources permit. Furthermore, neither the disposal of a site to a volume housebuilder in the case of LAW, nor the completion of a WDA-funded reclamation scheme, will necessarily guarantee an end to under-use or vacancy on the sites involved; additional conditions for use remain to be met. A more complete role in the process, in that successful participation will lead to development, is undertaken by housing associations, but here this apparent 'efficiency' is the result of the imposed administrative framework of grant aid rather than an intrinsic feature of their function. This relates to housing provision and management rather than to successful involvement in the process.

Where non-development agencies become involved in the process, land is required primarily as a physical support. Specific requirements, both current and expected, are defined by the operational arms who are also responsible for the primary function; in the case of Wales Gas, for instance, it is the engineering requirements of energy distribution which define land needs. Other agencies with primary non-development objectives, pressed by government expenditure limits and poor profit levels, may view their landholdings as assets whose disposal can realise useful capital receipts. This possibility is currently being exploited by the British Steel Corporation, while the British Rail Property Board has been pursuing the same aim through sale, letting or leasing since 1969. Such disposals may be a long way from re-use given the often poor physical condition of such land. Finally, the nature of the production process or prime activity may lead to a unique relationship to land. For the National Coal Board (NCB), the concern with inherent productiveness and the function of mineral extraction means that land must be held in reserve pending mining, and that worked out surplus is constantly being created. For the British Transport Docks Board (BTDB), the unique attribute of location is of predominant importance in determining land holding policy; this is reinforced by the existing investment in dock infrastructure at port locations, which must be protected if long-term trade prospects are not to be jeopardised. Pending use or disposal by the NCB or BTDB, of course, vacancy persists.

Basic agency roles are, in a sense, 'internal' to the development process. Also significant are the twin external influences of finance and the central political context. This latter influence is clearly important in determining the statutory basis for agency roles in the process, but also has important effects on the articulation of those roles and their relationship to land. For instance, the current trend towards 'privatisation' is manifested in the process by pressures which encourage the disposal of surplus land and other assets to the private sector. These pressures take a variety of forms: the establishment of land registers, the abolition of redundant lands procedure, moves to encourage or force the sale of council houses, and pressures on the nationalised

industries to dispose of capital assets to meet government
financial requirements. Complementary pressures exist which
limit the flow of land into the public sector development
process, such as the provision of land reclamation grants to
the private sector. Similarly, the external influence of
finance affects publicly held vacant land in several different
ways. These do not necessarily all relate to the availability
of development finance. As noted above, the sale or leasing
of such land may be required in order to generate capital or
revenue receipts with which to support an agency's main
function. Within the process, a shortage of funds may prevent
actual construction and lead to a period of vacancy, but
during this time the site may be the responsibility of an
agency other than the one concerned with development. The
shortage of grants for development by housing associations for
instance, is felt not at tender but at loan approval stage,
i.e. prior to site acquisition by housing associations. Where
local authorities shoulder the task of land supply for
associations, it is they who will be left to meet debt charges
and maintenance expenses pending development. Alternatively,
site preparation may be hampered by a lack of funds, as in the
case of recent cutbacks on the WDA reclamation programme; this
will prevent the removal of those constraints on site
development that can be expressed in financial terms.

These difficulties relate to a separation of the two
functions of finance provision and development which places
the developing agency in a vulnerable position, particularly
if land acquisition has already been accomplished with the
expectation of funds for construction becoming available.
This vulnerability stems not only from the reliance of many
agencies (such as the local authorities, the WDA, and housing
associations) on external central finance for successful
development, but also from the insertion of various grant or
fund-distributing bodies in the central government-agency
link. The WDA performs this latter function for land
reclamation schemes carried out by the local authorities; this
allocative role is also carried out for their respective
'clients' by the University Grants Committee and the Housing
Corporation. In these situations, the landowning agencies are
not only dependent upon an external source of finance, but
must also satisfy whatever criteria for allocation of funds
are laid down by the intermediate body.

Furthermore, within the development feasibility leg of the
process, contributions from several different agencies with
different objectives and different capital programmes may be
necessary to secure the development of a site. Indeed, those
agencies that do have a remit for development are ultimately

dependent on the decisions, actions and programming of other public bodies such as the statutory undertakers. Coordination, therefore is vital if sites are not to remain vacant pending their eventual effective release by some provision of service or infrastructure. In any event, such delays and difficulties relate to the structure of the development process rather than to 'administrative failures' or 'incompetence' on the part of any one development agency.

This account of the relationship of the study sites to the process has concentrated on the dimension of ownership in 'explaining' vacancy, but other approaches are possible (see Nicholson, 1983). For instance, a historical perspective is valuable in understanding processes of use cessation on sites formerly in an industrial use. Here, vacancy can be related to the wider economic context of demand and supply for goods and services, which supplied the rationale for former uses and also influenced their decline. This viewpoint stresses the role of the external economic growth box, as mediated by public policy, in creating land vacancy.

From the process perspective, land vacancy may be characterised as a transient feature of the urban environment, brought about by a variety of economic, political and social changes which in turn stimulate adjustments in land use. The same perspective also stresses the complexity of the development process; indeed, the one generalisation that may safely be made about the vacancy issue is that simplistic analyses, which reduce the phenomenon to one or two local 'causes', are not admissible. Given the complexity of development, the different interests involved, and the variety of pressures which may lead to land use change, such explanations are likely to disguise rather than clarify the processes at work.

However, while these case studies, together with the model used to analyse them, shed light on the complexities of the urban development process and on the place of public ownership of vacant land within it, they can only provide a limited perspective. By focussing on a sample of vacant sites and on the particular processes affecting each, 'external' influences such as central government social and economic policies are treated inadequately, remaining as 'black boxes' in the model, rather than being fully incorporated into the analysis. Clearly, to do this, a more comprehensive framework for the analysis of public landownership is required, addressing especially the ways in which the vagaries of the development process affect, and are articulated by, various public agencies, and the impact of this on all land in public ownership.

A FRAMEWORK FOR THE ANALYSIS OF PUBLIC LANDOWNERSHIP

Complementary investigations of this nature were conducted in South Wales during 1981-1982. A number of closely related premises have crucially informed this work. Firstly, it was felt that public ownership of vacant land could only be adequately analysed within the context of a given agency's overall landownership and of the particular characteristics of its development process. In turn, overall landownership and the development process of different agencies are best analysed in relation to their various operations and activities, and to the internal and external circumstances, forces and relationships that combine to shape these. This avenue suggests that the apparently simple term 'public landownership' is likely to mean different things to different bodies (see Massey, 1980), implying that research into the topic should adopt an institutional approach, aiming to highlight any differences or similarities that emerge with respect to landownership.

In order to examine the intricate web of forces and relationships involved, a clear analytical framework is required. This must be not only sufficiently flexible to accommodate the great variety of public bodies, but also sufficiently comprehensive to enable incorporation of the wide range of forces influencing their operations, especially with regard to landownership. The broad parameters for this framework are set firstly by the use of an institutional approach, as stated above; and, secondly, by the adoption of a 'relational' orientation, interpreting events as the result of a complex interaction of various elements and forces, which in themselves are extremely variable and complicated (see Jessop, 1982). The substantive content of the research reviewed here impels the examination of such interactions in terms of the wide range of public landownership patterns and practices.

To do this, a number of closely related components may be proposed for detailed investigation on an institution-by-institution basis:

1. Historical legacy and development: this involves both the inheritance of structures, conditions, forms of organisation and policies from previous administrations or from predecessors, and the way in which current institutions or recent administrations have retained, developed, altered or jettisoned such arrangements. This includes not only the inherited landownership patterns and practices and the way these have changed over time, but also the effects of changes in organisation, conditions, etc. on these patterns and practices.

2. Commodity production and service provision: public bodies are generally involved in either the production of a specific type of commodity (e.g. coal, electricity), or in the provision of specific services or sets of services (e.g. housing, transport), and occasionally in both (e.g. water authorities). The nature and organisation of the production of a given commodity or the provision of a given service, and the changes that have been effected in relation to them, will clearly have implications for landownership patterns and practices.

3. Statutory powers and obligations: all public bodies are established directly or indirectly under the provisions of parliamentary statutes, which also set out the powers, obligations and spheres of activity to be pursued by the respective institutions. In most instances such responsibilities are mandatory, but certain powers (most commonly given to local authorities) are only discretionary, so that their application varies over time and space. All powers of public land acquisition are similarly limited by statute, usually relating to a specified activity or type of operation. Moreover, the general rules governing public land acquisition furnish further checks in the form of ministerial approval, public inquiries into Compulsory Purchase Orders, and so on. Conversely, public bodies are also enabled to dispose of any interest in land, although the procedural channels for this are nowhere near as labyrinthine.

4. Institutional organisation: this includes not only the formal internal organisation adopted in order to carry out the specific functions allocated to each body by its governing statute(s), but also the forms of representation inscribed into this structure, and the various relationships that they entail. Of particular interest in this regard are the situation and scope of estate management within each body; the relationships between this and other departments in terms of land acquisition, development, management and disposal; and the extent to which formal and informal representation enables different social groups to promote or prevent activities that are seen as being in or against their interests.

5. Political context: the pre-eminent political influence over all public bodies is the policies and actions of central government, especially in terms of financial and operational controls imposed via the supervisory functions of its various departments. The latter themselves are to some extent affected in a similar manner. This overall

political/financial context, therefore, is likely to be of considerable significance in any examination of activities involving public land acquisition, development and/or disposal.

6. External relationships: public bodies are also subject to a wide range of external associations and forces. These include: relationships with those who perceive their interests being affected by overall operations or particular activities, but are unable to achieve their aims via the representative machinery (e.g. environmental groups); the varying levels of demand for the commodity or service in question; the alternative forms (and hence agents) of production or provision, particularly those in the private sector; and the general context set by trends and events in the wider economy and in civil society (e.g. changing employment levels, demographic fluctuations, etc). Again, any of these considerations may play a part in determining the nature of, and changes in, public landownership patterns and practices.

This division into six components is essentially a convenient way of summarising the proposed analytical framework. It should be clear from the brief discussion above that the stress rests firmly on the interrelationships between the various elements, rather than on the elements themselves. It should also be evident that application of the framework to any individual public body will necessarily involve a lengthy and detailed account. For this reason, the example presented here - British Railways Board (BRB) - is examined in summary form. The choice of BRB rested primarily on the frequent derogatory, though unsubstantiated, references to its landownership practices.

BRITISH RAILWAYS BOARD IN SOUTH WALES: AN ANALYTICAL ACCOUNT

General background

The expansion of the railways in the mid-nineteenth century provided an important outlet for the huge capital surpluses being generated at the time by industry and commerce (see Hobsbawm, 1969; Rose, 1981). This extensive investment resulted in a proliferation of railway companies in fierce competition for access to expanding towns and other sources of traffic. Consequently, much unnecessary duplication occurred, with certain industrial areas such as the South Wales coalfield having an extremely dense network of lines. Indeed, many valleys were served by two, and in places three, lines, which with their associated stations and yards occupied a sizeable proportion of the developable land in such areas.

By 1890 the system in South Wales was substantially complete; only minor additions were made after this date (see Barrie, 1980). The fixed nature of this network and the difficulties in securing new investment (mainly due to declining rates of return on capital employed) meant that adaptation to changing patterns of population distribution and of economic activity could only occur very slowly, if at all. These problems were further aggravated by the steady decline in the amount of traffic carried during the inter-war period, in the face of the slump in coal exports on the one hand, and of increasing competition from road transport on the other. As a result, revenue in real terms also decreased. These financial straits - declining revenue and low rates of return - meant that there was very little new or replacement investment in the railways before the Second World War. The heavy traffic carried by the system as part of the war effort - especially serving the ordnance factories built in South Wales - also took its toll, again without any expenditure on replacement equipment.

In other words, at the time of nationalisation in 1948, the railways in Britain faced severe financial and structural problems. As outlined above, their extent had been aggravated by the lack of action taken to deal with them in the past. However, the very nature of railway operations also contributed to their emergence and persistence. The major difficulty concerns the existence of peak demands, especially for passenger services, at certain times of the day or year. Unless the average density of traffic is high, enabling the fixed costs of providing services to be spread more evenly, the track and equipment required to meet peak demand must lie idle, and hence generate no revenue, for most of the time. Methods of reducing fixed costs include: more intensive use of rolling stock and track capacity by means of quicker and more frequent journeys, special excursions, etc; lower levels of track and equipment maintenance, a short-term expedient that often leads to deterioration and ultimately closures; decreases in track mileage and installations by means of layout modifications and rationalisation of activities; and complete line closure, thus eliminating fixed costs (and also revenue) for part of the network. All these strategies have different implications for the management of the railway estate, and a glimpse at the development of the railways under the stewardship of BRB reveals that all four approaches have been adopted at different stages, either separately or in combination.

Thus, between nationalisation and the 1962 Transport Act the main plank of railway policy was the 'Modernization Plan' (British Transport Commission, 1955), involving large investment in new track, equipment and rolling stock. This inevitably featured some rationalisation, with a large number of freight and motive power depots being closed, and a smaller number of station and line closures. However, such moves did little to ease British Railways' financial troubles, and it was concluded that a thorough economic reappraisal was needed. Thus, the famous 'Beeching Report' (BRB, 1963), heralded a massive programme of line, station, depot and yard closures, to the extent that a quarter of the passenger route mileage existing in 1963 had disappeared by 1967. While some of these closures eradicated duplicate facilities, the vast majority were justified solely in terms of the economics of railway operation. Although the plan also included schemes for main-line and suburban electrification, and for the containerisation of freight traffic, the enormous scale of the closure programme had a more dramatic impact on the railway network (and hence on the railway estate) than any other policy since nationalisation.

Although the contraction of the railway network continued into the early 1970s on a reduced scale, a series of concerted campaigns to prevent closures promoted the idea that provision of railway services could be justified on wider social and economic grounds rather than on narrow commercial criteria. This concept of the 'social railway' gradually gained acceptance, most importantly in the Department of Transport. It was enshrined in the 'Passenger Service Obligation' (PSO) introduced under the 1974 Railways Act, providing grants for the continuation of unremunerative services, either from central government or local authority sources. Such policies clearly had a stabilising effect on the extent of the railway network in the mid-1970s. However, at the same time BRBs financial position deteriorated further, reflecting the increasingly adverse conditions facing its operations. Problems included an appreciable rise in unit costs, related to wages, equipment, fuel, and inflation in general; a continued decline in market share for both passengers and freight; and, stemming from these, a growing deficit between revenue and total expenditure (including interest repayments). Three main strategies have been adopted in an attempt to counter these tendencies: measures to attract greater patronage (e.g. concessionary fares); measures aimed at increasing labour productivity (e.g. 'flexible rostering'); and stringing financial controls imposed by central government. 'External finance limits' were first introduced in 1978 for all nationalised industries (see Chancellor of the

Exchequer, 1978), **and relate to all externally-generated** finance, including borrowing, leasing and funds raised from local authorities under the PSO. While this strict financial discipline may well produce a satisfactory economic performance over the short term, the limits act as a strong brake on all investment, and thus may well have damaging long-term consequences. In other words, the investment required to continue and to improve existing services is unlikely to be forthcoming, and a further round of closures may ultimately be inevitable – again with obvious consequences for BRBs landownership pattern.

This brief historical outline of railway development points to the importance of the political motives underlying different policies. Thus, the current concern with productivity, plus the low levels of investment, are inextricably tied up with central government attempts to reduce public expenditure and indebtedness. Similarly, other aspects of transport policy may have a significant impact. In this sense, the massive capital investment involved in the motorway and road-building programmes of the 1960s and early 1970s provide a gauge of the favour with which road transport was treated at the same time as the extent of the railway network was rapidly contracting.

During this period the 'cheap energy' policies pursued by successive governments, based on imported oil, also had devastating effects on the railways. Not only did they support the ideal of universal personal mobility via the private motor car (and hence lend justification to the growth of the road network), but they also resulted in immense changes in the hitherto closely linked coal, electricity and gas industries, which were traditionally major railway customers. Thus the rundown of the coal industry was accompanied by a steady decrease in the number of coal-fired power stations and by the complete disappearance of town gas manufacture. Such trends not surprisingly took a heavy toll in South Wales, with closures of pits, power stations, gasworks and railway lines proceeding virtually hand in hand. These wider considerations help to pinpoint the political choices made by successive governments, choices which have dictated not only the level, but also the form of their influence over BRB affairs.

The railway estate in South Wales

What impact have these historical developments had on the landownership patterns and practices of BRB in South Wales? At

196

the time of nationalisation the region boasted a dense maze of lines, especially in the coalfield areas and around the main seaports. In terms of landownership, British Railways inherited an estimted 6,000 hectares (15,000 acres) from its predecessors in the area. At first the emphasis in the management of this railway estate was placed firmly on operational purposes, with the Western Region being given limits of authority for transactions, above which Executive ratification was required. In fact, at this time there was negligible activity in development or disposal of land, with the relatively small amounts of surplus land generated by closures receiving scant attention. Very few new acquisitions were made, with most new connections being built on customers' land (e.g. Aberthaw 'A' power station; Llanwern steelworks).

Apart from a brief interlude in the 1960s, when a new subsidiary, Railway Sites Limited (RSL), was formed to exploit the development potential of favourable surplus sites (Bonavia, 1971), this remained the position until the late 1960s, when it was realised that freehold disposal of surplus land was not only the best way of dealing with the vast acreage of redundant land released by the Beeching closure programme, but was also a means of generating short-term financial gains. However, the existing department responsible for managing non-operational property was too small to cope with the huge scale of this task, so a specialised estate and property organisation, the British Rail Property Board (BRPB), was established in 1969 to manage both operational and non-operational land and buildings. Its overall approach comprises three main elements: ensuring that there is sufficient land for current and future operational requirements; the development of favourably located sites in order to secure growth of rental income; and the disposal of surplus land on the best terms possible. In South Wales this role is carried out by the South-Western Region of BRPB, based in Bristol.

Where necessary land is acquired for the construction of new lines and connections, generally for freight traffic. In the last decade there have only been three such developments in the region (to a new mine at Treforgan; to the new Ford plant at Bridgend; and to the Fibreglass factory near Pontypool), all related to guaranteed bulk traffic and thus reflecting the switch from wagonload to trainload freight. Only the Ford factory connection has involved land acquisition by BRPB; the other two were completed on land owned by the respective customers. In operational terms, therefore, BRPB is seldom concerned with land acquisition; its main role is to advise and assist each Division and subsidiary in finding more

suitable locations for their activities. This may release
land or property which is better adapted to another kind of
railway use, or which may be surplus to operational
requirements. In the latter case it will either be developed
for a non-railway use, or sold. The general aim is that the
income received from such lettings or sales is at least
adequate to cover relocation expenses. Occasionally an unused
site is retained if potential exists for its future use by a
railway customer; a good example is the old Roath Goods Yard
in east Cardiff.

BRPB retains the freehold of those sites that possess
development potential; these usually enjoy a central location.
Most development schemes are undertaken in partnership with
private developers, using development leases and featuring
mainly commercial, retail and industrial uses. Two prime
examples are located next to Queen Street station in Cardiff -
Fanum House, on the site of the former Taff Vale Railway
headquarters; and Brunel House, on part of the old Rhymney
Railway line to the docks. Very few projects are funded and
managed by BRPB, mainly because of the difficulties of raising
finance. Existing buildings, on the other hand, are
demolished unless an alternative use can be found. Where old
railway buildings have been 'listed' by the local authority,
however, they are given enough maintenance to keep them safe,
even if left empty. Wherever possible, though, occupiers are
found: examples include the headquarters of the Butetown Steam
Trust at Bute Road station, Cardiff; and the conversion of
Abergavenny station house to offices.

BRPB's main business concerns the disposal of the vast
amount of surplus land produced by the closure and
rationalisation programmes of the last two decades. Most of
this is marketed in the conventional manner, although close
liaison with local authorities and other public bodies
sometimes results in sales without marketing. Sites with
development potential, however, are sold with the necessary
planning permission, at a price that reflects the nature of
the proposed development. This commercial approach has
occasionally engendered conflicts between BRPB and other
interested parties, such as local residents' groups and
planning agencies. The crux of the matter is that BRPB is
required to maximise its return from land sales, an objective
that is hampered by the massive amount of railway land that
suffers from poor location, inadequate access, awkward shape,
physical constraints and legal impediments. This is
particularly the case with redundant lines in the South Wales
valleys. Sales of such land merely realise nominal sums that
barely cover the administrative and legal costs of the

conveyance. Because of this, it is seen as important to
obtain the best price possible for those sites that are
attractive to developers.

   Clearly this approach fails to consider the social benefits
or disbenefits of proposed developments; it also results in
some very optimistic proposals. On the other hand, it does
seem to have been successful in terms of the record of
disposals in the South Wales region in recent years; as Table
1 shows, this has been impressive. Roughly 58 per cent of the
total sold represented land released by the operating

Table 1

BRPB Land Sales, South Wales, 1974-1981

Year	Number of Sites Sold	Hectares	Acres	Average size per sale (Hectares)	(Acres)
1974	143	175.8	434	1.23	3.03
1975	100	173.7	429	1.74	4.29
1976	116	138.5	342	1.19	2.95
1977	167	150.7	372	0.90	2.23
1978	155	135.7	335	0.87	2.16
1979	186	119.5	295	0.64	1.59
1980	154	116.2	287	0.75	1.86
1981*	43	25.5	63	0.59	1.46
Total	1064	1035.6	2557	0.97	2.40

* to 31st March only.

Divisions during the period; the rest stemmed from earlier
closure programmes. About 27 per cent took the form of bulk
sales to local authorities - a good example being the
conveyance of a large portfolio of sites to Swansea City
Council. The total receipts from these sales amounted to £2.3
million, an average of about £2,200 per hectare (£900 per
acre). All this meant that by March 1981 the estimated amount
of land in BRB ownership in South Wales was roughly 3,500
hectares (8,600 acres), which represents a 40 per cent

reduction in the size of the railway estate since
nationalisation. Of the 1981 total, only 133.9 hectares
(330.5 acres), or 3.8 per cent, was vacant; as Table 2
indicates, this land was at varying stages of the recycling
process.

Table 2

Status of BRPB Vacant Land, South Wales, 1981

Status	Hectares	Acres
Recently taken out of operational use	70.9	175.0
Under negotiation, on market, or being prepared for sale	15.0	37.0
Under active investigation	6.5	16.0
Held for future operational purposes	1.8	4.5
Without services or access	22.3	55.0
Awaiting planning consent	17.4	43.0
Total	133.9	330.5

    Finally, although no comprehensive information exists, in
South Wales it is possible to trace the fate of a considerable
amount of former railway land since disposal (for example,
Page, 1979).. The principal uses of a sample of such land are
summarised in Table 3, which reveals the predominance of new
roads in taking up the alignment of former branch lines.
These are used to a lesser extent for footpaths and
bridleways. Much remains vacant, especially in the valleys,
although it is perhaps significant that this relates
exclusively to intractable linear parcels, often incorporating
physical obstacles such as cuttings and embankments, rather
than the more developable nodal features like stations and
yards. These are more commonly occupied by extensive uses
like housing and industry. While this evidence helps to
reinforce the argument that mere disposal of an interest in
land by a nationalised industry in no way guarantees its
subsequent re-use, at the same time much of the land
relinquished by the extensive closure programmes in South
Wales has been successfully adapted for other purposes. In the
light of earlier comments, it is perhaps hardly coincidental
that the major replacement use has involved the construction
of new roads, so that in a sense the results of a political

choice, and of the complex chain of interactions that shaped it, may actually be seen on the ground.

Table 3

Principal Uses of Former Railway Land in South Wales

Subsequent Uses	Lines	Stations, Yards etc
Roads	24	2
Industry	3	7
Housing	4	9
Car parking	1	4
Footpaths	7	–
Recreation	5	1
Agriculture	2	–
University	–	3
Local Authority Uses	4	3
Land Reclamation	5	–
Vacant	17	–
Total	72	29

CONCLUSION

The case of BRB in South Wales provides a useful illustration of the way in which the analytical framework may be applied to a concrete example. A similar evaluation of the wide range of other public bodies active in South Wales, currently in preparation, indicates that their landownership patterns and practices to a large extent reflect the exigencies and imperatives of their productive and/or distributive operations, and of the particular way in which such operations have been and are organised. Furthermore, they relate clearly to the various investment strategies and programmes, forward planning statements and needs assessments produced by such bodies, which in turn fluctuate according to the variations in political control, institutional organisation and a host of other economic and social forces and relationships. The framework has essentially attempted to incorporate the extensive and variable range of elements and relations that impinge upon the public sector development process, and as such provides a broad analytical context for the examination of individual sites by means of the model outlined in the first part of the paper.

One of the major implications of the work presented here is that it is perhaps erroneous to think in terms of land policy 'per se', at least as far as public bodies are concerned. The whole direction of these two complementary approaches to the analysis of public landownership has been towards the mechanisms and relationships that interact to produce the patterns, rather than the patterns themselves. This means that any problem associated with public ownership and/or use of land should be tackled by measures that address the complex set of processes that produce the problem, rather than by 'ad hoc' or simplistic directives aimed merely at changing superficial characteristics.

10 The economics of planning gain

GEOFFREY KEOGH

INTRODUCTION

There has recently been a growing debate about the related and controversial practices of bargaining in development control, the use of planning agreements, and the realisation of planning gain. Although there are no firm data available, it is widely held that bargaining for planning gain has increased substantially in recent years. A survey undertaken by Jowell (1977) confirmed that the practice of negotiating for planning gain was widespread amongst planning authorities in the period 1974-1975, while the principle that planning gain should be demanded of certain categories of development has been formalised by a number of authorities through its inclusion in their development plans. Obviously the potential for planning gain will vary between classes of development and between areas, with things that might be viewed as a gain by one authority being seen as a loss by others (Loughlin, 1981). However, there are sufficient examples to show that the scale of benefits that could accrue to authorities which permit highly profitable development is considerable. The property boom in the early 1970s served to underline this point for local authorities, emphasising the possibilities for securing a share in development profits on behalf of the community. At the same time, the machinery for achieving planning gain has become more powerful, offering planning authorities greater scope for entering into planning agreements. The powers to undertake planning by agreement have existed in similar form since 1932. However, the Town and Country Planning Act, 1968 freed authorities from the need to obtain ministerial approval for such agreements while, more significant still, the Housing Act, 1974 (together with various other powers and a growing number of local enactments) strengthened local authority powers by ensuring that obligations of a positive nature could be enforced against successors in title to the land (Grant, 1975 and Jowell, 1977). Previously it had generally been held that only restrictive or negative agreements would be enforceable.

There are mixed feelings about the practice of bargaining for planning gain. Some argue that it is legally invalid, unethical, open to abuse, and completely outside the ambit of legitimate planning. The Property Advisory Group (PAG), in a recent report (Department of the Environment, 1981) which form the basis for a review of planning gain, contend that if the pursuit of public benefits from development goes beyond strict consideration of the planning merits of any proposal, the development control process 'becomes subtly distorted and may fall into disrepute'. They therefore do not accept that planning gain has any place in our system of planning control and conclude that, with only minor exceptions, 'the practice of bargaining for planning gain is unacceptable and should be firmly discouraged'. In contrast, others argue that the scope and flexibility of planning agreements, and the gains which they give rise to, represent a significant opportunity to pursue positive planning. This appears to be the prevailing view within the planning profession and the PAG report has attracted vigorous criticism from planners, from various local authority organisations, and even from some developers. The only point of broad agreement between the critics and advocates of planning gain lies in the widespread support for a review of current practice and for the establishment of broad principles within which bargaining should proceed.

The extensive debate which preceded the PAG report focussed largely upon the legal, procedural and, to a lesser extent, ethical questions which planning gain gives rise to. The debate cannot readily be summarised, although a recent review revealed the two major areas of disagreement to lie, first, in the appropriate definition of planning gain and, second, in the difficulties and dangers associated with the bargaining process (Keogh, 1982). To a considerable extent, these issues arise out of an apparent confusion about the proper purpose of planning and a failure to make explicit the perceived objectives of planning. In the absence of an analytical framework which includes a clear model of what planning is, or should be, attempting to achieve, planning gain has been evaluated primarily in terms of the policy instruments by which it is secured. This is obviously unsatisfactory since both planning gain and planning instruments must be judged in relation to an assessment of planning objectives. Nevertheless, the literature does highlight a number of common anxieties about planning gain, including the possibility that it could seriously undermine the planning process, giving rise to corruption and the unwarranted exploitation of monopoly power by planning authorities. Distributional questions also arise, although recent commentary has been less concerned with the principle of appropriating development profits than with the question of whether they should pass to the local community as planning gain rather than to the Exchequer in the form of Development Land Tax.

In this paper, an attempt is made to extend the existing debate by looking explicitly at the economic implications of planning gain, which have largely been ignored hitherto. The aim is to undertake an economic analysis of planning gain which will provide a framework for investigating some of the criticisms that have been levelled at it. In the next section, planning gain is reviewed in economic terms, concentrating on its implications for the efficient use of land and other resources, and on its distributional impact. In the concluding section, an attempt is made to draw together various economic and non-economic arguments in a reassessment of planning gain.

ECONOMIC ANALYSIS

Planning, whatever else it may be, is an economic activity. It uses resources to achieve specific objectives and must, since resources are scarce, pose a problem in constrained choice. Unfortunately, the objectives of planning are not always clear. Planning appears to have been used to pursue a wide range of goals, sometimes contradictory, which embrace technical, aesthetic, social, distributional and efficiency issues. Economists tend to see planning as an attempt to maximise, or at least improve, social welfare and this seems to be consistent with many of the statements made by planners (Crook, 1974). As Oxley (Oxley, 1975) observes:

"From the mixing pot of statements as to planning's purpose the odour that lingers longest surrounds those concerned with reaching a position which is 'best' for society".

It may be objected that such a broad goal is vacuous and Utopian, doing nothing to inform the analysis of planning practice (Scott and Roweis, 1977). However, most economists writing in this field have interpreted planning as a problem in welfare economics (see, for example, Evans, 1974; Oxley, 1975; Harrison, 1977; Moore, 1978; Willis, 1980; Walker, 1981). Certainly, as Evans (1974) clearly demonstrates, it is possible to interpret most of the problems tackled within the planning process as aspects of market failure: externalities, public goods, monopoly power and imperfect information. While welfare theory remains a doubtful basis for a substantive or procedural theory of planning, it has been advocated as a normative basis for the identification and analysis of planning problems (see Oxley, 1975; and Moore, 1978).

When this approach to planning is adopted, attention becomes focussed on the· initial distribution of resources, the efficiency with which resources are deployed and output is exchanged, and the distribution of output and welfare. The role of planning and any judgement of the planning process will therefore be assessed in terms of these issues. Oxley (1975) argues that this is appropriate since any planned intervention in individual activity must necessarily imply a challenge to the distribution of resources or the efficiency of production and exchange.

For the economist, the important questions posed by planning gain are whether it will improve or worsen the efficiency with which resources are deployed to provide the goods and services which contribute to welfare, and whether the distributional implications are satisfactory. The use of a socially approved welfare function is generally advocated for the purpose of judging distributional consequences. However, the identification of distributional effects is an essential prerequisite of any rational discussion of equity issues. Naturally these economic questions must then be brought together with the broader planning questions raised in the previous debate.

It is interesting to note that the economic argument, in contrast with much of the existing debate, begins with a hypothesis about the purpose of planning. This provides a basis for selecting an appropriate definition of planning gain. In particular, it leads to the rejection of those definitions which identify planning gain in terms of the instruments by which it is achieved (PAG in Department of the Environment, 1981; Ratcliffe, 1981). In an assessment of economic efficiency, planning gain should be defined in terms of the benefit and its source. Thus, Jowell's (1977) definition of planning gain, as:

"... the achievement of a benefit to the
community that was not part of the initial
application (and was therefore negotiated) and
that was not of itself normally commercially
advantageous to the developer",

is accepted, with the qualification that in some circumstances
planning gain may be offered within an application for mixed
development and would not then have to be negotiated
(Loughlin, 1981).

The Land Market

It is essential to begin with a model of land market processes
and for this purpose the neo-classical model of the land
market is used, with its extension through the work of Alonso
(1964), Mills (1972) and others to explain patterns of urban
location. The model envisages perfect goods and factor
markets with land allocated between competing uses on the
basis of its value in production. Land will differ in terms
of its characteristics (fertility in the classical theory of
Ricardo, but accessibility and physical attributes in the
urban adaptations of the land market model) such that a given
parcel of land may be more productive and profitable in one
use rather than another, while a given activity may be more
profitably carried on at one location rather than another.
Competitive bidding between perfectly informed individuals
should determine the overall level of rents throughout the
city and allocate specific plots between users so that the
highest and best (i.e. most profitable) use is made of each
parcel of land. One condition of this outcome is that land
will offer equal returns to competing uses at the margin
between uses. This outcome is illustrated in Figure 1 for the
simple Alonso model where the 'quality' of land depends only
upon proximity to the city centre so that competing land uses
will occupy concentric rings around the city centre. It
denotes the bid rent curves of four competing land uses,
commercial (CC), industrial (II), residential (RR) and
agricultural (AA), while the outer envelope of these curves is
the urban rent gradient. Despite the unrealistic assumptions
of the model, it emphasises the nature of land market
interaction and introduces the notion of efficiency in the use
of land.

Clearly the land market does not work in the smooth and
efficient way suggested by the model. Information is costly

Figure 1

Urban Land Values and Location

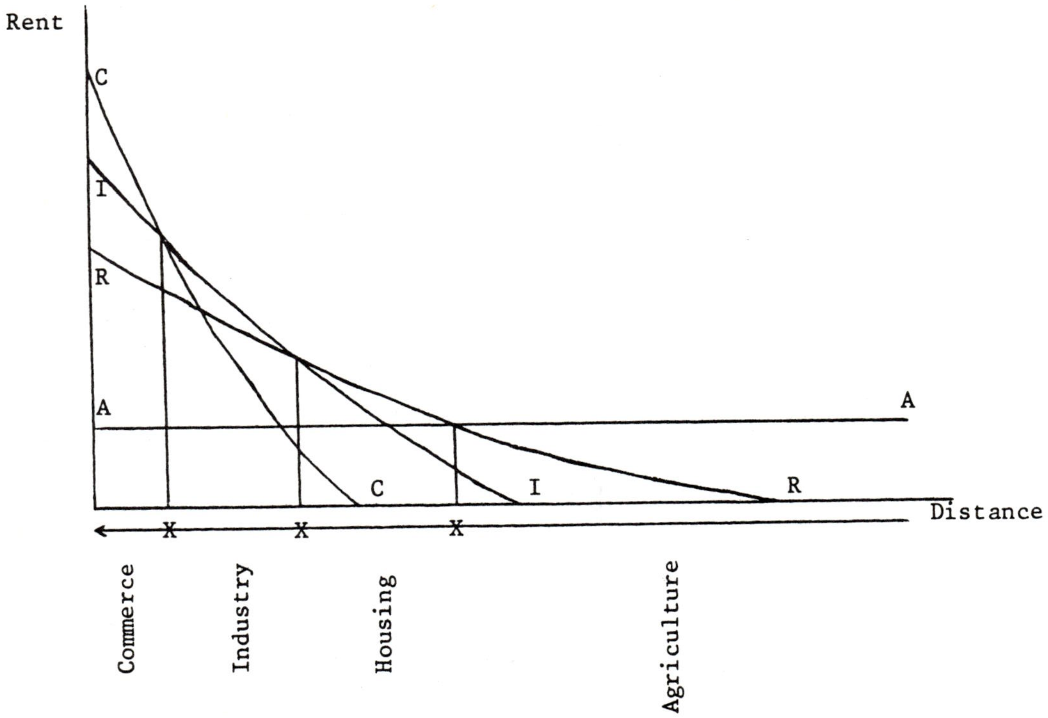

and imperfect, considerable inertia is brought about by high transaction costs and the structure of property rights, while the uniqueness of each parcel of land introduces an element of monopoly power. Of greater significance, land use frequently has public good characteristics, while specific land uses may have external, or spillover, effects on others. As a result, even an efficient market in the private rights in land would fail to achieve a pattern of land use that was socially optimal. Trade in land depends on the private returns (and profitability) to land use and ignores the external benefits and costs that are significant to society. Of course, these are amongst the problems that planning is designed to tackle, even if it is not always articulated in this way.

Planning controls act as a constraint on the market activities of individuals, and market participants will respond by attempting to minimise the impact of planning upon them. While controls on land use may reduce land value differences when used to deal with problems of imperfect information or market power, their use to correct externalities will distort the pattern predicted by the neo-classical model. If the total land allocated to specific uses is restricted it will tend to increase the price of land in those uses, and if the pattern of location is adjusted it will alter the price paid for specific parcels of land. If a private market in land is retained, subject to planning controls, competitive bidding for land on the basis of its profitability will open up discontinuities in the rent gradient (see Figure 2). If planning is concerned with the efficient use of land (subject to the efficient use of other resources, and a satisfactory distributional outcome), then it must be concerned not only with the value of land in production in the same way that an individual land owner would be, but also with the value of any losses or gains accruing to other land users or to the community as a whole. In the same way that private individuals are concerned with the private returns to land and will attempt to maximise them by equalising returns at the margin between uses, so the planner should be concerned with the social returns, which will be maximised by equalising the social return at the margin of land uses (McMillan, 1975). Thus, the difference in land values at the margin should represent any external costs or benefits associated with land use.

This is illustrated in Figure 3 where, for simplicity, the problem is to allocate a given area of homogeneous land, L, between industrial (i.e. developed) use and agricultural (i.e. undeveloped) use. The curve D_i denotes the demand for land in its developed use; the net present value of land, determined

Figure 2

Urban Land Values and Location with Planning Control

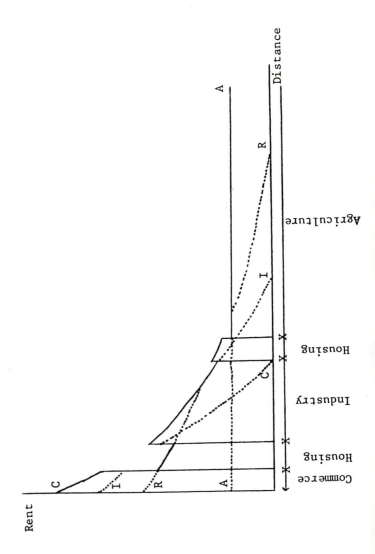

Figure 3

Optimal Rates of Development: Private and Social

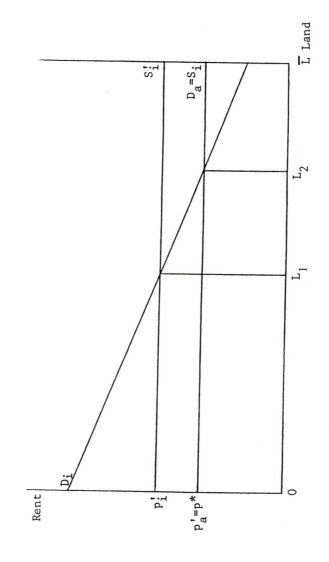

211

by its contribution to industrial profit. The demand for agriculture, D_a , carries similar information but also denotes the supply of land to industrial development, S_i , because developers must bid land away from agriculture, requiring them to offer at least the going price for agricultural land. In an efficient market, L_2 of land would be acquired for development and the value of the marginal land in each use would be equated at the equilibrium price p*. However, development might impose additional, external costs in terms of lost amenity, aesthetic loss, and so on. In these circumstances an assessment of relative social costs and benefits will be required to determine the allowable level of development. If one thinks of the external costs in terms of a money sum, the efficient use of land requires development to occur wherever the value of development exceeds the value of land in its existing use <u>plus</u> the external costs. In terms of Figure 3, the supply curve of land for development should shift upwards to S_i', by an amount equal to the external costs, implying a socially efficient level of development equal to L_1. If planners use development control to achieve this target, it will open up a gap between the return on, and price of, the marginal developed land (= p_i') and the marginal agricultural land (= p_a'). Since this price difference equals the amenity and aesthetic loss from developing the marginal land, the outcome is economically efficient because it equates the marginal social returns to land in each use.

In this model of the land market, planning controls create rental gaps and it is these gaps that signify betterment and the possibility of extracting planning gain. For the developer of marginal land, the value $p_i'-p_a'$ is an economic rent received simply as a consequence of the grant of planning permission. Since, in theory, development will occur provided the developer can earn normal profits, this introduces the possibility of imposing a tax on the unearned economic rent. In principle, any tax up to 100 per cent could be levied without inhibiting efficient development, although Development Land Tax presently stands at 60 per cent, while no estimate has been made of planning gain as a tax on development profits. In general terms it can be observed that, if the planning system allocates land to uses which are acceptable on planning grounds, the land market will, if it is reasonably efficient, allocate that land to the most profitable of the acceptable uses. Any development profits which result could then be taxed directly or by means of planning gain.

Planning Gain and Economic Efficiency

The land market analysis provides a concept of efficient land use and identifies the potential role for planning controls in achieving efficiency. Planning gain is the realisation of some or all of the economic rent as a benefit for the local community, and this section investigates the effect of planning gain on the efficiency of resource use. There are several aspects to this question concerning both the direct impact of planning gain on the efficiency of land use, and the efficiency with which resources are used to produce the specific community benefits that constitute the planning gain.

Concern about the process of bargaining for planning gain has highlighted two conflicting views of the planning system. On a 'rational-legal' view, planning is seen as a wholly negative and regulatory activity where legal rules are firmly established, planning principles predominate, and bargaining has little or no place (see Heap and Ward, (1980). In contrast, Jowell (1977) argues that a 'contractual' model of planning may be more tenable , emphasising flexibility and the scope for negotiation. There is considerable evidence to suggest a well established tradition of negotiation in the development control process (Harrison, 1979). In a recent paper, Davies (1980) suggests that development control is not merely a process by which development plans are implemented, but should be seen, amongst other things, as a means by which environmental policy is extended and updated through the interpretation of 'other material considerations'. On this view, development control

> "... moves away from a fundamentally straight-
> forward administrative process into a more
> complex negotiating process between the various
> interests concerned in development".

Under a regulatory approach to planning there is a danger that planning permission will be granted or refused on the basis of whether the proposed development is crudely categorised as acceptable or unacceptable. However, it seems more realistic to examine planning control in a trade-off formulation in which some developments have greater planning disadvantages, but also offer greater benefits. These benefits are reflected in the profitability of the land use and ultimately in the scope for the realisation of planning gain. The prospect of planning gain provides the planning authority with an incentive to evaluate the trade-off. This situation is illustrated for a simple example in Figure 4. The problem again concerns the allocation of a given quantity of

Figure 4

Rates of Development with Competing Developing Categories

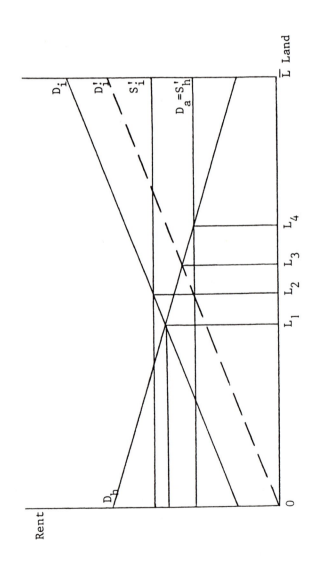

214

homogeneous land, $\overline{L}$, at present in agricultural use. However, there are now two categories of development, housing and industrial, competing to secure land. Agricultural use value is denoted D_a, with D_h and D_i showing the value of the land in housing and industrial use respectively. In a free and efficient land market, and assuming no externalities between residential and industrial uses, all land would be developed with L_1 allocated to housing and $\overline{L}-L_1$ allocated to industry. Marginal returns to land would be equated at p*. If it is now assumed that housing development generates no undesirable social costs but that industrial development does, appropriate supply prices can be specified to reflect social costs. Thus, housing need only cover lost agricultural use value S_h' while industrial development should be required to cover additional social costs reflected in the supply curve S_i'. In a regulatory planning system, the probable response to the external social costs of industrial development would be to permit housing development up to L_4 but forbid industrial use (the application of 'proper planning principles'?). If the problem is to secure efficient land use, the regulatory planning solution is unacceptable since much of the potential industrial development is sufficiently profitable to cover its social costs. If a trade-off were permitted between social costs and development value, planning consent would be granted for industrial development up to $\overline{L}-L_2$. With the planning authority willing to grant residential planning permission for L and industrial planning permission for $L-L_2$, the land market would bring about outcome L_2 as the allocation which maximises development profit subject to the constraint that all development must cover its full social cost. Subject to the same constraint, this also maximises the potential for planning gain which, in turn, provides the planning authority with its incentive. In the absence of planning gain, with social costs of development which are often borne locally, it would not be in the interest of any individual authority to permit development which generates social costs, even though the benefits from development might be extremely high. Clearly such an outcome would be inefficient.

It remains to add one qualification to this result. Although negotiation for planning gain will increase the extent to which planning decisions reflect net social benefits, it may not be sufficient to achieve an optimal pattern of development. This can be seen in Figure 4 by subtracting social costs from the value of land in industrial use to derive an adjusted industrial demand curve D_i'. D_i' and D_h are now comparable in that they both show development value net of external social costs. The intersection of these curves at L_3 denotes the allocation of land between housing and industry which would maximise the net social benefit from development.

The second efficiency argument raised by the critics of planning gain concerns the abuse of monopoly power by planning authorities. This is somewhat ironic since one of the apparent functions of planning is to overcome problems caused by private monopoly power in the land market. The problem envisaged by the critics appears to be one in which the planning authority acts like a monopolistic firm, restricting output, raising price and maximising profits (see Willis, 1981). In this case, output would be the flow of land for development, price would be the price of land in developed use, and profit would be the value of planning gain received by the authority. However, this is to misunderstand the operation of the land market. The monopolistic firm maximises profit in a given time period by determining the profit - maximising flow of output which, since all units of output are the same, sells for the highest price attainable in the market for that level of output. Whilst the planning authority undoubtedly enjoys a degree of monopoly, its power is as a discriminating monopolist, since the grant of planning permission is determined on a case by case basis. If planning authorities are allowed to bargain for planning gain, and respond to this possibility with effective negotiation, they will have every incentive to ensure that the rate at which land is taken for development is optimal, because planning gain in excess of social costs can be earned on every planning permission up to the marginal development at which the marginal social benefit is just equal to marginal social cost. By this means the planners would secure planning gain up to the value of the excess profits from development. It is clear that the flow of land to developed use is less likely to be unduly restricted where planning gain is permitted than it is under a system of absolute planning standards. If anything, there is a danger that permitted development might overshoot the social optimum by allowing some development that could not cover its social costs. In this event, planning gain could genuinely be said to have undermined valid planning principles, and safeguards would be required to avoid this outcome.

A further reason for discounting the monopoly argument lies in the competition between local authorities to secure development, especially if planning gain is permissible. Certainly there may be some developments that are immobile and must either occur at a given site or not at all. But development finance is not immobile and is likely to flow out of an area in which the price of development (in terms of planning gain) is too high. Real property is one form of investment and 'the location and character of development are determined by investment criteria' (Ambrose and Colenutt, 1975). Thus, the demand curve for development will shift to the left as the 'price' of development falls in other areas, although there is no empirical evidence concerning the size of this effect. Many forms of development will be highly mobile and it has been argued (by Broadbent, 1977, for example) that it is the developer who generally enjoys the stronger bargaining position. Planning authorities, in their desire to obtain planning gain, are unlikely to pitch their demands so high that they deflect development from their area. In the light of this, it is interesting to return to the point, made in the introduction, that what constitutes a gain in one area might be seen as a loss in another. In areas of low unemployment and high demand for industrial and commercial development, a planning gain could be obtained to offset any environmental costs involved. However, where unemployment is high and demand for industrial and commercial use is low, the reverse may be true. In this case, the marginal social costs of development may lie below the loss of existing use value once the social costs of unemployment are taken into account. Instead of extracting planning gain, the local authority would be justified in offering incentives to secure development. Thus, in the first area the ensuing environmental costs are the costs to be traded against planning gain while in the second area the increased activity is seen as the gain for which certain costs must be incurred. Subsidies and incentives to development are the obverse of planning gain.

Samuels (1978) argues that planning gain is illusory because, by increasing the costs of development, it will lead developers to charge a higher price for their product. Similarly, Tucker (1978) expresses the view that planning gain is inflationary. This is a fallacious argument. The price of office, factory or residential space will be determined by the market, with demand playing a key role due to the inelasticity of supply in the property market. Planning gain will simply reduce the residual that exists after the costs of development have been deducted from revenue. This residual is seen in conventional theory as flowing to the land owner so that it is the land owner rather than the consumer who gives up surplus to the planning authority. It is true, however, that if planning authorities restrict the release of land for development, that restriction in supply will push up the productive value of the land and hence the price of such land. If land prices rise by only the amount required to cover social costs, it merely means that developers, and ultimately

217

consumers, are being required to pay the social costs of their production and consumption, and this should improve the allocation of resources. It is important to note that this is an outcome of planning controls in general and should not be attributed to the extraction of planning gain.

Planning gain may be viewed as an alternative, and some would say unauthorised, tax on development. It was argued above that, in principle, a tax on development profits should not retard development provided it does not erode normal profits. In practice, it has been said of the various direct taxes on development that they reduce the rate at which development occurs below that which is optimal. It is appropriate to ask whether planning gain is likely to affect the rate of development. Evans (1983) has argued that the rate of development may be reduced due to supply side factors in the land market. He points out that land (and real property) will often be valued by their owners at above market price, reflecting consumer surplus. Thus, a farmer who owns his land would not be induced to sell by an offer equal to the land value in agricultural use. He would require, in addition, a sum to compensate him for the other benefits that he enjoys from his land; for example, historic, social and family ties, and so on. Since a development tax would look only at the difference between value in agricultural use and developed use, part of any such gain would be paid in tax. The farmer would therefore require a greater pre-tax price to obtain a given sum in compensation for the loss of non-pecuniary benefits, and this would reduce the rate of development below the social optimum. This is shown in Figure 5 where agricultural use value is denoted D_a and S is the supply curve for land, sloping upwards to show increasing consumer surplus earned by successive parcels of land. S_t shows the supply price required to cover a proportional tax on development profits while still allowing the vendor to recoup his consumer surplus. The tax will reduce the level of development from L_4, where the marginal returns to land are equal for developed and undeveloped uses, to L_2, where developed land is worth more than undeveloped land at the margin, signifying an inefficient use of land. If instead, development profits were appropriated as planning gain, no such effect would arise. The developer would have to pay above agricultural use value to secure the land, and the available planning gain would be constrained by the profitability of development. In other words, it is the pure rent signified by the gap between the necessary purchase price of land and its developed value that would be taxed, rather than the gap between agricultural use value and developed value.

Figure 5

Effect of Development Tax and Planning Gain on the Rate of Development*

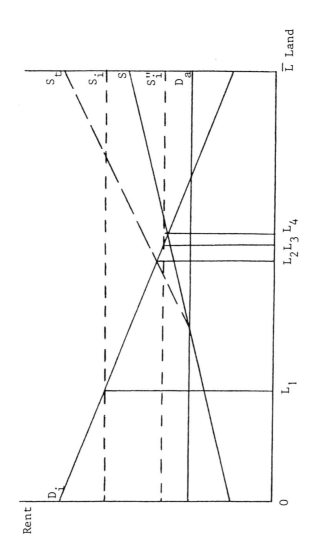

* adapted from Evans (1983, Figure 4)

219

This argument becomes further complicated when planning action to cover social costs is brought into the picture. If the social costs of development are very high (e.g. S '), land use controls designed to secure the socially optimal rate of development (L_2) will not be frustrated either by a development tax or by planning gain. However, if social costs at the margin are relatively low, with external costs less than any consumer surplus grossed up to cover taxation (e.g. S_i"), development tax will slow development below the socially efficient rate permitted through planning controls (L_3) whereas planning gain will not. Thus the outcome depends on the scale of the externality and the rate of tax on development (the slope of S_t increasing as the tax rate increases). The crucial point is that, when the development of land is restricted by planning control, development tax may sometimes permit an efficient outcome but, planning gain should always permit an outcome that is efficient in allocative terms.

Finally in this section, the discussion turns away from questions of efficient land allocation to issues concerning efficiency in the production of community benefits. It has been suggested that, while planning gain in the form of some physical community provision might be acceptable, cash payments to a local authority would not be. Similarly, it has been argued that community benefits provided on, or directly related to, the development site that gives rise to the gain might be acceptable, but benefits provided off-site or unrelated to the initial project would not be (Heap and Ward, 1980). It is difficult to see the logic of these arguments. Once one admits the principle of securing planning gain, defined as it is at the beginning of this section, the essential questions concern the efficiency with which any planning gains are secured, and not where and in what form they are secured. Harrison (1977) makes this point, using as his example a commercial development from which planning gain is secured in the form of housing. If the developer constructs the housing as part of the overall project it might be more expensive than if the local authority constructed it. Further, if it is isolated within a commercial development it might be of lower value than if it had been constructed in a wholly residential area. In these circumstances it would make more sense to secure a cash payment which the local authority could use to construct housing elsewhere, perhaps as part of a larger housing project. It is also important to remember that planning gain is limited by the profitability of a project. It might, therefore, be more effective to pool the gains from a number of sites, and this could again favour cash payment. For example, the limited provision of public open space as part of a number of individual developments might represent an insignificant public benefit, whereas a sizeable public park obtained by pooling planning gain could be of significant value to the community. The efficient provision of the community benefits which constitute planning gain may, therefore, depend on planning gain accruing to the planning authority initially in the form of cash to be used for facilities located elsewhere than on the original development site.

Planning Gain and Distribution

It would be insufficient to judge planning gain solely in terms of its implications for economic efficiency. Policies which secure a high degree of efficiency in the use of land and other resources could carry distributional effects that were wholly unacceptable. Indeed, it is possible for efficiency and equity to conflict, posing policy makers with the problem of trading one off against the other. It is easier to make *a priori* assessments of efficiency because economic efficiency is essentially a technical concept. But distributional judgements must rest on some form of social welfare function derived through the political process. The debate about planning gain must implicitly be concerned with the right of the community to appropriate some or all of the unearned increment in land value that follows from the grant of planning permission. The chequered history of policy designed to achieve this during the period since 1947 (for example, Cullingworth, 1982) illustrates the controversial nature of this issue. However, in recent years a broad consensus appears to have emerged favouring a community share in development profits. The area of dispute has now shifted to the size of that share and the method of its achievement. Clearly to include the pursuit of planning gain as an instrument of planning policy is to concur with the crucial distributional judgement that the community should participate to some degree in development profit. Subject to this underlying judgement, there are three main observations that should also be recorded on the question of distribution.

First, referring back to the economic theory of rent and land use, it is assumed that the owner of land will secure the whole of any excess profits that are generated on his land. Land values will be determined as a residual and competition between users will ensure the outcome for the land owner. In terms of the simple theory, planning gain will be secured at the expense of the land owner rather than the developer since it will reduce the residual revenue after development costs have been met. Ratcliffe (1981) suggests that most developers accept the inevitability of the 'planning gain game', while Heap and Ward (1980) argue that developers who do not wish to jeopardise present or future planning applications perpetuate the planning gain process by their acquiescence. But if the land market works with a reasonable degree of efficiency, this could explain why developers are so ready to acquiesce in the surrender of planning gain. The real conflict would be between the planning authority and the initial land owner rather than between planner and developer. With or without planning gain, the developer expects to receive near normal profit. The fear that a redistribution of income away from the developer towards the community would reduce the incentive for development activity would seem unjustified on this view. In practice, as Ball (1981) notes, there is a struggle between land owner and developer to secure development profits, and the outcome of that struggle is uncertain. In assessing the distributional implications of planning gain this could be significant. Clearly, Ball's observation alters the distributional perspective and indicates a much more complex bargaining model. In particular, the land owner's share in development profit will depend on his likelihood of obtaining planning permission. An experienced developer may possess the expertise and resources required to obtain a planning permission that the original land owner would find difficult to secure.

Second, planning gain has been described as an ad hoc local tax with an arbitrary impact on the process of development. However, it is not planning gain which is arbitrary but planning itself. The effect of planning is arbitrary in the way in which, by the granting of planning permission, it creates value for some but not for others. In particular, it is inevitable that planning based on absolute planning standards will be arbitrary in its impact. Jowell (1977) expresses concern that planning gain may undermine the principle of even-handed justice. But planning gain is only arbitrary because different authorities hold different positions in the present confused climate. If bargaining for planning gain were the normally accepted practice, it would cease to be arbitrary as local authorities automatically bargained to secure development profits and to ensure that the development at least met its social costs. This would be even-handed in the sense that all developers would face a similar tax on development profit. It would be somewhat more just since it would raise the possibility of trading community gains against any environmental disbenefits.

The third aspect of distribution arises once the practice of 'taxing' development profits is accepted. This relates to the

distribution of 'revenue' between central and local government. Heap and Ward (1980) argue that planning authorities
have no right to pre-empt the government by taking a first-
slice of development profits as planning gain. But it could
be argued that this is best judged in relation to who bears
the costs of development. If development profits arise
because planners attempt to ensure that social costs are
covered, planning gain can be viewed as a payment to compensate for social costs. Since it is likely that many of the
environmental costs of development will be borne locally, it
seems reasonable that, if the community agrees to permit the
development, any compensating benefits should accrue to the
local community rather than to the Exchequer. This is clearly
related to the efficiency argument above where it was stated
that, unless there is an opportunity to secure planning gain,
no authority will have an incentive to permit 'undesirable'
development no matter how profitable it may be. It is in
situations of intra-marginal development, where there are
substantial development profits over and above any social
costs of development, that problems could arise. It is then
not so obvious that local authorities should benefit from
these gains in preference to central government. Indeed,
there may be a case for redistributing such gains to those
areas which have little to offer potential developers and
would benefit from providing 'negative planning gain' in the
form of development incentives.

Summary

From the analysis developed above it can be seen that
conventional economic theory offers no justification for
objections to planning gain. There is scope for argument
about the extent to which the distributional outcome would be
desirable but, in terms of economic efficiency, planning gain
appears likely to improve, rather than worsen, the allocation
of land and other resources. It is, however, important to
make clear the limitations of this mode of analysis. It is a
partial analysis with all the difficulties which that implies
concerning inefficiency in markets beyond the control of
planners (i.e. second best problems). It ignores certain
realities of the land market such as imperfect information and
the pursuit by land owners and developers of goals other than
the maximisation of profit, and it fails to take complete
account of the complex bargaining process between land owners,
developers and planners to which Ball (1981) alludes.
Finally, it inevitably begs many questions about the political
and social dimensions of planning which underly the earlier
comment that welfare economics and neo-classical rent theory

may represent a poor framework for analysing what planners actually do. To see planning practice as a welfare maximising, optimising activity may be a serious misrepresentation of the truth.

It may also be objected that the values of the market place are too dominant in this analysis. In many respects this conflicts with conventional attitudes to planning. However, planning controls exist within a market economy and the ability of the market to dissipate the impact of planning inevitably forces planners to pay heed to the forces of the market place. Furthermore, the operation of decentralised market processes probably provides the best available assessment of social preferences and values for use as data in some aspects of planning. As Kirk (1980) notes, planning gain is at odds with certain important principles of planning but this is not a situation of the planners' making.

> "It is the fundamental limitations of land use planning in a capitalist economy, where the rules of the market make the running, which give rise to this sort of bargaining in the first place".

Under the existing planning regime, the right to develop land has been nationalised in the social interest. Rights to use and to own land remain in private hands and trade in these rights is permitted through the land market. It seems inconsistent to allow the owners and users of land to exchange property rights while denying the community the ability to trade in development rights, to its greater advantage. There is nothing objectionable in the 'sale of planning permission' (subject to certain constraints to be discussed in the concluding section). It would simply place the local community on an equal footing with the existing participants in the land market.

CONCLUSIONS

In this paper an attempt has been made to extend the existing debate to include the economic aspects of planning gain. The economic arguments were developed by reference to a number of simple theoretical propositions which doubtless do not do justice to the complexity of urban problems or planning activity, and for this reason the legal-ethical problems and the economic arguments must be drawn together in this concluding section.

Foremost amongst the anxieties of those who criticise planning gain are the twin dangers of corruption and coercion. Many people find the idea of selling planning permission abhorent because it suggests an abuse of power. This is slightly odd in a society where we sanction as a matter of common practice the sale of the other rights in land enjoyed by individuals. However, it is clear that what is envisaged is a situation where some wholly unacceptable planning request is acceded to simply because of the planning gain that is offered. In terms of the analysis above, this would represent a situation in which the social costs of development were considered to be infinite (as when development would destroy an irreplaceable and vital environmental resource) or at least so high that the proposed development could never cover its social costs and should therefore not be allowed. Naturally, the danger of corruption is always present, although Jowell (1977b) found no evidence of corruption in the pursuit of gains and Harrison (1979) found no significant evidence of corruption in the general sphere of development control. It arises in a situation where the identification and judgement of social costs and benefits will frequently be highly subjective and controversial. Often the problem will involve intangible and immeasurable items of cost and benefit. There will therefore be room for argument over the values that should attach to such items. But this is no justification for adopting a system of rigid rules, because any planning choice between acceptable and unacceptable development must itself imply a valuation of social costs and benefits. Rather, it is a case for bringing such valuations into the open where they can be the subject of public debate. The way to avoid corruption is not to hide behind a series of allegedly clear regulations and guidelines, but to ensure that the procedures of planning, including bargaining for planning gain, are open and legitimate. On these grounds, there should be greater formalisation of planning gain in the planning process, with planning agreements subject to appeal either on the grounds of unreasonable demands by planning authorities or on the grounds of their unwillingness to enter an agreement. This would not be a completely new departure since it already occurs implicitly in the case of mixed developments which include elements of social provision in combination with normal commercial development. It is also important that the public should play an active role in the procedure. It has been shown that public participation is feasible although, as always, care must be taken to ensure that participation is real rather than a cynical token exercise (Loughlin, 1978, Durrant, 1982). In a recent paper, Loughlin (1981) argues that public participation could be secured through the discussion of any planning gain criteria which are formally specified in Development Plans, and in the preparation and use of Development Briefs. These procedures would not altogether eliminate the dangers of corruption and the abuse of power, but these dangers arise in the general operation of the town planning system rather than as a specific adjunct of planning gain. There is always the possibility that planners and elected councillors will be tempted to pursue goals other than 'good planning'.

The existing debate raises a number of questions of legality concerning the use of agreements to secure planning gain. These legal issues are beyond the scope of this paper, but one important comment should be made. There is no apparent case, on economic grounds, for rejecting the pursuit of planning gain. If the legal instruments are not adequate or not suitable, then changes should be made to the powers of planners in preference to throwing aside the legitimate pursuit of planning gain on the grounds of legal uncertainty. Much of the existing debate is deficient because it takes no clear position on what planning is attempting to achieve. But it is that point of reference which is essential to any rational consideration of the efficacy of planning gain, and the legal requirements should follow from it.

The need for guidance on the issue of planning gain has been recognised by the Secretary of State and a circular on the subject has recently been issued (Department of the Environment, 1983). This sets out a number of tests of reasonableness to be applied to any requirement for planning gain, and encourages planning authorities to offer formal guidance within their Statutory Development Plans. These tests imply a restrictive interpretation of the legitimate pursuit of planning gain.

"The essential principle to apply is that the facility to be provided or financed should be directly related to the development in question or the use of the land after development".

In general, the economic arguments raised in this paper have not been incorporated in the circular.

Official guidance should be based on a thorough analysis, both theoretical and empirical, of the effects of bargaining for planning gain. The PAG report, and many of the responses to it, totally failed to provide an adequate basis for formulating advice. This paper offers a theoretical perspective of the economic problems raised by planning gain but it is important to emphasise that very little is known at present about the importance of planning gain in practice or the behaviour of planning authorities in securing gain. Among the empirical questions that should be answered are, first, to what extent do local authorities compete for development through variations in the 'planning gain price' of development, second, to what degree does planning gain capture development profit and, third, who pays in practice?

On the theoretical evidence of this paper, there appear to be grounds for establishing the pursuit of planning gain as a legitimate responsibility of local planning authorities. To perform this role effectively they would need to acquire the negotiating and analytical skills required to bargain effectively and this implies an expansion of the range of professional inputs into planning. Kirk (1980) suggests that:

> "Development control officers should be as adept
> at calculating financial margins and likely
> profits to be made if planning permission is
> granted as the developer's own staff".

On the evidence of Jowell (1977b), some authorities are already moving in this direction. His study revealed two London Boroughs which were in the habit of employing independent valuers to assess potential development profits for this purpose. Bargaining for planning gain should ensure a pattern of development which is more nearly socially efficient, while ensuring that benefits accrue to the local community which permits the development and which, in many cases, will bear much of the social cost. It offers the additional advantage of avoiding both the need to compute Development Land Tax liability, which can be complex (Hoyes, 1982), and the associated difficulty of dealing with those offers of planning gain which are merely 'superficial gloss 1981). Grant (1976) argued that the Community Land Act would have formalised the practice of bargaining for planning gain. By the same logic, it is interesting to note that the outcome of a comprehensive pursuit of planning gain should be the same as the intended outcome of the Community Land Act, but without the intervening stage of land ownership by the local authority.

Heap and Ward (1980) ask rhetorically, in the sub-title to their paper, 'how much can the system stand?' This illustrates the seriousness with which they regard planning bargaining, which is of course the means by which major planning gains are generally achieved. The implication is that the development control process is in danger of collapse through being used for what Heap and Ward consider to be inappropriate purposes. However, while one could dispute the distributional consequences of planning gain and the legal validity of some of the means by which it is obtained, there seems to be little support for the view that development control is endangered by the pursuit of planning gain. If anything, the efficiency of land use is likely to be enhanced. As Grant (1975) says:

> "... the use of agreements <u>in itself</u> does nothing to lessen the overall control of undesirable development: if anything they serve to supplement and strengthen control".
>
> (emphasis added).

This conclusion can be extended to apply not only to planning agreements but also to the realisation of planning gain in general.

11 Apportioning the infrastructure costs of urban land development

MARTIN LOUGHLIN

URBAN LAND MARKETS

Urban land markets function as a system of differential locational advantages in which a major determinant of the value of any particular land parcel is the result of decisions made concerning the use of neighbouring sites. This inter-dependent quality of urban land is referred to by economists in terms of <u>externalities</u>: those impacts (whether positive or negative) of a land use decision which are not reflected in the pricing system of the firm or individual responsible for them. The decision to build a factory in a particular location may, for example, have a negative externality impact on a neighbouring residential area as a result of the increase in the levels of air-borne and noise pollution resulting from its operation. That same decision, however, could have positive externality impacts on other sites in the area, whether because a site thereby becomes a suitable location for secondary industrial processes or because it is devoted to commercial use and benefits from the custom of the factory's employees. The existence of significant externalities in the functioning of urban land markets is generally given as a major reason for state intervention. State regulation of the land development process thus aims to minimise the disruptive effects of externalities on the efficient functioning of market processes.

The state, however, does not intervene in the functioning of urban land markets merely to regulate these processes but also directly provides many services which are vital to the efficient functioning of the urban system but which the market either cannot or will not provide. Economists generally refer to these services as public goods and merit goods. Public goods have two defining characteristics: non-excludability (which means that it is impossible to charge consumers for the use of goods) and non-rivalness (which means that more of the goods can be consumed without adding to the costs of the service). Merit goods are those goods which are provided more cheaply than the consumer may be willing to pay, on the assumption that they are felt to be desirable:

> "it is presumed that consumer sovereignty is not working - that the individual fails to perceive the full benefits of consumption and therefore public policy should correct the bias"
>
> (Lee, 1981).

On this analysis state provision of urban services can realistically be presented as falling into one of the following categories:

(1) Those services (street lighting and street cleaning for example) where it is either impossible or inefficient to charge for use. That is, disproportionately large administrative costs would be involved if any attempt were made to charge consumers for the use of these services.

(2) Services, such as museums and art galleries, community centres, streets and parks, which exhibit the characteristic of non-rivalness insofar as the marginal cost of use, once the service is provided, is virtually zero.

(3) Services such as sewage and refuse disposal, water services and other public utilities, which are extremely capital extensive, which consequently tend to have decreasing average and marginal costs over the entire range of their output and which therefore have a tendency to monopoly. Such monopoly power, particularly in relation to any service which is crucial to the functioning of the economic system, is generally regarded as unacceptable and consequently state intervention is required.

(4) Finally, there are certain urban services, which

neo-classical economists label merit goods, which are underwritten by the state because otherwise they will not be consumed in quantities sufficient to render them functional to the needs of the society. Libraries and other cultural facilities are generally given as examples, although more basic services include the state provision of housing, education and health care. The history of state provision of these services shows that, as a result of the operation of the labour market, a large proportion of the workforce are, at any particular time, unable to afford to purchase such services in sufficient quantity or quality as would be functional for the existing needs of society.

In all these cases the tendency in Britain has been for the state to intervene by directly assuming responsibility for the provision of such services. These services may be referred to as infrastructure services: those services which either render possible land development (service roads, water, sewerage and utility services and street lighting); or make it acceptable in terms of contemporary standards (parks and amenity areas, street cleaning and refuse services) or which are rendered necessary as a result of the development (schools, health and welfare services, libraries and other cultural facilities and public transport). For the above reasons few of these services are financed primarily through user charges. Rather it is felt that the more efficient means of financing such services is by providing them free of charge and raising the costs of service provision through taxation. Consequently to the extent that these services are provided by the state they have a tendency to underwrite the profitability of any particular development scheme.

LAND VALUES AND THE LAND DEVELOPMENT PROCESS

The state, therefore, through the functions of providing infrastructure and regulating development, occupies a key role in the land development process. As a result the process is itself politicised. Because of the importance of the state's role the distribution of advantages in the urban system can no longer be seen as a result of the 'impartial' processes of the market. This is particularly critical in the context of land values. Land values in the urban system are both shifted among sites (from state regulation of development which operates to grant development permission on some sites and refuse it on others) and increased (from state investment in the production of vital urban infrastructure) as a result of

state intervention.   **The entire question of land values   thus**
becomes politicised.   Should value and movement in value rest
where it falls (on the view that engaging in any form of
economic activity involves the assumption of risk)?   Should
landowners be compensated by the state for state action which
reduces land values (due to the fact that, given the powers
available, the state is in a special position, its actions
therefore often cannot be predicted by 'normal' market signals
and consequently it should underwrite any losses it causes)?
Should the state recoup increases in value resulting from
state provision of infrastructure (to obtain a contribution
towards this massive expenditure outlay from those who
directly benefit from it)?   Should the state recoup all
increases in value resulting from the state action (on the
grounds that all such increases are 'unearned' by landowners)?

In Britain several unsuccessful attempts have been made
since the establishment of a comprehensive planning system to
deal with the issue of land value movements arising from its
operation (Cullingworth, 1982).   The focus on this aspect of
land value movement, however, has diverted attention from the
question of the possibility of recouping increases in land
values resulting from the provision of infrastructure by the
state.   Such recoupment mechanisms existed in the late
nineteenth century (Parker, 1965) although some were not very
successful in realising their objectives (Turvey, 1953).

Nevertheless, many contemporary development projects require
a heavy expenditure outlay by public agencies on various forms
of infrastructure.   Although these services may directly
benefit the project it is often assumed that this expenditure
outlay should be financed through general taxation.
Consequently, given the failure successfully to resolve the
land value question arising from the operation of the
regulatory planning system and given also the existence of a
statutory system of compensation for the depreciatory impact
on land values arising from the provision of public
infrastructure (Grant, 1982b), the question of whether there
are, or ought to be, mechanisms for recouping land value
increases attributable to the provision of public
infrastructure should be systematically examined.

As a result of certain recent political and economic
developments this question is of topical significance.
Firstly, there has been a steady shift in the location of new
units of production, leading to a deindustrialisation of
cities (Massey and Meegan, 1978; Young and Mills, 1982).   This
shift has reinforced the trend towards depopulation of the
cities which has occurred since the war.   The favoured

232

locations have either been on the perimeters of cities or in small towns. In either case a heavy outlay in new infrastructure is likely to be required. Given that somewhere in the region of one-quarter to one- third of the overall development area may be required to provide infrastructure and that public agencies acquiring land for such purposes may have to pay a price which incorporates its increased worth because the infrastructure is being provided (DoE 1972) a growth programme could impose a very heavy capital burden on a local authority.

Secondly, the period since the mid-1970s may be characterised as one of significant public expenditure restraint. Consequently, since local authorities have been severely constrained in the services they may provide, there may be a tendency for authorities to refuse permission for development on the ground that it is premature and would impose a severe strain on the existing infrastructure of the area (1). Finally, this period of expenditure restraint has, since 1979, coincided with a period in which Government policy has been to encourage development activity and exhort local authorities to take a more positive attitude to planning applications (Department of the Environment, 1980b).

The combination of these political and economic developments (the restructuring of the space economy during a period of fiscal entrenchment and in the context of a Government policy encouraging private development) has resulted in the question of the recoupment of land value increases attributable to the state provision of infrastructure emerging primarily through the attempt to impose on developers a greater share of the infrastructure burden of new development. Since it is in this context that the issue has emerged, the mechanisms available to enable public authorities to transfer responsibility for the provision of infrastructure will now be examined.

MECHANISMS AVAILABLE FOR TRANSFERRING INFRASTRUCTURE COSTS TO DEVELOPERS

Conditions attached to a grant of planning permission

A local authority has substantial development control powers. Under Section 29(1) of the Town and Country Planning Act 1971 the authority may grant or refuse permission and in granting permission may do so either unconditionally or subject "to such conditions as they think fit". This general power to impose conditions is not limited by any other provision in the statute and rather is clarified by Section 30(1) which states that "without prejudice to the generality of Section 29(1)" where the authority considers it expedient in connection with the application, it may impose conditions "regulating the development or use of any land under the control of the applicant (whether or not it is land in respect of which the application was made) or requiring the carrying out of works on any such land". These sections appear <u>ex facie</u> to sanction the transfer, in many cases, of a significant proportion of any infrastructure burden to the developer. Conditions could be attached requiring the provision of the necessary infrastructure (roads, sewers) and those services required by current planning standards relating to layout, access and amenities (landscaped areas, play spaces etc). It could even be argued that the statutory provisions enable the local authority in, say, a major housing development to require the developer to build any school or community facility required as a result of the development. This analysis suggests that conditions could be used to impose a significant proportion of the infrastructure cost of new development on to the developer.

In practice, however, the analysis is not so clear cut. Although there are no signicant statutory constraints on the use of conditions the courts have applied basic principles of administrative law to the use of conditions. In particular the courts have required that any condition imposed must further a planning purpose and not an ulterior purpose, that conditions must fairly and reasonably relate to the permitted development and that they must not be so unreasonable that no reasonable authority could have imposed them (2). The exercise of this function ultimately requires the courts to make a determination, however implicit, about the nature of the planning system (to determine the difference between a "planning" and an "ulterior" objective) and to determine precisely the manner in which common law private property rights in land have been modified by the regulatory planning system (to assess whether or not the condition is "unreasonable"). In the absence of clear statutory guidance the courts have adopted, although not without some measure of ambiguity and contradiction (Loughlin, 1980b), a fairly restrictive approach which operates to protect established common law private property rights. The impact which the adoption of this orientation has had on the ability to use conditions to transfer infrastructure responsibility is fairly subtle and may be illustrated only by examining cases.

In <u>Adams & Wade v. Minister of Housing and Local Government</u> (1967) 18 P&CR 60 the applicants, on appeal, had been granted permission for housing subject to a condition requiring them to provide an amenity strip of trees and shrubs. The houses were built and sold off. The developers then applied for permission to build houses on the land set aside as an amenity strip. Once permission, hardly surprisingly, had been refused the developers, arguing that the land was "incapable of reasonably beneficial use in its existing state", served a purchase notice on the local authority (Grant, 1982a). This notice was rejected by the authority and also, on appeal, by the Minister, but in the High Court the Minister's decision was, as a result of formalistic reasoning, successfully challenged. Widgery, J. held that, in determining whether the land was capable of reasonably beneficial use, the test was whether the current owners of the housing land would be interested in acquiring it for amenity purposes.

The purchase notice implications of that decision have subsequently been nullified by Section 184 of the Town and Country Planning Act 1971 but the general issue of the adoption of highly formalistic reasoning by the courts remains. Surely, it might be argued, the appropriate procedure in such circumstances would be for the local authority to serve an enforcement notice for breach of a condition subject to which the planning permission was granted. The difficulty in the use of the enforcement procedure in this context, however, is demonstrated by Lucas & Sons Ltd v. Dorking & Horley RDC (1964) 17 P&CR 111 in which Winn J. held that a planning permission for a development project is in law to be construed as a series of permissions for its component parts. Consequently it was held that the developers were able, after partially implementing a planning permission for a small housing estate, to rely on an earlier permission to build houses on the undeveloped part of the site in accordance with the terms of the earlier permission.

Following the logic of the decision in Lucas, the failure, contrary to a condition of the permission, to provide an amenity strip in the Adams & Wade case did not constitute a breach of planning control: everything that was built was in accordance with the terms of the permission and nothing was built which was not in accordance with that permission. While the logic of this decision has been questioned in relation to the building of a single dwelling house (3) it seems still to stand in relation to a permission which authorises the building of distinct units within a development scheme (4). These decisions do not demonstrate the impossibility of requiring, by conditions, that the developer provide amenity areas and the like in the development scheme. Provided a condition is imposed which requires that any such areas should be provided before any of the houses are occupied or sold, control should still be effective. What the cases clearly demonstrate is the pro-established rights orientation of the courts which results in the adoption of the narrowest interpretation of the nature of the local planning authority's power.

The implications of this general approach by the courts for the issue of the limits of the power to transfer infrastructure responsibility through the use of conditions is seen most clearly in Hall & Co Ltd v. Shoreham-by-Sea UDC (1964) 1 WLR 240. In this case the plaintiffs were granted planning permission to develop industrially part of a site allocated in the development plan for industrial purposes. The site lay alongside a busy main road and therefore, in order to reduce access points to that road, the plaintiffs were given temporary access, but by conditions were required to build a road along the frontage of the site when required to do so by the authority. They would then be required to give a right of passage across it from the road sections built on adjacent land. The object was to create a single access road from the industrial estate by requiring individual plot owners each to construct a section of the access road rather than all obtaining separate road access. The plaintiffs sought a declaration, inter alia that the conditions which sought to achieve this objective were ultra vires the local planning authority.

The Court of Appeal considered the key issue in this case to be the question of whether the conditions imposed were so unreasonable that no reasonable authority could have imposed them. And, while they thought that the objective sought to be achieved by the authority (limiting the points at which traffic could enter the main road) was a perfectly reasonable one, they held that the actual terms of the conditions were in fact so unreasonable as to be ultra vires. The crux of the issue was the fact that, although once the ancillary road was constructed the owners could require the authority to adopt the road as a highway maintainable at public expense (thereby relieving themselves of maintenance obligations), the owners would receive no compensation for the land surrendered for the purposes of road construction. Since there was an alternative way of achieving this objective (by using powers of compulsory purchase to acquire the strip for a road) and that under this alternative procedure compensation would be paid for the land taken, the Court of Appeal considered that the use of the land in such circumstances was ultra vires.

The precise rationale for the decision in Hall is not easily ascertainable. The court placed a great deal of weight on the fact that there was an alternative method of achieving the objective sought by the use of conditions and that that method required the payment of compensation. But then this argument could be used in relation to every condition requiring the provision of service roads or amenity areas. Furthermore, the House of Lords have explicitly rejected the proposition that the fact that there is an alternative method, requiring the payment of compensation, of achieving a planning objective does not per se render the exercise of development control powers improper (5). The rationale for the decision seems more clearly to lie in the fact that, in focusing upon the strip required for the road, the court considered that effectively the land was being taken without compensation to achieve a benefit not solely in favour of the application site.

The general position on the use of conditions to achieve infrastructure contributions thus seems to be this: responsibility for the on-site infrastructure which renders possible the development (sewers, service roads) is that of the developer; some on-site physical infrastructure may be required of the developer through landscaping and layout arrangements (amenity areas, open space) but where it constitutes a distinct area a condition ensuring that it is provided should be attached; and that a condition requiring physical infrastructure provision which even minimally, does not ensue solely for the benefit of the application site may be beyond the powers of the authority. Thus, despite the broad powers in Sections 29 and 30 of the 1971 Act (general power to attach such conditions as the authority thinks fit and specific power to require the carrying out of works which are necessary in connection with the development) the decisions of the courts, particularly in Adams & Wade (effectively requiring the authority to purchase the land on which they had legitimately required certain works to be carried out) and Hall (holding ultra vires the attempt by the authority to require the provision of certain works for the purpose of making the development acceptable by reference to legitimate planning objectives), clearly demonstrate the restrictive approach taken to the use of conditions to require infrastructure contributions from developers.

Statutory charges for infrastructure

As a general principle public agencies are under statutory duties to provide all the necessary off-site infrastructure to service any new development. Thus a developer may require the water authority, the gas corporation (in certain areas) and the electricity board to provide the necessary supplies. However, these agencies may in certain circumstances obtain contributions from developers towards the expense of providing this supply. Most of the cost of laying pipes to provide a gas supply can be recovered from the owner by the corporation (6) as can the cost to the water authority of providing a public sewer needed to service the development (7). With electricity, although capital costs are not directly recoverable, the board may refuse to supply unless the owner guarantees, for at least three years, to take electricity amounting to a certain annual sum fixed by the board, up to a maximum of 20 per cent of the expense of providing the works necessary for providing the supply (8).

Developers may also require the water authority to lay the necessary mains to enable the developer to make a connection thereto at a reasonable cost. Under this requisitioning procedure the authority may require the developer to contribute for a period of twelve years the difference between one-eighth of the capital cost of the provision of the mains and the total charges levied on the premises for that year (9). If such contributions are levied the courts have held (10):

(1) That the mains must take the most appropriate route having regard to proper water engineering practice, but may not deliberately deviate so as to serve other customers;

(2) If the most appropriate route is taken, the size of the main may be such as is necessary to take account of the needs of potential customers along the route of the pipe;

(3) However, the size of the main may not be gauged with a view to making subsequent further extensions beyond the point necessary to supply the developer.

Under these provisions significant contributions may be made by developers to the costs of providing the necessary off-site infrastructure. The main necessary service not included in statutory contribution arrangements is that of road improvements required as a result of the development. However some local authorities have used Section 278 of the Highways Act 1980 to obtain contributions towards the expenses of the necessary roadworks. This section enables the highway authority proposing to execute any works to:

"enter into an agreement ... with any other

person who would derive a special benefit if those works incorporated particular modifications, additions or features or were executed at a particular time or in a particular manner".

Consequently, although these various provisions could be placed on a simpler or more rational basis, it seems unlikely that public agencies will be required to make a great expenditure outlay for the provision of necessary physical infrastructure. Contributions to capital costs can be required: authorities then generally assume responsibility for the maintenance of all infrastructure services (including on-site infrastructure provided by the developer which is passed on to the authority through adoption agreements (11)). Thus, in terms of statutory contributions to infrastructure costs the relevant distinction seems to be between those services which render possible the development (for which contributions to capital costs of service provision can be obtained) and services which, while not immediately essential for the functional viability of the development, are nevertheless required as a result of the development.

The use of agreements

Despite the existence of statutory provisions enabling contributions to certain types of infrastructure to be made, local authorities have felt, particularly with the inflation in land prices in the 1970s, that developers do not contribute sufficiently to the infrastructure costs of new development. This feeling, combined perhaps with the feeling that the increase in land values attributable to the grant of planning permission was not being sufficiently taxed by the state, led many local authorities, through informal negotiations with developers, to seek further contributions by developers to infrastructure costs borne by the authority. Contributions received through such negotiations were generally embodied in legal agreements entered into under Section 52 of the Town and Country Planning Act 1971.

Because there were doubts about the extent to which Section 52 agreements enabled authorities to enforce positive undertakings against developers, many authorities sought additional powers in local acts, particularly in the late 1960s and early 1970s (Jowell, 1977b). This issue was also highlighted in the Report of the Sheaf Committee (DoE 1972). which stated:

"[Section 52 agreements] can supplement normal

planning control by regulating the phasing of development and where appropriate, cover matters such as contributions to servicing costs necessary to make development possible or the transfer of sites to local authorities for community facilities. Amending legislation should, however, be considered to provide for positive convenants to bind successors in title".

In response to the Sheaf Committee's recommendation the Government announced that they were consulting with local authority associations and the housebuilding industry about provisions to be included in legislation which would require developers to contribute to the costs of services provided by authorities in connection with new development DoE 1972b). The Government's original proposal for a compulsory infrastructure charge was later abandoned but a provision enabling local authorities to enter into positive covenants with developers was enacted in Section 126 of the Housing Act 1974, which is now superseded by Section 33 of the Local Government (Miscellaneous Provisions) Act 1982.

The context in which these legal developments have taken place clearly suggest that these powers were vested in local authorities to enable infrastructure contributions to be received. This view has been accepted by the Government on more than one occasion. Nevertheless in recent years a certain amount of concern has been expressed about these practices. Such concern arises because of the lack of any formal structure governing the circumstances in which, or the procedures by which, contributions may be negotiated, with the result that the types of infrastructure contributions obtained may not clearly be related to the extra infrastructure burden generated by a particular development project (Loughlin, 1981). In particular it has been felt that the process of bargaining for infrastructure contributions may lead local authorities to grant planning permissions in circumstances in which the strict planning merits of the scheme dictate otherwise and, as a result, it may be viewed as a buying or selling of permission. Also it has been argued that local authorities are using these powers to recoup betterment arising from the existence of the regulatory planning system and thereby are undertaking a role which would more appropriately be performed by general taxation.

This expression of concern culminated in a Report from the Property Advisory Group of the DoE on 'Planning Gain' (DoE, 1981) which sought to provide tests to limit the circumstances

240

in which infrastructure contributions may be received. Essentially, this widely-criticised document (Grant 1982a, Jowell, 1982, Loughlin, 1983) attempted to establish limits to the legitimate use of agreements similar to those adopted by the courts in relation to the use of conditions: viz, that the agreements must fairly and reasonably relate to the permitted development. This, however, raises the difficulty that agreements are being used to obtain infrastructure contributions partially because of a perceived narrowness of the courts in construing the limits to the legitimate use of conditions. The use of agreements for the purpose of obtaining infrastructure contributions thus remains a matter of controversy.

REFORM OF THE MECHANISMS FOR TRANSFERRING THE INFRASTRUCTURE COSTS

This examination of the mechanisms available to enable a local authority to transfer the infrastructure burden of new development to the developer demonstrates that the view that public authorities are responsible for infrastructure provision and must finance this expenditure from public resources is far from accurate. However, there seem to be several problems with the existing procedures. Certain difficulties exist with the use of conditions for the purpose of transferring responsibility for infrastructure; statutory powers enabling charges to be made for infrastructure provision have grown in an incremental fashion and cover only certain types of infrastructure; and the use of agreements to obtain contribution to infrastructure costs has in recent years been the subject of a great deal of controversy. This section therefore examines the range of reforms which might be made to the use of these mechanisms.

The use of conditions

If contributions to the cost of infrastructure were felt desirable it may be asked whether it might not be better to empower local authorities to incorporate such a requirement in the grant of planning permission.

This view has recently been advocated by the Royal Institute of Chartered Surveyors (RICS, 1983) who have suggested that the best way of resolving the uncertainty in negotiating over responsibility for offsite infrastructure is by extending the power to impose conditions "to make it possible to grant permission contingent upon the prior completion of off-site work or the making of cash payments in lieu". According to the RICS this would have the advantage of bringing "a wide range of planning gains into the mainstream of the development control machinery and to allow their planning merits and legality to be tested on appeal". The RICS probably consider also that the dominance of the pro-established rights orientation of the courts will serve to limit the range of infrastructure contributions which may legitimately be obtained.

The root cause of this restrictive approach by the courts seems due in large part to the dominance of an individualistic conception of private property rights in land. This individualistic conception assumes that private property may be divided and subdivided into any particular parcel over which full rights of property (by which is meant rights to use, benefit from and dispose of the land) may be exercised. In Adams and Wade this individualistic conception is evident in the refusal to recognise the prior bond between the amenity strip and the housing land; in Lucas, in the refusal to recognise that planning permission is a permission for a specific integer of land; and in Hall in the way in which the court focuses on the proposed road strip as a separate and distinct unit rather than examining it in the context of the larger unit for which permission was sought.

One key issue, therefore, is whether this individualistic conception is appropriate and, if not, whether it can be transcended. We have already seen that in an urbanised economy there is a growing inderdependency between land parcels because of the existence of externalities and because land development is heavily dependent on state provision of infrastructure. Consequently, the economic value of private property rights has in a sense become increasingly socialised. In this context, it may be argued that the maintenance of an individualistic legal conception of private property rights is quite inappropriate. The objective then is to discover a legal principle which will enable us to transcend the individualistic conception of private property rights in development land and will also provide clear guidance to help resolve some of the difficulties concerning disputes in this area of law.

One legal concept which may be of assistance is that of the planning unit. The planning unit is a concept used to aid in the evaluation of whether or not the activities carried out on, or changes in use made on, land constitute development. It operates to identify the relevant geographical area for analysing the legal nature, effect and consequences of those activities. The function of the planning unit can be seen by examining the case of Percy Trentham Ltd v. Gloucestershire C.C (1966) 1 WLR 506. In this case, the appellants had bought an area of less than two acres comprising a farmhouse and farm buildings previously part of a 75 acre farm. Without obtaining planning permission, they used the farmhouse as offices and the buildings, which previously were used for the storage of agricultural equipment and farm produce, for the storage of building material and equipment. The local authority served an enforcement notice alleging, inter alia, that there had been a material change of use from farm buildings into buildings for storage. The appellants argued, however, that the previous use of the buildings was as a repository for the storage of agricultural equipment, that the present use was a repository for the storage of building equipment and that as the use of buildings as a repository for any purpose was permitted without the need for planning approval under Class X of the Use Classes Order, the changes in use did not constitute development.

The Court of Appeal in dealing with the arguments considered that the authority were entitled "to look at the whole area which is used for a particular purpose including any part of that area whose use was incidental to or ancillary to the achievement of the purpose". In so doing, the Court of Appeal held that the buildings did not have a use as repositories but merely as buildings for storage in relation to the use of the whole (i.e. 75 acre) unit as a farm. Consequently, the use of the buildings for purposes unconnected with the use of that whole unit as a farm was a material change in use for which planning permission was required.

The Percy Trentham case, then, provides a clear indication of the importance of the planning unit and, although it is a concept which has been fashioned in a different area of planning law and for different purposes, it may nevertheless provide a useful conceptual tool to help overcome some of the difficulties in relation to the power of local authorities to control development for which permission has been granted. In this case the courts identified a particular geographical area as the unit of analysis, not by reference to any particular parcel an owner may care to present, or even the parcel over which the owner at the time of the dispute happens to exert control, but by examining the historically determined social function of that area of land. We have seen that the courts, in adopting the individualistic conception, tend to consider the issues raised in any case by reference to the smallest discrete land parcel they can identify. The concept of the planning unit, by focusing on a unit of land chosen by reference to social function, can, if applied to this issue, provide the basis for a socialised conception of private property rights in development land. This would require the courts, in determining whether conditions regulating the permitted development were legitimate, to adopt as the unit for analysis, a conception of private property based on what Denman and Prodano (1972) have called the "proprietary land unit".

The implications of the adoption of this socialised conception of private property rights can be seen by examining the likely result of its adoption in the cases examined. In Lucas it is clear that a different result would have been reached because the permission would refer to the integer rather than constitute a collection of discrete licences to implement each individualised unit of development. In Adams & Wade the position is a little more complicated because by the time the purchase notice dispute emerged the developer had sold the housing land. Nevertheless it seems clear that the courts should in such circumstances, as they did in the Percy Trentham case, look to the planning history of the site. If they did it seems unlikely that the purchase notice would have been confirmed. Furthermore, given the effect of this conception on the Lucas decision, it is likely that an enforcement notice could be served in the Adams & Wade case because the permission should be read as authorising the provision of the complete development package.

The effect of the adoption of this conception on issues such as those raised in Hall is potentially more far-reaching. Assuming that in that case the plaintiffs would have required the local authority to adopt the road, the main issue of controversy was the fact that the local authority would have acquired the land at no cost. The Court of Appeal's approach in this case was effectively to isolate the area of land required for road construction and to treat it as a separate unit of analysis. By so doing, they were able to conclude that in effect this amounted to a taking of land without payment of compensation and as such was so unreasonable as to be ultra vires. If the socialised conception is adopted, however, the nature of the conditions attached to the permission should not be examined in the context of the small area required for the road (under which a taking is effected) but rather in the context of the larger unit of land owned by the plaintiff company (from which perspective the conditions constitute a regulation of part of the land). The role of the court would thus be to review the reasonableness of this regulation in this broader context. In Hall, given that the authority's objective of minimising access points to the busy

main road is reasonable and that the need for the road arises
purely as a consequence of the development for which
permission was granted on that unit of land, it would seem
highly unreasonable for a court to conclude that this amounts
to an unreasonable regulation.

The adoption of a socialised conception of private property
rights in development land should therefore enable the courts
to develop a more appropriate framework for dealing with the
adjudicative issues arising under the regulatory planning
system. Conditions which require developers to provide
infrastructure would be acceptable provided it was on land
under the control of the applicant and the infrastructure to
be provided fairly and reasonably related to the permitted
development. This would enable local authorities to require
developers to provide only a small proportion of
infrastructure costs in some cases. Statutory reforms could
be enacted enabling local authorities to obtain greater
contributions through the use of conditions (RICS, 1983), but
a rejection of the pro-established rights orientation and the
adoption of a socialised conception of private property rights
seem pre-conditions to the adoption of a more coherent and
appropriate approach to the infrastructure issue by the
courts.

Infrastructure charges

The main problems with the present system of obtaining
statutory contributions to infrastructure costs seem to be
threefold. First, only certain types of infrastructure are
covered. Second, since the formulae for obtaining contributions have apparently been fixed in an ad hoc fashion for each
service the system for obtaining contributions is perhaps not
as coherent as it might be and third, when contributions are
obtained through the requisitioning procedure, since there is
no provision for cost apportionment, the infrastructure may
not be provided as efficiently as otherwise it might be: as a
result, the burden of contributions might be disproportionately weighted on the developer opening up an area.

It could be argued that these problems may be resolved by
introducing a comprehensive national system of infrastructure
charges. This charge presumably would take the form of a levy
on every grant of planning permission for a notional amount
towards the cost of infrastructure services which would be
generated by the development. It could easily be implemented:
a sliding scale of charges could be drawn up for particular
categories of development and the process would be open, non-

discretionary and an intrinsic part of the regular process of development control. This compulsory infrastructure charge was considered by the Government in 1973 but was not proceeded with in this form (DoE, 1972b). This approach seems preferable to related suggestions of the RICS (1974) and Lichfield and Darin-Drabkin (1980, p.235) which would require developers automatically to vest a proportion of their land in local authorities for infrastructure services. The charge would give local authorities more flexibility to plan the location of such services.

The main drawback with such a proposal seems to lie in the fact of its compulsory nature. In many circumstances the local authority would not wish a developer to bear the full infrastructure burden of the permitted development. That is, local authorities desire flexibility and discretion in seeking contributions. This stems from their perception of their role as managers of urban change. This requires that proposals be evaluated within the context of market dynamics and socio-economic policies. Many developments felt to be necessary or desirable may not be economically viable if the infrastructure burden of the development would automatically have to be carried by the developer. This management function therefore seems to require the adoption of a bargaining strategy towards developers in order to obtain contributions from profitable development and to provide subsidies and other benefits to induce private development under conditions in which development is otherwise not an attractive proposition. The need for this degree of flexibility might suggest the preferability of using agreements to achieve these objectives.

Agreements

As we have seen, however, the use of agreements to achieve these objectives has been the subject of some controversy. This arises primarily because the powers vested in local authorities to achieve such objectives have been in the form of enabling powers which do not impose significant restraints on the circumstances of their exercise. Authorities may, as a result, adopt · widely different policies on the basis of the existence of such powers.

Studies of the use of agreements to obtain various types of infrastructure contributions have therefore advocated the imposition of substantive limits to the use of agreements. Any tests so far proposed, however, seem either too restrictive or quite unworkable. It seems, therefore, that if there is felt the need to confine and structure the discretion of local authorities in the use of agreements, procedural safeguards (such as identifying policies on infrastructure contributions in development plans, using development briefs and giving applicants the power to appeal to the Secretary of State against the terms of agreements) may provide better solutions (Loughlin, 1981).

The DoE Consultation Paper (1983), its response to the Property Advisory Group Report, and DoE Circular 22/83 are the latest official contributions to this issue. Criticisms of the Property Advisory Group Report seem superficially to have influenced the DoE's view on the use of agreements to obtain infrastructure contributions since the guidelines are expressed in more general terms. Nevertheless, as has been pointed out (Grant, 1983b; Grant and Jowell, 1983b), the guidelines are just as ambiguous and unworkable as those attempted by the Property Advisory Group. The Circular proposes two tests for ascertaining the reasonableness of the developer's obligations. Firstly, that the extent of what is required must be "fairly and reasonably related to the proposed development" and secondly, that any facility "provided or financed should be directly related to the development in question". If the applicant successfully appeals to the Secretary of State because of what seems to be an unreasonable demand by the local authority then any application for the award of costs will be considered sympathetically. It hardly seems likely that this Circular will do much to alter current practices among local authorities.

CONCLUSIONS

There has now emerged a wide spectrum of opinion that, in appropriate circumstances, developers should make significant contributions to the infrastructure costs of new development. A great deal of disagreement exists, however, over the precise circumstances in which contributions may be required, the nature of those infrastructure contributions to be made and the legal mechanisms which should be used to achieve them. Furthermore, very little is known about the impact which a policy of negotiating or requiring infrastructure contributions is having, or may have, on the land development process. Are developers buying profitable permissions cheaply by offering infrastructure "goodies" or are they being held to ransom by powerful local authorities? What impact do these practices have on certainty and stability in the planning system (and what are the efficiency implications of this)? What is the redistributional impact of the practice (does it release public funds for redistributional services or does it constitute a tax on new housing which ultimately benefits existing houseowners and penalises new entrants)? Can infrastructure management attract firms back to the city or are the underlying economic forces too powerful? These questions raise key issues concerning the nature of the planning system which require detailed investigation. The recent DoE guidelines ignore most of these important questions and do little to further our understanding of the issues.

Notes

1. See, e.g. Geo. Wimpey & Co. v. Secretary of State for the
        Environment (1978). 250 E.G. 241.

2. Newbury D.C. v. Secretary of State for the Environment
        (1981). A.C. 578.

3. Copeland B.C. v. Secretary of State for the Environment
        (1976). 31 P&CR 403.

4. Pilkington v. Secretary of State for the Environment
        (1973). 1 WLR 1527.

5. Westminster Bank Ltd v. Minister of Housing and Local
        Government (1971). AC 508.

6. Gas Act 1972. Schedule 4, para.2.

7. ss. 14-19, 34, 36 Public Health Act 1936; ss 14, 16
        Water Act 1973.

8. s25(1), Schedule Electricity Lighting (Clauses) Act 1889;
        s57(2), Schedule 4, Part III Electricity Act 1947.

9. s37 Water Act 1945.

10. Royco Homes Ltd. v. Southern Water Authority (1978).
        77 LGR 133.

11. ss17, 18 Public Health Act 1936 (Sewers); ss37, 38
        Highways Act 1980 (roads).

12 The achievement of specialist agencies in rural development

GWYNDAF WILLIAMS

INTRODUCTION

Since the war the explosion of urban influence, and growing conflicts over rural resource development, has put the countryside under increasing social, economic and physical pressures. The impact of such changes however have been extremely variable. The traditional areas of upland Britain have continued to suffer from the long term consequences of selective migration, the sharp decline of primary industry employment, and the withdrawal of public services in the fields of transport and social welfare. In lowland Britain on the other hand, pressures of metropolitan expansion and urban overspill have had radical social and physical consequences, while coastal villages and hamlets in areas of outstanding landscape character have often succumbed to retirement migration and large scale tourist development (Countryside Review Committee, 1977b). Public policy response to combat such changes had largely been to structure public investment programmes into 'key' settlements, and to exercise tight land use controls.

In employment terms, whilst labour productivity in agriculture and forestry, and employment in tourism, have all increased dramatically in recent years, opportunities offered by the manufacturing sector have generally been substantially under-represented. It has traditionally been characterised by its subsidiary lower tier nature, low incomes, a limited range of job opportunities, and being extremely vulnerable to economic recession (Hodge and Whitby, 1981; Watts, 1981). The last decade however has seen dramatic changes, and the 1981 census reveals that some of the fastest growing areas have been located in the rural and remoter areas, with the lowest density areas growing faster than the national average (Champion, 1981). Such counter-urbanisation trends have also been taking place in terms of manufacturing employment, with no other trend in industrial location being so powerful as the shift from cities to small towns (see Table 1).

Fothergill and Gudgin (1982) argue that traditional explanations relating to the attractions of rural locations are inadequate. Evidence on labour costs and militancy are inconsistent when applied to measuring urban industrial decline, while it is more likely that migration occurred in response to rising rural employment than that the jobs followed people into small towns and rural areas. Explanations which rely on residential preference are most relevant to the location of new factories, while, they argue, urban-rural differences primarily reflect disparities in the growth of existing factories.

They feel that this shift has little to do with industrial structure or movement, but suggest that surviving city based firms are growing more slowly than their competitors elsewhere due largely to the problems of 'constrained location', resulting from expensive land and site assembly costs, and green belt policies. Rising capital intensity in manufacturing accelerates job losses in factories with no room for expansion, and increases profitability outside cities. This balance between constrained and unconstrained location thus provides an explanation which can differentiate cities from small towns and rural areas. It means that a study of the development process for the provision of industrial land and premises in rural areas, is an especially valuable area of enquiry.

Resulting from such population and employment changes, growing concern has been expressed at the appropriateness of existing administrative structures and decision making processes in rural areas (Wright, 1982). The piecemeal, sectional approach of public agencies with decision making responsibilities for the countryside, has increasingly focussed attention on the institutional context, particularly in relation to the methods adopted for the achievement of policy aims. This chapter is concerned with one such institutional approach, namely, the use of specialist agencies

Table 1

Sources of Manufacturing Differential Shifts 1959-75

	Manufacturing employment change Percent	as % 1959 manufacturing employment		
		Industrial[1] movement	Indigenous performance	Differential[2] shift
London	− 37.8	− 12.1	− 28.7	− 40.8
Conurbations	− 15.9	+ 1.5	− 7.8	− 6.3
Free standing cities	+ 4.8	+ 1.1	+ 7.9	+ 9.1
Industrial towns	+ 16.3	+ 4.2	+ 17.7	+ 21.9
County towns	+ 28.8	+ 7.3	+ 25.5	+ 32.8
Rural areas	+ 77.2	+ 29.4	+ 54.7	+ 84.1

Source: Fothergill and Gudgin 1982, p.73.

1 estimates based on Department of Industry figures

2 1959 base: year, 99 industry disaggregation

as administrative instruments to facilitate the implementation of a specifically industrial development programme.

The increasing complexity of government has been accompanied in recent years by the rapid growth of both advisory and executive agencies, intermediate in their independence to central government - quangos (Barker, 1982). This has been reinforced by the general abandonment of an essentially reactive regional industrial policy, and the proliferation of a variety of agencies concerned with the promotion of local economic initiatives (Mawson and Miller, 1983). A number of such bodies have been established to tackle the development problems of the more marginal rural areas of Britain - Highlands and Islands Development Board (1965); Mid-Wales Development (formerly, Development Board for Rural Wales, 1976); Development Commission (1909) and its agency Council for Small Industries in Rural Areas (1968); and the short lived Northern Pennines Rural Development Board (1969-1971) (see Figure 1, 2).

Rural development agencies are undoubtedly intended as instruments for increasing policy flexibility and innovation, but their operation is bound to be influenced by wider policy considerations. Increasing government emphasis on small business development, evident in the expansion of industrial building allowances and various business 'start up' schemes, has been reinforced by the advice outlined in Circular 22/80, on the need for local planning authorities to balance environmental objectives with the encouragement of economic activity in rural areas (JURUE, 1983).

The sharp reduction in regional incentives announced by government in July 1979 has undoubtedly had significant effects on Britain's rural areas not only in terms of existing central government policies, which focus investment on Assisted Areas, but also in terms of their eligibility for EEC Social and Regional Fund assistance (see Figure 2). However, in Mid Wales, a compensatory package of rural measures has been announced to counter the loss of Development Area status, possessed by the region since 1966.

This chapter will concentrate on the contrasting approaches to rural industrial development adopted by Mid Wales Development (Development Board for Rural Wales) and the Development Commission. Mid Wales Development is a <u>regional</u> development agency, possessing executive powers which are promoted within the context of an overall regional development strategy. The Development Commission, in contrast, has an <u>area</u> based perspective; working through the existing

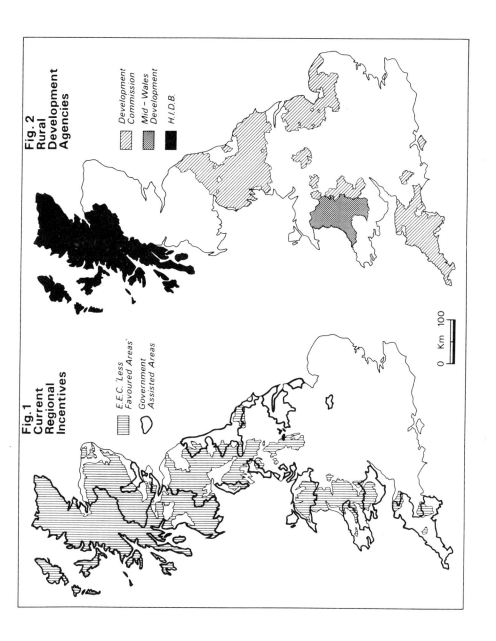

structures of local government, and with its offshoot COSIRA
possessing a local presence. A detailed study of their major
policy instrument, namely the advance factory programme, will
elucidate information concerning their relationships over land
and development issues with central and local government, and
the local community, and their success in promoting specific
development initiatives.

An initial concern with the development of an appropriate
conceptual framework, is followed by a discussion of the
legislative and financial context to the operation of these
agencies, and their experience of programme implementation.
The concluding section will attempt to discuss the value of
using such specialist agencies as a policy response, and
future directions that such responses might take.

THE PROBLEM OF PERSPECTIVE IN DEVELOPMENT POLICY

Development Models

A variety of theories have been developed over the past few
decades relating to the need for appropriate development
strategies in peripheral regions. An early concern by
economists with growth pole strategies - with development
diffusing outwards from core regions of innovative change -
was added to during the 1960s by the work of various political
scientists on the notion of 'internal colonialism' (Hechter,
1975). They argued that peripheral areas suffered not only
from disadvantages arising out of being located outside the
economic core, but also from being perceived as being part of
a subordinate culture.

Current work has shown growing dissatisfaction with the
notion that the development of peripheral regions is
essentially a technocratic and apolitical exercise in
'problem' solving. This has been replaced by the notion that
the real need is to accommodate and democratise a basically
irreconcilable contradiction between territory and function
(Friedmann and Weaver , 1979). Thus the development of
peripheral regions should essentially be considered as a
process of widening opportunities for individuals, social
groups and territorially organised communities, internally
mobilising the full range of their capabilities and resources.
The nature of the relationship between the implementers and
recipients of development programmes is thus critical, and it
is within such context that the value of specialist agencies
should be seen in relation to the promotion of rural
industrial development (Wenger, 1982).

254

Specialist Agencies as Administrative Instruments

The number of appointed public agencies established by statute, or Ministerial decision, to perform executive tasks in place of central departments or elected local authorities, has grown rapidly over the past twenty years under both Labour and Conservative administrations. Their piecemeal development, more a reflection of opportunistic pragmatism than any specific doctrine, is generally seen to represent a compromise of day to day executive independence, while remaining within the general ambit of Ministerial control. Many, however, have been established with little guidance on how their objectives are to be achieved, or their impact on existing administrative structures of assessment of government.

Hood (1978) in attempting to explain the form of such agencies, argues that they represent four basic approaches. Under his 'roulette wheel' theory it may be argued that the factors governing their characteristics and function are so difficult to articulate, their form will be random. Second, they may demonstrate 'administrative fashion' reflecting continually changing beliefs in governmental integration versus diversity, rather than responses to differences in problems or tasks. The 'managerialist' thesis argues that the constitutional status of an agency is in some sense functional for the performance of a specific operational task. This suggests that many new aspects of public policy need a different administrative style, more flexible and adaptive than normally seen in the Civil Service, and such agencies are often found performing 'business' type activities, and tasks requiring innovation and speed.

The final explanation of agency type is that of 'political logic', in that as the machinery of government becomes over institutionalised, resulting in conflicting demands between agencies, unorthodox constitutional machinery may be used for bypassing or flanking movements. In the case of rural development agencies this may not necessarily be against the wishes of the local authorities, being seen as a source of additional resources, and a forum for inter-authority co-ordination. However, in Scotland and Wales attempts to diffuse political pressures for devolution, whilst articulating concern for the problems of peripheral areas, clearly underlay the establishment of the Welsh and Scottish Development Agencies, and the Development Board for Rural Wales. Politically, such agencies may additionally mobilise support outside the regular bureaucracy, harnessing it for beneficial public action. However, this sector undoubtedly affords the opportunity for government by co-option rather than by election or merit, and has borne increasing criticism lately over Ministerial patronage (Lowe, 1983).

Agency Evaluation

There are three major areas of policy implications - financial effectiveness, political control and local accountability. It is often implied that such agencies are the most cost effective means of distributing public funds, but few attempts have been made to provide a 'performance appraisal', either in financial terms, or in terms of alternative approaches using the existing arms of central/local government.

Such low profile development agencies may receive little direct governmental involvement, an attitude often actively supported by the agencies themselves on the grounds that their independence of operation might be compromised. They may thus have discretion not only to implement and interpret the general intentions of legislation under which they were established, but also to determine the parameters and impact of their functions.

Specialist agency committees and boards are continually faced with criticisms relating to local democratic accountability, with their power base and financial resources being derived from a central government often perceived as remote. They will however, attempt to promote notions of partnership in their relationships both with the local authorities and the local communities in their areas. While local authorities may have nomination rights over a minority of agency membership, they may nevertheless use their statutory functions, for example, over land release, as bargaining mechanisms.

INSTITUTIONAL BASIS OF INTERVENTION

Agency Objectives and Development Strategies

Whilst both agencies may be perceived as relatively radical responses to the needs of 'traditional' rural communities, they differ in evolutionary form, executive powers and policy responsibilities.

Mid Wales Development (Development Board for Rural Wales), possessing executive powers and a regional operational base, grew out of local authority frustration at governmental inactivity, which culminated in their establishment of the Mid

Wales Industrial Development Association (1957), to promote inward investment. The region was ill equipped to handle development at this stage, due to the lack of suitable sites, premises and infrastructure, but this initiative was clearly a significant early attempt at local 'self help' (Broady, 1980).

The gaining of Development Area status (1966) and the Development Commission's willingness to build advance factories as a direct counter to depopulation, led to an increasingly politicised development movement. Criticisms of its preoccupation with factory development mainly centred on outside business interests, and a growth centre policy actively seen to threaten rural community life, did not disappear with the establishment of the Development Board for Rural Wales. Indeed, the Board's presence and profile has tended to spawn a diffuse community based development movement, opposed to many of the Board's policy emphases (Wenger, 1980b).

The Board inevitably inherited the existing policy commitments and the general strategy of its predecessor, which, subsequent to the rejection of a proposed new town for the region in 1967, had adopted a growth town strategy. In reviewing this policy (DBRW, 1979), the Board, whilst accepting the principle of concentration, felt the need to widen the impact of growth. Their overall strategy (1979-1984) thus selected five major growth areas within which 250,000 sq.ft. of industrial premises is expected to be built, particularly involving units of over 10,000 sq.ft. In a further nine special towns, additional factory space of 150,000 sq.ft. is planned, with individual factories being less than 5,000 sq.ft. In eight key towns, 50,000 sq.ft. of factory space is contemplated, predominantly in the form of small factories/workshops. A network of 25 villages were selected for an experimental programme of initiatives including co-operatives, village tourism and small shopkeeper training programmes, although this has not yet progressed very far. The geographical focus of the Board's activities has inevitably been on Newtown, which has accounted for over half the Board's total investment, but with the culmination of this new town programme in 1985, development opportunities are expected to spread (see Figure 3 and Table 2).

More wide ranging in impact, but lacking executive power until it gained full grant-in-aid status in April 1984, has been the work of the Development Commission and its agent COSIRA. Established as early as 1909, it was given the task of advising government on the spending of the Development Fund, by recommending schemes which would directly or

257

Table 2

Approved Factory Workshop Programme

	Sq.Ft
Pre 1 April 1984	136,879
1974/75	28,500
1975/76	141,700
1976/77	378,900
1977/78	700,124
1978/79	599,700
1979/80	376,500
1980/81	186,655
1981/82	388,933
1982/83	122,989

Figure 3

Development Commission: Mid Wales Development
Areas of Operation

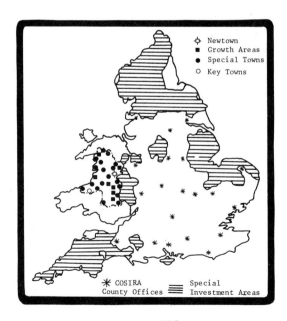

indirectly benefit the rural economy. Whilst originally concerned with the promotion of traditional craft industries, its scope has considerably altered over the last twenty years, its resources now being concentrated on:

- Devising and implementing rolling programmes of small scale factory/workshop building in rural towns of less than 15,000 population.

- Providing, through COSIRA, a business management, technical advice, training and credit service to small manufacturing and service industry employers of less than 20 skilled persons, in towns generally under 10,000 population.

- Encouragement of voluntary initiative, and pioneering rural community experiments, through its active support of 36 county based Rural Community Councils (RCC).

The Commission's constant lobbying of government during the 1960s for more positive policy instruments, led to the development of an experimental 'Trigger Areas' programme (Mid Wales, Eastern Borders, North East Scotland). This was followed in the early 1970s by a focus on what increasingly became known as Special Investment Areas, and these form the central concern of current Commission activities.

Following a review of its work in 1975, and a government report on depopulation (Treasury, 1976) which stressed the cost-effectiveness of factory building as a rural support measure, the Commission's remit was expanded to include the creation of an additional 1500 jobs/annum in depopulated areas of rural England (Clarkson, 1980). Its function in Wales and Scotland were diverted at this stage to the Scottish and Welsh Development Agencies, and the DBRW. COSIRA, formed by the amalgamation of a number of existing agencies in 1968, and wholly funded by the Commission, whilst initially concentrating on the larger market towns, has latterly become heavily involved with the building and conversion of small units and workshops in the smaller settlements. In order to accomplish this, local authorities are requested to prepare local 'Action Plans' denoting settlements possessing good prospects of recovery as a result of Commission investment. Such plans set out the area's existing economic and physical infrastructure, the availability of suitable light industrial sites, and the phasing of local factory and house building programmes over the plan's five year duration. This interactive partnership continues into the implementation phase, through collaboration between the Commission, Department of Industry, English Industrial Estates, COSIRA, and the relevant local authorities.

259

The Commission/COSIRA's functions were reviewed by the current government, the results of which were announced in March 1982. They were given greater operational freedom to meet the social and economic needs of rural areas, with the Commission being given the task of designating its own priority areas. These new, centrally designated, Rural Development Areas are expected to accommodate areas of high unemployment, unfavourable population structure and employment opportunities, and suffering from problems of accessibility. They will replace existing designations drawn up in co-operation with, and often on the specific initiative of, local authorities (Williams, 1984).

Management Structure and Accountability

Until the current financial year, the Commission acted as a permanent Royal Commission, advising government on the spending of the Development Fund, its finances annually voted by Parliament and overseen by the DoE. Whilst able to frame schemes for financial support, it could not directly initiate development; could only give assistance to non-profit organisations; and possessed no remit over tourism, agriculture or forestry. Under the Miscellaneous Financial Provisions Act 1983 however, the Commission has achieved greater operational freedom as a grant-in-aid body, enabling it directly to fund its own programmes, to own land and buildings, and to assist profit making bodies. It will also have a statutory duty to advise government on rural matters in England. Through COSIRA, concessionary loans are available for small firms within the Commission's priority areas, as are rent free periods, where necessary, for tenants of their factories. Half of the Commission's current budget of £19.5 million is expended on its factory/workshop programme, while a further third is spent on COSIRA's budget.

Mid Wales Development is directly responsible to the Secretary of State for Wales, funded by the Treasury, and has been given a mandate to keep under review, promote and implement schemes for the industrial, commercial and social development of its area. It has been given powers of acquisition/disposal of land, erection of buildings, and powers to make grants and loans at preferential rates to potential growth industries and commercial ventures. It cannot, however, get directly involved in agriculture and forestry. In addition, non-economic grants and loans are available for projects designed to strengthen social infrastructure. While it interestingly combines the functions of a new town development corporation and a rural development agency, it may also engage in the provision of key worker housing, and provide rent guarantees to local authorities and housing associations. Its current budget is £10 million, largely expended on the construction of industrial premises and housing.

No study of local impact can fail to take account of the sensitive area of accountability, and both agencies possess a formal board structure, with membership lying at the discretion of Ministers, on advice from central government departments. The Commission has a staff complement of 35, and a Board of eight members appointed under Royal Warrant. It has no locally based presence, and its credibility is largely based on its close working relationship with local authorities, and its financial support for Rural Community Councils. COSIRA possesses a national board of six directors, each responsible for a particular geographic region. This facilitates liaison between the national and local arms of COSIRA, provided by thirty voluntary, county based Small Industries Committees, made up of members from the local professions, business and local authorities. When approval is given by COSIRA headquarters for the five year county strategy, each Small Industry Committee is responsible for drawing up an annual programme to carry out the work outlined in the strategy.

Out of a staff complement of 300, COSIRA's local presence is facilitated by the existence of fifty Small Industries Organisers, based on a network of twenty-five local offices. Their role is essentially one of seeking out and maintaining contact with small firms in their areas, and channelling assistance to them as required from their advisory and credit services. Local community participation in the Commission's 'Action Plans' and COSIRA's 'County Strategy' is limited, but both documents are expected to fit into the provisions of established Structure and Local Plans.

Mid Wales Development has a staff complement of ninety, with a management board comprising a full time Chairman, and twelve part time members, five of whom are suggested by local authorities. It highlights extremely well the contradiction inherent in 'development', and conflicts between territory and function, in that the Board has consistently promoted an outward looking development process, and is only now beginning to stimulate indigenous social and economic identity.

EXPERIENCE OF IMPLEMENTATION

A central focus of agency objectives is undoubtedly employment creation, the balance of emphasis however being somewhat different. Whilst both agencies have direct responsibilities for providing premises and industrial sites, supported by a range of business advisory services, Mid Wales Development has attempted to fit this into a wider regional settlement strategy.

The focus of agency industrial activity lies with the provision of advance factories, a long established instrument of sub-regional development in Britain. Slowe (1981) argues that the longevity of such an instrument results from its politically uncontroversial nature, involving no compulsion, relatively little subsidy, and no encouragement for firms to locate to their disadvantage. Such units are currently provided by English Industrial Estates (EIE), various development corporations, private developers, and increasingly directly by local authorities.

The Development Process - The Achievements

(a) Factory Development: Subsequent to the withdrawal of Development Commission responsibilities from Scotland and Wales, and the new remit given to the agency in 1975, the factory development role of the Commission has dramatically expanded, with 3 million sq.ft. of factory space having been approved in its thirty Special Investment Areas (see Table 3). The Commission's units range in size from 1,000 - 15,000 sq.ft., spread through twenty counties and over 220 sites, and while each thousand square feet of factory space has the potential of four jobs, the current occupancy rate is around 2.85.

Table 3

Development Commission Factory Programme (March 1983)

	Number	Square Feet
Units completed	689	1,652,504
Under construction	157	226,453
Planned for 1983-85	573	1,112,923
Approved programme taken over by the private sector	28	69,000
Total Approved Programme	1,447	3,060,880

Source: Development Commission. Forty First Report (April 1982-March 1983) p.16.

The sharp decline in mobile 'footloose' industry, and the increasing demand for rural workshops has led the Commission to concentrate its recent efforts on providing units under 2,500 sq.ft. usually grouped in clusters. Factories are usually built for lease at current market rents, with the Commission being given the authority in July 1980 to dispose of the freeholds of sites and factories to the private sector at market value.

Early problems, mainly over the requisition of suitable sites, have largely disappeared, with recent local authority involvement in the process having positive results, not only in ensuring the success of the rolling programme, but also in terms of the Commission's overall credibility (Minay, 1981). Although the Commission's approval is needed for expenditure at particular stages in every project, its agent, English Industrial Estates, is responsible for ensuring that approved factories are designed, built and managed. Thus the Commission's role is as a catalyst stimulating local activity, providing guidelines and resources, but delegating detailed planning and design (see Figure 4).

The Commission has recently begun to diversify the range of its employment initiatives, and during 1982 it introduced its first Rural Workshops Design Competition in an attempt to produce adaptable low cost workshop designs acceptable in rural locations. To enable more buildings to be built or converted for use by small firms particularly in remoter locations a Partnership Workshop Scheme was introduced in February 1981, the Commission providing half the finance, with the local authority being responsible for their design, letting and management. This scheme has recently been extended to include contributions towards site assembly, for eventual sale or lease to the private sector.

Grants of 35% are also available for projects costing under £50,000 overall, for the conversion of redundant buildings for craft and light industrial use available as workshops for at least five years. Constraints on such schemes in the past have included the lack of suitable buildings being identified, concern of the owners at the consequences for their farm operations, their liability to changed rates and tax assessments, and high costs of conversion resulting from environmental/servicing constraints. The Commission has additionally begun to support, through pump-priming grants, a number of local enterprise trusts - e.g. Mendip and Wansdyke Local Enterprise Group, West Somerset Small Industries Group. Wiltshire Small Industries Trust, funded by Hambro Life, Burma Oil and the County Council, has received Commission support to

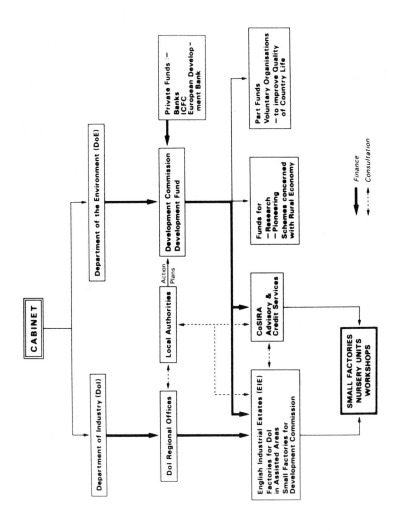

CABINET

Department of the Environment (DoE)

Department of Industry (DoI)

Private Funds :-
Banks
ICFC
European Develop-
ment Bank

Development Commission
Development Fund

Local Authorities

Action
Plans

DoI Regional Offices

English Industrial Estates (EIE)
Factories for DoI
in Assisted Areas
Small Factories for
Development Commission

CoSIRA
Advisory &
Credit Services

Funds for
– Research
– Pioneering
Schemes concerned
with Rural Economy

Part Funds
Voluntary Organisations
– to improve Quality
of Country Life

SMALL FACTORIES
NURSERY UNITS
WORKSHOPS

Finance
Consultation

set up a revolving fund to convert disused buildings in
villages to starter workshops (National Council for Voluntary
Organisations, 1982).

The Commission has recently been urged to seek private
sources of finance for its factory building programme,
although this is largely in settlements not traditionally seen
as commercially attractive. Continuing delays in financial
procedures and the annual basis of Development Fund allocation
has reinforced the Commission's wish for a change in status to
that of a 'grant-in-aid' body, a status finally attained in
April 1984.

Mid Wales Development is similarly involved in a programme
of advance factory building, and business advisory services,
currently amounting to nearly 300 units (over 2 million
sq.ft.), and directly providing nearly 7,000 jobs. However,
the momentum of development is beginning to slow down, and
during the summer of 1982, 59 completed factory units were
available for rent within the region. The vulnerability of
the whole process was further shown by the recent withdrawal
of GKN from a 200,000 sq.ft. factory unit, as a result of
company rationalisation. Thus the agency is increasingly
paying as much attention to stimulating existing businesses as
to promoting new enterprises. The existence of a wide range
of factory sizes and locations enables well established firms
to 'trade up' within the region, and new firms to take up some
of the seventy starter factories, based in twelve locations.
The agency is additionally marketing a 'package' for small
entrepreneurs, linking such units with a modern three bedroom
house, for a combined rental of £35 per week. Unlike the
Commission, Mid Wales Development, possessing Compulsory
purchase powers in relation to development opportunities, has
got involved in commercial development - designing and
building a shopping centre, office block and a combined
shops/office development in Newtown.

(b) Business Management and Technical Advice: Both agencies
provide a package of direct and indirect business development
services, advising on finance, marketing and technical
problems, and evaluating new product ideas.

COSIRA's remit of reinforcing the Commission's general
strategy, has resulted in nearly 14,000 small businesses being
on their books, two thirds of the 3,000 helped during 1981/82
being new businesses. Their work is dependent on the
activities of their field staff, particularly their fifty
Small Industries Organisers, and supported by a field advisory
staff of sixty technical production and forty business

265

management advisers, who charge small firms a daily rate for their advice. An apprenticeship scheme (New Entrants Training Scheme) has proved particularly successful over the last decade in stimulating small business development and COSIRA's training work has recently begun to attract a growing amount of assistance from the European Social Fund (£187,000 in 1981/82).

COSIRA has limited funds available to make loans to small firms in relation to buildings, purchase of plant and equipment, working capital, and since March 1982 this has been extended to include some retail purposes. Government commitment to private enterprise and finance however means that COSIRA can now only provide half of project costs in their priority areas, and a third outside. The use of the Loan Fund is virtually a 'topping up' source of finance, ensuring the applicant's credibility, and has grown over the last decade from £2.7 million to £18.7 million. Thus, for example in 1981/82, COSIRA approved loans of £2.5 million to finance projects in 290 firms. Such a comprehensive small firms support scheme has undoubtedly gained considerable admiration for the Commission's activities, and wide ranging support for its main policy objectives. Concern over possible duplication between COSIRA services, and the Department of Industry's Small Firms Service, led to a recent management review of the operation of both. The report, published in May 1983, concluded that the agencies had different operating methods, with little overlap in practice, and that few benefits would accrue from a merger.

Mid Wales Development's business advisory services is similarly widely used, and the agency, in addition to helping local companies to take part in national trade exhibitions, is also involved in producing promotional films and business directories. Concerned at the lack of an indigenous business sector the agency has given particular emphasis to attempting to encourage and develop local entrepreneurial skills. Thus, in addition to publishing a Small Business Kit, and running a range of local seminars, it has linked with Manchester Business School in its New Enterprise Programme. It is also devising a Business Development Programme for selected companies with growth potential.

Overall therefore, the work of such agencies has been remarkably successful in relation to the supply of premises, and the necessary business advisory support services. However, this has not traditionally been an area of much local government involvement, thus enabling the agencies to cut out a clearly defined niche for themselves.

The Development Process - Site Planning and Design

Basic concerns over internal flexibility and external adaptability of industrial units are reinforced by traditional problems of remoteness, infrastructural costs and communication weaknesses. Both agencies have policies of providing high quality units with high capital outlay and low maintenance costs, on the assumption that completed factories will be for rent. However, recent governmental encouragement for the sale of such units has created problems in that their capital cost is usually above market value for some time after completion (Oxford Polytechnic, 1982).

(a) Site Assembly: The identification of sites for factory development is an integral part of local authority submitted Action Plans, and local authorities have increasingly begun to purchase, service and sell plots for industrial development. The development process is extremely complex, the ideal eighteen months timescale being dependent on an uncomplicated process of site purchase, design, tender and building. However, the submitted Action Plans, encouraging a five year forward planning exercise, do facilitate the building up of a suitable land bank in most cases.

All potential sites earmarked in the Action Plans are subjected to a feasibility study by EIE/COSIRA covering both technical and environmental constraints, and positive community support. Feasible sites are valued by the District Valuer, usually purchased directly by the local authority, serviced by them, and then resold to English Industrial Estates acting on behalf of the Commission. Obtaining outline planning permission for Commission factories rarely causes difficulties, both due to the Action Plans themselves, and their agency's credibility in building high quality units.

Mid Wales Development has direct powers under the 1976 Act to acquire, service and develop, manage and dispose of land, subject to approval from the Secretary of State. Similarly, although it prefers voluntary agreement, it may appropriate land (using compulsory purchase powers) for the purpose of undertaking any of the agency's functions, and force landowners to declare their interest in land. Specific industrial schemes are planned in consultation with local authorities, with agreed projects being submitted to the Welsh Office for approval. In order to ensure a supply of sites in the locations designated for industrial development, a land bank was initially acquired, but this is diminishing as development goes ahead.

The size and number of units on any site is decided in accordance with the regional strategy, taking into account existing units, how quickly these are being let, housing availability and whether any such units are being built for specific firms. However, as with the Commission's programme, there is an increasing tendency to build more of the smaller sizes.

(b) <u>Factory Design</u>: When an Action Plan has been approved, the Commission makes a formal request for both EIE and COSIRA's involvement in a specific factory project and this in turn in delegated to the agency's regional offices. Design of Commission factories may be undertaken in house but is usually undertaken by local architects' practices commissioned by EIE. They attempt to balance advantages of standardisation and repetition, with a degree of flexibility to blend into the particular rural environment. Thus careful consideration is given to materials used, particularly in villages, with repetition of unit designs usually found only on town sites, resulting in village units being proportionately more expensive. It is generally accepted that whilst portal frame construction is appropriate for most advance factories, more traditional methods of construction have advantages for small units up to 2,000 sq.ft., largely based in villages. In addition, for all factories over 1,000 sq.ft., 100% expansion space is allowed for possible future extensions.

Mid Wales Development's approach is similar to that of EIE factories, in that design is both undertaken 'in house' and by local architects, to a standard design brief, with additional information for specific schemes. Local contractors are used wherever possible, but the lack of choice of contractors within the Board's area may increase building costs appreciably.

(c) <u>Leasing Policies</u>: Both agencies undertake checks on potential tenants in terms of their financial viability, technical feasibility, and number of jobs likely to be created. COSIRA's awareness of the needs of local firms, and their direct link with available Commission units, ensures a painless move into new premises, with minimum loss of production. For factory units under 5,000 sq.ft. leasing policies are flexible, with rent reviews at change of tenant stage, but with larger factories EIE has a twenty-four year lease with five year rent reivews. In Mid Wales the smaller units tend to be on 'easy in - easy out' licenses, while units over 3,000 sq.ft. are on a twenty-five year lease with five year rent reviews, with, wherever necessary, rent free periods of up to two years. Rents currently range from £1.10 - £1.25 per sq.ft.

(d) User Satisfaction: Various empirical studies have shown
that over three quarters of Commission tenants are independent
businessmen with their owners working in the advance factory.
Additionally, the majority of tenants are existing businesses,
previously located within a ten mile radius of their new
units, located in premises either not intended for industrial
use (garages, sheds, military buildings), or in unsatisfactory
conditions (see Table 4).

Table 4

Development Commission Advance Factory Tenants

Empirical Studies Sample		Newly Estab- lished Business	Established Business Relocated
Welsh Border	10	2	8
Norfolk/Lincs	31	7	24 (6 branch plants)
Eastern Borders	20	5	15 (4 branch plants)

Thus the major reason for moving in most cases is the search
for more space and improved facilities.   Choice of unit size
is dependent however on the complexity of the industrial
process, the number of employees, and the flexibility of
various units in terms of work areas (Hillier, 1982).

For newly established businesses, there is a narrow field of
search for suitable premises, based on the owner's existing
home, and his dependence for help on family and friends. The
Commission's ability to offer up to two years rent free
premises has proved extremely attractive for new firms in
their initial development period, while for established
businesses it enables them to make a quick recovery and
promote growth after moving. However, a vital financial
consideration for new firms starting up in an advance unit is
the cost of modifications to the unit needed to accommodate
their process.

Advance factory units undoubtedly fill a need for temporary
premises for up to five years, while a viable firm goes
through a period of consolidation before its next phase of
expansion.   Viable firms may thus be expected to expand into
other larger premises, thus liberating the nursery units for

,

269

younger and smaller concerns. The impact of economic recession has undoubtedly slowed down this ladder of opportunity, with demand for units often varying greatly over small geographical areas.

Housing as a component of Development Policy

Both agencies have a role in the field of rural housing, as a way of reinforcing their industrial development initiatives. Both are empowered to guarantee rents to local authorities and housing associations for up to two years, for housing kept vacant for incoming key workers.

Mid Wales Development in particular possesses powers to construct housing, and, as part of its role as a new town development corporation, has constructed 1300 units at Newtown. Since housing for key workers is becoming an increasingly important issue in Mid-Wales, the Board completed its first direct development outside the new town area at Tywyn in 1981, with further housing being planned both at Tywyn and Dolgellau. The Board feels that the region needs around 100 key worker houses annually, and while a number of authorities have already built units on an agency basis (Bala, Llandrindod, Manchynlleth), they would prefer the Board to build such units directly.

The Development Commission, becoming increasingly diversified in its approach to rural development, has recently begun to focus its attention on the need for low cost housing in the countryside. Since 1977, the Housing Corporation has agreed to finance small housing association schemes in or near factory locations, provided that the Commission supports the bids for funds by District Councils, and agrees, where necessary, to guarantee rents up to first lettings.

In advocating an experimental housing role it has grant aided numerous local housing studies, a feasibility study of timber framed starter homes, and is currently undertaking an experimental construction programme of 'craft homes' in Alnwick, Eden and South Shropshire districts. These have been built for sale (£45,000 each) but the Housing Corporation has also agreed in principle to join with the Commission in building some craft homes for rent, to be managed by housing associations in Cornwall and North Norfolk. Craft homes however are a specialist market, and there are doubts over their high costs, marketability and their need for special environmental controls.

In an attempt to promote new tenure forms, the Commission

has agreed to participate with the National Federation of Housing Associations in the promotion of a shared equity scheme. As part of this experiment relating to a combined rental/mortgage scheme, the Commission intends to lend £5,000 per house for 100 houses, the balance of the mortgage component being provided by building societies. Since these houses are unlikely to cost less than £30,000 they will undoubtedly be beyond the reach of a significant minority of rural dwellers. The Commission is also investigating ways of helping local authorities with the cost of acquiring and servicing sites in villages that might otherwise be too expensive to develop for low cost private housing, and which could be sold under license to private developers to encourage the construction of more starter homes.

However, unlike industrial development, housing is a well established local authority function, and the long term influence of the Commission in this field is likely to be extremely limited.

THE RESULTS OF AGENCY EVALUATION

Any detailed study of the impact of rural development agencies, depends essentially on the evaluation framework adopted - political, institutional, economic or social. In physical terms, however, both agencies reveal considerable achievement in supporting a wide range of development opportunities, with their demand for both industrial land and premises, and in the promotion of new initiatives. The current slowing down of growth stimuli may lead however to a more fundamental questioning of their future programmes. Additionally, their inability to intervene over wider rural land use issues may limit their long term effectiveness.

With increasing positive discrimination by government in favour of small businesses, and the rapid expansion of such advance factory/workshop programmes over the last decade, it is important to make a comment on the real impact of such activity. While the Commission believe that the success of their programme rests on their close collaboration with local authorities in the development process, the attraction of locally determined rent structures to small businesses, and the intensive support services offered by COSIRA, attempts to develop local economic impact assessments have proved extremely difficult.

A number of such evaluation projects have however been attempted. An early study by Law and Howes (1972) in Mid

Wales, and later studies by Whitby (1981) and JURUE (1983), attempting to extend the financial evaluation of the factory programmes to consider the net social benefits of the initiative, have all concluded positively on the cost-effectivenes of the programme as a rural support measure. Medhurst (1982), in a recent critique of such studies, argues that there are a number of unresolved issues relating to future evaluations of such local initiatives - the consideration of social opportunity costs, the importance of clear and explicit agency objectives, and the proper balance between quantitative analysis and qualitative judgement. Ultimately the policy maker requires evidence upon which to choose between alternative initiatives requiring public investment.

It is clearly one of the major attributes of any specialist agency, that it possesses the ability to innovate and experiment in a flexible manner, and where such ideas prove successful, they may subsequently be more widely adopted. Such 'incubator' or 'catalyst' roles are clearly critical, but they may provide antecedents for local conflict, based on the perspective adopted by the agency and their local perception as devaluing existing social constructs. The Development Commission is less vulnerable to such charges through its direct involvement with voluntary Small Industries Committees, Rural Community Councils and local authorities. Nevertheless, both agencies have a clear view of initiatives that they are prepared to support.

Whilst such agencies have undoubtedly facilitated an increasing competence and rationality in development processes in rural areas, a number of current changes will undoubtedly effect their future activities. The slowing down of development programmes, increasing conflicts between central and local government over control and accountability in policy making, the promotion of market 'realism' and the encouragement of private sector involvement, will inevitably create increasing tensions.

The evidence of the 1981 census relating to diminishing rural depopulation due both to counter-urbanisation pressures, and the impact of national recession on migration flows, will increasingly beg the question as to whether such agency activities are becoming programmes in search of a policy. This will inevitably raise questions relating to the appropriateness of existing administrative instruments in facilitating comprehensive long term development opportunities in rural areas, and the relationship between economic development and broader land use policies.

13 Government agencies in land development

URLAN WANNOP

THE RELEVANCE OF THE SCOTTISH CASE

Since the reorganisation of local government and creation of
the Scottish Development Agency (SDA) in 1975, Scotland has
become distinctive in the degree to which Government has used
public agencies to stimulate urban regeneration and the
redevelopment of urban land. Although other agencies are
involved including the Housing Corporation and the Scottish
Special Housing Association most notably, it is the SDA which
dominates with the following significant characteristics:

(i) the adoption by the Agency of the traditional role
for local authorities in planning and initiating
urban renewal and improvement projects;

(ii) innovating attitudes and practices in urban
regeneration schemes;

(iii) implicit uncertainties about the relative weight of
economic and social objectives in projects,
associated with difficulties in evaluating their
'success';

(iv) a challenge to the relevance of the Development
Planning system;

(v) ambiguity within Government as between initiatives
by the Scottish Economic Planning Department and the
strategic role of the Scottish Development
Department.

This special Scottish experience contributes evidence in
relation to the latter three of the four areas of concern in
land policy identified by Barrett and Healey in part 1 of this
book; their phraseology has been paraphrased for brevity:

A. Understanding land ownership and management practices and
the development process.

B. Evaluation of state intervention in the land development
process.

C. Forms of organisation of land development and their effect
on the outcome of policy initiatives.

D. Methodological problems in evaluating the impacts of land
policy and initiatives.

In the Scottish case, Barrett and Healey's areas of concern B
and C overlap so considerably that they are combined for the
purposes of this chapter. Indeed, the overlap is spreading
through England as the Task Forces and Urban Development
Corporations proliferate.

THE SCOTTISH DEVELOPMENT AGENCY AND THE EMERGENCE OF AREA
INITIATIVES

Although the political case for the SDA and its principal
purposes incorporated in the SDA Act of 1975 aimed at the
regeneration of the Scottish economy, the enacted scope of the
SDA contained a potential to participate in urban development
which few observers at the time may have expected to become so
significant. The SDA was to seek:

(1) the furthering of economic development;

(2) the maintenance, provision and safeguarding of employment;

(3) the promotion of industrial efficiency and international
competitiveness; and

(4) the improvement of the environment.

Aside from its paramount political priority of industrial

restructuring, the SDA was quickly involved in 1976 in a major area initiative: in the role of co-ordinator of the Glasgow Eastern Area Renewal (GEAR) Project. Despite the initial reluctance of its Chief Executive, the SDA accepted the role of coordinating the multi-agency renewal programme for the East End of the City as well as participating in its own right to carry out environmental improvement, some social initiatives and factory building (Table 1). The GEAR programme has been variously criticised especially in terms of accountability (Nelson, 1980) and value for money (Orton, 1981), yet it laid the ground-rules for a new style of local planning and development in urban Britain, whereby a government agency coordinated the capital programmes and some other local initiatives of a diverse range of local and central governmental bodies. Indeed, within six months after GEAR began it was argued that the experience would "enable the Agency in the future to offer help ... in other parts of Scotland", (SDA, 1978). Even so, there was significant opinion within the SDA at this time which was unconvinced that the structure and style of the GEAR Project was the best model for economic recovery elsewhere in Scotland.

The emerging area focus of the SDA's industrial policies and of previously separate land renewal and factory-building programmes became sharper in the 1978/1979 period, when the Scottish Economic Planning Department introduced the SDA to assist with areas of "special need" requiring an "in depth" approach. The closure of the Glengarnock steelworks led to a Taskforce with the remit to "prevent the further decline of the Garnock Valley Community", (SDA, 1979). Working with BSC (Industry) Ltd and the local authorities, the Task Force was given preferential support within the SDA to accelerate industrial, social and environmental investment in the Garnock Valley. An initial target of 800 jobs by 1982 was set, but a termination date for withdrawal of the Task Force was left to be determined later. The Task Force model was repeated in Clydebank, where the closure of the Singer works had compounded the collapse of the town's staple industries. The Task Force launched the Clydebank Business Park which became the centrepiece of the Enterprise Zone designated in 1981.

The SDA's new-found confidence in the economic potential of area renewal initiatives gained from its Glengarnock and Clydebank initiatives, led to "comprehensive integrated projects" first conceived for Leith and Blackness (Dundee), where the SDA launched a variety of projects in support of local economic development programmes. The understanding between the participants as to their respective contributions became "Project Agreements" (Table 1) between the SDA and

275

Table 1: AREA INITIATIVE OBJECTIVES, TARGETS AND SDA EXPENDITURE, AS AT 31 MARCH 1983

NAME	BASIS	STARTING DATE	TARGET DATE	OBJECTIVES	SDA EXPENDITURE TO 31.3.83	SDA EXPENDITURE TOTAL EXPECTED	TARGET EMPLOYMENT	TARGET FIRMS
GEAR Glasgow Eastern Area Renewal	Co-ordination of urban regeneration	1976	1987	"physical, social and economic regeneration ... for the benefit of both residents and business community"	£43m	Capital: £73m Revenue: £1m + other not specified	not specified	–
GARNOCK VALLEY	Task Force	1979	1984	regeneration of local economy; assistance to local industry; re-use of steelworks	£14.2m	Capital: £19.0m Revenue: not specified	c.2000	80–100
CLYDEBANK	Task Force	1980	1985	promotion of Enverprise Zone, development of 'Business Park' and extension of industrial estates to create new employment	£15.0m	Capital: £21m Revenue: not specified	5000	200+
DUNDEE (1) Blackness	Project Agreement	1981	1984	co-ordinated implementation of Business Development Area	£2.7m	Capital: £5.6m Revenue: £0.4m	not specified	–
(2) City	Project Agreement	1982	1985	commercial development of Waterfront and wider industrial initiatives	£0.1m	Capital: £18m Revenue: not specified	1200 created + 3500 created 1986–91	–
LEITH	Project Agreement	1981	1984	stem decline in business activity; realise potential; assist residents in gaining access to jobs; improve environment	£5.3m	Capital: £7m Revenue: not specified	800 created and safeguarded	–

Name	Type			Objectives	Cost	Capital/Revenue	Jobs	
ASSET Ardrossan, Saltcoats and Stevenston	Self-Help	1981	1984	business development; factory building and environmental improvement	£1.8m	Capital: £3m Revenue: not specified	—	—
MOTHERWELL	Project Agreement	1982	1987	removal of development constraints, develop 'unique advantages', increase job opportunities, diversify economic structure	£5.0m	Capital: £37m Revenue: not specified	3000 permanent created 300-500 temporary	—
KILMARNOCK	Project Agreement	1983	1986	stem decline in business activity; increase job opportunities; diversify economy and avoid dependence upon externally controlled firms	—	Capital: £0.15m p.a. Revenue: £0.03m p.a.	1000 permanent created	—
COATBRIDGE	Project Agreement	1983	1986	stem decline in business activity; stimulate new business; increase job opportunities; upgrade infrastructure	£1.4m	Capital: £10.7m Revenue: £0.05m	800 permanent created	—
WIGTOWN	Project Agreement	1983	1986	generate local commitment and 'self-help'; create new employment and improve rural services	—	Capital: £0.49m Revenue: £0,15m	500 created and protected	—
DENNY and BONNYBRIDGE	Project Agreement	1983	1986	stimulate business through diversification, new starts and entrepreneurship; improve image by renewing land, premises and environment	—	Capital: £2.8m	200 new protected	—

Sources: Annual Reports, Project Agreements, Task Force Reports, GEAR Reports

local government, with negotiated but legally unenforceable financial commitments by the signatories. The projects were seen as three to five year pump-priming exercises with the setting of employment targets. All the Project Agreements made up to Summer 1983 covered areas experiencing decline in manufacturing employment, including the Wigtown Rural Project area, but the SDA has almost no other kind of area available to it and declining areas are not inevitably inconsistent with the adoption of "a planned and selective approach ... (and the) emphasis will be their potential for improved performance" (SDA, 1981). How the extent of improved performance could be measured and the return on SDA expenditure evaluated is a difficult conceptual issue, as is the effectiveness of the associated land development - unless measured by the very limited criterion of merely achieving any reuse of vacant urban land, regardless of the inherent opportunity costs.

The rising importance of area projects was reflected in the restructuring of the Agency in 1982 with the formation of an Area Development Directorate, whose projects were now absorbing approaching 60 per cent of the Agency's annual capital expenditure. The Ardrossan, Saltcoats, Stevenston Enterprise Trust (ASSET) was formed in 1981 and, subsequently, the Motherwell Project Agreement was signed early in 1982 and an Agreement covering the whole City of Dundee was made in November of that year. Within the first weeks of 1983, Project Agreements followed for the district of Kilmarnock and London and for a central part of the town of Coatbridge; projects were imminent for Port Dundas (Glasgow), Denny-Bonnybridge (Central) and Wigtown (Dumfries and Galloway) and the Agency had also commissioned a major study of the potential for a project embracing the whole City Centre of Glasgow.

EVALUATING AGENCY INTERVENTION AND THE ORGANISATION OF LAND DEVELOPMENT: THE CASE OF GEAR

To discern criteria by which the quality and achievement of their interventions can be properly evaluated, the origins of the SDA involvement in urban regeneration and land development must be understood. Some might see the SDA as a means of Government with-holding certain public expenditure from local authority hands and, on this basis, the rate of expenditure or the quality of the assets created by the SDA would be enough by which to judge the whole performance of their projects. This would suppose that the SDA was being introduced merely to organise better a product which would also emerge in its absence, later perhaps rather than sooner. However, this would mean evaluating only the means and effectiveness of the organisation of the product; the question as to whether the product was worth creating at all would not be faced.

In the origins of SDA intervention, three notable threads can be seen to have become more strongly entwined over a period of perhaps fifteen years, from the mid-1960s. There was a thread of growing Government dissatisfaction with the quality and speed of urban renewal as conceived and managed by Scottish local government, and by Glasgow Corporation in particular; there was a thread of real concern for long-established problems of poverty, deprivation, physical decay and economic re-adjustment in the older towns and cities; there was also a thread of political aggrandisement as central government's thirty year role in regional development through the new town programme was sharply curbed in the mid-1970s.

By comparison with progress of the new town programme, civil servants could speak disparagingly not only of the aesthetic and social quality of Glasgow's renewal, but also of the quality of its councillors and its administration. The attitude was shared not only amongst civil servants but, also, with both Labour and Conservative Ministers whose origins were in local politics in Glasgow. When Glasgow's successive claims for central government to specially fund the cost of deficiencies in local facilities were to be at least partially met during the 1970s, Government could turn to the SDA because it was not disposed to channel extra finance through the hands of councillors or of unimaginative designers.

With regard to experience after 1974/1975, of course, it can be argued that any local failure was fundamentally that of central government, whose reform of local administration had seriously misjudged the nature of the planning and development problems which local authorities would have to tackle in the 1970s and 1980s. The two-tiers introduced to local government in the major towns and cities and the separation of housing from other strategic responsibilities, inefficiently fragmented efforts for urban renewal and thereby reinforced the prospects of central government stepping in.

Similarly, the division of what had originally been designed as a unified development planning system is also attributable to central government, and is a partial answer to Government criticism of the slowness of local authorities to make coherent plans for urban renewal. Narrow interpretation by central government of the purpose of Structure and Local Plans also tended to confine their concerns to the use of land, unquestionably helping them come to seem peripheral to the management and execution of urban renewal and of land development.

It remains that whomsoever is to blame for past impediments to renewal and land development, a project is likely to deserve some credit in an organisational evaluation if it ensures a faster rate of investment than would otherwise have occurred, or if it gives some satisfaction to the participants and to the clients who live or work or have some other stake in the area. GEAR was started without anything to compare with the Project Agreements introduced for later projects, and had no in-built targets against which its performance could be evaluated. Although six basic economic and social objectives were later adopted, they were unquantified, far from explicit and not immediately open to evaluation. Even so, GEAR suggests that although prone to an initial hiatus, projects are able to create a greater impetus of development than local authorities would have done unaided and, whatever any missed opportunities to have brought even greater satisfaction, they may also organise a generally more acceptable product within their terms of reference.

Over six years after the Project began, GEAR was still unique. There had been no previous instance in Britain in which government agencies and local authorities had attempted such a large coordinated programme of physical, economic and social initiatives over such a major sector of an existing City. Nowhere beforehand had the leading responsibility been placed on a government agency. GEAR remained a very different arrangement to the Partnership and Programme initiatives pursued since 1978 in England. Continuation of the full administrative responsibilities of Strathclyde Regional Council and Glasgow District Council in GEAR differed significantly from the arrangements whereby in 1981, the London and Liverpool Dockland Development Corporations assumed planning and certain other powers from the established local authorities.

In drawing conclusions about the progress of GEAR, considerable reservations have to be made. In its coordinating role, the SDA lacked the statutory powers and responsibilities which town and country planning or local government legislation provides to Regional Councils, District Councils and New Town and Urban Development Corporations. The Agency could choose how to spend the extra resources it itself brought to the Project, but it could not direct the other participants in any way. It is accordingly not always possible to separate the direct influence of the GEAR team from the influence of the GEAR Project. It appears probable, for instance, that the Shettleston and Parkhead Health Centres were retained within the Health Board's programme as might not have been the case in the absence of the GEAR Project. Whether the Board's initiative arises from their commitment to the spirit of the Project, to the willingness of Government to increase financial allocations to participants able to accelerate investment in the area or to the persuasion of the GEAR team, is a matter of speculation.

In the Review of GEAR (Wannop, 1982) commissioned by the SDA, it was impossible to assess precisely what developments had been introduced to programmes or accelerated or protected from the trend of public expenditure cuts because of participants' commitment to GEAR. A tentative assessment is that some £33 million of a total of £149 million of capital investment by the participants over the first five years of the Project, would have been spent elsewhere in Strathclyde or Scotland but for the fact of GEAR. Of this additionality, some £26 million is attributable to the Agency and the balance to the other partners - Strathclyde Regional Council, Glasgow District Council, the Greater Glasgow Health Board, the Scottish Special Housing Association, the Housing Corporation and the Manpower Services Commission.

It was inevitable that criticisms (Booth, 1982) would tend to focus on the GEAR coordinating team, in circumstances in which the SDA had more responsibility than power. However, two essential points must be made. First, the SDA were given a managerial role which satisfied few of the precepts of effective administration and which was little more familiar to any of the other participants than it was to the SDA. Secondly, the number of issues in dispute were small in number and some certainly arose because participants could not instantly adjust to the exceptional role they had agreed for the SDA, although they wished to see immediate results.

In its first five years, GEAR was certainly unsuccessful in re-thinking the whole future of the East End in the light of changing circumstances and of current prospects for economic change, for resources, for land for different urban activities and for the further restructuring which may occur in the Clydeside Conurbation in early years and in the longer term. The 1982 Review by the Agency of the future of GEAR threw up strategic issues about land and the potential for development of a kind in which action should have been taken four years before. In the two Docklands, similar issues were more quickly faced.

By 1982, GEAR had earned support amongst the principal
participants sufficient to demand the Project's extension, for
a limited period of years at least. On the basic measure of
additional expenditure, the Regional and District Councils
could regard GEAR as a successful extension of action to renew
Glasgow at a time when overall local authority expenditure was
being reduced, and when it was difficult to discriminate even
marginally in favour of deprived areas. Similarly, central
government could regard the Project as successful because it
had brought a faster rate of spending than the local
authorities and other agencies could otherwise have achieved.
Central government had also gained greater influence in local
matters such as housing policy, because the District Council
had been more rapidly displaced by SSHA and the Housing
Corporation as the balance of local housing was altered. It
is uncertain to what extent the finance made available to GEAR
through government agencies was diverted from elsewhere in
Scotland or, indeed, was at the expense of allocations to the
local authority sector. It remains that the Regional and
District Councils perceived the financing to be a supplement
to their own resources as some of the agencies, similarly,
believed GEAR to have permitted them a higher ceiling on
expenditure. To a degree, therefore, central government was
able to buy support for its agency intervention in the East
End.

Criticisms made of GEAR that much of what has been built or
invested in was already programmed or planned beforehand, are
misplaced. The Project's immediate purpose was to accelerate
and improve the quality of programmes which, prior to 1976,
had run behind schedule and had led to long periods elapsing
between the publication of plans and proposals, the vacation
of buildings, their rehabilitation or clearance and their
reoccupation by new households, new firms, new buildings, or
new uses of vacant sites.

The GEAR Review (Wannop, 1982) considered other forms of
management of renewal in urban areas elsewhere in Scotland and
England, suggesting that GEAR had been comparatively
successful in an organisational sense. It had been associated
with a higher rate of expenditure than would otherwise have
occurred in the East End. It had produced a higher quality of
physical environment and probably more public and private
initiatives to change conditions than were previously
promised. It appeared to have protected the East End from
public expenditure cuts more successfully than had been
possible in the comparable Maryhill Corridor of Glasgow, where
a special approach to coordination lay entirely in the hands
of the local authorities without direct Ministerial

encouragement. It had overcome difficulties of poor relations between participants which have persisted in many Partnership arrangements in English cities, although perhaps at some cost to long-term strategy by evading some issues of inter-participant priorities. None of the other cooperative models of area renewal tried in Britain were thought by the Review to suggest any better structure on which the advanced case of GEAR could be usefully recast, although the land brokerage role of the Docklands Development Corporations appeared very relevant to the need to arrange more flexibly and quickly the transfer of land from obsolete uses or inactivity into beneficial uses.

METHODOLOGICAL PROBLEMS IN EVALUATING THE IMPACTS OF INITIATIVES IN LAND DEVELOPMENT

The area projects are ostensibly aimed at economic improvement, either sooner through direct assistance to firms by finance or premises, or later through the indirect benefits of environmental action. So, although Project Agreements incorporate programmes of readily monitored intentions in such regards as the quantity of floor space, area of drainage schemes, lengths of road and size of other infrastructural contributions, these permit evaluation only of managerial performance and not of the objective success of the enterprise. Only so far as the Project Agreements set employment targets, do they provide any tangible criterion by which the effects of the projects can be evaluated. This is to again assume that the mere re-occupation of vacant urban land or of abandoned buildings is not sufficient objective in its own right, regardless of cost. A wide evaluation must assume that there are alternative ways of disposing of public investment in urban and land development, which can produce different levels of economic and social return. Yet, the Project Agreements provide a potential measure of their economic impact only so far as they incorporate job targets, and these are specified in a variety of conceptually different terms.

How then can a start be made on evaluation? McNicoll and Swales (1982) argue that ambiguity in the SDA's objectives demands greater flexibility in evaluating investments than could be reflected in measured rates of financial return based on 'commercial principles'. Clearly, the political origins of the SDA complicate evaluation, as does the inevitability that some area projects may be stimulated as much by the SDA's need to keep its balance in the geographical politics of Scotland, as by strict comparisons of geographical needs and opportunities. However, even the narrowest interpretation of the principal objectives of economic and environmental improvement immediately faces the overriding problem in evaluating the area projects. Neither objective is given primacy in the SDA Act and each, to some degree, contributes something to the other. It might be unwise to suggest that environmental returns are less readily measured than economic returns, but there are familiar difficulties in comparing the two and in considering them within the same framework.

The SDA has itself contributed to environmental evaluation through cost-benefit appraisal, when at an early stage considering relative priorities as between the reclamation of pit bings and other semi-rural projects and the recovery of vacant and degraded urban land, to which it subsequently switched the emphasis of expenditure. It appears that the area projects are not yet appraised in advance in a comparable fashion, nor has a basis for longer term evaluation been established either in economic terms or in relation to the impact of projects on strategic urban development.

Commentary on some of the economic and strategic implications of area projects has already surrounded GEAR (Orton, 1981; Booth et al, 1982). While some of this discussion appears unaware rather than neglectful of the political origins of GEAR, it has touched on economic and strategic questions which become even more significant as a single demonstration project (GEAR) is extended into a programme of urban investment spreading across Scotland. Booth et al underestimated the innovative significance of GEAR and its catalytic influence in aspects of Glasgow's administration, including the acceleration of new housing policies, as well as hinting at an unfavourable judgement on the performance of GEAR on grounds on which contrary evidence may be becoming available. Orton underestimated the growing indications that since 1977, collective investment in Glasgow's East End had run at a higher level than would have occurred in the absence of GEAR.

The SDA's dilemma is wider than the uncertainty over whether the Area Projects are to be principally regarded as initiatives for ecnomic recovery, or as programmes to re-occupy more rapidly vacant land and eliminate environmental squalor in Scottish towns and cities. By defining a boundary, job targets and a programme of action for the projects, the Project Agreements tend to imply that evaluation should be similarly confined. Many of the common criticisms of too narrow an application of the area approach are relevant to an economic evaluation. The problems are exemplified by differences of approach within the Project Agreements so far concluded.

The first target set was for Leith and was to create and safeguard 800 jobs over three years, primarily in manufacturing. At the end of two years, the SDA considered that over 450 jobs had been created and provided for. But what jobs were eligible for counting under the terms of the target? The terms did not specify how many of the jobs were to be newly created as against being safeguarded. Should the jobs counted as being safeguarded be only those in existing firms receiving SDA support, through financing or the provision of new or improved premises; if so, should any offsetting count be made of jobs lost in other firms through stronger local competition offered by the firms selected for support? If the count were confined solely to firms receiving some sort of direct aid, it would amongst other omissions, neglect the economic significance of stone-cleaning, tree-planting and rehabilitation of derelict and degraded land which are principal elements in the environmental programme, seen by the Agency as supporting the economic thrust of the Project. Because these environmental benefits will not be very localised, it might be argued that as most jobs in Leith would receive some support, the terms of the project target would even be met if only 800 of the 11,500 manufacturing jobs recently in Leith remained after the three years of the Project. While this latter outcome would presumably leave all participants in the project gravely unhappy, it characterises the difficulty of measuring the impact of policy and of defining satisfactory criteria.

The second Project Agreement was for Blackness, a small part of inner Dundee where the avoidance of a job target can be argued as wholly appropriate, because it would be difficult to show that jobs created in the area would have been additional to those which would have been created elsewhere in Dundee in the absence of the Project. Similarly, any jobs 'safeguarded' for Blackness by the Project might in its absence have moved to another part of Dundee, so causing little or no loss of employment in the City nor perhaps to the Dundee economy. Questions on what firms have done because of the Project or would not have done in its absence could, of course, be put through a direct survey, but a much wider evaluation would be required placing the Project Area in the context of its city or urban region, if not also in a national context. The problem is well covered by Ashcroft (1982).

The Motherwell Project Agreement returned to the setting of a job target, for 3,000 jobs which were not necessarily to be primarily in manufacturing as in Leith but were specified as being "permanent". While the very large extent of the Motherwell Project Area, including most of the District, presents a sounder basis for measuring the Project's economic impact, the definition of a "permanent" job presumably could include the stabilisation of a temporary or vulnerable one, and might therefore include job safeguarding as well as job creation. The Kilmarnock and Coatbridge Project Agreements adopted a similar approach to that of Motherwell, by respectively aiming for 1,000 'direct permanent' jobs and for 800 "permanant" jobs.

The Dundee Project was distinctive, not only because after an original expectation that the Project would be confined to the Waterfront it was extended to the City as a whole, but because its target had now been simplified as the creation of 1,200 jobs. The Wigtown Rural Project reverted to the "creation and protection" of 500 jobs in manufacturing and services, of which 350 would be generated from indigenous sources, including existing firms, new starts, cooperatives and community businesses, and 150 secured from non-indigenous sources by inward investment. This is the most specific target, although still posing large conceptual problems for any evaluation.

These issues of the objectives and means of evaluating urban renewal and regeneration are not unique to SDA projects. The questions sketched out have crystallised because the SDA has introduced financial and management approaches to small area development of a kind which local authorities are unaccustomed to, are disinclined to take, are not statutorily required to follow or find difficult because of their financial or administrative structures. The designation of areas for the two English Docklands Development Corporations has similarly produced targets and accounts for small areas, for which local authorities have had no reason to produce their own accounts. Although Government agencies accordingly do invite an evaluation of what they achieve by the fact of their style and necessity to produce accounts and data for their operations, these help only so far as agency effectiveness in a fairly narrow managerial sense is concerned. The much larger question remains of whether they and others could use their resources in different and even more constructive ways, to the greater benefit to either their inner city or of their enveloping urban system.

THE POLITICAL CONTEXT OF AGENCY INTERVENTION AND SOME IMPLICATIONS

The developing pattern of the SDA's urban interventions lies within a Scottish political and administrative context which, in matters of planning and urban development, has since the late 1970s become less distinctive in relation to England, where there has been a spread of the kind of Government intervention in urban regeneration previously characteristic of Scotland. It is accordingly possible to draw on the longer Scottish experience to suggest some implications of possible widespread significance.

Agency interventions have now largely moved away from the 'comprehensive' approach to locally concentrated urban problems, characteristic of the mid-1970s and of GEAR in particular. Social elements remain and a reduced Urban Aid programme persists, but the tokenism of £50,000 assigned for community projects in the Coatbridge Project Agreement by comparison with £10,700,000 earmarked for capital investment, characterises the shift of emphasis from the late 1970s. Of course, the Docklands projects contain a community budget and even in GEAR the weight of expenditure was always heavily towards capital projects. So, it may have been past rhetoric rather than the expenditure accounts which spoke of a comprehensive, community based approach, but there is no doubt but that property and land development is now unequivocally central to urban initiatives. This is acknowledged by the SDA (1983) in referring to "the Agency's quickening interest in the development of property, in addition to industrial premises, as a means of generating economic activity" and to "this end results of much of our environmental improvement work in the stimulation of industrial, commercial and residential development by the private sector were evident throughout the country and none more so than in Leith".

Taking a long perspective, it might be said that a full circle has been achieved in British regeneration policy. The SDA area projects and the two Dockland projects could be seen as contemporary forms of the Comprehensive Development Area (CDA) approach, which dominated urban renewal policy twenty years ago. The areas of the current individual local initiatives are larger, action is more selective, approaches incorporate a large element of rehabilitation and are more sensitive in other important respects. Yet, in relation to all the experiments and social concern of the intervening period, we had returned in 1983 to policy from which much of the social concern of the mid-1970s had been shaken-out, and in which physical renewal appeared again near to being an end in itself. Notwithstanding the expansive economic aims freely surrounding the projects, it was uncertain as to what degree they created new economic wealth to the benefit of either the project area or of their surrounding urban or metropolitan systems. The Conservative Government's priority for capital rather than revenue expenditure had been well established in most fields of public policy, but the preceding Labour Government - in Scotland at least - had through the GEAR project and the emerging policies of the SDA also put the emphasis on capital investment.

For the statutory system of development planning in Britain - already criticised for tardiness and marginal effects upon structural urban change and administration - the recent operations of the SDA and of other Government agencies have been an additional challenge. For example, five years after Strathclyde Regional Council had given Clydebank District Council approval to prepare a local plan for the core of their District, the Council had twice thought it necessary to modify the boundaries of the plan but had not achieved a draft for public consultation. In the intervening period, an SDA Task Force had been introduced to execute a major programme of public investment, an Enterprise Zone had been designated on the basis of the speedily-prepared planning statement demanded by the enabling Act, and a nationally-promoted Business Park had been conceived of and established. All this without the benefit of a statutory local plan.

From the experience here and, also, from the Project Agreements integral to SDA participation in the area projects, important pointers have arisen to the future of the development planning system. The Review of the Future of GEAR (Wannop, 1982), confirmed for Glasgow the gap between strategic and local planning in major cities which has been encouraged by the separation between the two tiers of local government. The gap was not closed very substantially during the first five years of the life of GEAR, but the subsequent SDA area projects brought the Agreement approach, which has characteristics of immediacy and attention to resources which have been amongst the deficiencies of statutory development plans. So, we might see that after the failure over the past decade of attempts by some planners to translate statutory development plans into social and economic development plans, statutory development planning is now being superseded in many circumstances by other forms of land development programme. Furthermore, this is occurring in some of the most important and urgent instances of urban development. Having failed to gain a foothold on the ground which they sought in the 1970s, statutory development plans have fallen back to consolidate their interest in regard to physical development, only to find their neglected position increasingly occupied by new public approaches to planning and executing urban regeneration.

In the return to an emphasis on physical action as the centre-piece of urban regeneration, the initiative in Scotland and in priority areas in England has, in the process, passed very considerably from local authorities to central government. Principal projects are now increasingly steered and initiated by central government or their agencies. There has been a nearly straight-line development in this characteristic of policy. Government moved from the days of its 1960s negotiation and approval of CDA projects initiated by local authorities, through sponsorship of the Community Development Programmes and Inner Area Studies, to SDA's coordination of the GEAR Project, to the Partnership arrangements chaired by Ministers, to the Glengarnock and Clydebank Task Forces formed at central government's instigation, to the Merseyside and London Docklands Development Corporations, to the SDA's area projects and to the Merseyside and other Task Forces of other English towns and cities. The content of central government management and input in urban development projects has progressively increased, whether devolved to an agency as in Scotland or, in England, shared between the two Dockland Corporations and Task Force teams of civil servants and secondees from financial institutions.

Another interpretation of the agency tendency, of course, is that the interventions are a means of one branch of central government – the Department of Environment in England and Wales and the Scottish Economic Planning Department – establishing an ascendancy over other branches, which may otherwise not be biddable in regard to their policies as they affect urban areas. There is probably more truth in this interpretation in England and Wales than in Scotland, where although there may be no Department of Industry disputing urban policy with a Department of the Environment, different Departments of the Scottish Office can also put central government in a superficially ambivalent position. The strategic influence of the urban interventions of the SDA under the aegis of the Economic Planning Department, can be compared with the Development Department's overt position – as expressed in the National Planning Guidelines – eschewing any guidance to local authorities over urban priorities, which are asserted to not be a matter for central direction. As the SDA imply an order of priorities and a national significance in their projects for urban regeneration, the overt stance of the Development Department appears false in regard to central government as a whole.

It is part of both the reversion to the physical and land development focus of urban regeneration projects and of the growing participation of central government, that the benefits from the projects may now go increasingly not to people previously established in the areas but to outsiders. Of course, it could be said that this was common even twenty years ago when local communities were being displaced by CDA schemes, but when filling vacant land, rehabilitating and building new industrial buildings and private housebuilding bulks so large in current agency interventions, they connect much less clearly with local needs and provide much more opportunity for outside gain. The most readily and accurately measurable criteria by which their performance can be evaluated relates to the volume of construction achieved, not to employment or other local economic measures or any direct local social progress. Of course, if a full evaluation of the impact of projects must reach beyond their defined area, it must be recognised that local social and economic progress cannot be entirely based upon local physical development. So, the area foci again attract primarily physical action and, as with the CDA approach of twenty years ago, their prospective benefits are not clearly nor possibly substantially gained by the local residents. The Conservative Government has, of course, shifted the focus of property development substantially towards private investors, most notably through the site servicing and land brokerage roles of the Docklands Development Corporations. The opportunities for this shift may have hitherto seemed fewer in GEAR and the other Scottish projects, but are likely to be more determinedly pursued in future.

Of other implications of the high-profile agency area interventions, that of their diversion of attention from background reductions in investment in other fundamental elements of urban regeneration and of land and regional economic development, has been raised (Lawless, 1981) elsewhere in the general context of inner city initiatives. The Scottish initiatives add to the evidence both in relation to priorities within the SDA's budget and to other public expenditure. The urban renewal role of the SDA has been taking a larger share of the growth of investment than has industry. The Scottish dimension of the national rise of urban policy at the expense of regional policy has also been noted elsewhere (Ashcroft, 1982). The rise of the SDA's initiatives in the project areas can be compared to the considerable real reduction in Scottish new town investment and, in relation to public expenditure in Scotland in Trade, Industry and Employment, the scale of the overall decline has overwhelmed the scale of all the SDA's activities. Investment in GEAR and the area projects is of small importance beside the greater economic and social significance of the reductions of spending in industry and employment at large. When expenditure in GEAR and the area projects by the Scottish Special Housing Association (SSHA) and the Housing Corporation is added into the count of SDA investment, the relative deflation of the new towns in Scottish strategic development becomes more considerable. We thereby see a shift of central government influence into established urban areas but without any real increase of urban investment.

It is more difficult to compare the size of the SDA role in urban development to that of local authorities than it is to other arms of policy of the Secretary of State, or of central government departments. Certainly, the precise degree to which Scottish area projects encroach on the traditional responsibility of Scottish local government for urban renewal is unclear, because local authorities do not present their own accounts in terms of renewal projects as the SDA does. The figures suggest, however, that the substantial reductions in recent years of local authority capital expenditure are unlikely to be made good by SDA investment. Similarly, the real reduction in Rate Support Grant for the Districts within which the Scottish projects have been launched offsets the new investment brought by the SDA, SSHA, Housing Corporation, Health Boards and Manpower Services Commission who are variously associated. So, if the share which central government takes of the urban regeneration effort cannot be exactly measured, the significance of the trend of growing central intervention is nonetheless great.

PART III
THE STATE AND LAND DEVELOPMENT: WESTERN EUROPEAN EXAMPLES

Introduction
PATSY HEALEY

The previous papers in this collection have discussed a variety of British land policy programmes. Yet the parameters which govern British land policy, some well-recognised and others less evident but long-established in ideologies and practices, are most clearly revealed when comparisons are made with other countries. The next two papers discuss industrial land policies in the Netherlands and housing land policies in Sweden, countries which in several respects have similarities with the UK.

Both countries are well-known in the land policy literature for their use of state control of the conversion of rural to urban land through municipal land ownership. Needham shows that 70% of all new industrial land is provided by municipalities, and Duncan finds that 75% of housing and public services are built on land already owned by communes.

British planners often look enviously at both countries because of this, but frequently assume that their traditions are so distinctive that there is little to be learnt of relevance to British land policy. Needham and Duncan show that this is not so. Both authors argue that in all three countries, private ownership and investment is the norm in most economic spheres, modified by economic and social welfare programmes. So why are the land policies of the Netherlands and Sweden so different, and what do these differences mean in terms of making land and property available for production and consumption purposes?

Needham concentrates on the differences in approach to industrial land supply between the Netherlands and Britain. He notes that the economic problems of both countries encourage policies which seek to use land to promote industrial development. But in the UK, local authority activity is limited to filling perceived "market gaps", with public sector land and property prices firmly linked to market values. In the Netherlands, by contrast, municipalities own and service most development land. They thus have a monopoly over land supply. Needham then examines the way the price of this land is established. He claims that, because municipalities are by far the biggest buyers of development land, they can acquire land at prices only a little above agricultural value. The minimum price at which municipalities then supply land is established by administrative procedure to ensure that costs are covered. However, municipalities can set prices above this. Needham argues that in doing so, they are effectively acting in a market place composed of all municipalities. Until recently, this tended to force prices up, to obtain returns for use on other municipal projects. With an increasing concern to attract development, municipalities are now undercutting each other, with those who bought and serviced land many years ago at a considerable advantage. Many British urban authorities do, of course, own substantial amounts of land, acquired for various reasons over the years. Like their Dutch counterparts, they are now juggling with the potentially contradictory pressures to maximise the asset value of the land they own and to use cheap land to attract employment-generating activity. In the Netherlands, however, municipalities capture development gains, and have the powers, and commitment, to ensure a continued and varied supply of industrial land.

Duncan shows that in Sweden, commune ownership of development land has contributed to holding down land prices, by, as in the Netherlands, cutting out the private capturing of development gain. He stresses that most of the land in Sweden remains in private ownership. The commune acts as the land developer, purchasing and servicing development land which is then passed on to builders. These in turn are pressed to acquire cheap land since the selling price of housing (and consequently land) is controlled as a condition of State Housing Loans which provide construction capital to builders. Thus builders make profits through construction, not development, a sharp contrast to the British case, where the builder/developer has always played a major role in the private housing field.   In effect, Swedish communes have been able to use a more effective form of the Community Land Act backed by finance for land purchase, support in housing finance policies and in selective capital gains taxes.

Duncan concludes from a variety of evidence that the result has been to keep down new house prices, but that there is considerable variation between communes in the extent to which they have used legislation allowing long term land banking and expropriation.   He then goes on to ask why such a different approach to housing land has been adopted in Sweden, compared to Britain and many other developed capitalist economies. Needham claims that for the Netherlands, the answer lay in the distinctive Dutch topography and the necessity for controlling ground water levels.   Duncan argues that in Sweden, the reasons are socio-political. He suggests that in Sweden, landed interests have been weak throughout this century.   The powerful interests determining land policy have been farmers, largely interested in production;   a highly centralised industrial sector, closely linked to financial interests; and a well-articulated labour movement.   The farmers have opposed the use of rural land for investment returns, industrial and labour interests have supported low cost housing programmes, and financial interests have been able to realise returns from industrial investment.

Both papers serve to highlight how confused and fragmented British land policies have come to be in recent years, as many of the other papers have illustrated.   They also illustrate the importance of looking in detail at the way particular policies actually work, and at the sources of support for programmes. Duncan concludes by stressing the important point that to design effective land policies we need to beware of being blinded by ideological commitments, whether to land nationalization (on the left), or the "free market" (on the right).   Both are merely possibilities among a range of measures, from which to construct appropriate land policies to support economic and social development programmes.

14 Local government policy for industrial land in England and the Netherlands

BARRIE NEEDHAM

INTRODUCTION

A number of local governments in both countries are pursuing
active policies for stimulating their economics and for
countering unemployment in their areas, and in many of them
the provision of industrial land and buildings is an important
part of their package of measures. In this paper I shall be
comparing those local policies for industrial land and –
because the two are sometimes difficult to separate – making
some related comments about the policies for industrial
buildings. My main argument is that in <u>England</u>, local
government policies for industrial land are based upon the
concept of the market. There is an active market for
industrial land, and local government land measures tend to be
justified in terms of "filling market gaps" or "compensating
for market deficiencies": moreover, the price of such
publicly provided land is always set by reference to "the
market price". In the <u>Netherlands</u>, on the other hand, there
is hardly any private market in building land of any sort (for
industrial use or otherwise) so "the market" cannot be used so
easily as a reference-point and the public provision of

---

*   Important information and ideas have been obtained from
     Professor dr. Bert Kruijt and from the "land departments"
     of several municipalities.

industrial land is justified differently. It must not be
thought, however, that the market discipline is totally
absent, nor that the absence of a private market gives Dutch
local governments wide freedom in their industrial land
policy, for they are subject to two other strong disciplines –
competition with other municipalities and supervision by the
provinces. Nevertheless, Dutch municipalities are freer to
use land measures as part of their economic and employment
policies than are their English counterparts. From that
argument I refrain from drawing any detailed recommendations.
If they are made it will be because people are perhaps
stimulated to view in a different light the policies of their
own country. In particular, I hope that English readers will
be stimulated by the knowledge that in at least one other
country (see Duncan's paper in this volume) an important part
of land policy is pursued (and, on the whole, successfully)
without reference to "the market" and "the market price".
This paper is based upon research done by the author (Needham,
1982; Kruijt and Needham, 1980) and on research in which the
author took part (JURUE, 1979; Geraets, 1980), and most of the
statements made here are supported by the author's own work or
by the work of others referred to there. In this paper, the
stately academic game of citing sources will be restricted to
works not already mentioned in the above studies.

England

In the local authorities that we studied it was the express
aim of the Councils not to compete with private developers, to
complement and not compete with private enterprise provision,
and the authorities' land measures were consistent with this
principle. Land was acquired and then made available only if
the Council thought:

- that there was a demand for industrial land in that location
  at the supply price as set by the market

- that something was preventing that land from being brought
  on to the market privately

- that that public provision was not competing with private
  provision elsewhere within the local authority (provision
  outside was fair game for competition) or with the private
  provision of land inside or outside the local authority on
  which could be provided workplaces for some of the local
  unemployed.

In other words, by bringing that land on to the market, the

local authority was contributing to reducing unemployment locally or to making possible extra output locally, and that was a contribution which the private market could not or would not make.

That seems to me to be a good way of describing the industrial land policies of the four West Midlands local authorities that I studied in detail (Birmingham, Coventry, Dudley and the Metropolitan County Council) and the policies can be understood as being the outcome of three factors:

- the physical conditions in the area

- the discipline of the market

- political attitudes.

In the West Midlands region there is no general shortage of industrial land , but within the districts studied the only land which could be put to industrial use was derelict or abandoned and could be made usable only by a large and unprofitable expenditure. The only industrial land which could profitably be made available privately was on greenfield sites on the edge of the conurbation, too far away from the worst concentrations of unemployment to offer workplaces to the unemployed there. There was a strong demand for the reclaimed industrial land within the conurbation: estate agents reported the demand for land, and experience showed that the publicly provided land was snapped up quickly.

In England, the market in land is active, and independent of public authorities (perhaps with one or two exceptions: it is sometimes said (e.g. RTPI 1979) that in the inner areas of Liverpool and in some of the older London boroughs the local authority determines price and supply). Local authorities are just one of the actors in land markets, they do not determine prices, the concept of market price is firmly rooted in statutory and case law and in valuation practices, and public authorities are obliged to buy and sell at market prices (an obligation enforced by the District Valuer) with a few exceptions - e.g. within areas designated for New Towns, and the leasing of industrial land in certain circumstances (Local Government Act 1972, S.123). If public authorities have to buy and sell at market prices then the only possible reasons for their supplying industrial land are that something is hindering the private supply or that they want to compete with private suppliers.

That brings us to the political attitudes. In the cases

studied, the first reason had been chosen and the second rejected. It might be expected that such a political choice was right-wing, and it is true that three of the local authorities were Conservative-ruled in the period for which I investigated them (up to April 1980). But one was not (Coventry) and that expressed the same attitude, and even when Labour took over the West Midlands County Council it justified its interventionist West Midlands Enterprise Board with the same argument - filling gaps in the market (in this case, financial markets - see Mawson, 1982).

That same general argument can be applied equally well to the local authorities' provision of factories. There is no general shortage of industrial buildings in the region, but the private market will provide them only on greenfield sites, and in the West Midlands conurbation that can mean a long journey to work. However, because of the history of the area, there is a stock of old vacant factories, some of which can be rehabilitated to provide cheap industrial space but not in such a way as to be financially attractive to private developers. Moreover, the latter are (were?) not interested in providing the smaller units although those were strongly demanded. And what did we find? - that local authorities were supplying small factory units, new or rehabilitated, on difficult to develop sites within the built-up area, with the justification: we are filling gaps in the market. Moreover, the publicity over the lack of small factory units and over the speed with which those provided by public authorities were sold or let alerted private developers in some areas and they discovered that they could supply such units profitably: then the local authorities withdrew, for there was a market gap no more.

The Netherlands

In the Netherlands, the supply of building land for industry (and for all other uses) is dominated by the municipalities: between 1965 and 1978 for example, 70% of all new industrial land was provided by municipalities. It is clear, then, that the local government provision of industrial land cannot be motivated by the desire to fill "market gaps". Rather, it is the case that the necessity in the past for concerted action in order to bring into use low-lying or inundated land has given rise to a tradition, and the necessary legislation, which keeps the supplying of building land largely in local government hands. So the reason why the municipalities provide industrial land is simply: if we don't do it, no one else will, so there will arise a shortage in our area. And while that puts the municipality in a strong monopoly position, it puts them also under a strong moral obligation to ensure that industrial land is always available: in the older conurbations of Amsterdam, Rotterdam and The Hague, that can be a very heavy obligation to fulfil.

The market form is therefore very different than it is in England: within one local government area (the "gemeente") the local government has a near-monopoly in the supply of land. "Market price" has, consequently, a different significance than it has in England, and it plays a much smaller part in the practice of or the legislation about land policy. How, then, are industrial land prices set?

There is a bottom limit, enforced by central government regulation: the supply price must be such as will cover the costs. But how are those costs determined? Municipalities usually supply plots on industrial estates, and it is the revenue from a complete estate which must cover the costs. The latter consist of:

- acquisition costs

- costs of plan preparation, making the ground fit for building on, and putting in services

- interest charges

- costs of extra works (roads, bridges, etc) outside the industrial estate but necessitated by it.

In England and other countries where market prices rule, the price at which land is bought adjusts to the price at which it will be sold ("land prices are price-determined, not price-determining", the residual or surplus land-price theory: see, for example, Needham 1981). It is in that way that acquisition costs are determined. Where acquisition in any one area is in the hands of a monopsonist, that cannot happen. What determines acquisition costs in the Netherlands, then? Current use value (in most cases, agricultural value) is the floor, but most acquisition (both amicable and compulsory) is at the so-called "market value". That is a misleading term, for it means in practice a price which is a multiple of current use value, where the multiple is set by convention and case law. And whereas in England the acquisition price of building land is usually very many times agricultural value (a factor of 40 or higher for housing land in the later 1970s), in the Netherlands acquisition tends to be at three or four times agricultural value. That, and the very high costs of making land fit for building on (often, very expensive drainage is necessary), means that acquisition costs are a small part of total supply costs: the minimum supply price of industrial land is largely determined by "production costs", however odd that might sound to English ears.

Municipalities are not supposed to dispose of industrial land for less than those production costs, and the provinces check that that does not happen. In the smaller "gemeenten" (less than 100,000 inhabitants) every land transaction has to be approved by the province, so minimum disposal prices can be easily enforced. In the larger local authorities, however, that control is very much laxer: it is the annual accounts of the "land department" of the "gemeente" which are checked.

In that way, minimum prices are established: but a maximum price or a way of determining that is not specified. And many authorities "mark up" their minimum prices in order to supplement their income with profit on the land account. When land is being provided for housing, that is frowned upon and regarded as "not cricket", understandable attitudes in view of the monopoly which a local government has in its own area and the desirability of keeping down housing costs. "As regards the making of profits, a municipal real estate department may in my opinion be compared to a department of public utility, such as for instance the municipal water-works, where the primary consideration is to supply a good quality of drinking water at a reasonable price and not to make profits, although some profit at the end of the year would certainly not be unwelcome" (Rotterdam Municipality, 1959). As a result, such profits on land deals which are made by municipalities unable to withstand the temptation are carefully "laundered" and there is no clear picture of the relationship between land disposal prices and the supply costs of that land.

When land is being provided for industry, the situation is rather different, for municipalities find it much less objectionable to make a profit on land supplied to industry than on land supplied to housing. However, no municipality dares to set industrial land prices too high, and it receives "signals" about land prices elsewhere: firms are not interested in locating within the local authority, the local Chamber of Commerce points out the prices that are being asked for elsewhere, the larger local authorities occasionally talk to each other, and so on. Furthermore, it sometimes happens that prices are set by negotiation: the municipality will not go below cost price and has an idea of what the plot might be worth to the firm, and the firm wants the land as cheaply as possible and is prepared to locate in another municipality if land there is cheaper, taking into account differences in location and services.

In these ways, industrial land prices are indeed set in a market, but a market which is far from transparent and in which knowledge was until recently very imperfect. (In September 1982 a survey was published of disposal prices – maximum, minimum and average – on all industrial estates in the Netherlands – V.G.M., 1982). And it is noteworthy that the municipalities are not doing anything to change that: the results of negotiations are kept secret and profits on land deals are "lost" in the accounts or (at the most) a profit or loss on all land transactions is published in the end-of-year accounts. And one of the results is, as one might expect, an apparently meaningless variety of prices for industrial land in one region.

One might think that the market in "second hand" industrial land would impose a discipline on the price of building land for industry. By that I mean the industrial market (land + buildings): such a market undoubtedly exists and in it prices are set. By taking the market price of a (land + building) and subtracting the (written-down) value of the building, the residual value of the land can be deduced. That can be said to be its market value. And one might imagine that it would "discipline" the price at which a municipality supplied industrial land:

- if the supply price was set higher, there would be no demand for the land

- if the supply price was set lower, the municipality would be handing a quick resale-profit on a plate to a developer.

The fact that in practice the supply price of industrial land does not appear to be affected systematically by those considerations can probably be explained by the very small part land plays in an industrialist's total development costs.

That is the system, then, but it has begun to creak badly in the last few years. For even the once prosperous Netherlands are now in the grip of a recession, and municipalities compete seriously against each other to retain existing firms and to attract new ones. The power to set industrial land prices is one of the few obvious weapons in the hands of a municipality and although the small financial significance of land costs to an industrialist (see above) would seem to blunt that weapon, in practice the psychological significance of land prices seems to be high.

A modest land-price battle has broken out among municipalities. Some have even broken the rules and offered industrial land at below-cost prices, only to be rapped firmly on the knuckles by the all-overseeing provinces. Others have frozen the price of the industrial land: Groningen, for example, was raising prices by 1% a month ("to cover interest charges", it said), then it froze prices, then it elevated the holding of prices at that level into one of the aims of its economic policy. Municipalities now preparing new industrial estates have become keenly cost-conscious in order to hold down "production costs" and some try to pass off some of the costs onto other accounts. Municipalities with existing industrial land can do no more than ensure that their supply prices do not exceed historical production costs (but what to do about the steadily mounting interest charges?) and to compare nervously their prices with those of their competitors (for Arnhem 1978). Minimum prices, which means production costs, have become maximum prices.

A similar change has become apparent in the <u>conditions</u> under which Dutch local governments dispose of industrial land: they are no longer able to exploit their monopoly position in order to impose strict conditions. Rather surprisingly, not many municipalities tried to do that even when theirs was a sellers' market. For example, few tried to insist upon leasehold disposal instead of freehold, although the city of Amsterdam has the experience of doing that since 1896. Of course, a combination of leasehold disposal and "covering the costs" for each industrial estate separately can cause financial difficulties: the costs are recouped only very slowly and without the help of (high) profits. Nevertheless, leasehold disposal was never common (only 12% of gemeenten operate a leasehold system) and in the present circumstances municipalities are even less likely to want to insist upon it. Arnhem provides a good example. In 1978 the Council resolved to dispose of industrial land by leasehold only "provided that the interests of the city would not thereby be damaged". In practice almost all firms taking industrial land managed to buy it freehold, presumably by threatening to withdraw otherwise, and in 1981 the policy of leasehold-only was rescinded.

Another of the conditions which some Dutch local governments have tried to impose on the disposal of industrial land is called a "sociaal vestigings-statuut". Firms are allocated land only if they enter into an agreement with the municipality about such matters as the accommodation of foreign workers, the provision of social facilities at work, negotiations with the trade unions, etc. Rotterdam was the

first to apply such conditions (in 1974) and since then a few
other municipalities have followed suit. But many more
deliberately decided not to, for fear of scaring away existing
or new firms. More common is a policy for selective disposal
of industrial land, under which firms must satisfy conditions
of high employment density, a portion of the workplaces going
to women workers, a positive contribution to the economic
structure of the area, low environmental damage. Even in
better times, those conditions had little effect because they
were not applied to firms relocating within the municipality,
and those firms occupied the largest part of the new
industrial land. Nowadays, most local governments prefer to
negotiate "flexibly" with applicants rather than rigidly to
apply the criteria. Beggars can't be choosers.

I say very little about the provision of industrial
buildings by Dutch local governments, partly because it is
largely unconnected with their policy for industrial land and
partly because it is not done very often. Only in the older
larger conurbations of the Randstad where physical conditions
are in some ways similar to those in the West Midlands County
do you find joint industrial land/building measures, and that
for the same reasons as in the West Midlands: in the older
areas of the city, land can be brought into industrial use and
new or rehabilitated factory space provided, but not
profitably by private developers, and it is important that
workplaces be available within the city and not only around
its edges.

Conclusions

My conclusions concern the role of the market in determining
the disposal price of industrial land, both the problems
caused when disposal has to be strictly at market price and
the problems when it does not.

The latter set of problems is illustrated by the Netherlands
where the market form makes it very difficult to establish
market prices for industrial building land. That means that,
when municipalities supply into a seller's market, they can
charge prices above production costs: that they thereby make a
profit I find not at all objectionable, but that there is no
check on the size of the profit and that the book-keeping is
kept secret, I do. But the particular market form, which municipalities can put to their advantage in good times, puts them
in a weak position in bad times. Under the present-day
conditions of a buyer's market, the competition between municipalities and the lack of transparency in the market leads the

municipalities to supply at cost, which gives a purely
fortuitous advantage to those municipalities which were able
to buy and service industrial land at the much lower prices of
several years ago. And in some areas - the city region of The
Hague, for example - production costs have become so high that
disposal costs of new industrial estates on the periphery are
higher than the market price of "second hand" industrial land
in the city. It would make no sense to try to introduce the
concept of free market price into the Dutch practice: much
more practicable would be for the municipalities in one area
to form a price-fixing cartel in order to prevent industrial
land prices from falling too low. It is interesting that this
has already been arranged in the city region of Nijmegen. The
industrial estates in the city itself are filling up and more
industrial land must be provided in the surrounding local
government areas. But production costs there are higher than
those in Nijmegen of a few years ago. So a co-operative
agency has been set up between the municipalities involved in
order to provide that extra land and to avoid a land-price
competition.

In England, it is the obligation to supply strictly at
market price that is, in my opinion, the problem. It is too
rigid and it does not allow local authorities to pursue an
economic or employment policy by offering land at reduced
prices to selected firms. And if a local authority has been
fortunate enough to acquire land at less than its current
market value, then supplying it below market price entails -
it is true - an income foregone, but there is no actual
expenditure. More generally, it has never been part of land
policy in England to supply land below market price, even for
"social uses" such as subsidised housing: even if that land
had been acquired below its (residual) value, it must be
disposed of at full market price with the profit going into
the public purse (once again, the New Towns are an exception
to this statement). The argument is made that selling at
lower prices would allow the buyer to make a profit on resale.
That is a danger, but it could be prevented by including a
restrictive covenant that resale within a given number of
years must be back to or approved by the local authority (the
Dutch call this an "anti-speculation" clause and they apply it
quite widely). This argument cannot, therefore, be the only
reason for the practice. Rather, it seems that the ideology
of the market reigns supreme in English land policy, including
local government policy for industrial land. In my opinion,
that reign is too rigid.

15 Land policy in Sweden: separating ownership from development

SIMON DUNCAN

1 INTRODUCTION: SCOPE AND AIMS

1.1 British political debate and Swedish evidence

An emerging political orthodoxy in Britain, supported by the present Conservative government and fuelled by the "New Right", asserts that state intervention in economic life is unnecessary, unsuccessful and inefficient. Rather, it is claimed, the creation of a supposedly "free" market will result in greater economic efficiency and social welfare. This assertion is taken to be as true for development land provision as much as anything else (see Chapter 3 in this volume, for instance), despite the mass of empirical and theoretical evidence showing that this idealised world is least likely to happen, if it can happen at all, in the distressingly real world of land ownership and development in Britain. Nonetheless, this is the direction in which land policy in Britain is being pushed (see Chapter 6 in this volume).

In this chapter, I will help refute this emergent "free market" orthodoxy. The example of development land supply in Sweden shows how state intervention in the urbanisation process can be administratively, socially and economically efficient. This intervention has not only resulted in a greater degree of social welfare and social justice (something often dismissed as unimportant by New Right theorists). It has also led to greater economic efficiency. In both these ways state intervention has enlarged the scope for future social progress.

The next section (1.2) will briefly sketch how Swedish state intervention in development land supply has these effects. Before this, however, I will anticipate two major conclusions. First of all, note that state land policy in Sweden is more thorough, pervasive and wider-ranging than the relatively weak British system, still largely based on the 1947 planning legislation. Whereas the British system is essentially negative, and even this is being diluted, the Swedish system has a strong prescriptive side with positive powers over land ownership and urban development itself. It is not so much the case that the British experience since 1947 shows state intervention into land supply inevitably fails, as the new orthodoxy likes to claim, rather, the British experience shows that state intervention has never gone far enough. Secondly, the chapter reinforces the conclusion (already adumbrated in Chapter 6) that the logical and empirical deficiencies of the new 'free market orthodoxy' are in fact well appreciated by some of its proponents. Rather this new orthodoxy is used as a smokescreen under which particular economic and social interests can be advanced.

Finally, this chapter is not saying that Sweden shows us the ideal society, even as far as development land supply is concerned. There are of course many deficiencies and problems with the Swedish system and its ideals may also run in advance of its practice. I will refer to some of these problems later. But I do claim that the Swedish system of development land supply is in quite a different class to Britain as far as social welfare and economic efficiency is concerned. It is a qualitative leap, similar to the sea-change between pre- and post-war planning systems in Britain.

1.2   The supply of development land: Sweden and Britain
      compared

In the last section I claimed that Swedish state intervention into the supply of development land had increased social welfare and economic efficiency. This is because speculation in land to be used for building permanent housing or public services is severely constrained, and the appropriation of development gains by landowners and/or builders is severely circumscribed. (There are specific exceptions and qualifications to this general statement - we will come to

309

some of these later). Most development land is acquired by state authorities in publicly owned land banks for release to developers (public and private). Land ownership is separated from land development in the housing/public service sector.

This has three major results. First of all, the costs of purchasing raw land, as a proportion of the production costs for new dwellings, average less than 5% (often as low as 1%). The substantial part of land development gains are, in effect, socialised and/or passed on to housing consumers in the form of cheaper housing, better quality housing, better planned environments, more accessible housing and capital gains to owner-occupiers. Secondly, as a corollary, a major source of unearned income for private landowners and/or builders is substantially reduced. This encourages more properly capitalist behaviour, where financial reward follows the efficient investment of capital in the productive process, rather than rewarding unproductive political influence or speculative skill. Specifically, for builders in Sweden, raw land costs are only a very minor part of total production costs and are in any case usually dealt with by state authorities. Unlike Britain, builders cannot make significant profits via land development gains but must instead invest in increasing productivity, technical and organisational innovation, and product development. In other words they invest in the building process itself and the contrasts between the British and Swedish house building sectors are quite dramatic in this respect. Among other things, the Swedish construction industry is more capable of building large amounts of cheaper housing as well as providing an increasingly important export sector. And finally, for urban planners it is more possible to plan rationally – sufficient land will be available in advance – rather than according to the dictates of the land market.

All this is in stark contrast to Britain. In this country raw land costs as a proportion of new house prices can be anything up to 40% (boom periods in Outer London), development gains are a major source of income to landowners, developers and builders, and the house-building sector remains something of an exception to the normal laws of capitalist economic rationality. The severe constraints on urban planning produced by the land market are well known.

1.3 Outline of the paper

I do not have the space here to follow up all these themes in detail. Rather, the paper will concentrate on a description of Swedish land policy and its results in terms of land prices and availability. I will focus in turn on:

: a brief description of geographical and demographical issues, concluding with a brief sketch of the main elements of the development land supply system in Sweden (Section 2)

: housing land acquisition costs, land costs as a component of building costs and public land bank acquisition costs (Section 3)

: the legislation which enables the Swedish state (largely through local authorities) to pursue an active land policy separating private land ownership and urban development. This section concludes with a brief balance sheet of the successes and failures of Swedish land policy (Section 4)

: the political and social factors which have allowed this situation to emerge (Section 5)

: a brief discussion of how far this experience may be possible in Britain (Section 6).

Further details on the interaction between land supply and the construction industry in Sweden and Britain can be found in Dickens et al (1985), and a description of housing provision as a whole in Sweden is available in Duncan (1978). Ball (1983) provides a good account of the political economy of house-building in Britain including the role played by land.

The next section (Section 2) will briefly establish that land policy in Sweden is not exceptional because Sweden is an exceptional place. Indeed, in many ways Sweden can be seen as an ideal type of capitalist development. It is perhaps more the case that Britain is the deviant society.

2. SWEDEN: EXCEPTIONAL PLACE OR EXCEPTIONAL POLICY?

The relative success of Swedish housing land policy, outlined in Section 1.2, seems exceptional in comparison to Britain and other advanced capitalist countries. It is important to stress at the outset that this success is not the result of geographical or demographic differences which make Sweden an exceptional place. Rather, it is the particular set of policies and their application which are exceptional. As

Section 5 will show, there is a specific social and political history explaining how these policies have come about. Nonetheless, this specificity of Swedish society is itself akin to the normal model of capitalist development (Dickens et al, 1985).

This claim will be supported here in two ways. First of all Sweden is not particularly different, in relevant geographical or demographic respects, to other advanced capitalist countries. Secondly, it is only the supply of development land to be used for housing and public services which behaves exceptionally; other land market sectors - such as those for agricultural land or second homes, behave in less exceptional ways.

Sweden's overall population density is low compared to Britain (20 inhabitants per sq.km as opposed to 326 in England and Wales and 65 in Scotland). It is, however, about the same as the USA (24 per sq.km) and substantially higher than in Canada (0.2 per sq.km). Neither Canada nor the USA are noted for the absence of land speculation, and in both the land component of housing costs is often rather high. This is partly because the "wide open spaces" of the prairies or tundra have little direct relevance for land supply in metropolitan regions. The same goes for Sweden. It is not the case that most Swedes live in isolated huts in the woods. Sweden is, of course, a modern capitalist country - in most respects more modern and capitalist than Britain.

Nearly 85% of the population is classified as "urban" and over 35% live in the three large city-regions of Stockholm, Gothenburg and Malmö. All three cities are located in important agricultural areas, indeed the area around Malmö is one of the most productive arable plains in Europe. Vast areas of northern Sweden, in contrast, are effectively inaccessible. At the urban scale, population densities and land conversion pressures are similar to those in other large and medium sized city regions elsewhere in Europe and North America. As we shall see, it is the social and political accessibility of land, rather than some "natural" determinant, which is crucial.

As far as underlying demographic demand is concerned, household numbers, building standards and space standards have risen considerably since 1945 and continue to do so, even if total population levels have only increased slowly. Within Sweden, however, there was a significant redistribution of population in the 1950s and 1960s from dispersed industrial villages and small towns to larger cities, especially to the three metropolitan regions. Together with household formation and house size trends, this led to massive land conversion pressures around the larger cities. This pressure is exacerbated by high disposable household incomes (about 40% higher than the British average) with relatively high economic growth rates until the 1970s. Only about 4% of the 'economically active' population is currently unemployed, although another 3-5% are absorbed into various state supported employment schemes etc. Relative economic stability and household prosperity - in contrast to the much more sickly position in Britain - also help maintain land conversion pressures.

Partly because of higher real incomes - and also because of lower relative costs for permanent housing - many Swedish families (over 20%) do in fact own houses in the woods besides their permanent urban dwellings, although these too are concentrated in the more accessible scenic areas and sometimes appear like summer cottage conurbations. Land for recreation house development is not subject to the policy measures available for permanent housing development. Tellingly, as we shall see below, land prices for recreation house development have increased substantially - and plot size has decreased - at the same time as land prices for permanent housing has fallen in real terms. Indeed, by 1979 rural land for recreation houses cost more than suburban land for permanent family houses - an interesting reversal of normal land value gradients. Again, it is not so much overall "natural" demographic factors that directly create the demand and supply of development land. It is more a question of the way in which these factors are given effective meaning through the development of specific social and political institutions which control how land is owned and developed.

It is important in this context to note that land in Sweden is overwhelmingly in private ownership. Only around 10% of agricultural land, 20% of forestry land, and 20% of industrial/commercial land (by taxation value) is owned by state institutions (counting the national church and the crown as well as central, regional and local authorities). Even including the semi-autonomous public housing companies, only a quarter of permanent dwellings (and hardly any recreation dwellings) are owned by state authorities.

The state dominates land ownership in one category only: development land banks. Over 80% of new housing is built on land released from local authority (commune) land banks. This land has usually been acquired at stable or declining real costs under legislative and financial conditions which favour

313

local authorities rather than private landowners. Local authorities usually dominate local development land markets. On development most of this land is sold to the developer (including public developers) or the owner-occupier. (About 20% is disposed of leasehold, with 10 year revision). But it remains difficult for builders to appropriate housing development gains at this stage, for around 90% of new housing is subject to price regulation - and other development controls - by state authorities. final regulated prices - as specified in local authority/developer contracts - should reflect actual production costs including the actual acquisition costs of development land. Development approval and the allocation of State Housing Loans to the developer depends on these conditions being met. The normal land conversion chain in Sweden is that of private ownership - local authority land bank - housing developer - consumer, and each of the links in this chain come under some degree of state regulation. State management of the land conversion process has not been achieved by <u>replacing</u> private ownership, but by <u>separating</u> private ownership from urban development.

3. HOUSING LAND AND LOCAL AUTHORITY LAND BANKS: PRICES AND RELATIVE COSTS

3.1 <u>Data problems and perceptions of land costs</u>

Published statistics giving a comprehensive picture of development land over a long period are not available. I have had to use a number of sources which, because they have been collected in different ways for different purposes, are not usually directly comparable. However, I think a reasonable picture of trends and significance can be established. Major statistical sources were the Housing and Construction Series (SM Bo) and the Housing and Construction Statistical Yearbook (BBA), both published by the Central Statistical Bureau. These abbreviations will be used henceforth.

Why this statistical gap in the otherwise exemplary Swedish information system? The answer can give us some clues about development land in Swedish society. For raw land costs are an insignificant part of housing construction costs (as this section shows). The relative lack of statiscal concern probably reflects this insiginificance. In talking about <u>raw</u> land costs to practitioners in Sweden, I usually received a somewhat nonplussed response - why all the interest in something rather insignificant and passive in effect? What was much more meaningful for them was the costs of land development and site development. That is the costs prior to construction of land clearance, preparation, planning, roads, services provision etc (land development) and the costs subsequent to construction of providing communal play areas, car parks, green spaces, etc. It is significant for the argument that land and site development are in fact productive processes, requiring real inputs of labour and capital equipment. In the Swedish context this amounts to much more than the mere transfer of ownership leaving the land involved completely unimproved. It is not so surprising then, that there are good data series on land development costs and site development costs in contrast to the relative paucity of information on raw land costs.

3.2 Housing land acquisition costs

This section will describe price movements and levels for land used in new housing development. This represents the penultimate stage in the land conversion chain (landowner - public land bank - developer - consumer), the price paid by developers for raw land as one element in total dwelling production costs. (In reality this price is sometimes transformed into leasehold payments).

It is perhaps most instructive to begin by comparing unit land prices for plots sold for permanent housing and recreation housing. For the former, the state normally intervenes in the land conversion process as described in Section 1.2. For recreation housing, development land is sold under much freer market conditions. Table 1 presents this information.

As usual, several qualifications must be made. I could not find data for before 1976. Even then, the data does not include all housing land sold in those years as homes without plots (presumably terraced housing etc) are excluded. Furthermore, the identification of permanent houses/state intervention, recreation houses/no intervention does not always hold true. Although very few recreation houses are built within the state land system about 15% of "small houses" (i.e. single family detached, terraced etc) are built outside this sytem.

Nonetheless, even with these qualifications the contrasts between the "state" and "non-state" sectors is remarkable (and the data deficiencies will, if anything, act to underestimate such differences). For small house plots, unit land prices decreased by 5% over the period, while for recreation house plots unit land prices increased by a massive 52% (using

315

Table 1

Plot prices by housing sector, 1976-1979

	Average price paid by 1979 (7) (Krm^2)	1979 price as percentage 1976 price (1976 values) (%)	Average annual percentage price change (1976 values) (%)
Multi-dwelling housing (i.e. flats maisonettes)	59.5	106	+ 2.1
Small houses with plot(2) (i.e. det-ached/terrace)	34.5	95	- 1.3
Recreation houses with plot(2)	40.2	152	+ 17.3

(1) 11 Swedish kroner (kr) = approx £1 (1983)
(2) i.e. houses without plots, presumably terraced housing,
     were excluded.

Source: Calculated   from BBA, 1981.

recreation houses cost more than suburban plots for small
houses. As we might expect, unit land prices for multi-
dwelling housing plots were still most expensive in 1979.
Much of this land is in central cities, often redevelopment
land and sometimes including commercial uses (ground floor
shops etc). Nonetheless, constant price increases were
relatively stable in this sector also, at 6% over the period.

Note that 1976 to 1979 was a period of relatively stable
demand for house plots, as recorded by the total annual number
of sales. (There was some decrease in 1976-1977). I have
data for 1980 but excluded this from the calculation due to a
slump in plot purchase that year (decreases of 40% for small
house plots, 60% for multi-dwelling and 70% for recreation).
Indeed, in 1980 recreation house plot prices declined to 117%
of the 1976 price (constant prices) again below the 1980 small

house plot price. Nonetheless, the latter prices remained
stable at 96% of 1976 prices, despite a fall in demand.
Multi-dwelling plot prices rose massively in 1980, due to the
inclusion of a number of very expensive Stockholm purchases in
an abnormally low level of total purchases for that year.

Table 1 indicates the gross differences between housing land
sectors where the state actively intervenes (permanent
housing) and where it does not (recreation housing). In the
"state sector" land prices are relatively stable in real
terms, even decreasing. In the non-state sector prices show
the more familiar British boom and slump pattern, with all
this implies in terms of market instability and economic
inefficiency (see Ball, 1984).

Information for a 3 or 4 year period cannot tell us very
much about long term trends. Unfortunately, I can find a long
data series for small house plot prices only. However, this
is useful as "small houses with plots" come nearest to the
British definition of "private sector housing plots" (in
Sweden 85% of small houses are built for owner-occupation, and
90% are built by private developers or individuals. Multi-
dwelling buildings are rented and are now mostly built by
public housing companies and cooperatives). Table 2 presents
this information.

Table 2

Small house plot prices, 1957-1980

	% 1957 prices at end of period (kr m^2, constant 1949 values)	% annual change (kr m^2, constant 1949 values
1957-65	109	1.3
1965-70	113	0.6
1970-73	107	-1.6
1973-76	128	6.7
1976-80	123	-1.3
	Average 1957-80	0.9

Sources: Calculated from Svensson 1978 (up to 1976), BBA
1981.

There are many possible factors influencing these land price movements. Two features however, suggest the importance of control over development gains. One is the relative stability of real land price movements compared to the usual notorious boom and slump patterns. (In Britain private sector plot prices increased by 82% in constant prices between 1969 and 1979, with extremes of a 105% increase in 1973 and a 139% decrease in 1975; the average annual percentage change over these ten years (plus or minus) was a staggering 53%). The other feature in the Swedish data is the small real price increase over the period (23%, or 0.9% pa) in a period of mostly expanding demand. (Land purchases for small house building was increasing until 1973, with slumps in 1974/75 and 1980). Indeed, in the 1965-73 period, when small house construction was increasing dramatically, real price increases were stable or declining. These price changes do not seem to reflect substitution between housing sectors; land purchase for multi-dwelling housing was also at a high and expanding level up to 1973, but has declined significantly since then. Compare the total increase during 1970-80 of 9% in Sweden compared to 82% in Britain during 1969-79 (both in constant prices).

Some incidental figures are available for other housing sectors in Sweden. A government inquiry into housing construction cost increases in the late 1970s (SOU 1982:34) provides figures for plot price increases for multi-dwelling houses and "group built" small houses (the latter term signifies the bulk owner-occupation sector where houses are not built individually). Controlling for plot size increase over the same period (unlike Britain, this increased significantly especially for public and coop rented housing) reduces these increases to about 20% during 1974-78 (constant prices). The overall conclusions of the inquiry, incidentally, were that the increase in housing construction costs were mainly due to increasing dwelling quality and size, building standards and norms, and the loss of economies of scale after the "million programme" of house construction ended in 1973. Raw land costs were of little relevance. The same conclusions were reached by an inquiry into housing construction cost increases in the cooperative sector (BPA/RK 1978). Normal raw land costs for housing construction by RK (Riksbyggen - a housing cooperative largely owned by the building unions and now the developer for about 5% of total annual dwelling completions) were estimated at the very low level of 2.50kr m^2 in 1965 rising to 6.50kr m^2 in 1978. In constant 1965 prices this represents an increase of less than 6% over the 13 years.

My overall conclusion of the efficiency of state intervention in controlling land prices (as well as removing land market instability) is supported by information on land sold to developers from local authority land banks as opposed to that sold direct by private landowners. Table 3 summarises this information for 1977 and 1978, the only years for which I could find published data.

Table 3

Sales from local authority land banks compared to sales by private developers, 1977-1971(1)

	Small house plots		Recreation house plots		Multi-dwelling housing plots	
	1977	1978	1977	1978	1977	1978
1. Average plot price of land sold by local authorities (kr m^2)	20.9	26.8	12.3	18.3	29.8	31.6
2. Commune sale price as % average plot price for land sold by private persons and trusts	76.6%	80.2%	61.2%	77.5%	21.7%	12.2%
3. Commune sale price as % average plot price for land sold by limited companies	52.3%	31.2%	33.8%	37.8%	8.6%	10.1%

(1) The table refers to greenfield land sold for house building, and to "normal cases of normal sales". That is redevelopment land, non-normal sales (e.g. by expro-priation) or non-normal cases (e.g. sold by relatives) are excluded.

Source: Calculated from SMBo 1979.

Again, relative price differences between the three seller categories will reflect many factors including plot location, land quality, sub-market variation etc. For instance, the huge differential between prices for multi-dwelling plots probably reflects the split between private developers/ rentiers in the small specialised luxury markets (e.g. in prime inner-city locations with some commercial development) and the bulk low and middle income rented housing built for public and cooperative deelopers. However, one of the aims of state intervention in Sweden is to obtain cheaper housing land and, by preventing appropriation of development gains by landowners or builders, to pass this on to housing consumers. This seems to have happened, at least over these two years. In this way the Table supports the conclusions taken from Table 1, that land prices within the state system behave differently from those outside it. Note in particular the contrast in land sold for small house building, where commune sale prices were 20-25% cheaper than land sold by private persons or trusts, and as much as 50-60% cheaper than land sold by companies.

Important legislative changes increasing state control over the housing land market and the capacity to appropriate development gains through land ownership were introduced (1) in the late 1940s/early 1950s (planning monopoly, increased local authority expropriation powers, state housing loans which involve price controls over new housing including land costs), (2) the late 1960s (tougher taxation and expropriation measures, encouragement of local authority land banks and public leasehold) and (3) 1974 (the "land condition" where the 90% of new dwellings which use State Housing Loans should be built on land released from local authority land banks). I will discuss these measures in more detail in Section 4. Before this, however, it is important to establish how important land costs are as a component of total housing construction costs.

3.3 Land costs as a component of housing construction costs

The last section was concerned with the landowner-developer part of the land conversion chain. In this section, which estimates land costs as a component of total dwelling construction costs, we move on to the last stage in the land conversion chain, the developer-consumer link.

Note that in Sweden over 90% of new housing since the war has been built under conditions of price regulation by state authorities. This is one part of the State Housing Loan intervention apparatus. The agreed construction cost includes the building cost itself – and thus the building company's profits – as well as most capital costs, development costs, land preparation costs and raw land costs. In other words builder's and developer's profits and/or capital accumulation (in the case of "non-profit" public and cooperative developers) are already accounted for in the final agreed construction cost. This cost is then passed on to the consumer in the form of rents or a purchase price. Housing in Sweden is sold more like a normal commodity in that it is not usually possible for builders or developers to appropriate development gains on sale to the consumer. In other words the familiar British model of "speculative building" is largely restricted to less than 10% of new house production, chiefly luxury owner-occupied housing. In estimating land costs as a component of total dwelling cost, therefore, I am also estimating final land costs to the consumer. (The speculative 10% of the new housing is excluded).

A sophisticated housing production and building cost series runs from 1965 to date, measuring these costs by several unit indices as well as in total for both multi-dwelling housing and 'group-built' small houses (SM Bo). Estimates of the land cost component of total dwelling production cost can therefore be calculated by relating the plot prices, discussed in the previous section, to this series. Table 4 presents the results of this calculation.

Table 4

Plot costs as a percentage of total house production costs, approximate figure

	Small houses	(% kr m^2) Multi-dwelling housing
1965	1.1%	
1970	1.0%	
1973	1.3%	
1976	1.4%	2.1%
1977	1.3%	2.1%
1978	1.3%	2.3%
1979	1.2%	1.7%
1980	1.1%	4.0%

Source: Calculated from SM Bo 1982, BBA 1981, Svensson 1979.

These figures are remarkable in comparison to the British situation where land component costs are much higher and are also subject to violent swings. For private housing in England and Wales, for instance, plot prices as a percentage of selling prices ranged between 15% and 27% over the 1970s. (Compare to the small house sector in Table 4, that is predominantly private, single family dwellings). Judging from the small amount of data available, a similar story is true for British public sector housing (compare to the multi-dwelling sector in Table 4).

We must again make a statistical caveat. Both British and Swedish figures are approximate in measuring raw land component costs. For instance, plots must presumably incorporate some initial planning work etc. The Swedish figures are calculated from two overlapping, but different, data sets (small houses with plots and group built small houses – although this will, if anything, overestimate the land component). The British and Swedish figures are not directly comparable even in statistical terms. (The former is calculated from costs per dwelling, the latter in cost per m^2 dwelling, although re-calculating the Swedish figures on dwelling terms – when possible – gives very similar results to Table 4). Nonetheless, the gross differences between the two countries are quite clear. The British figures suggest an unstable market where landowners can appropriate development gain – and ask for more as builders' profits go up. The Swedish figures suggest a stable market where land is an insignificant element in the costs of housing production. Land ownership is separated from development.

Some actual examples support these statistical estimates. Riksbyggen (RK) the union-owned housing cooperative building mostly multi-dwelling housing, calculates its raw land costs as amounting to less than 1% of total production costs during the whole period 1965-1978 both in unit area and dwelling terms (BPA/RK 1982). For one particular RK development I studied in 1982, land acquisition cost – including some initial site planning and preparation – were below 4%.

This example brings us to the issue of regional differences. In Britain these are very great in land market boom periods, and still significant, if smaller, in slumps. In the 1973 boom average plot prices in Greater London amounted to 43.3% of average selling prices, compared to 9.8% in Wales. This again reflects the landowner's ability to appropriate development gain in proportion to builders' speculative profits. Clearly, such potentially massive regional variations in the ability of landowners to extract development gains – up to 30% of total

house prices - cannot exist in Sweden. Important regional
differentials in housing land prices do exist, however, <u>at the</u>
<u>Swedish scale</u>. Thus by the late 1970s in Stockholms County
(approximately Greater Stockholm) plot prices for small houses
averaged around 3.5% of total production costs. This compares
to a national average of under 1.5% or figures of less than 1%
for parts of norther Sweden. See Table 5 for these regional
variations.

Such differences are insignificant in British terms.
However, these figures do show that a limited possibility does
exist for landowners to achieve some sort of development gain,
at least in the metropolitan areas and especially Greater
Stockholm. (Although some of the regional differences shown
in Table 5 will result from inherent land quality differences.
Thus much land taken for urban development in South Sweden is
Grade I agricultural land, while much in North Sweden is
forestry land).

Table 5

Regional variations in plot prices as a proportion of small
house production costs, 1980

County groups	Plot price (kr m^2)	Plot price as a proportion of production costs (1) (% kr m^2)
Stockholms County*	136.5	3.5%
Eastern Central Sweden	34.1	1.0%
Smaland and the Islands	28.3	0.9%
South Sweden*	58.2	1.7%
West Sweden*	36.7	1.0%
North Central Sweden	23.1	0.7%
Middle Norrland	24.4	0.7%
Upper Norrland	24.4	0.7%
Sweden	39.3	1.1%

*   Contains major metropolitan region
(1) The regional units used in the two sources do not always
     exactly correspond.

Sources: Calculated from SM Bo 1982, BBA 1981.

Brodin et al (1979) describe how this may occur. Much of the land used for Stockholm's expansion in the 1950s and 1960s had been acquired by the city council in the 1920s and 1930s, and this was bought at low prices from the then depressed agricultural sector. By the time this land was developed, raw land costs could be described as costing almost nothing in current terms. However, by the 1970s this supply of land had largely been used up. An alternative source was a peri-urban ring of recreation house land, often in pleasant wooded or lake/sea-side environments and very attractive to development for higher income groups. Because this land was already "built up" by holiday cottages (and a few permanent houses) this land was classified as "redevelopment land" and so different, more generous terms for previous property owners operated. However, in effect the land was more like greenfield land, most of the country cottages were surrounded by large plots of vacant land, enough for up to 10 or even 20 permanent houses. Given also the swing from predominantly public sector house building in the post war period up to 1973, to predominantly private sector development since then, the conditions existed for making considerable development gain.

This counter-example is very much the exception that proves the rule - especially when compared to the way in which the bulk of Stockholm's post-war development took place. And even by 1980 raw land costs in Greater Stockholm were only 3.5% of total costs. Only in exceptional circumstances can they reach 10%. As I claimed in the introduction, this is indicative of the great qualitative differences between the British and Swedish land conversion systems.

Finally, what of the costs of changing land from its "raw" state to built-up land. These are the costs of employing capital and labour to make real physical changes and are much more meaningful in the Swedish context. Land preparation costs (surveying, site planning, clearance, demolition and evacuation costs if necessary, ground preparation, water, sewage, streets etc) have averaged 23% of total dwelling production costs since 1973, showing a slightly declining share over this period (SMBo 1982). Site development costs (play areas, planted areas, grassed areas, pathways, parking) have increased since the mid 1960s, largely due to increased quality and quantity. The provision of several well equipped play areas in each housing development is now standard, for instance. These costs are now fairly stable at around 7-8% of total production costs (BPA/RK 1978; SOU 1982:34).

The contrast between the attention given to raw land costs

in Britain, and to land and site preparation costs in Sweden underlines the contrasts in social efficiency promoted by the two land conversion systems. In Sweden it is more possible to make productive changes in housing land, to use it better for the benefit of the eventual consumers. Similarly, average plot sizes and dwelling sizes have increased significantly in Sweden since the mid 1960s.

Note that if development gains are passed on to the consumer (in cheaper or better housing services), the degree of social-isation of these costs is partly determined by housing tenure. In the 1945-1973 period, 60-70% of new housing built each year was consumed in "non-profit" public rented and cooperative tenures. Development gains were socialised among tenants. Some of this "development windfall" could be spent on other consumer goods — ironically enough, owership of holiday cottages is higher among tenants than among owner-occupiers in Sweden.

After 1975, however, more than 60% of annual completions have been for owner-occupation. Development gains will be privatised for owner-occupiers, and realised in trading up, higher rates of consumption (more space etc), or capital gains. Nonetheless, although this distributional change in consumption has important social consequences, it remains that landowners and builders are kept away from development gain. "Privatisation" since 1973 has meant privatising consumption, not production. There has not been a return to large scale speculative housing which was last seen in Sweden – and seen to fail – in the 1930s. It was a series of war-time inquiries on the social and economic mal-effects of speculative building, as a means of mass housing provision, that ushered in the post-war state regulated system (see Dickens et al 1985).

3.4 Local authority land bank acquisition costs

So far we have been dealing with the end stages of the landowner-local authority land bank-developer-consumer conver-sion chain. On the prima facie evidence of Sections 3.2 and 3.3 we can conclude that local authorities are not paying substantial development gains to landowners in activating the first link in the chain. However, there is some evidence to back this up directly, evidence which is also useful in showing how this works and how it may fail.

Swedish local authorities have a statutory duty to build up land banks sufficient for between 7 and 10 years estimated

development - backed up by favourable loan facilities from
central government. (In practice however, around 20% of land
released from public land banks has been in local authority
ownership for less than 7 years). Since 1974, all housing
development receiving State Housing Loans - about 90% of
annual completions - has to be built on land released from
commune land banks. However, because of various exceptions
and transitional arrangements in practice only about 80% of
dwellings are built on such land. Even before this "land
condition" was imposed in 1974, local authority development
land banking was the norm. Some local authorities -
especially the large urban councils with a "municipal
socialist" bent - had been building up land banks since the
1920s or before, and most large communes were involved by the
1950s. From 1965-1969 as much as 63% of new housing was built
on land from public land banks, rising to 71% in 1970-1974
(SOU 1972:42).

Local authority land banking is supposed to control
development gains in two major ways:

(i)   Speculation will be circumscribed and communes will be
able to purchase land nearer use value than possible
development value. The local authority is the dominant
development land owner and the dominant buyer. Nor is there
any direct user who must have a particular piece of land as
soon as possible for a given purpose, for public ownership is
justified by the duty of building up land banks for future
urban development in general. If the landowner wants to sell
there are few apart from the local authority who want to buy,
if the local authority wants to buy it has a range of options.
This opportunity for local authorities to dictate terms is
enhanced by their possession of a realistic expropriation
threat which will place the landowner in a worse position. In
the last resort this threat can be activated to enforce
supply.

(ii) When development does take place, land prices will be 7-
10 years out of date. The taxpayer will have subsidised the
housing consumer in providing the capital and management costs
to achieve this. But at least this is more socially just than
the British system of indirectly subsidising landowners and
builders from taxation, through housing consumption subsidies.
The Swedish system is also more economically efficient in
providing cheaper unit housing costs and encouraging productivity gains in construction (see Section 3.5).

Although land banking by local authorities is ensured by
statute, the relative level and success of the operation will

be crucially affected by the degree and nature of their activity. In fact large variations exist between communes of different political and structural characteristics, with extremes between the larger urban authorities controlled by the left and small peri-urban authorities dominated by the Conservative Party.

No published national data on commune land banking seem to exist. Instead I will use Svensson's (1976) field study of the Gothenburg region from 1960-1974. This study is particularly useful in showing how development gains are controlled through public land banking, as well as illustrating commune variations.

Svensson found that the real prices of commune land bank purchases fell in 25 of the 44 pre-1974 communes studied over the period. Even in those 19 communes showing increases, these were usually only small. This was a region containing Sweden's second largest city as well as several free-standing industrial towns, and the area experienced considerable urban growth, redevelopment and suburban expansion throughout the period.

The two major factors affecting purchase prices, according to Svensson, were (i) the time period between purchase date and planned construction date and (ii) the degree of certainty of the use planned for the purchased land. More traditional land price factors, such as distance from urban centres, high levels of demand, and existing high use values were still important. It is significant for my argument, however, that the two most statistically important factors refer to commune land purchasing activity. The importance of policy, rather than given characteristics, is underlined. I will briefly summarise some of Svensson's individual commune studies to illustrate this further (see also Figure 1).

1. Gothenburg Over half a million population by 1974, and considerable growth between 1960 and 1973. The GA sector identified in Figure 1 was an area of suburban expansion, and by 1960 most commune owned land was used up. Local politicians formed a front company so as to keep this fact hidden and bought land in a neighbouring commune at rock bottom prices (1kr m^2). These purchases then formed the basis for future low prices, for they gave a precedent for compensation prices if the commune were to use expropriation and broke up the landowners' monopoly position. This appears like a combination of traditional "speculation" (but here for the public gain) with state control.

Figure 1: Housing Land Prices in the Gothenburg Region, 1960 - 1974

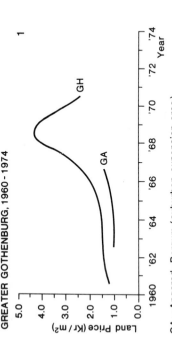

GREATER GOTHENBURG, 1960 - 1974

GA – Angered - Bergum (suburban expansion area)
GH – Hisingen (central industrial area)

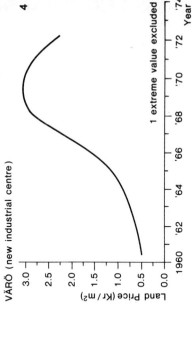

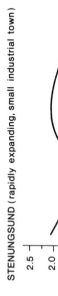

STENUNGSUND (rapidly expanding, small industrial town)

N.B. 2 year running average

Taken from Svensson (1976)

The GM area, in contrast, is a centrally located industrial area still containing some high grade agricultural land. Existing use values and competition from industry increased land prices - housing land prices could not be insulated from the wider land market and here real prices rose by 4.5% per annum.

2. Uddevalla   A free-standing industrial and holiday town, population 30,000 (40,000 in summer). Commune owned land was used up by the late 1950s, and subsequent expansion was blocked when a dominant local landowner refused to sell at a "reasonable price". The commune expropriated the holding with compensation below this level. The precedent now established, as well as the commune's increased land supply, set future prices at the very low level of 0.5kr m^2. This was the lowest price recorded by Svensson and approximated a 35% real decrease over 10 years.

3. Stenungsund   A small commune originally based on agriculture and tourism, but experiencing rapid industrial and population development during the study period (from 5 to 15 thousand). At first no commune land whatsoever was available to accommodate this expansion, and local landowners stuck out for high prices. The commune expropriated and gained a price of 2kr m^2. This also set a precedent for future prices as well as freeing the commune from immediate supply constraints. Real land prices fell by 94% over the study period and by 1975 the commune had amassed a 20-25 year land bank.

4. Vårö Like 3, a small commune experiencing rapid indus-trialisation over the study period, although population expansion was not so marked due to commuting. Unlike 3, however, commune land purchases showed a 250% real increase in prices over the period (19.2% per annum). This was because the commune did not pursue an active land policy or establish land market dominance. In particular (i) expropriation was not used, (ii) the commune did not amass a land bank, but merely bought for current needs and hence stoked up land prices, (iii) the commune failed to establish a team of land market specialists. This is, of course, similar to most British local authorities. Existing agricultural use values were also higher than in 3.

These individual commune histories illustrate very well the potential efficiency of local authority land banking in Sweden (see also Figure 2). Real prices collapsed when communes acted decisively to control landowners' development gains, and large land banks could be established, even in a period of substantial urban growth. Significantly, very large real

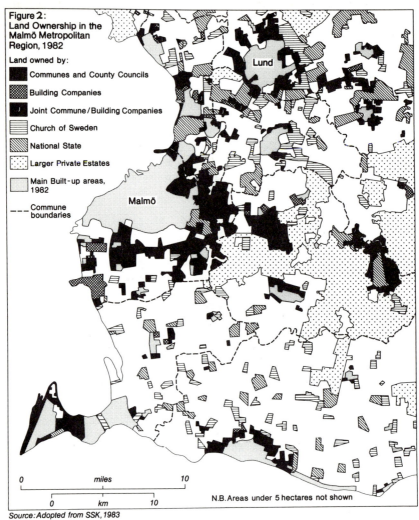

Figure 2:
Land Ownership in the
Malmö Metropolitan
Region, 1982

Land owned by:

Communes and County Councils

Building Companies

Joint Commune / Building Companies

Church of Sweden

National State

Larger Private Estates

Main Built-up areas,
1982

- - - Commune
       boundaries

Lund

Malmö

0   miles   10

0   km   10

N.B. Areas under 5 hectares not shown

Source: Adopted from SSK, 1983

330

price increases were recorded in a commune where demand
increased less, but where the commune was passive towards
landowners and in effect stoked up land prices through its
actions. Variations in political will, as well as the
availability of policy instruments, were crucial. Note also,
however, that these conclusions refer only to greenfield land
and that public land banking was less successful in areas of
multiple development uses. I shall return to these issues
later.

3.5   Land ownership and efficiency in construction

One important effect of the Swedish land conversion system is
to stimulate productive gains in the house building sector.
This is one important strand of the argument for the economic
efficiency of state control over development land supply and
development gains.

Certainly house building in Sweden stands in some contrast
to British experience. In Sweden the unit area building costs
(i.e. excluding land development costs etc) for small houses
stood at 98% of 1965 levels by 1980 (constant prices). Multi-
dwelling building costs had only reached 116%. These figures
include increases since the mid 1970s largely due to improving
dwelling quality and size as well as lower economies of scale
(SOU 1982:34). If these product changes are excluded,
building costs for small and multi-dwelling construction would
today stand at about 80% or 90% of 1965 prices, respectively,
in constant terms. This achievement reflects considerable
productive gains in construction and building material
production due to industrialisation (on site as well as off
site), capitalisation, technical innovation and organisation
efficiency. As one illustration, labour productivity (volume
of building per hour worked) increased by almost 250% between
1950 and 1980, much higher than British levels. Indeed,
percentage productivity increases in house building in Sweden
have often been higher than in manufacturing as a whole over
the post-war period.

There are a number of reasons for this productive gain in
Sweden - the integration of industrial capital (including
construction) with finance capital facilitating high rates of
capital investment, the strongly organised and high waged
labour force, the tripartite compromise of
state/labour/capital for social and economic management,
direct state intervention in the construction process itself,
the use of sub-contracting for division of labour purposes
rather than financial speculation. I have no space to pursue

these themes here (but see Dickens et al 1985, chapter 3).
However, one other important contributory factor is the
severely circumscribed ability of builders to realise profits
through development gains. Rather profits are taken directly
in production, and builders therefore take the path of
restructuring the building process itself, improving the
productivity of labour and/or establishing product and process
innovations. In Britain, a substantial proportion of
builder's profits from building can often be realised through
the agency of land banking and release. Speculative skill in
both land banking and sale timing is therefore paramount;
there is less incentive to increase productivity in the
building process itself.

Such technical innovation as occurs in British building is
often more attuned to development trading than production.
The recent expansion in using pre-fabricated timber frame
houses (used in Sweden over a long period) has as much to do
with increasing the builder's ability to sell quickly when the
market is right as with increasing building productivity
itself. Productivity may even decline when stocks of timber
frames are left half-erected on building sites waiting for the
right moment. There is already an important export pene-
tration of Swedish produced building material and components
into the British market. Significantly exports of complete
houses into Britain are becoming more common as well. Perhaps
British house building will eventually go the way of British
motorcycles.

3.6 Conclusions

In Section 3 I have presented evidence on housing land
acquisition costs, land costs as a component of house
production costs, local authority land bank costs, and
suggested some links between these and house building itself.
Some of this evidence is indirect. Moreover, much of this
evidence is indicative only - it does not directly show land
policy in operation - although Svensson's commune studies are
a useful exception here. Finally, there are many other
factors beside policy which influence development land prices.
However, the evidence does show that housing land prices in
Sweden are relatively low and stable, even when other land
market sectors (e.g. recreation housing) show steep increases.
Raw land costs are an insignificant component of total
dwelling production costs and active state intervention does
make a difference to these costs. The separation of ownership
from development can have important economic benefits in the
construction industry. As Svensson himself concludes in a
later - somewhat pessimistic - article:

"it is not hopeless to attempt to
influence the land market, in free enterprise economies, through state intervention", (Svensson, 1979).

I will now go on to describe in more detail how this state
intervention is achieved.

4. STATE CONTROL OVER DEVELOPMENT GAIN - THE LEGISLATION

4.1 Sources

This section uses government reports (BOS 1969, 1980) and
inquiries (SOU 1966:23/24, 1972:40, 1980:49) as well as
published accounts (Durin-Drabkin 1977; Svensson 1976, 1979).
Individual references will not be made in the text.

4.2 Pre-war policy: weak legislation but a more favourable balance of social interests

Pre-war policy was essentially as in Britain. Local
authorities entered the land market as just another purchaser,
without the benefit of planning powers. Although they
possessed weak rights of compulsory purchase these were
confined to very specific circumstances.

Although the legislative situation was similar to the
British case, the balance of political and social strengths
was not. I will describe this difference in Section 5. One
result in the pre-war period was that the larger and richer
urban authorities were both more able and more willing to
build up development land banks. Local authority income taxes
also gave local authorities a more buoyant income than in
Britain. Stockholm is a major example where left and centre
city governments bought land far in excess of current needs as
prices fell in the 1930s. Subsequently, this land was used
for major suburban expansion during the 1950s and 1960s, which
could proceed comparatively unconstrained by land costs or
acquisition problems. The international fame of suburban
planning in Sweden during this period (e.g. Vällingby near
Stockholm, see Popenoe 1977) owes much to this planning
freedom.

This underlines the importance of seeing public land policy
as a long term policy, with substantial benefits accruing over
a period of decades. I will comment later (Section 5) on the
political and social conditions necessary to achieve this.

4.3 Post war reforms – stronger control over development, but indirect control over land supply

As in Britain, the Swedish government went through a period of reform and welfare state building during and immediately after the war. Planning and housing provision were also important parts of this reform movement (see Dickens et al 1985. While showing strong parallels with British planning legislation, the Swedish reforms were more extensive in scope and less favourable to property interests. Crucially, they allowed a measure of control over land prices.

4.3.1 State planning monopoly The 1947 Building and Planning Act gave communes planning monopoly with negative control over land use changes and responsibility for drawing up town plans. Unlike Britain, only property owners directly affected by plans can make legal objections, and they only have three weeks to do so.

4.3.2 Expropriation In 1949 commune expropriation rights were extended to cover land necessary for ongoing building plans. Although rarely used (it was both time and cost consuming) this did provide a threat and dampened development induced price rises – as Svensson's study shows (Section 3.4).

4.3.3 Taxation Capital gains and wealth taxes were introduced, and these extended to land sales and holdings. No CGT was payable on land sales over 10 years in one ownership. Nor did these taxes provide any active way of intervention in the land market.

4.3.4 State Housing Loans This was perhaps the crucial innovation as far as development control was concerned, and provides the major contrast with British legislation. Under the 1947 Housing Provision Act communes were given statutory responsibility for planning and organising all housing development (public and private). The chief policy instrument giving this practical meaning was the State Housing Loan (SHL) system first introduced in 1942. Unlike simple planning powers, this allows direct regulation of the development and construction procedures themselves.

SHLs provide 10-30% of developers' total costs (the more "social" the tenure, the higher the proportion). These loans allow developers to avoid the uncertainties and instability of the private capital market (although this is also subject to a degree of state regulation in financing house building). They have usually been provided at below market rates and in effect act as a subsidy for construction interests. Over 90% of all housing built since 1945 has been financed in this way.

334

This subsidy is not open ended. Conditions for loan provision, established in developer/commune contracts, include approval of development timing, quality, location and costs, including land costs. Loans are allocated through the chain of Parliament - Central Ministry - County Board - Communes, and this allows operation of a five year rolling construction plan. The SHL system was strengthened in 1974 (Section 4.42). Together with public land banking it is the major means by which the state directly intervenes in the development land market.

4.4   Strengthening state intervention - 1965-1975

4.4.1   Land costs as a political problem

The history of local authority land banking, combined with the post-war State Housing Loan apparatus, prevented land supply or costs becoming a stranglehold over urban development in the 1950s. However, the 1960s was a period of substantial urbanisation with a reconcentration of population in the larger urban areas. The balance of social forces affecting land development was also changing with the emergence of oligopolistic building companies. It became apparent that local authorities would not be able to fulfil their responsibilities for planning and housing provision without increased state control over development land. This realisation was made politically effective because of the importance of housing to the electoral success of the ruling party, the Social Democrats, as well as radicalisation in the labour movement as a whole. Another wave of reformist government inquiries provided the basis for further legislation. I will group this into four categories - land banking and release, expropriation, public information and taxation.

4.4.2   Land banking and land release

(a)   Local authority land banks   Under the 1967 Housing Act communes are responsible for maintaining land banks sufficient for 7-10 years estimated development. State loans for commune land purchases were introduced in 1965 (for land to be leased by communes) and 1968 (all commune owned land). These loans are subsidised and allocated only for land bought at approved prices. (Since 1981 they are "in abeyance" for redevelopment land).

The costs of land banking are usually only a minor part of commune expenditure. Acquisition costs are broadly balanced by disposal gains (sales and leases). It is only in the first few years, before turnover is established, that costs are significant and it is then that central government support is crucial. This again shows the importance of seeing land policy in the long term.

(b) Leasehold from commune land banks is particularly encouraged in the legislation. This is seen as giving local authorities the ability to share in future development gains as well as to control future development through their freehold rights. Leasehold ("tomträtt") disposal by communes has been encouraged in a number of ways: (i) since 1958 freehold rights have been extended indefinitely (previously 100 years only), (ii) from 1966 leases must be for 10 year periods or less. Appeal on lease levels is now heard by the land expropriation courts (compare with comparatively meaningless 100-200 year local authority leases in Britain), (iii) from 1967 leasehold disposal means lower interest rates on State Land Loans.

Despite these measures, only about 15-20% of commune owned land is now released to developers through leasehold. This is partly because the financial advantages (return on leasehold v. equal investment elsewhere + cash sales) are not clear cut. Partly leasehold becomes an issue of social values rather than financial gain, and it is the more left communes that use it most.

Most debate on land policy in Sweden concerns leasehold, and it is here that electoral changes can produce dramatic policy changes. Unlike Britain, state land banking is generally seen as a sensible way to regulate and aid development, and is relatively uncontentious.

(c) The "Land Condition" for State Housing Loans Since 1974 the "land condition" links SHLs (Section 4.34) directly to commune land banking. For loan approval (remember that 90% of housing is built with SHLs) development should take place on land released by the communes (with transitional arrangements up to 1984). This provision is potentially very important but has not yet applied in a boom period. In July 1981 the "bourgeois" centre-right government rescinded the land condition for redevelopment. This is now an increasing part of new housing development. It is also here that development gains are more easily appropriated by builders or property owners, because use values and development values are less easy to separate.

4.4.3 Expropriation rights

As Section 3.4 showed, the threat of expropriation is of some importance to state regulation of development gain. For the threat to have much effect, its actuality must be possible and fairly drastic. Before 1949 this was not the case, as in Britain (CPOs). Expropriation was too time consuming, cumbersome, expensive or specific to be of any general use as a land policy instrument. This situation was only partially resolved in 1949 and since 1966 the scope and flexibility of commune expropriation has been extended. Small or low value land parcels (covering most owner-occupied housing) are excluded. Thus:

(a) Extension of expropriation scope. Expropriation can be justified by inclusion in long term land use plans or even housing need or population growth estimates. No specific or immediate use need be shown. Nor, since 1972, can the landowner claim similar development plans as grounds for exception. The expropriation threat covers all land needed for development and/or commune land banks.

(b) Extension of expropriation efficiency. Communes can now take over expropriated land before appeals are heard. Before 1966 landowners could use appeals to delay acquisition by as much as six years and to raise compensation in proportion. These possibilities are now removed, in practice the original compensation level only is subject to appeal. (There are some specific exceptions). The introduction of specialised expropriation courts has also improved efficiency.

(c) Strengthening expropriation penalties. Compensation is now supposed to exclude development gains. Before 1971 this was set at a "reasonable price" (not necessarily market price). Since 1971 compensation is set at land prices current 10 years before expropriation with allowance for monetary inflation and capital investment. (Up to 1981 transitional arrangements set compensation at 1971 values). Rather than take this risk, the landowner might as well sell at the price first offered by the commune.

The effect of the expropriation threat appears to be a stagnation of land values without a stagnation in land release. This suggests the efficiency of exemplary control rather than blanket control.

4.4.4 Public information. Since 1968 all intending land sellers must inform the commune "in good time". Together with much the better registration of property ownership, financial

control and earnings in Sweden, this gives communes added control possibilities. As the history of office speculation in Inner London shows, knowledge is as important a resource as financial or legal power (Wates, 1976). This information right is linked to the "pre-emption prerogative" where the commune can replace any prospective buyer as justified by planning proposals etc. In practice expropriation is used instead, as this is cheaper for the commune.

4.4.5 <u>Taxation</u>. Taxation is not itself a part of "active" land policy. That is, instead of allowing state intervention to alter the structural effects of land ownership (what the land can be used for, and how), tax measures are largely restricted to intervening in the redistributive effects of land ownership (see Massey and Catalano (1978) for a useful discussion of this distinction). Nonetheless, tax will also indirectly affect the development process through its impact on owners' expectations. This is important where private ownership is dominant outside development land itself. In Sweden, income from land value appreciation is usually seen as undeserved, and its taxation is probably tougher than in Britain. (It is certainly more stable over electoral periods, which almost amounts to the same thing).

(a) <u>Capital gains tax</u> is the major taxation instrument. CGT is levied at 75% of profits on land sales, or 100% if the land has been owned for less than 2 years by the seller. Profits are calculated with reference to the vendor's original purchase price, with the sale price depreciated in line with money inflation and a notional maintenance rate for dwellings. These measures relax taxation on land held for a long period, especially residential land, but increases it dramatically for rapid turnover of land. Remaining profits are taxed as revenue under normal income tax arrangements.

(b) <u>Other taxes</u>. Wealth tax is levied at 1-2.5% of taxation value (usually below 80% of market price). Local authority property taxes are levied at 2% of taxation value for owner-occupation, 3% for non-profit rented housing and at higher rates for private rented housing and commercial uses. Neither tax is important as a land policy instrument.

4.5 <u>Successes and failures in Swedish land policy</u>

The conclusion so far is that the measures outlined above allow the Swedish state to control the level and distribution of development gains in the case of greenfield land for permanent housing and public services. This improves social welfare and economic efficiency and stands in some contrast to the British situation. However, problems remain in other land conversion sectors and Swedish state intervention itself produces further problems. Specifically:

(a) Redevelopment. It is difficult to separate land prices from property prices and housing development from commercial development. Control over development gain appropriation by landowners and private developers is more difficult – especially after the recent "bourgeois" government repealed the "land condition" and removed State Land Loans for redevelopment areas in 1981.

(b) Recreation house land. This is excluded from most of the measures described above and has shown steep price rises (Section 3.2).

(c) Development gains and owner-occupation. Since 1975 over 50% of new housing production has been for owner-occupation, which in 1982 accounted for about 40% of the total stock (38% in 1945). Most of this is built with State Housing Loans and on land banked by communes, with low raw land costs as part of a controlled price. With rented housing, the "development gains" removed from landowners/builders and passed to consumers could be socialised. (Rents in the private sector are linked to the dominant public sector levels). In contrast owner-occupiers can privatise development gain when selling in the open second-hand market. They even receive mortgage tax relief in doing so. (Although the tax differential between owners and non-owners is lower than in Britain).

4.6 New policy demands

These problems have led to further policy demands:

(a) From the left

   1. To bring recreation house land into the orbit of effective state control.
   2. Increased public expenditure on State Land Loans.
   3. Strengthening leasehold.
   4. Reducing the excessive state subsidy to owner-occupation or equalising benefits for tenants and coop -owners (partly answered by raising SHL subsidies for rented dwellings, and decreasing mortgage tax relief in 1983).
   5. Increase taxation on property and income from land sales.

6. Land nationalisation. This would solve those problems inherent in trying to separate development land from the land market as a whole, as well as tackling problems in other sectors.

(b) From the right

1. Freeing business from over excessive state regulation, including land. This demand does not always extend to regulation which is seen to support private sector profits – such as commune land banking for mass housing provision. This is seen by large construction companies and industrial/financial interests of which they are part of being one means of allowing efficient restructuring and demand management. "Rolling back the state" is more a response to less central private sector interests in sections where profits can do well anyway – such as city centre redevelopment. The 1982 centre-right government's repeal of the "land condition" for redevelopment areas was one result.

2. Return to a free market in all categories of land. In Sweden this idea is identified with the "loony right". The next section shows why this is so.

5. LAND POLICY AND THE BALANCE OF POLITICAL FORCES

All the measures discussed in Section 4 are perfectly possible to operate in Britain in technical terms. Nor would they be particularly expensive, even in narrow public sector borrowing terms. Similar social and economic gains to those occurring in Sweden should be quite easy to achieve.

It is, of course, political and social conditions which favour such measures in Sweden and militate against them in Britain. (Compare the short and ineffective life of the Community Land Act). This section will describe these conditions very briefly for Sweden. This is of more than historical interest for it is here that the key lies to implementing and maintaining change in Britain. (The section is based on Dickens et al 1985, Chapter 2; see also Castles 1978, Duncan 1982a, b; Korpi 1978; Scase 1976).

5.1 Weak landed interests and capitalist values

Aristocratic landed interests have been weak in Sweden since the late 17th century, both politically and in terms of land ownership. Nor, as in Britain, was landed capital important to the emergence of capitalism - in Sweden this was a matter of the rise of an indigenous bourgeoisie and the exogenous effects of English capital. So from Sweden's industrialisation in the 1840-70 period landowners have not been culturally important - again unlike Britain. Rather the cultural and political pace has been set by capitalist dynasts (Sweden's version of the Rockefellers or Vanderbilts) and the "people's movements" - the labour movement, non-conformism, and the cooperatives. There are few large landed estates and little concerted political power representing the interests of large landowners. Nor have such interests been important to the composition, success, or image of any modern political party in Sweden.

This is in obvious contrast to the British case, where 40% of all land is still owned by "landed property", the Country Landowners' Association acts as an effective and influential lobby, and where the Conservative party still retains important linkages and bases in these interests. Moreover, in Britain the values of a society dominated by landed property seem to have been crucial to the emergence of dominant political and cultural ideologies. In Sweden it is a social democratic mixture of "efficient capitalist" and social welfare that still dominates culturally and politically - perhaps expressed best in the notion of Sweden as "the people's home".

5.2   Reformist agricultural interests

The major "landed interests" in Sweden are those of owner-occupying farmers, originally based on a mass of small farmers. Well organised politically, these groups were interested in production oriented issues (e.g. food prices) and the survival of their ownership rights in the face of big business, rather than rent (e.g. development gain). They were actively opposed to large landowning interests and politically - through the Farmers' Party - supported reformist Social Democrat governments. Direct action by farmers and peasants forced legislation controlling investment in land by financial and industrial interests, and introducing tax rates favouring small land owners (1880-1920). Farmers are now below 5% of the employed population, but they still own most agricultural land and maintain some important political impact in the Centre Party (previously the Farmers' Party and now a strongly conservationist organisation). In short, landed and agricultural interests hold neither a political nor an ownership stranglehold over state intervention in land.

5.3 Strong labour and the 'labour movement housing coalition'

The Swedish labour movement is probably the strongest in any capitalist country, measured by access to state power, organisational and numerical strength. Its political traditions exhibit a mixture of pragmatic reformism in workers' interests combined with social democratic socialism. The Social Democratic Party itself held government power continuously from 1932-1976 (and regained it in 1982). Together with almost complete unionisation of the labour force, this means that many state institutions are built around labour movement involvement and/or social-democratic ideology. The National and County Housing Boards are good examples of the latter, while the "labour movement housing coalition" (the building workers' union, the tenants' union, the cooperatives, the large urban authorities - all Social Democrat organisations) has been the dominant influence in formulating housing and land policy over the 1940-1970 period. In contrast "bourgeois" political interests are split into a Conservative party and two reformist centre parties. The Conservatives last formed a one-party government in 1920 and right wing interests have had little concerted long term influence on housing policy since 1940.

5.4 Progressive and integrated industrial/financial capital

"Right wing interests" do not usually include big industrial and financial interests in Sweden. This is because they have followed a "pragmatic progressive capitalist" path to match the strength of labour's "pragmatic reformism". Unlike Britain, industrial and financial interests are highly integrated, and the small firm sector is weak. This integration extends to building materials and construction companies. Hence the Swedish "city" (effectively three large financial-industrial empires which dominate the Swedish economy) has been largely concerned with production, rather than investment in property.

Unlike the British situation this means that financial interests are not threatened by state intervention to control development gains and indeed welcome reforms that support demand for their manufactured products - such as house building and suburban expansion. Ironically enough, in comparison with Britain, when the Social Democrats regained government power in 1982 share prices rose, especially for construction and building material companies. The structure of capital, no less than the strength of labour, has allowed a "historic compromise" favouring both at the expense of weaker

interests like small firms and property owners. Unlike
Britain's relatively backward capitalism, the land question
sticks out like a sore thumb and is not crucial for either
dominant interest. Landownership rights are socially,
economically and politically weaker than in Britain.

6. CONCLUSIONS

My overall conclusion is that Swedish state intervention to
control the provision of development land is "better" than in
Britain, on the criteria of creating a more socially just and
economically effective society. This is not to say that
Sweden shows some perfect or unchanging model, as I have tried
to indicate. The contrasts with Britain are, however, quite
large and probably widening (this is nicely symbolised by the
Urban Development Corporations' power to vest local government
owned land for release to private owners, compared with the
power of Swedish communes to "vest" privately-owned land for
development purposes). None of the Swedish measures described
above would be technically difficult to introduce into
Britain. Rather, the problem is a political one. Clearly it
is not possible to go back in history and change Britain into
Sweden, by removing the political power of landed interests in
1680 for example. However, some political conclusions can, I
think, be drawn.

1. Housing land policy should not be approached in a
piecemeal way. To have a chance of success, it should be
linked to changes in construction, taxation and housing
finance. (Of course, as Sweden's legislative history shows,
it may be better not to introduce the measures themselves as
one dramatic package).

2. But, paradoxically, land nationalisation is not necessary
to effect substantial improvements. In principle, this is a
superior method of socialising and/or redistributing
development gain, and there is a problem of isolating a
housing land market from the land market in general. But a
sectoral land policy as part of housing and construction
policy can be effective and is probably politically easier to
achieve.

3. Housing land reform might be developed as one part of a
"social democratic compromise" between the British labour
movement and "progressive capital". As part of an integrated
land-construction-tax-finance policy, this would include pay-
offs to "progressive capital" (e.g. large construction firms)
as well as consumers on the Swedish model. This of course

depends on such a "social democratic compromise" again becoming possible in Britain - but this possibility can be influenced by the presence or otherwise of workable compromise policies. In contrast the present direction of British land policy is likely to lead to substantial economic and social inefficiencies.

ACKNOWLEDGEMENTS

Thanks to Ingemar Elander, Gert Nilsson and Jörgen Schultz for their help in Sweden. Thanks also to participants in the Housing Workshop Meeting (Sheffield, March 1983) and the 'Land Policy, Problems and Alternatives' conference (Oxford, March 1983) for their stimulating appraisal of an earlier version of this chapter. Some of the original research was carried out for an SSRC funded research project "Housing and the State in Britain and Sweden" (HR 5180) based in the Urban and Regional Studies Division of Sussex University.

PART IV
CONCLUDING REVIEW

PART IV

16 Priorities for research in land policy

SUSAN BARRETT AND PATSY HEALEY

In this concluding section we attempt to draw together important issues and themes emerging from individual contributions and to consider how far they help to clarify the 'problem' of land policy and thereby to redefine our original agenda of areas needing further research. Whilst the papers reflect the diversity of disciplinary backgrounds and perspectives outlined in our introduction, there are a number of complementary strands that run through them which point to some convergence in the issues which are seen as important areas for further investigation and debate.

Common issues in Land Policy Research

First the papers demonstrate clearly the growing polarity of economic opportunity between different regions of the country, and the importance of the local or regional economic context in influencing the manner in which land is perceived as an issue and upon the scale, purpose and mechanisms of government intervention in the land market or development process. Few of the papers have attempted a 'national' view; in most the focus of research attention appears to reflect the dominant economic problems of the local area or region studied. By and large, papers concerned with more traditional land use planning and regulatory aspects of policy intervention have drawn upon empirical data from relatively buoyant areas of the country or sectors of the economy (for example, Elson, Hooper, Barras). By contrast, papers located in situations of economic decline tend to emphasise more innovative and active state involvement in, or promotion of, development activity as part of an overall strategy for economic regeneration (for example, Morphet, Robbins, Cameron et al, Williams, Wannop). Here we see both central and local government agencies participating in the land conversion and development process; assuming the roles of developer and financier as well as land supplier; working in partnership with various private agencies, and bearing a substantial part of the investment risk (if not direct financial rewards) in the interest of stimulating demand and further investment, or with the ultimate objective of job creation.

The emergence (or re-emergence) over the past decade of more promotional policy initiatives produces a complex and fragmented picture of state intervention directly or indirectly related to land. These initiatives tend to be targetted at specific sectors or particular areas, and to be operated through a variety of public agencies. Promotional policies operate in parallel with the national land use planning framework, and have often been designed specifically to supersede or bypass it. They include a mix of financial incentives to encourage land conversion and development through grants and tax reliefs to individual firms and development companies (e.g. in EZs, UDGs), the grant of parallel powers and the direction of public resources to special agencies (e.g. LAW, UDCs, SDA), and the relaxation of regulatory controls (e.g. EZs).

Several of the papers point to the increasing centralisation of policy, particularly evident in the promotional arena — where new central initiatives are accompanied by the creation of special central government agencies to implement the policy, or where central financial resources are linked to particular policy initiatives (such as the Inner City Partnership and Programme areas, or Urban Development Grants) which bypass or undermine local political decision making. At the same time, central government has progressively reduced the financial autonomy of local government (culminating in the current rate-capping legislation), which directly affects the capacity of local authorities to pursue local developmental priorities. In relation to the regulation of land use and development activity, recent central government circulars appear to be increasingly directive and often linked to specific sanctions embodied in legislation. Whilst central government has always used circulars to convey policy, their status is, in theory, advisory. They are especially important in the arena of land use planning where the legislation vests policy responsibility in local planning authorities via the production of development plans (although these are framed in the context of national and regional policy priorities). There has been an increasing tendency in England and Wales to use circulars as the means of specifying and implementing policy in contrast to the Scottish practice of producing National Planning Guidelines. More than ten circulars were produced during the three year life of the Community Land Scheme; most of these were in practice directive rather than advisory since they provided the basic policy criteria and procedures by which resources were to be allocated to local authorities. Similarly, recent land use circulars (e.g. DoE Circulars 9/80 and 22/80) have been used to change the overall orientation of local planning policies, in some cases clearly undermining local control over the scale and location of development. This is most evident in the field of housing land availability (see Hooper's paper), but the attitude of local authorities to industry was also significantly changed by Circular 71/77.

In our Introductory Review, we suggested that land policy should embrace urban and rural land, and policy concerning the ownership, value, use, management and development of land. The papers, and discussions during the conference suggest the extension of this definition to include a crucial dimension, the process of land conversion from one state to another. It is this process of change which interrelates all the other dimensions; for example, change in land ownership involves establishing value as the basis for negotiating price, change in use may involve change in value, management and ownership and also development. The process of land conversion (whether upward or downward in value terms) forces consideration of the interacting effects of one dimension upon others. Whilst change in land use has been the traditional focus of the British planning system, it is the combination of change in ownership and use that lies at the heart of much of the political debate on the land question. It is at this point that individual expectations and aspirations meet the collective framework of legal rules and policies which, as state intervention, provide either opportunities or constraints to individual action. This meeting point has tended to be viewed as a straightforward confrontation between the 'public' and 'private' sectors, the legislative and policy framework of the statutory planning system either limiting the 'free' operation of the land and property market, or regulating 'private' action in the 'public' interest.

The statutory planning system, centred as it is on the spatial allocation of land for particular uses, and the regulation of land use and development activity within the framework of development plan policies, tends to presuppose continuing pressure for new uses and development and the operation of market price mechanisms which will encourage land owners to release land for development. Although local authorities have general powers to acquire compulsorily land needed for development, no financial resources are specifically earmarked for this purpose. The system is thus oriented to a context of economic growth and less able to respond to situations requiring promotional intervention. The kinds of promotional policy initiatives illustrated in this volume can be viewed as a necessary complement, rather than an alternative, to the planning system, in areas of economic decline.

The centrality of the development process

As well as emphasising the importance of the economic context on the operation of different mechanisms in the land conversion process, the papers suggest that the process itself is far more complex and varied than conventionally assumed. (This reinforces our own research findings - see Barrett and Whitting 1983, Healey et al 1982, Healey 1983, Chapter 8).

The development process involves two main elements. There is the bringing together of the physical resources required - land, infrastructure, development/investment finance, professional advice and skills, construction materials and manpower - the assembly job. But preceding this, though linked with it, is the essential process of calculating risk and reward in terms of the estimated cost and time-scale of the assembly process in relation to assessed future demand and expected returns on investment.

Whilst it may be relatively easy to describe the 'ingredients' or resources to be assembled for development to take place, it is more difficult to find a way of describing the development process itself that encompasses the interaction of the different activities, the range of agencies involved in the process and, particularly, the complexity of their inter-relationships. Conventional descriptions of the development process either categorise the functions involved, or adopt a 'pipeline' approach, listing the stages involved in the conversion of land from one state to another. For example, the 'Pilcher Report' on Commercial Property Development used a functional description of the activities involved in achieving a commercial development:

"i) the perception and estimation of demand for new commercial buildings of different types;

ii) the identification and securing of sites on which buildings might be constructed to meet that demand;

iii) the design of accommodation to meet the demand on the sites identified;

iv) the arrangement of short and long term finance to fund site acquisition and construction;

v) the management and design of construction; and

vi) the letting and management of the completed buildings".

(DoE, 1975)

In practice, the functions are combined and performed in different ways for different sectors by a range of agents including land owners, local authorities, developers, builders, investors and financial institutions, occupiers and professional advisors. Another way of looking at the development process is to try and classify the agents according to the functions of the roles they assume in the process. The conventional approach here is to see the process as essentially private sector and market based, with the public sector as fulfilling certain regulatory activities. On this basis the roles might be characterised thus:

The Developer: the key actor who orchestrates the assembly of inputs; sites, finance, advice, production inputs;

The Funder: who provides development and, where relevant, investment finance;

The Builder: who carries out construction;

The Advisers: who provide professional advice and services to the other agents, e.g. market analysis, financial appraisal, design,

                         site appraisal, legal trans-
                         actions etc;

The Public Sector: which regulates the use of land
                         and   coordinates the   provision
                         of infrastructure.

    In reality, none of these roles is so clear cut, and there
is certainly no one-to-one correspondence between particular
kinds of agency and the roles outlined.   Most importantly, as
illustrated by several of the contributions to this volume,
public sector activity is not confined to the regulation of
development or provision of infrastructure.   Both local and
central government agencies may adopt a variety of additional
roles, separately or in combination, including:

    - land   purchase and site assembly for disposal to
      the private sector (with or without site services);

    - provision of buildings on publicly owned land for
      sale, lease, or rent;

    - related financial assistance;

    - development partnerships.

This suggests that:

    i)   roles are not static but evolving over time, and
          thus cannot be assumed or assigned to particular
          agencies on the basis of historic functions;

    ii)   roles in the development process cannot be divi-
          ded up between the 'public' and 'private' sector
          in any clear way; in particular, public agencies
          may be performing any or all of the   functions
          identified as part of the process of achieving
          development.

    In other words, whilst the development process may be viewed
as a series of <u>functions</u> or <u>activities</u> that bring together
<u>resources</u>, the <u>agencies</u> that carry out functions will vary and
may to a greater or lesser extent be <u>substitutable</u> for one
another in fulfilling roles in the process.   Thus to
understand the way in which functions and agencies relate to
one another in the development process, it is important to go
beyond a simple description of who does what in particular
circumstances.   As well as considering the resources and

                              352

functions involved in the process of land development, it is necessary to focus on actors and agencies with potential roles in the process and explore the factors which determine their involvement, including objectives, interests and conditions affecting their scope for action and the way in which that scope is perceived and used in different circumstances.

The absence of any papers at the conference attempting to conceptualise the development process may well be a reflection of this complexity. There is not a development process to be described and explained, but many; the nature of the process varying sectorally and spatially depending on the configuration of agencies involved, and the nature of their economic interest in land and property. Nevertheless, several of the papers take us in this direction (for example, Hooper, Cuddy and Hollingsworth, and the comparative perspectives in the contributions from Needham and Duncan) and some important conclusions can be drawn which question the conventional view of the public/private sector relationship in the land market and development process.

First, it can be seen particularly in situations of economic uncertainty that there are commonalities of interest across the 'public/private' divide. For example, locally or regionally based private sector developers and construction firms dependent on economic buoyancy to create demand for property will share the local authorities' concern with promoting the local economy. Faced with problems of economic survival, they will be willing to enter into industrial or housing partnership with the local authority (or other state agency) involving perhaps taking a lesser reward in return for the sharing of the high risk inherent in undertaking development where demand is uncertain or unproven (see Boddy 1982). Similar principles are involved in the Urban Development Grant initiatives. Second, conflicts of interest may be just as acute within both the state and private sectors as between the state and private individuals or agencies. The papers dealing with the operations of central government development agencies point to potential conflicts of interest between these agencies and the local planning authorities; equally within the 'private' sector there are likely to be conflicts of financial interest between the institutions providing development and investment funding seeking low risk and long term rental and asset growth, and both developers looking for low cost development funding and occupiers seeking low rental premises. This reinforces earlier points concerning the need to understand the individual nature and motivation for agency involvement in the development process, rather than imputting interests and behaviour from generalised institutional labels.

353

Third, the preceding discussion suggests that the planning system is not the only, or necessarily the most important, policy influence on land use outcomes. We have already drawn attention to the increasing use of financial incentives targetted at the individual or firm rather than policy attached to land as the basis of promotional policy initiatives. Less is known about, for example, the indirect effects of fiscal policy in influencing the behaviour of individuals or companies in their approach to land and property acquisition or disposal, where land or buildings represent a capital asset. Such issues as the relative demand for different types of land and property in different tenures; whether land is made available on the market – and by whom; the encouragement or discouragement of particular land use categories and forms of development; systems of equity sharing between agencies involved in development; organisational arrangements for land management – are likely to be influenced by a wide variety of government interventions. Fiscal, economic, social and even welfare policies may have as much, if not more, influence on the behaviour and scope for action of particular agencies in relation to land, than policies directed to the land itself. The multiplicity of legal and policy influences on the stance and behaviour of a single agency is particularly well illustrated by Gore and Nicholson's case study of British Rail land holdings in South Wales.

Finally, it is clear that land conversion and development activity specifically involves a range of transactions between the different agencies, roles and interests involved in the process – developer, owner, financier, planning authority, statutory undertaker etc. These transactions focus around the differential possession or control of the resource 'ingredients' necessary for achieving change – legal rights and powers, land, money, skills – and may be seen as processes of resource exchange in a situation where each of the agencies is more or less dependent on others for assembling the whole. Several of the papers look at the nature of interactions taking place in the transaction process, and conclude that the kinds of bargaining and negotiation formally associated with private transactions in the market are equally to be found in the interactions between public and private agencies. Whilst in some areas, such as the negotiation of partnership arrangements, UDGs, or in discussions about land availability, a negotiative approach is explicitly accepted and formalised, it is also taking place perhaps more implicitly in the operation of what is conventionally seen as the 'regulatory' planning system in the negotiations around the control of development.

The significance and complexity of the land conversion process reinforces our original concern about the split in education, research and practice between those disciplines and professions interested in land use and urban and economic spatial change (i.e. in understanding and managing change in the urban and rural environment), and the professions concerned with land and property valuation and estate management. The kinds of issues emerging in these papers emphasise the gap in contributions, to both the conference and this volume, which address the relationship of estate management principles and practice to wider issues concerning the utilisation and management of land resources. This in turn may reflect the relative academic neglect of the estate management/valuation arena from which to derive broader approaches to analysis.

But, should an attempt to bring these diverse elements together be pursued further? What is the unifying principle, if any? In our introductory review we created a definition of land policy to embrace a variety of disciplines and professional activities. We now look again at our starting definition in the light of the conference papers and discussion.

The Dimensions of Land Policy

The conference itself generated considerable debate and differing views about the validity, or even the feasibility of defining land policy as a policy area or research topic in its own right. At one end of the spectrum were those arguing that almost every aspect of government intervention has a relationship with land since any activity in which the state engages occurs in space on land, and has a range of indirect effects on the occupation and use of land by others.

At the other end of the spectrum were those challenging our position in the introductory paper, and arguing that the term 'land policy' can only be defined operationally in terms of specific implements directly related to the control of physical property and development rights, within a wider framework of economic and social policy governing the uses of land resources. On a slightly different tack, there were also differences between those tending to see patterns of land ownership, use and value as essentially structurally determined, only susceptible to alteration through fundamental changes in societal structure and relations, and those regarding land policy as the means for intervening in these areas to deal with market externalities or ensure the provision of services 'in the public interest'.

These, and subsequent, discussions(*) have helped us to clarify our original eclectic starting point for the conference. We would argue that the ultimate <u>objective</u> of land policy is to influence the way in which land is used as a resource for economic and social activity. However, the <u>policy mechanisms</u> used must reflect an understanding of the factors and processes which combine to influence land use outcomes. This implies going beyond the traditional concerns of either land use planning or estate management to consider:

i)   the role played by land in different areas of economic and social activity, in particular the relationship between land ownership, value creation and the processes of capital accumulation;

ii)   the way in which demands and needs for land are mediated by those influencing or controlling the 'supply of land and premises' – notably the development industry and the state in a variety of roles;

iii) the degree to which the attitudes and behaviour of those actively involved in the land market and development process (whether 'public' or 'private' agencies) are influenced by forms of government intervention aimed at managing the economy at a national and regional level.

Central to this approach are questions about who has control of, or access to, land resources, i.e. the patterns of interests in land, the aspirations and motivations of those seeking access to land resources and the criteria or constraints which influence changing patterns of access. Traditionally these issues have been approached in terms of the ongoing political debate concerning the availability of land for development, in particular, the supply of land for housing. As illustrated by Cuddy and Hollingsworth, some of the more simplistic aspects of the debate have been removed through the institution of the joint Housebuilders Federation/local authority availability studies. Hooper's paper shows that there is still considerable misunderstanding of the issues involved. However, there is now generally a better recognition that 'availability' is a relative, rather than absolute, concept, incorporating three distinct dimensions varying in time and space:

---

* notably in the RTPI Working Party on Land.

i) political priorities for land use in specific areas;

ii) physical development feasibility;

iii) economic development feasibility – itself incorporating the relationship of timing and cost of infrastructure provision and the concept of 'marketability', and the organisation of building firms.

However, two aspects of land supply have not been adequately researched: first, the relationship of land ownership to land 'availability'; and, second, the relationship of supply to demand in the land conversion process.

In Britain the structure of land ownership is individualistic rather than social (whether the 'individual' is a single person, company or department of a public agency). Individuals compete for access to a scarce resource. There is thus a market basis for the transfer of control of land resources. Much attention has been paid to the policies and practices of state planning agencies in allocating land for development and the effects of state intervention on the land market and conversion process. Less attention has been paid to the behaviour (policies and practices) of land owners and how this affects the operation of the land market.

The planning system treats land as a resource for production and consumption processes to be managed in the collective interest. However, whilst land is undeniably a resource, it is also a commodity which is held or exchanged for its asset value. This is recognised even at the level of the individual owner/occupying householder, and is reflected in the language used by estate agents when advertising freehold properties. Massey and Catalano (1978) in their analysis of ownership categories, highlighted the importance of the purpose for which land is owned in affecting attitudes to its use, value and management. They distinguish between owners to whom land is an essential production resource and those for whom land is essentially a financial investment, and suggest an increasing tendency towards the 'commodification' of land because of its inflation-beating characteristics as a financial investment. Perhaps the most obvious example of this tendency is the increasing ownership of both commercial property and agricultural land by pension funds and insurance companies. This leads on to the issue of the relationship of supply and demand for development and the mediating role of the development industry.

The basic assumption, generally promulgated by the development industry, is that the supply of space or premises produced by speculative development companies reflects and responds to the market demand of end users. However, there is some evidence, for example, in the case of successful industrial developments let on commercial terms (see Boddy 1982), that not all economic demand is satisfied or responded to by the market sector. Whilst it is clear that development is unlikely to take place if there is no demand for activity in a particular location, the existence of demand will not necessarily ensure development. The intervening criteria are not well understood - even amongst estate management professionals. More attention needs to be given to the internal structure of particular segments of the development industry and the kinds of factors which will be considered in investment decisions concerning survival, risk and profitability. There are also a variety of issues concerning the relative dependence between different agencies - in particular the reliance on institutional funding for both development and investment funding and the degree to which this constrains or influences the type and cost of development activity undertaken.

The relationship of supply and demand is further complicated by the complexity of land markets, with distinct markets both sectorally and spatially, which nevertheless overlap in important respects. An important research task is the interlinking of work on individual sectoral land markets with that on the structure of the development and building industries, and on forms of land ownership.

Our approach to land policy also implies looking more closely at the appropriateness of types of policy intervention for achieving desired outcomes. In our introduction we referred to Lowi's categorisation of policy according to its purpose (Lowi 1978). We argued that whilst some aspects of land policy can be regarded as procedural mechanisms to further policy ends defined elsewhere (constituent policy in Lowi's terms), many of what appear to be regulatory or constituent policies in fact have underlying ends related to the distribution or redistribution of property rights and benefits arising from the ownership and use of land and property. However, we also need to take on board policies with specific spatial and sectoral outcomes in mind, for example green belt policies, policies for inner city physical renewal or housing land availability policies. Here we have what might be described as distributional policies, with redistributional ends.

Going beyond this kind of classification, it is necessary to ask what sort of policy instrument will actually be effective in achieving the desired outcome? In land use terms, regulatory policies may be effective in directing or redirecting where there is demand or pressure for land conversion. It is not surprising that most of the criticism, and defence, of the statutory land use planning framework relates to its operation in areas of development pressure and maximum development gain i.e. the urban fringe. But if land policy is seeking to direct or encourage particular activities in specific locations, then, as discussed earlier, it may be necessary either to provide incentives or to take direct action to substitute for the agencies that are not willing or able to produce the pattern of uses desired.

There is a tendency for different mechanisms to have particular ideological associations. The Labour party has traditionally been associated with the substitution of state for private control and with direct state action, whereas the Conservatives are seen as favouring market incentives. However, this distinction is less clear at the local level (see Barrett et al. 1979, Saunders 1979), and over the past decade both Labour and Conservative national governments have increasingly moved towards a mix of policy instruments in their attempts to respond to the differential spatial and sectoral impacts of economic recession and the need for economic restructuring. (The recent history of legislation regarding development land illustrates this).

The Community Land Scheme represented an attempt by the 1974 Labour administration to give more positive 'community' control over land use and land conversion via the public ownership of development land. This was effected by the Community Land Act 1975 which enabled local authorities in England and Scotland and the Land Authority for Wales to buy and sell land needed locally for development as defined in Land Policy Statements derived from the framework of Statutory land use development plans. The scheme also provided for the appropriation of a percentage of development value 'created' by the designation of land for development, and the distribution of the benefits between central and local government (under the provisions of the Development Land Tax 1976). Although seen in political terms as the 'nationalisation' of the market in development land, in practice the Scheme itself was predicated on the continuing existence of the land and property market, and on the continued operation of a private sector development industry to carry out developments. In parallel the same administration initiated the Inner City Partnership and

359

Programme arrangements - incorporating and extending the Urban Aid Programme, and including a wide variety of grants available to state and private agencies, individual firms and community groups - to encourage job creation, economic and physical regeneration in decaying inner urban areas.

Subsequent Conservative administrations have committed themselves to the 'rolling back' of state intervention and the reduction of public expenditure, with the aim of stimulating economic activity via the creation and investment of private wealth. The 1980 Local Government Planning and Land Act repealed the Community Land Act (though retaining the Land Authority for Wales), made slight modifications to the 1971 Town and Country Planning Act (in particular generalising the compulsory purchase powers to embrace land needed for development), and introduced a range of new initiatives aimed at urban regeneration:

- the requirement to establish registers of vacant and underused land in public ownership available for sale;

- the creation of Enterprise Zones;

- the creation of Urban Development Corporations with wide powers of intervention to control the ownership, use and management of land in the Merseyside and London Docklands areas.

This legislation, together with subsequent circulars, represented a major shift of land policy emphasis towards the promotion and facilitation of private development activity. There has also been a progressive reduction in financial resources available to local government for direct intervention in the land and property market. However, the government is still employing a wide range of fiscal and financial measures and direct public intervention via the activities of its own agencies, all of which involve substantial public expenditure. Thus in practice the difference in approach lies less in the scale of state involvement and expenditure, but more in the policy instruments and agencies chosen and in the distributional objectives and impacts of intervention.

What is clear from the evolution of policy over the past decade is the growing imperative of positive intervention to mitigate the differential economic and social effects of economic recession. In particular, central government has been faced with a continuing withdrawal of private investment on a massive scale, not just in the collapse of traditional industries, but also in the shift in investment patterns of the major financial institutions. In responding to this imperative, administrations with totally opposed ideological perspectives have found themselves taking a more entrepreneurial stance to encourage private sector investment. With regard to land policy this means state participation in, as well as regulation of, market processes, and the use of a wider range of policy instruments applied selectively in different sectors and locations. What was seen earlier as the fragmentation of land-related policy might be regarded as necessary and appropriate variety in response to differing local circumstances. It may also be seen as experimentation; a recognition of the need to learn how to operate new policies in new conditions.

Given this situation, some practitioners have argued that land policy can only be defined and operated at the local level. But whilst a particular problem or need may be manifest in a particular way in a specific locality, the origins of the problem and the solution may lie elsewhere. For example, a local authority may identify a local demand for small workshops, and wish to encourage or to undertake their development. However, it may not be possible for the authority to influence the capital priorities of the water authority to obtain necessary new sewerage infrastructure for the area in which sites are available, or to influence the investment policies of financial institutions to provide development or investment funding, or indeed to obtain the resources to do the job itself. Similarly, apparently local conflicts over the use or release of particular sites for housing development versus conservation for agriculture or green belt use may be resolved with reference more to the national or regional policies of MAFF, DoE or the Housebuilders Federation than in terms of the specific characteristics of the site itself or the planning policies of the local authority. In other words, the chances of policies for the development and use of particular sites or areas being implemented will be contingent upon interaction with other policies and constraints impinging upon the operating environment of those on whom the policy depends for action. Those agencies may be operating at a different level – for example regional, national or even international – with quite different policy constituencies and access to resources.

Thus, when considering land policy, it is more than usually difficult to isolate our field of concern both substantively and in terms of the level of operation. We are centrally concerned with the inter-relationships between spheres of economic and social activity as they affect land, and with the interaction between policy sectors as they involve land and development. It is for this reason that those involved in land policy are so much concerned with interagency relationships both within the collection of agencies which constitute the public sector, and between the public and private sectors.

The necessity of considering how land policy relates to other policy sectors does not invalidate our case for a focus of attention upon land as a field of public policy. No policy fields can be defined in terms of precise boundaries. Rather, our definition spreads outwards from a central core of concerns. A similar fluidity of boundaries is increasingly being recognised in other traditionally separate policy fields, such as housing (see Merrett 1982). One reason for this is the general reconsideration of the strategy, role, modes of intervention and internal organisation of the state associated with the search for a way forward out of recession. Thus the shift in modes of intervention, and the combination of tendencies both to centralisation and fragmentation noted above in the land policy field can be echoed in most other policy fields.

This emphasises the importance of locating the discussion of land policy, and of any policy field, firmly within the context of general tendencies in the organisation of the economy, and of political structures and processes. Thus, the growth of an increasingly centralised property sector, the expanding role of the financial institutions in land and property investment, the emphasis on land as a commodity and a store of value rather than as a resource, and the search for ways of recycling abandoned land, all reflect fundamental changes in the organisation of the national and international economy. Equally, the attempts to change what the state does and how it does it must be understood at least in part in terms of the struggles by various interest groups to come to terms with changes in the economic sphere, and the particular balance of interests that gains control of the institutions of central and local government over time.

Research for Land Policy

If the conference encouraged us to reaffirm our view that there was a distinctive field of land policy worth concentrated attention, we also believe the agenda of concerns outlined in the introduction still provides a valuable basis for progressing work in this field. It is, however, important to recognise that different levels of explanation and generalisation are required if we are to relate the detailed land and development issues and the operation of land policies to the wider questions of state intervention in the economy and society. At one level, land policy is merely an example of a policy field, and we should be aware of the wider literature on policy processes and the role of the state and the conceptual basis this offers us. In order to translate this meaningfully into the land policy field, however, we need a body of middle-range theory which will allow us to relate broad generalisations to the particular institutional forms and processes associated with land ownership, land markets and development processes. We have already stressed that theorising the development process more adequately is a key task at this level.

Benson (1982) has also stressed the importance of distinguishing different levels of analysis if the detailed operation of policy processes is to be related to inter-organisational analysis. He sees one as concerning policy paradigms, administrative arrangements and inter-organisational dependencies, and a second concerned with deeper interest power structures and rules of structure formation. Benson argues that both levels have tended to be treated analytically in isolation. The main task is to find a way of connecting and relating them.

Our immediate concern might seem to be with the second level especially in orienting research activity to current policy and practice priorities as we concluded in the introduction. But without the first level to underpin our work, we are in danger of being deceived by what is immediately evident, missing some of the structuring factors which shape the objects of our primary concern. On the other hand, if we remain at the higher level, or treat structuring factors in too mechanistic and determinate a way, we will be unable to provide adequate explanations of the range of land policy "events" discussed in this collection of papers. The important task, as generally in contemporary political economy work, is to develop a sensitive and productive relationship between the two levels. In the land policy field, this should give us a much more robust explanatory base, which in turn should improve the quality of ideas about land policy alternatives.

1. Land supply, land ownership and land markets

As stated earlier, what is needed here is more detailed work investigating land ownership tendencies in different sectors of the economy, the factors influencing land acquisition and disposal practices amongst different agencies and the relationship of ownership patterns to the availability of land for the changing space needs of different social and economic activities. Whilst recent work has contributed to a greater understanding of the complexity of land markets – both spatially and sectorally, less attention has been given to the changing nature and geography of the needs and demand for land and space (though this is central to current work by Barras and Broadbent at the Technical Change centre, and is an important element of the Economic and Social Research Council Environment and Planning Committee's major research initiative on the Changing Urban and Regional System in the UK). Equally, detailed sectoral and institutionally based studies are needed to further understanding of land and property market processes; in particular the nature of the relationship between types of demand and need for land and premises and the mechanisms for supply.

2. Roles and interests in the development process

Earlier in this chapter we emphasised the centrality of the land conversion process in bringing together, and high-lighting, conflicts of interests relating to the ownership, use, management and value aspects of land. In particular we pointed to the complex and dynamic interaction of function, role and agency in the process, especially where development activity is involved. Whilst a number of studies have been carried out looking at particular sectors of the development industry, more work is needed on the question of who does what and why in the development process. This involves considering the varying way in which roles and agencies come together between sectors, in different scales of development, and over time. Specifically, we need more investigation of:

(i) the degree and dynamics of dependency of different agencies in the development process and the relative dependency and substitutability of agencies providing different resource 'ingredients'; and

(ii) the commonalities and conflicts of interests within and between the 'public' and 'private' sectors as a basis for improved understanding of the scope for, and likely response to, policies influencing the development process.

3. Purposes, types of state intervention in land, its use and development

In the Introduction we suggested that more work was needed to evaluate state interventions explicitly or indirectly affecting the land and property sector. We argued that much of the current framework of policy tends to be taken for granted - at least in relation to land use and land management, yet national intervention strategies establish important dimensions of the power relations within which the various public and private agencies with land and property interests operate in respect of land use and development change.

Many of the papers in this collection arise from work directed at the evaluation of particular interventions, and they tend to raise fundamental questions about interpreting the purposes of state intervention as well as the normative basis for defining the role of the state in relation to land and property in the context of the British political economy. We would therefore suggest that our previous agenda needs to include headings relating to the purposes of state intervention, and the critical evaluation of assumptions embodied in alternative intervention strategies regarding impact and outcome. It is, perhaps, from investigations directed to the latter, that the former may be deduced - and conceptually appraised. For example, we have already pointed to the dominance of a neo-classical view of the role of the state in relation to regulating the land market and the provision of public goods. Yet the present picture is one of active state participation and intervention to promote particular activities and uses as well as traditional regulatory functions. Many of the papers point to the increasing influence of national and regional economic concerns in the shift to promotional intervention; yet they also raise questions about the degree to which the kinds of development oriented measures being promulgated are likely to have any substantial impact on local economic 'health'. This leads to the question of whether land or development related interventions can (or should be) aimed at the major restructuring of activity and redistribution of benefits arising from differential use and value patterns, or whether this policy sector can only (or should only) be seen in terms of marginal adjustments to the impacts of structural change determined elsewhere. It may well be that these kinds of questions can only be addressed through comparative analysis which would enable researchers to stand outside their own system - as illustrated in this volume by the contributions from Needham and Duncan.

In a similar manner, we also need more work which looks critically at assumptions embodied in alternative approaches to intervention. For example, the nationalisation of land has tended to be seen by the left as the solution to 'the land problem'. Yet whilst ownership may increase control of land use and management, there are still fundamental conflicts of interest concerning such issues as: long term versus short term benefits to be gained from different use/management strategies; problems of determining use and development priorities; managing the process of land supply. State ownership per se will not remove such conflicts, merely transfer them to a different arena. Similarly, the removal of state intervention will transfer into the market arena a range of issues concerning the provision of indivisible goods (infrastructure being the prime example) and the inefficiencies of excessive 'free' competition. The kind of approach we have been advocating, which focusses on sectors, agencies, roles and interests, is, we believe, a useful starting point for improving our understanding of the nature of 'interests' and the way in which different kinds of intervention strategy serve or constrain them.

4. The internal organisation of the state as it relates to land questions, notably relations between central and local government, and intersectoral relations

Our original agenda placed emphasis on the need for studies of the way in which policy instruments are realised in organisational terms, i.e. the choices made about organisational structure and procedure, and the extent to which these exert an independent influence on outcomes. From the issues raised in this connection, we would extend this to include the specific question of agency choice – notably between centrally or locally accountable agencies, and questions concerning the nature of inter-agency relations as a dimension in the policy process. In many ways the issue of the way the state itself is organised forms an integral part of the questions being posed on both the purposes of state intervention and roles and interests in the development process. The important dimensions to be added are political autonomy and accountability, and the priority to be placed on local democratic processes and local accountability relative to national control and accountability in relation to different policy issues. Whilst much policy may in effect be determined centrally but implemented locally, there is an important distinction between the local administration of national policy and local policy making discretion. More attention has been been paid over the past few years to the

366

nature and scope of the local state (e.g. Cockburn 1977, Saunders 1981, Dunleavy 1980), but there is still a need for both empirical and conceptual work which ties this in with specific policy arenas and with different theoretical formulations of inter-organisational relations.

These four groups of issues provide four different ways of cutting into the complex social processes which constitute the field of land policy. Inevitably researchers from different disciplinary traditions and conceptual perspectives will address these issues in different ways. As we noted in the Introduction, the different conclusions and ideas this will reveal are important. But what is equally important is that we continue the effort at communicating and interrelating different approaches to the analysis of land policy. This book, and the conference which gave rise to it, was underpinned by our conviction as to the importance of such a combined effort. We look forward to the outcomes in terms of both research and policy ideas.

List of papers given at the conference

Author and Institution	Title
R. Barras (CES Ltd)	Development of Profit and Development Control: the Case of Office Development in London.
C. Brook (Leeds City Council)	The Rapidly Changing Field of High Technology Development and Science Parks.
S. Cameron et al (University of Newcastle).	The Supply of New Industrial Premises by Public and Private Agencies.
M. Cuddy and M. Hollingworth (Land Authority for Wales	The Review Process in Land Availability Studies: Bargaining Positions by Builders and Planners.
S. Duncan (London School of Economics and Sussex University)	Land Policy in Sweden Separating Ownership from Development.

M. Elson (Oxford Polytechnic)	Land Release and Development in Areas of Restraint.
S. Fothergill, M. Kitchen & S. Monk University of Cambridge)	The Supply of Land for Industrial Development.
A. Gore & D. Nicholson (University of Wales Institute of Science and Technology)	Frameworks for the Analysis of Public Sector Land Ownership and Development.
G. Hallett (University College, Cardiff	The Rule of Law in the Planning System: A Comparison of California, W. Germany and England.
O. Hetzel (Wayne State University)	Enterprise Zones in the U.S.
A. Hooper (University of Reading)	Land Availability Studies and Private House Building.
C. Howick (Roger Tym & Partners)	Enterprise Zones
D. Johnson & N. Bozeat (Joint Unit for Urban and Regional Research)	Can Peripheral Restraint Revert Development to the Inner City?
G. Keogh (University of Reading)	The Economics of Planning Gain
M. Loughlin (Warwick University)	Apportioning the Infrastructure Costs of Urban Land Development.
S. Markowski (South Bank Polytechnic)	Urban Land Policies for the 1980s: An Economist's View.
S. McGill and C. P. Walker (Leeds University)	The Control of Development Around Hazardous Installations in a Major Metropolitan Planning Authority.

P. McNamara (Oxford Polytechnic)	Development Control Data: An Underused Resource.
N. Moor (Nigel Moor and Associates)	Inner City Areas and the Private Sector.
J. Morphet and J. Robbins (London Borough of Tower Hamlets & Roger Tym & Partners)	The Use of Land for Employment: a Study of Policy Making and Implementation in Inner London 1975-1982.
J. Muller (University of Witwaterstand)	Land Policy and the Public Interest: South Africa.
B. Needham (University of Nijmegen)	Local Government Policy for Industrial Land in England and the Netherlands.
Y. Rydin (London School of Economics)	State Intervention in the Residential Development Process through the Operation of Development Control.
J. Short & S. Fleming (University of Reading)	Evaluating Land Use Planning.
M. Shucksmith & G. Lloyd (University of Aberdeen)	Land Policies in the Highlands and Islands of Scotland.
M. Simmons (Kent County Council)	Monitoring Housing Development: Review-ing Housing Policy.
H. Smyth (School for Advanced Urban Studies, Bristol)	A New Approach to Theorising the Development Process: A Theory of Ground and Building Rent.
W. Solesbury (Department of the Environment)	How the National Interest in Land is Pursued.
J. Underwood (School for Advanced Urban Studies, Bristol)	Policy Systems, Organisation and Procedures for Interests: A View of Local Planning.

U. Wannop
(University of
Strathclyde)

Government Agencies in Land Development.

G. Williams
(University of
Mnchester)

The Achievement of Specialist Agencies in Rural Development.

A. Woolery
(Lincoln Institute
of Land Policy)

Land Reform: American Style.

Bibliography

Alonso, W. 1964. Location and Land Use. (Harvard University Press, Cambridge, Mass).

Ambrose, P. and Colenutt B. 1975. The Property Machine. (Penguin, Harmondsworth).

Arnhem, Municipality of, 1978. De concurrentiepositie van Arhem m.b.t. bedrijfs-vestiging. (gemeente Arnhem).

Ashcroft, B. 1982. "Spatial policy in Scotland", in ed Cuthbert M. Government Spending in Scotland. (Paul Harris Publishing, Edinburgh).

Association of Metropolitan Authorities 1982. Land for Private Housebuilding.

Ball, M. 1981. "Land use planning and suburban development – the land values question revisted". Paper presented to conference on Structural, Economic Analysis and Planning in Time and Space. (University of Umeo, Sweden, June 1981).

Ball, M. 1983. Housing Policy and Economic Power. (Methuen, London).

Barker, A. (ed) 1982. Quangos in Britain. (Macmillan, London).

Barras, R. 1979a. "The new property boom". Estates Gazette, 6th October, pp.41-43.

Barras, R. 1979b. The Development Cycle in the City of London. Research Series 36. (Centre for Environmental Studies, London).

Barras, R. 1981. "The causes of the London office boom" in The Office Boom in London, CES Paper 1. (Centre for Environmental Studies, London).

Barrett, S. 1981. "Local authorities and the Community Land Scheme", in eds Barrett, S. and Fudge, C. Policy and Action. (Methuen, London).

Barrett, S. 1982a. "Policy characteristics and the implementation of the Community Land Scheme", paper presented to the International Working Group on Policy Implementation, Umeo, Sweden, June 1982. (Unpublished mimeo).

Barrett, S. 1982b. "The 1980 Act and the supply of develop-
ment land", in ed Markowski, S. Land policies for
the 1980s. Occasional paper EM 1/82. (Department of
Estate Management, Polytechnic of the South Bank).
Barrett, S. Boddy, M. and Stewart, M. 1978. Implementation
of the Community Land Scheme. SAUS Occasional Paper
No.3. (School for Advanced Urban Studies, Bristol).
Barrett, S. and Fudge, C (eds) 1981. Policy and Action.
(Methuen, London).
Barrett, S. M. and P. Healey 1983. "Land Policy: Towards a
Policy and Research Agenda", Paper to Conference on
Land Policy: Problems and Alternatives. (Oxford).
Barrett, S. Stewart, M. and Underwood, J. 1978.
The Land Market and Development Process, A Review of
Research and Policy. Occasional Paper No.2. (School for
Advanced Urban Studies, University of Bristol).
Barrett, S. and Whitting, G. 1981. Local Authorities and the
Supply of Development Land to the Private Sector.
Working Paper No.19, (School for Advanced Urban Studies,
University of Bristol).
Barrett, S. and Whitting, G. 1983. Local authorities and land
supply, Occasional Paper 10. (School for Advanced
Urban Studies, University of Bristol).
Barrie, D. S. M. 1980. History of the Railways of Great
Britain, Vol. 12: South Wales. (David and Charles, Newton
Abbot).
Batley, R. and Edwards, J. 1978. The Politics of Positive
Discrimination. (Tavistock, London).
Benson, J. K. 1982. "A Framework for Policy Analysis", in
Rogers, D. and Whetton, D. eds Interorganisational
Coordination. (Iowa State University Press, Iowa).
Bernard Thorpe and Partners 1981. Development in London 1967-
1980: A Special Study. (Bernard Thorpe and Partners,
London). p.32.
Blowers, A. 1980. The Limits of Power. The Politics of
Local Planning Policy. (Pergamon, Oxford).
Boddy, M. 1981. "The property sector in late capitalism: the
case of Britain" in ed Dear, M. and Scott, A. J.
Urbanisation and Urban Planning in Capitalist Socitety
pp.268-286. (Methuen, London).
Boddy, M. 1982. Local Government and Industrial Development
Occasional Paper 7. (School for Advanced Urban Studies,
Bristol).
Boddy, M. and Barrett, S. 1979. Local Government and the
Industrial Development Process. SAUS Working Paper No.6.
(School for Advanced Urban Studies, University of Bristol).
Bonavia, M. R. 1971. The Organisation of British Railways.
(Ian Allan, London).

Booth, S.A.S, Pitt, D. C. and. Money, W. J. 1982. "Organisational redundancy? A critical appraisal of the GEAR project', Public Administration, Vol.60, No.1, pp.56-72.

BOS (Bostadsstyrelsen) 1969. Kommunal markpolitik (BOS 1), Stockholm.

BOS (Bostadsstyrelsen) 1980. Kommunal markpolitik, Stockholm.

Bow Group 1978. Saving our Cities.

BPA/RK (H. Almgren) 1978. Bygg och Bokostnad 70-tal (BPA/RK) Stockholm.

Bramley, G. 1976. Lambeth Inner Area Study. Paper to CES Inner City Employment Conference, York.

British Railways Board 1963. The Reshaping of British Railways. (HMSO, London).

British Transport Commission 1955. Modernisation and Re-equipment of British Railways. (HMSO, London).

Broadbent, T. A. 1977. Planning and Profit in the Urban Economy. (Methuen, London).

Broady, M. 1980. "Mid Wales: A case of rural self help". The Planner, Vol.66, pp.94-96.

Brodin, I., Chambert, H., Dahlin, P. 1979. Utredning om förnyelse av aldre villa- och fritidsbebyggelse. (Lanstyrelsen i Stockholms Län).

Brown, J.H, Phillips, R.S, and Roberts, N.A. 1981. "Land markets and the urban fringe: New insights for policy makers", Journal of American Planning Association, Vol.47(2).

Bruton, M. and Gore, A. 1980. Vacant Urban Land in South Wales. Final report to the Land Authority for Wales and the Prince of Wales Committee. (Department of Town Planning, University of Wales Institute of Science and Technology, Cardiff).

Bruton, M. and Gore, A. 1981. "Vacant urban land", The Planner, Vol.67(2).

Burrows, J. W. 1977. Vacant Urban Land and its Planning Implications. Unpublished M.Phil thesis. (School of Environmental Studies, University College, London).

Cadman, D. 1979. "Private capital and the inner city". Estates Gazette, Vol.249, March 31st.

Cadman, D. 1983. Property Finance in the U.K. Paper presented to the Anglo-American Land Policy Conference "The Re-use of Land and Buildings", June 1983.

Camden, London Borough of 1979. District Plan Written Statement: A Plan for Camden. (London Borough of Camden, London).

Cameron, S. Dabinett, G. Gillard, A. Whisker, P. Williams R. and Willis, K. 1982. Local Authority Aid to Industry. An Evaluation in Tyne and Wear. DoE Inner City Research Programme Report No.7. (HMSO).

Cantell, T. 1977. Urban Wasteland. (Civic Trust, London).

Castles, F. G. 1978. The Social Democratic Image of Society (Routledge and Kegan Paul, London).

Cawson, A. 1982. Corporatism and Social Welfare. (Heinemann, London).

Champion, A. G. 1981. "Population trends in rural Britain". Population Trends, Vol.26. (Winter). pp.20-24.

Chancellor of the Exchequer 1978. The Nationalised Industries. Cmnd 7131. (HMSO. London).

Clarkson, S. 1980. Jobs in the Countryside. Occasional Paper No.2 (Wye College, Department of Environmental Studies and Countryside Planning).

Clawson, M. 1971. Suburban Land Conversion in the United States: An Economic and Governmental Process. (John Hopkins University Press, Baltimore, Maryland).

Cockburn, C. 1970. Opinion and Planning Education. (Centre for Environmental Studies, London).

Cockburn, C. 1977. The Local State. (Pluto Press, London).

Community Development Project (CDP) 1974. Inter-Project Report. (CDP Information and Intelligence Unit, London).

Community Development Project (CDP) 1977. Gilding the Ghetto. (CDP Inter-Project Team, London).

Coopers Lybrand Ltd 1980. Provision of Small Industrial Premises. (Department of Industry).

Council for Industry in Rural Areas (CoSIRA) Report 1975-78 (CoSIRA).

Council for Industry in Rural Areas (CoSIRA) Report 1978-79 (CoSIRA).

Council for Industry in Rural Areas (CoSIRA) Old Buildings - New Opportunities (CoSIRA).

Countryside Review Committee 1977a. The Countryside - Problems and Policies. (HMSO, London).

Countryside Review Committee 1977b. Rural Communities. Topic Paper 1. (HMSO, London).

Cox, A. 1980. "The limits of central government intervention in the land and development market: the case of the Land Commission". Policy and Politics 8(3), August.

Crook, G. R. 1974. "Physical planning", in ed Bruton, M. The Spirit and Purpose of Planning. (Hutchinson, London).

Cullen, M. and Woolery, S. (eds) 1982. World Congress on Land Policy. (D.C. Heath, Lexington, Massachusetts).

Cullingworth, J. B. 1982. Town and Country Planning in Britain. (George Allen and Unwin, London, 8th edition).

Dabinett, G. 1982. The Supply of New Industrial Premises in the Northern Region 1974 to 1980. Centre for Urban and Regional Development Studies Working Paper. (University of Newcastle upon Tyne).

Dabinett, G. and Whisker, P. 1981. The Declaration of IIAs and the Provision of Advance Factories and Loans and Grants by Local Authorities in Tyne and Wear 1974-1979. I.C.E.P. Working Paper No.2. (University of Newcastle upon Tyne).

Dacorum District Council 1982. Dacorum District Plan: Proposed Modifications. p.31.

Dacorum District Council 1980. Draft Local Plan: Written Statement. (Dacorum District Council, Hemel Hempstead).

Daniels, W. W. 1972. Whatever Happened to the Workers in Woolwich? (PEP, London).

Darin-Drabkin, H. 1977. Land Policy and Urban Growth. (Pergamon, Oxford).

Darke, R. 1982. "The dialectics of policy-making: Form and content", in ed Healey, P. McDougall, G. Thomas, M.J. Planning Theory: Prospects for the 1980s. (Pergamon, Oxford).

Davies, H. W. E. 1980. "The relevance of development control". Town Planning Review. 51, pp.7-17.

Davies, T. 1981. "Implementing employment policies in a district authority", in eds Barrett, S. and Fudge, C. Policy in Action (Methuen, London).

Dear, M. and Scott, A. (eds) 1981. Urbanization and Urban Planning in Capitalist Society. (Methuen, London).

Deloitte, Haskins and Sells and Roger Tym and Partners 1982. GEAR Review: Business Development and Employment Strategy. Final Report for the Scottish Development Agency.

Denman, D. R. and Prodano, S. 1972 Land Use: An Introduction to Proprietary Land Use Analysis. (Allen and Unwin, London).

Dennis, N. 1970. People and Planning. The Sociology of Housing in Sunderland. (Faber, London).

Dennis, N. 1972. Public Participation and Planners Blight. (Faber and Faber, London).

Dennis, R. 1976. The decline of inner city manufacturing employment. Paper given to CES Inner City Employment Conference, York.

Department of Education and Science, 1967. Children and their primary schools, Plowden Report. (HMSO, London).

Department of the Environment 1970 Land for Housing. Circular 10/70. (HMSO, London).

Department of the Environment 1972. Land Availability for Housing. Circular 102/72. (HMSO, London).

Department of the Environment 1972. Report of the Working Party on Local Authority/Private Enterprise Partnership Schemes. (Sheaf Report) (HMSO, London).

Department of the Environment 1972a. The new Local Authorities: management and structure (The Bains Report). (HMSO, London).

376

Department of the Environment 1973. "The New Water Industry: Management and Structure". (Ogden Report). (HMSO, London).

Department of the Environment 1973a. Widening the Choice: the next steps in housing. Cmnd 5280. (HMSO, London).

Department of the Environment, 1973b, The New Water Industry Management and Structure, (Ogden Report). (HMSO, London).

Department of the Environment 1975a. Vacant Land. Liverpool Inner Area Study, report of consultants to the steering committee. (HMSO, London).

Department of the Environment 1975b. Commercial Property Development (The Pilcher Report). (HMSO, London).

Department of the Environment 1976. Office Location Review. (HMSO, London).

Department of the Environment 1977a. Inner Area Studies: Liverpool, Birmingham and Lambeth: Summaries of Consultant's final reports. (HMSO, London).

Department of the Environment 1977b. Policy for Inner Cities. (HMSO, London).

Department of the Environment 1977c. Local Government and the Industrial Strategy. Circular 71/77. (HMSO, London).

Department of the Environment 1977c. Hertfordshire County Structure Plan Examination in Public: Report of the Panel. (Department of the Environment, London). pp.88-89.

Department of the Environment 1978. Private Sector Land. Requirements and Supply. Circular 44/78. (HMSO, London).

Department of the Environment 1980a. Land for Private House-building. Circular 9/80. (HMSO, London).

Department of the Environment 1980b. Circular No.22/80. Development control: Policy and practice. (HMSO, London)

Department of the Environment 1981. Planning Gain. Report by the Property Advisory Group. (HMSO, London).

Department of the Environment 1983. Planning Gain Guidelines. Consultation paper. (DoE, London).

Department of the Environment 1983. Town and Country Planning Gain. Circular 22/83. (HMSO, London).

Department of the Environment 1983. Planning Gain, Circular 22/83. (HMSO, London).

Department of the Environment/House Builders Federation 1979. Study of the availability of private housebuilding land in Greater Manchester, 1978-1981. 2 volumes. (HMSO, London).

Department of the Environment/Housing Research Foundation 1975. Housing land availability in the South-East: a consultant's study. Economist Intelligence Unit Ltd and Halpern and Partners. (HMSO, London).

Department of the Environment/Housing Research Foundation 1978. Land Availability: A study of land with residential planning permission. Economist Intelligence Unit Ltd. (HMSO, London).

Department of Health and Social Security 1968. Report of the Committee on Local Authority and Allied Personal Services Seebolm Report (HMSO, London).

Derthick, M. 1972. New Towns In-Town. (The Urban Institute, Washington DC).

Development Board for Rural Wales 1979. Board Policy Statement.

Development Board for Rural Wales 1981. Finance for Business in Mid Wales.

Development Board for Rural Wales 1982. Sites and Premises.

Development Board for Rural Wales. Annual Reports (various).

Development Commission. Annual Reports (various).

Dickens, P. Duncan, S. S. Goodwin, M. and Gray, F. 1985. Housing States and Localitys. (Methuen, London).

Dobson, M. 1981. Land release for housing: the view of the housebuilding industry. (Surveyors Technical Services, London).

Donnison, D. 1982. GEAR Review: Social Aspects. Final Report for the Scottish Development Agency.

Dror, Y. 1968. Public Policy Making Re-examined. (Chandler, Scranton, Pennsylvania).

Dror, Y. 1971. Design for Policy Sciences. (Elsevier, New York).

Duncan, S. S. 1978. Housing Provision in Advanced Capitalism: Sweden in the 1970s. Working Paper in urban and regional studies. (University of Sussex).

Duncan, S. S. 1982a. Class Relation and Historical Geography: The Creation of the Urban and Regional Problems in Sweden University of Sussex Research Papers in Geography, 12. (University of Sussex).

Duncan, S. S. 1982b. Class Relations and Historical Geography: The Transition to Capitalism in Sweden. LSE Discussion Paper in Geography, 4. (London School of Economics, London).

Dunkerley, H. Wakis, A. Courtenay, J. Doebele, W. Sharp, D. and Rivkin, MN. 1978. Urban Land Politics and Opportunities. (World Bank, New York).

Dunleavey, P. 1980. Urban Political Analysis. (MacMillan, London).

Dunning, J. H. and Morgan, E. V. 1971. An economic study of the City of London. (Allen & Unwin, London).

Durrant, L. 1982. "How development can pay for a bypass". Chartered Surveyor. February, pp.396-397.

Ellis, R. 1983. Office market review: City of London. January. (R. Ellis & Partners, London).

Estates Times 1977. "Hypermarkets: A Bargain for Shopper and the Inner City". September 25th.

Estates Times 1981. "Retail Centres Stabilise Inner Cities - URPI". April 3rd.

Evans, A. W. 1974. "Economics and Planning" in ed Forbes, J. Studies in Social Science and Planning. (Scottish Academic Press, Edinburgh).

Evans, A. W. 1983. "The determination of the price of land". Urban Studies, 20. pp.119-129.

Fielding, N. 1982. "The volume housebuilders". Roof, Vol.7, Number 6. November/December.

Flynn, R. 1983. "Co-optation and strategic planning in the local state", in ed King, R. Capital and Politics. (Routledge and Kegan Paul, London).

Forshaw, J. H. and Abercrombie, P. 1944. The County of London Plan. Prepared for the LCC. (Macmillan, London).

Fothergill, S. and Gudgin, G. 1982. Unequal Growth - Urban and Regional Employment Change in the UK. (Heinemann, London).

Fothergill, S. Kitson, M. and Monk, S. 1983a. Changes in Industrial Floor-Space and Employment in Cities, Towns and Rural Areas. Industrial Location Research Project Working Paper No.4 (Department of Land Economy, Cambridge)

Fothergill, S. Kitson, M. and Monk, S. 1983b. The Industrial Building Stock and its Influence on the Location of Employment Change. Industrial Location Research Project Working Paper No.5. (Department of Land Economy, Cambridge).

Fothergill, S. Kitson, M. and Monk, S. 1983c. Industrial Land Availability in Cities, Towns and Rural Areas. Industrial Location Research Project Working Paper No.6. (Department of Land Economy, Cambridge).

Friedmann, J. and Weaver, C. 1979. Territory and Function - The Evolution of Regional Planning. (Edward Arnold, London).

Geisse, G. 1982. "Urban land-market studies in Latin America: Issues and methodology", in ed. Cullen, M. and Woolery, S. World Congress on Land Policy. (Lexington, Massachusetts).

George, V. and Wilding, P. 1976. Ideology and Social Welfare. (Routledge and Kegan Paul, London).

Geraets, M. 1980. Het Werkgelegenheids- en het Werkloosheidsbeleid van Enkele Grote Gemeenten in Nederland (Het Economisch Instituut, Katholieke Universiteit, Nijmegen).

Gordon, I. Lewis, J. and Young, K. 1977. "Perspectives on policy analysis". Public Administration Bulletin. 25th December.

Gower Davies, J. 1972. The Evangelistic Bureaucrat. (Tavistock, London).

Grant, M. 1975. "Planning by agreement". Journal of Planning and Environment Law. pp.501-508.

Grant, M. 1976. "The Community Land Act: An overview". Journal of Planning and Environment Law. pp.738-748.

Grant, M. 1982a. "False diagnosis, wrong prescription". Town and Country Planning. May.

Grant, M. 1982b. Urban Planning Law. (Sweet and Maxwell, London).

Grant, M. 1983. "The bargaining business". Town and Country Planning, 128.

Grant, M. and Jowell, J. 1983a. "Guidelines for planning gain?". Journal of Planning and Environment Law, 427.

Grant, M. and Jowell, J. 1983b. "Planning gain". Submission to the DoE on the Planning Gain Guidelines Consultation Paper. May.

Grassie, J. 1983. Highland Experiment. (Aberdeen University Press, Aberdeen).

Gray, C. 1982. "Corporate planning and management: a survey. Public Administration Vol.60, No.3, pp.349-355.

Greater London Council 1978. Greater London Development Plan. (GLC, London).

Greater London Council 1982a. Economic Policy for London: Progress to July 1982. (Industry and Employment Committee, GLC, London).

Greater London Council 1982b. The Changing Social Structure of Greater London. Reviews and studies series: No.15. (GLC, London).

Gripaios, P. 1976. "A new employment policy for London". National Westminster Bank Quarterly Review. August.

Gripaios, P. 1977. "Industrial decline in London: an examination of its causes". Urban Studies, Vol.14, No.2.

Hall, P. (ed) 1981. The Inner City in Context. (SSRC, London).

Hall, P. Gracey, H. Drewett, R. and Thomas, R. 1973. The Containment of Urban England. (Allen and Unwin, London).

Hallett, G. 1977. Housing and Land Policies in West Germany and Britain. (Macmillan, London).

Hallett, G. 1979. Urban Land Economics. (Macmillan, London).

Hallos, P. 1977. "Industrial decline in London: an examination of its causes". Urban Studies, Vol.14, No.2.

Hammersmith and Fulham 1979. District Plan Written Statement. (London Borough of Hammersmith and Fulham, London).

Harloe, M. ed 1977. Captive Cities. (Wiley, London).

Harrison, A. J. 1977. The Economics of Land Use Planning. (Croom Helm, London).

Harrison, M. L. 1979. Land Planning and Development Control. Department of Social Policy and Administration Research Monograph, University of Leeds.

Harvey, D. 1981. "The urban process under capitalism: a framework for analysis", in Dear, M. and Scott, A. J. (eds).Urbanization and Urban Planning in Capitalist Societies. (Methuen, London).

Harvey, D. 1982. Limits to Capital. (Blackwell, London).

Healey, P., Davis, J., Elson, M. and Wood, M. 1982. The Implementation of Development Plans. (Department of Town Planning, Oxford Polytechnic).

Healey, P. 1983a. Local Plans in British Land Use Planning. (Pergamon, Oxford).

Healey, P. 1983b. "'Rational Method' as a mode of policy formation and implementation in land use policy". Environment and Planning B.

Healey, P. 1983c. "British planning education in the 1970s and 1980s" in Davies, H. W. E. and Healey, P. British Planning Practice and Planning Education in the 1970s and 1980s. Oxford Working Paper No 70. (Town Planning Department, Oxford Polytechnic).

Healey, P. and Underwood, J. 1979. Professional Ideals and Planning Practice. Progress in Planning Vol.9(2). (Pergamon, Oxford).

Heap, D. and Ward, A. J. 1980. "Planning bargaining - the pros and cons: or, how much can the system stand?" Journal of Planning and Environment Law. pp.631-637.

Hechter, M. 1975. Internal Colonialism - The Celtic Fringe in British National Development. (Routledge and Kegan Paul, London).

Heclo, H. 1972. "Review article: policy analysis". British Journal of Political Science, Vol.2.

Her Majesty's Treasury 1976. Rural Population - Report by an Inter-Departmental Group (HMSO, London).

Hertfordshire County Council 1972. Hertfordshire 1981: Planning Objectives and Policies. (Hertfordshire County Council, Hertford).

Hertfordshire County Council 1976. Structure Plan: Written Statement (Submitted). (Hertfordshire County Council, Hertford).

Hertfordshire County Council 1980. Hertfordshire County Structure Plan: Alterations 1980: Report of Survey - Employment, 6.1. (Hertfordshire County Council, Hertford).

Hertfordshire County Council 1981. Hertfordshire County Structure Plan: Alterations 1980. (Hertfordshire County Council, Hertford).

Hertfordshire County Council 1982. Annual Structure Plan Statement. (Hertfordshire County Council, Hertford).

Hertfordshire County Council 1983. Annual Structure Plan Statement. (Hertfordshire County Council, Hertford).

Higgins, J. 1978. The Poverty Business in Britain and America. (Blackwell/Martin Robertson, Oxford and London).

Hillier, J. 1982. "The role of CoSIRA factories in the provision of employment in rural Eastern England", in ed Moseley, M. J. Power Planning and People in Rural East Anglia. (Centre for East Anglian Studies, University of East Anglia).

Hobsbawm, E. J. 1969. Industry and Empire, Pelican Economic History of Britain, Vol.3. (Penguin, Harmondsworth).

Hodge, I. and Whitby, M. 1981. Rural Employment - Trends, Options, Choices (Methuen, London).

Hood, C. 1978. "Keeping the centre small - explanations of agency type". Political Studies, Vol.26(1).

Hooper, A. 1979. "Land availability". Journal of Planning and Environment Law. pp.752-756.

Hooper, A. 1980. "Land for private housing". Journal of Planning and Environment Law. pp.795-806.

Hooper, A. 1982. "Land availability in South East England". Journal of Planning and Environment Law. pp.555-560.

House of Commons 1978. Report of the Functioning of Financial Institutions. Evidence on the Financing of Industry and Trade. (Wilson Committee). (HMSO, London).

House of Commons 1983. Third Report from the Environment Committee 1982-1983: The Problems of the Management of Urban Renewal. (HMSO, London).

House Builders Federation, 1984. "Initial Land Register Inspections". The House Builder (February).

Hoyes, T. 1982. "Development Land Tax: The basis of value". Journal of Valuation, 1, pp.153-159.

Humber, J. R. 1980. "Land availability - Another view". Journal of Planning and Environment Law. November, pp.19-23.

Humphries, H. C. 1980. Vacant Urban Land and the Development Process. Unpublished M.Sc. thesis, Department of Town Planning. (University of Wales Institute of Science and Technology, Cardiff).

Islington, London Borough of 1975. Draft Employment Topic Paper. Unpublished.

Islington, London Borough of 1978. Draft Written Statement.

Islington, London Borough of 1980. Written Statement and Proposals Map. (London Borough of Islington, London).

ILCEG 1976. Report on Employment Policies of Constituent Authorities. Unpublished.
ILCEG 1977, 1978, 1979, 1980, 1981, 1982. Annual Report.
ILCEG 1980. A Review of Progress 1975-1980.
Investors Chronicle/Hillier Parker 1982. Rent Index. November.

Jenkins, W. 1978. Policy Analysis: A Political and Organisational Perspective. (Martin Robertson, London).
Jessop, R. 1982. The Capitalist State: Marxist Theories and Methods. (Martin Robertson, Oxford).
Johnson, J. H. and Pooley, C. G. 1982. The Structure of Nineteenth Century Cities. (Croom Helm, London).
Joint Land Requirements Committee 1982. Is There Sufficient Housing Land for the 1980s? Paper I: How Many Houses Should We Plan For? (Housing Research Foundation, London)
Joint Land Requirements Committee 1983. Is There Sufficient Housing Land for the 1980s? Paper II: How Many Houses Have We Planned For: Is There A Problem? (Housing Research Foundation, London).
Joint Unit for Research on the Urban Environment (JURUE) 1976. Planning and Land Availability. Interim Report. (University of Aston in Birmingham).
Joint Unit for Research on the Urban Environment (JURUE) 1977. Planning and Land Availability. Final Report. (University of Aston in Birmingham).
Joint Unit for Research on the Urban Environment (JURUE) 1979. Local Authority Employment Initiatives. (University of Aston in Birmingham).
Joint Unit for Research on the Urban Environment (JURUE) 1980. Industrial renewal in the inner city: an assessment of potential and problems, DoE inner cities research programme report No.2.
Joint Unit for Research on the Urban Environment (JURUE) 1982. Planning Problems of Small Firms in Rural Areas. (University of Aston in Birmingham).
Joint Unit for Research on the Urban Environment (JURUE) 1983. An Evaluation of the Effects of Development Commission Activities. (University of Aston in Birmingham).
Jones, G. W. et al 1979. Central-Local Government Relationships. (SSRC, London).
Jones Lang Wootton 1982. Central London Offices Research Monitoring Report. December.
Jowell, J. 1977 "Bargaining in development control". Journal of Planning and Environment Law. pp.414-433.
Jowell, J. 1982. "Giving planning gain a bad name". Local Government Chronicle. 12th February, p.155.

Keeble, D. 197 . New Firms and Rural Industrialisation Study. (Geography Department, University of Cambridge).

Kensington and Chelsea (no date). Draft District Plan. (Royal Borough of Kensington and Chelsea, London).

Kent Planning Officers Group/House Builders Federation 1981. Residential Land Supply in Kent 1980 1984. (NFBTE, London).

Keogh, G. 1982. Planning Gain: an Economic Analysis. Discussion Paper in Urban and Regional Economics, Series C, No.12. (Department of Economics, University of Reading).

King and Co. 1982. Industrial Floorspace Survey. (King and Co., London).

Kirk, G. 1980. Urban Planning in a Capitalist Society. (Croom Helm, London).

Koenigsberger, O. H. and Groak, S. (eds) 1980. A Review of Land Policies. (Pergamon, Oxford).

Korpi, W. 1978. The Working Class in Welfare Capitalism: Work, Unions and Politics in Sweden. (Routledge and Keegan Paul, London).

Kruyt, B. and Needham B. 1980. Grondprijsvorming en Grond-prijspolitiek, Theorie en Praktijk. (Stenfert Kroese, Leiden).

Land Commission 1968, 1969. Annual Report.

Law, D. and Howes R. 1982. Mid Wales − An Assessment of the Impact of the Development Commission Factory Programme. (HMSO, London).

Lawless, P. 1981. Britain's Inner Cities. (Harper and Row, London).

Leather, P. 1979. "Housing investment programmes and housing strategies". The Planner. Vol.65, No.6. December. pp.186-188.

Lebas, E. 1977. "Movement of capital and locality: Issues raised by the study of local power structures", in ed Harloe, M. Urban Change and Conflict. Conference Paper 19. (Centre for Environmental Studies, London).

Lee, D. B. 1981. "Land use planning as a response to market failure", in ed. de Neufville, J. I. The Land Use Policy Debate in the United States. p.149. (Plenum Press).

Lichfield, N. 1980. "Towards a comprehension of land policy". Habitat International. Vol.4, pp.375-395.

Lichfield, N. and Darin-Drabkin, H. 1980. Land Policy in Planning. (George Allen & Unwin, London).

Lichfield, N. Kettle, P. and Whitbread, M. 1975. Evaluation in the Planning Process. (Pergamon, Oxford).

Local Government Act 1972.

London Council for Social Services 1977. Employment and Industry in Greater London – A background document. (LCSS, London).

London Evening Standard 1978. "London's wasted acres". February 6th.

Loughlin, M. 1978. "Bargaining as a tool of development control: a case of all gain and no loss?". Journal of Planning and Environment Law. pp.290-295.

Loughlin, M. 1980a. "Planning control and the property market". Urban Law and Policy. Vol.3, pp.1-22.

Loughlin, M. 1980b. "The scope and importance of 'material considerations'". Urban Law and Policy, Vol.3, p.171.

Loughlin, M. 1981. "Planning gain: law, policy and practice". Oxford Journal of Legal Studies, 1, pp.61-97.

Loughlin, M. 1982. "'Planning Gain': Another Viewpoint". Journal of Planning and Environment Law. p.352.

Loughlin, M. 1983. Local Government: The Law and the Constitution. (Local Government Legal Society Trust, London).

Lowe, P. 1983. "A Question of Bias". Town and Country Planning, Vol.52(5), pp.132-134.

Lowi, T. 1978. "Public policy and bureaucracy in the United States and France", in ed Ashford, D. Comparing Public Policies. (Sage, Beverley Hills).

McAuslan, P. 1980. The Ideologies of Planning Law. (Pergamon, Oxford).

McIntosh, A. and Keddie, V. 1979. Industry and Employment in the Inner City. (DoE Inner Cities Directorate, London).

McKee, W. and Martinos, H. 1981. "Office development in the London Borough of Hammersmith and Fulham", in The Office Boom in London, Centre for Environmental Studies Paper 1. (CES Ltd, London).

McMillan, M. 1975. "Economic rules for planners: a reconsideration". Urban Studies, 12, pp.329-333.

McNamara, P. F. and Elson, M. J. 1981a. The Evolution of Restraint Policies in Hertfordshire. SSRC Project Paper No.2. (Department of Town Planning, Oxford Polytechnic).

McNicoll, I. and Swales, J. K. 1982. "Public expenditure on industry in Scotland", in ed Cuthbert, M. Government Spending in Scotland, (Paul Harris Publishing, Edinburgh).

Marriott, O. 1969. The Property Boom. (Pan Books, London).

Martin, J. E. 1966. Greater London: An Industrial Geography. (G.E. Bell and Sons, London).

Massey, D. and Catalano, A. 1978. Capital and land: Private Landownership by Capital in Great Britain. (Arnold, London).

Massey, D. and Catalano, A. 1982. The Anatomy of Job-loss. (Methuen, London).

Massey, D. and Meegan, R. 1978. "Industrial restructuring versus the cities". Urban Studies, Vol.15, p.273.

Massey, D. 1980. "The pattern of landownership and its implications for policy". Built Environment, Vol.6, No.4, pp.263-271.

Mawson, J. 1982. Changing directions in regional and local economic policy: the West Midlands experience. Paper to Conference, Managing the Metropolis. (Eindhoven).

Mawson, J. and Miller, D. 1983. Agencies in Regional and Local Development. Occasional Paper No.6. (Centre for Urban and Regional Studies, University of Birmingham).

Mayo, M. 1979. "Radical politics and community action", in ed Loney, and Allen, The Crisis of the Inner City. (Macmillan, London).

Medhurst, J. 1982. A Critique of the Evaluation of the Development ommission Factory Programme. Working Paper No.32. (JURUE, Aston University, Birmingham).

Merrett, S. and Gray, F. 1982. Owner-Occupation in Britain. (Routledge and Kegan Paul, London).

Meyerson, M. and Banfield, E. 1955. Politics, Planning and the Public Interest. (Free Press of Glencoe, New York).

Mills, E. S. 1972. Urban Economics. (Scott Foresman, London).

Minay, C. 1981. Partnership between Central and Local Government in Rural Development. Sixth International Seminar on Marginal Regions, Norway.

Ministry of Housing and Local Government 1955. Green Belts. Circular 42/55. (HMSO, London).

Ministry of Housing and Local Government 1957. The Green Belt. Circular 50/57. (HMSO, London).

Ministry of Housing and Local Government 1960. Royal Commission on Local Government in Greater London, 1957-1960. (Herbert Report). (HMSO, London).

Ministry of Housing and Local Government 1966. Our Older Homes. (Dennington Report). (HMSO, London).

Ministry of Housing and Local Government 1967. Report of the Committee on the management of local government. (Maud Report). (HMSO, London).

Ministry of Housing and Local Government (MHLG) 1969. Act of 1968: Time-Limited Planning Permissions. Circular 17/69. (HMSO, London).

Moore, T. 1978. "Why allow planners to do what they do?". Journal of the American Institute of Planners, 44, pp.387-398.

Moss, G. 1980. Britain's Wasting Acres. (The Architectural Press, London).

Munton, R. 1983. London's Green Belt: Containment in Practice. (Allen and Unwin, Hemel Hempstead).

Nabarro, R. and Richards, D. 1980. Wasteland. Thames Television Report. (Associated Book Publishers Ltd, London).

National Council for Voluntary Organisations 1982. Country Work - A Guide to Rural Employment Initiatives. (NCVO).

Needham, B. 1981. "A neo-classical supply-based approach to land prices". Urban Studies, Vol.18, pp.91-104.

Needham, B. 1982. Choosing the Right Policy Instruments (Gower, Aldershot, Hants).

Nelson, S. 1980. Participating in GEAR: Public Involvement in an Area-based Urban Renewal Programme. Strathclyde Area Survey. (University of Strathclyde, Glasgow).

Newby, H. 1980. Green and Pleasant Land. Social Change in Rural England (Penguin, Harmondsworth).

Nicholson, D. J. 1983. Vacant Urban Land in South Wales, An Analysis of the Extent and Causes of Public Sector Holdings. Unpublished Ph.D.Thesis, Department of Town Planning. (University of Wales Institute of Science and Technology, Cardiff).

Nicholls, D. C. Turner, D. M. Kirby, ?. Smith, R. and Cullen, J. D. 1981. Private Housing Development Process: A Case Study. (Department of the Environment, London).

Offe, C. 1975. "The theory of the capitalist state and the problem of policy formation", in ed Lindberg, L. N. and Alford, R. Stress and Contradiction in Modern Capitalism. (Lexington, Massachusetts).

O'Malley, 1975. Canning Town Community Development Project, Canning Town in North Woolwich: The Aims of Industry? The study of industrial decline in one community.

O'Riordan, T. 1982. Putting Trust in the Countryside. (World Conservation Strategy Committee, National Conservation Committee).

Orton, I. 1981. 'Whatever happened to GEAR?' Fraser of Allander Institute Quarterly Economic Commentary, Vol.7, No.3, pp.27-30.

Oxford Polytechnic Building Research Team 1982. Small Advance Factories in Rural Areas. (Oxford Polytechnic).

Oxfordshire County Council and Oxfordshire District Councils/House Builders Federation 1982. Housing Land Supply in Oxfordshire 1980-1989. (NFBTE, London).

Oxley, M. J. 1975. "Economic theory and urban planning". Environment and Planning A, 7, pp.497-508.

Page, J. 1979. Forgotten Railways: South Wales. (David and Charles, Newton Abbot).

Parker, H. R. 1965. "The history of compensation and betterment since 1900', in ed Hall, P. Land Values, (Acton Society Trust, London).

Pickvance, C. G. 1976. "On the study of urban social movements",. in ed. Pickvance, C. Urban Sociology.
(Tavistock, London).

Planning 1982. 'Growth Generated by Land Supply Circular'.
Planning 479. 30th July, p.3.

Popenoe, D. 1977. The Suburban Environment: Sweden and the
United States (University of Chicago Press, Chicago).

Purdue, M. 1982. "Notes of cases, Town and Country Planning".
Journal of Planning and Environment Law. pp.575-580.

Ratcliffe, J. 1981. "Planning gain - an overview".
Estates Gazette, 2nd May.

Reade, E. J. 1978. "Planning as a mode of decision-making".
Sociologists in Polytechnics. Conference paper.

Rhodes, J. and Kan, A. 1971. Office Dispersal and Regional
Policy. Occasional Paper No.30 (Department of Applied
Economics, Cambridge University Press).

Rhodes, R. A. W. 1981. Control and Power in Central-Local
Relations. (Gower, London).

Robson, W. A. 1961. The Greater London Boroughs. (London
School of Economics, London).

Rose, D. 1981. "Accumulation versus reproduction in the Inner
City: "The recurrent crisis of London" revisited", in
eds Dear, M. and Scott, A. J. Urbanisation and Urban
Planning in Capitalist Society. (Methuen, London).

Rotterdam, Municipality of 1959. Municipal Eeal Estate Policy
in the Netherlands. (Gemeente, Rotterdam).

Royal Commission on the Distribution of the Industrial
Population 1940. Report (Barlow Report). Cmnd 6153.
(HMSO, London).

Royal Institute of Chartered Surveyors 1974. The Land
Problem: A Fresh Approach. (RICS, London).

Royal Institute of Chartered Surveyors 1983. The Use of
Planning Conditions. (RICS, London).

Royal Town Planning Institute 1978a. Report of the Working
Party on Employment. (RTPI, London).

Royal Town Planning Institute 1978b. Land Values and Planning
in the Inner Areas. (RTPI, London).

Royal Town Planning Institute 1979. "Land Values and Planning
in the Inner Areas". (RTPI, London).

Samuels, A. 1978. "Planning agreements: their use and misuse,
Town and Country Planning Act, 1971, Section 52". Local
Government Review, 4th and 11th November, pp.609-612
and pp.624-626.

Saunders, P. 1979. Urban Politics. (Hutchinson, London).

Saunders, P. 1981. Social Theory and the Urban Question.
(Hutchinson, London).

388

Scase, R. 1976. Social Democracy in Capitalist Society: Working Class Politics in Britain and Sweden. (Croom Helm London).

Scott, A. J. 1980. The Urban Land Nexus. (Pion, London).

Scott, A. J. and Roweis, S. T. 1977. "Urban planning in theory and practice: a reappraisal". Environment and Planning A, 9, pp.1097-1119.

Scottish Development Agency 1977, 1978, 1979, 1980, 1981, 1982, 1983. Annual Reports 77, 78, 79, 80, 81, 82, 83. (Scottish Development Agency, Glasgow).

Scottish Office 1973. The New Scottish Local Authorities: Organisation and Management Structure. Paterson. (HMSO, Edinburgh).

Selznick, P. 1966. TVA and the Grass Roots. (Harper & Row, New York).

Shankland Cox Partnership 1972. Land Availability for Housing. (Housing Research Foundation, London).

Shankland Cox Partnership 1973. Land Availability for Residential Development: the West Midlands. (Housing Research Foundation, London).

Shepley, C. 1982. "Talking to the housebuilders". Planner News, (9) April.

Shoard, M. 1981. The Theft of the Countryside. (Temple Smith, London).

Skewis, J. 1978. "Opportunities for rural based industries in upland Wales", in ed Tranter, R. B. The Future of Upland Britain. (Centre for Agricultural Strategy, Reading University).

Slowe, P. M. 1981. The Advance Factory in Regional Development. (Gower, Aldershot).

Smith, B. 1973. Perspectives on Planning, Employment and Industrial Location. Proceedings of a seminar. Working Paper No.20. (Centre for Urban and Regional Studies, University of Birmingham).

Smith, B. 1977. The Inner City Economic Problem A Framework for Analysis and Local Authority Policy. Research Memorandum 56. (Centre for Urban and Regional Studies, University of Birmingham).

Smith, R. M. 1979. The Demands of Industry in Hertfordshire Diploma in Town Planning Special Study. (North London Polytechnic).

Smyth, H. 1982 Land Banking, Land Availability and Planning for Private Housebuilding. Working Paper No.23. (School for Advanced Urban Studies, University of Bristol).

South East Dorset District Council/House Builders Federation 1982. outh East Dorset Land Supply Study 1981-1986. (NFBTE, London).

South East Joint Planning Team 1970. Strategic Plan for the South East. (HMSO, London). pp.80-83).

Statens Offentliga Utredningar. SOU 1966:23/24 <u>Markfragan</u>, Stockholm.

Statens Offentliga Utredningar. SOU 1972:42 <u>Konkurens i bostadsbyggandet</u>, Stockholm.

Statens Offentliga Utredningar. SOU 1982:34 <u>Prisutveckling inom bostadsbyggandet och dess orsaker.</u> (Stockholm).

Standing Conference on London and South East Regional Planning/Housebuilders Federation 1981. <u>Housing Land in South-East England.</u> SC 1600. (SCLSERP, London).

Stevenson, D. 1981. "Westminster's limited contribution to the new office boom", in <u>The Office Boom in London</u>, Centre for Environmental Studies, Paper 1. (CES, London).

Sunday Times 1981. "Insight", 12th July.

Sutcliffe, E. 1981. <u>Towards the Planned City.</u> (Blackwell, Oxford).

Svensson, R. 1976. <u>Swedish Land Policy in Practical Application.</u> Document D5:76. (Swedish Council for Building Research, Stockholm).

Svensson, R. 1979. "Gar det att fora en social markpolitik i ettkapitalistisk samhalle". <u>Plan.</u>

Swann, P. and Long, T. 1982. "The Numbers Game". Planning 197, 3rd December, p.7.

Sydvästra Skånes Kommunalförbund (SSK). 1982 <u>Markdgare i Sydvästra Skåne</u> (SSK), Malmö.

Tabb, W. K. and Sawers, L(eds) 1978. <u>Marxism and the Metropolis.</u> (Oxford University Press, New York).

Terry, S. and Elson, M. J. 1981. <u>Restraint and Employment: An Analysis of Development Control Decisions in Dacorum and North Hertfordshire 1974-1979.</u> SSRC Project Paper No.4. (Department of Town Planning, Oxford Polytechnic). Report No.47. (Edinburgh University).

Townsend, A. 1983. "The scope for intra regional variation in the 1980s". <u>The Planner.</u> Vol.69, No.4. July/August.

Tucker, L. R. 1978. "Planning agreements: the twilight zone of ultra vires". <u>Journal of Planning and Environment Law.</u> pp.806-809.

Turvey, R. 1953. "Recoupment as an aid in financing nineteenth-century street improvements in London". <u>Review of Economic Studies</u>, Vol.21, p.53.

Tym, R. and Partners 1980. <u>Living by the Yard.</u> (R. Tym, London).

Town and Country Planning 1979. Vol.48(1).

Underwood, J. 1980. <u>Town Planners in Search of a Role.</u> SAUS Occasional Paper 6. (School for Advanced Urban Studies, Bristol).

Underwood, J. 1981. Development Control: A Case Study of
    Discretion in Action, in Barrett, S. and Fudge, C. (eds),
    Policy in Action. pp.143-162.(Methuen, London).
United Nations (Department of Economic and Social Affairs)
    1973. Land Policies and Land Use Control Measures. Vol.I
    (United Nations, New York).
University College London, 1979-1982. Production of the Built
    Environment. Papers of the Bartlett Summer School.
    (University College, London).

VGM 1982. Vestigingsplaatsen in Nederland, Vastgoedmarkt,
    nr.9B. (Amsterdam).

Walker, B. 1981. Welfare Economics and Urban Problems.
    (Hutchinson, London).
Wandsworth, London Borough of 1976. Prosperity or Slump?
    The Future of Wandsworth's Economy (London Borough of
    Wandsworth).
Wannop, U. A. 1982. The Future of GEAR. Report for Scottish
    Development Agency.
Wannop, U. A. and Boyle R. M. 1982. "Area initiatives and
    the SDA: The rise of the urban project". Fraser of
    Allander Institute Quarterly Economic Commentary. Vol.8,
    No.1.
Ward, M. 1980. Job Creation by the Council: Local Govern-
    ment and the Struggle for Full Employment. (Institute
    for Worker's Control, Nottingham).
Wates, N. 1976. The Battle for Tolmers Square. (Routledge
    and Kegan Paul, London).
Watts, H. D. 1981. The Branch Plant Economy - A Study of Ex-
    ternal Control (Longman, London).
Weatheritt, L. and John, O. N. 1979. Office Development and
    Employment in Greater London, 1967 to 1976. GLC Research
    Memorandum, RM 556. (Greater London Council, London).
Wenban-Smith, A. 1980. "Supply of Housing Land". Planning
    No.369, 23/5, p.2 (letter).
Wenban-Smith, A. 1983. "Structure Plan Reviews in the
    Metropolitan Counties - A District View". Planner News
    (February), p.20.
Wenger, G. C. 1980a. Mid Wales - Deprivation or Development.
    Board of Celtic Studies, Social Science Monograph.
    (University of Wales Press, Cardiff).
Wenger, G. C. 1980b. Self Help Initiatives - Some Welsh
    Examples. Welsh Multi-Purpose Rural Co-Operatives Con-
    ference. (Plunkett Foundation, Oxford).
Wenger, G. C. 1982. "The problem of perspective in
    development policy". Sociologica Ruralis, pp.5-16.
Westminster, City of 1977. City of Westminster District Plan:
    Draft Written Statement. (City of Westminster, London).

Williams, G. 1984a. "The contribution of development agencies to the promotion of rural community development", in Gilg, A. Countryside Planning Yearbook, Vol.5.

Williams, G. 1984b. "Rural advance factories". The Planner Vol.70(3), pp.11-13.

Willis, K. G. 1980. The Economics of Town and Country Planning. (Granada, London).

Willis, K. G. 1981. "Planning agreements and planning gain". Planning Outlook. (Department of Town and Country Planning, University of Newcastle-upon-Tyne).

Woodrow, P. 1982. Speech quoted in "Planning", 17th December, 1982 (16).

Wright, S. 1982. Decision Making in Rural Areas. (Dorset East Lindsay, West Cleveland). Bartlett School of Planning. (University College, London).

Wright, S. 1982. From Parish to Whitehall: Administrative Structures and Perceptions of Communities in Rural Areas. OP 16, (Department of Planning, Gloucester College of Art and Technology).

Young, K. and Garside, P. 1982. Metropolitan London: Politics and Urban Change 1837-1981. (Edward Arnold, London).

Young, K. and Mills, L. 1982. "The decline of urban economies", in ed Rose, R. and Page, E. Fiscal Stress in Cities. (Cambridge University Press).